European Advertising Academy

The objective of the European Advertising Academy (EAA) is to provide a professional association to academics and practitioners interested in advertising and its applications that will promote, disseminate and stimulate high quality research in the field.

More information about this series at http://www.springer.com/series/12465

Martin K. J. Waiguny · Sara Rosengren
Editors

Advances in Advertising Research (Vol. XI)

Designing and Communicating Experience

Editors
Martin K. J. Waiguny
IMC Krems, Krems an der Donau
Austria

Sara Rosengren
Center for Retailing, Stockholm School
of Economics, Stockholm, Sweden

ISSN 2626-0328   ISSN 2626-0336 (electronic)
European Advertising Academy
ISBN 978-3-658-32200-7   ISBN 978-3-658-32201-4 (eBook)
https://doi.org/10.1007/978-3-658-32201-4

© The Editor(s) (if applicable) and The Author(s), under exclusive license to Springer Fachmedien Wiesbaden GmbH, part of Springer Nature 2021

This work is subject to copyright. All rights are solely and exclusively licensed by the Publisher, whether the whole or part of the material is concerned, specifically the rights of translation, reprinting, reuse of illustrations, recitation, broadcasting, reproduction on microfilms or in any other physical way, and transmission or information storage and retrieval, electronic adaptation, computer software, or by similar or dissimilar methodology now known or hereafter developed.

The use of general descriptive names, registered names, trademarks, service marks, etc. in this publication does not imply, even in the absence of a specific statement, that such names are exempt from the relevant protective laws and regulations and therefore free for general use.

The publisher, the authors and the editors are safe to assume that the advice and information in this book are believed to be true and accurate at the date of publication. Neither the publisher nor the authors or the editors give a warranty, expressed or implied, with respect to the material contained herein or for any errors or omissions that may have been made. The publisher remains neutral with regard to jurisdictional claims in published maps and institutional affiliations.

Lektorat: Marija Kojic

This Springer Gabler imprint is published by the registered company Springer Fachmedien Wiesbaden GmbH part of Springer Nature.

The registered company address is: Abraham-Lincoln-Str. 46, 65189 Wiesbaden, Germany

Contents

Construct Confusion in Advertising Research 1
Lars Bergkvist and Tobias Langner

**Does a Lack of Control Alter Associative Structure of Brands?
The Effects for Positioning Familiar and Unfamiliar Brands** 13
Alicja Grochowska, Magdalena Gąsiorowska, and Piotr Hajda

**Which Message Frames and Forms Best Promote Political
Campaigns via Social Media?** 31
Meily Mei Fung Cheung, Wai Han Lo, and Benson Shu Yan Lam

**Can It Hurt to Be Honest About Nudging? the Impact
of a (Disclosed) Social Norm Nudge on Food Preferences and Choice** .. 47
Lotte Hallez, Rob Van Roy, Bieke Zaman, and Tim Smits

**The Impact of Source Credibility on Irish Millennials' Brand
Attitudes and Perceptions of Brand Credibility: A Study
of Instagram Influencers' Health and Fitness Endorsements** 63
Andrea Manning and Laurent Muzellec

**General Language Use, Language Proficiency and Language
Attitudes as Predictors of Consumer Response to the Use
of Spanish and English in Advertising in Chile and Mexico** 77
Andreu van Hooft, Frank van Meurs, and Qudsiyah Braaf

Disclaimers in Real Estate Print Advertisements 91
Emmanuel Mogaji

***"Trust Me, I'm an Advertiser"*. The Influence of Message Sidedness and Advertiser Credibility on Readers' Perceptions of Native Advertisements** 105
Dr. Simone Krouwer, Prof. Dr. Karolien Poels,
and Prof. Dr. Steve Paulussen

A Thematic Exploration of Strong Emotional Appeals Based on Evolutionary Psychology 119
Serena D'Hooge and Patrick Vyncke

Half a Century of Super Bowl Commercials: A Content Analysis of Humorous Advertising Styles 137
Artemis Timamopoulou, Leonidas Hatzithomas, Christina Boutsouki, and Maria C. Voutsa

Should Companies Use Tattooed Models in Their Advertisements? 151
Antonia Heberle and Heribert Gierl

Creating Branded Entertainment that Resonates: Perspectives of Multinational Award Winners 167
Marthinus J. C. van Loggerenberg, Carla Enslin, and Marlize Terblanche-Smit

Advertising Music and the Effects of Incongruity Resolution on Consumer Response 183
Morteza Abolhasani, Steve Oakes, and Zahra Golrokhi

The Sound Factor in Autoplay Mobile Video Ads 195
Eunah Kim and Jisu Huh

Battle-Weary Women: The Female Creatives Fighting for Leadership in Advertising Management 213
Helen Thompson-Whiteside

Can Market Mavens Be Negative Word of Mouth Senders? the Moderating Role of Assumed-Competence and Gender 225
Keigo Taketani and Kei Mineo

Gender Responses to Emotional Appeals in Advertising: Comparing Self-Reports and Facial Expressions 241
Eirini Tsichla, Maria C. Voutsa, Kostoula Margariti, and Leonidas Hatzithomas

Sustainability and Diversity Labels in Job Ads and Their Effect on Employer Brands 255
Denise F. Kleiss and Martin K. J. Waiguny

Children's Perceptions of Sponsorship Disclosures in Online Influencer Videos 273
Esther Rozendaal, Eva A. van Reijmersdal, and Margot J. van der Goot

Family Decision Making and Vacation Functions in Summer Tourism – The Case of Austrian Families 289
Stephanie Tischler

Replicating the CSR-Advertising-Effectiveness Model: Do Consumers' Attitudes Towards Corporate Socially Responsible Behavior in the Pharmaceutical Industry Change Over Time? 305
Isabell Koinig, Sandra Diehl, and Barbara Mueller

Empowering Claims in CSR Tweets: The Moderating Role of Emotion, Fit and Credibility 321
Paula Fernández, Patrick Hartmann, Vanessa Apaolaza, and Clare D'Souza

A Cognitive Approach to the Argument Strength × Message Involvement Paradigm in Green Advertising Persuasion 337
Jason Yu

Construct Confusion in Advertising Research

Lars Bergkvist and Tobias Langner

1 Introduction

Whether advertising research is successful or not as a field depends to a large extent on the precision of construct measures and whether results are comparable across studies. Measures should be designed to measure constructs as precisely as possible and enable comparisons across studies. This motivates research on advertising research practice, that is, systematic studies of how advertising researchers go about their business. To date, there are only few studies of this kind (e.g., Bergkvist and Langner 2017; Bruner 1998). These studies have found considerable heterogeneity in the measurement of frequently used constructs such as *attitude toward the ad* (A_{Ad}), *brand attitude* (A_{Brand}), and *brand purchase intention* (PI_{Brand}). This suggests that marketing researchers rely on convergent validity. If two measures are correlated, they are considered to be interchangeable and results are assumed to be comparable. However, this is not necessarily the case. As demonstrated by Rossiter (2016), the fact that two measures are correlated does not automatically mean that they share a similar correlation with a third construct. Even at commonly accepted levels of convergent validity (e.g., 0.70 or

---

L. Bergkvist (✉)
College of Business, Zayed University, Abu Dhabi, United Arab Emirates
E-Mail: Lars.Bergkvist@zu.ac.ae

T. Langner
Schumpeter School of Business and Economics, Bergische University Wuppertal, Wuppertal, Germany
E-Mail: langner@wiwi.uni-wuppertal.de

0.80) there is a considerable risk that research results will be significantly different if different measures of the same construct are used. In practice, this means that research results will vary depending on what measure is used and studies with different measures of the same construct will frequently not be comparable.

The present study investigates the heterogeneity of measurement operationalizations of the frequently measured construct *ad credibility* that has been overlooked by previous research. In addition, the study aims to identify similar constructs that appear under different names, and constructs whose measurement overlap with the measurement of A_{Ad}. The study contributes to advertising research by calling for a consequent execution of valid and comparable construct measurement. As a result, this will improve measurement practice over time and, thus, ensure achieving the primary aim of advertising research, the accumulation of advertising knowledge.

2   Method

The present study is based on searches and analyses of a database listing the constructs measured in all articles published in the *International Journal of Advertising (IJA)*, the *Journal of Advertising* (JA), and the *Journal of Advertising Research (JAR)* between 2012 and 2014. The number of research articles with construct measurement during this period was 285 and the total number of constructs measured in these articles was 1086. For each construct, the database listed the construct name and definition (both as stated in the article), and the items included in the construct measure (except in 84 cases when no or only partial item information was provided in the article).

The search focused on the items used in measures of ad credibility and aimed to identify constructs whose items overlap. Complete or partial item overlap would identify those cases in which the same construct appears under different name in different studies.

3   Findings

Diversity in Construct Operationalizations

The operationalizations of *ad credibility* were analyzed with respect to the number of items and the diversity of the items. There were seven studies which operationalized *ad credibility* (Table A1). These studies employed between two and nine items to measure the construct, demonstrating limited agreement on how many items are needed to measure the construct. Most of the *ad credibility measures* used a semantic-differential type of answer format, only two studies relied on a Likert-type answer format, and all but one study used a seven-point answer scale. It is of some interest to note that most "semantic-differential" items were unipolar rather than bipolar (i.e., the two adjectives that made up an item were not polar opposites but rather indicated the presence or absence of the attribute). There was considerable diversity in the items used in the measures. The total number of items across the seven studies were 19. Out of these, one item ("believable") was included in all seven studies and one item ("convincing") was included in six studies. Remarkably, the item "credible," arguably the most content valid item, was included only in two out of the seven studies. Of the remaining items, six were included in one study and five were included in two studies. Thus, the use of idiosyncratic items to measure *ad credibility* appears to be common practice.

The diversity in operationalizations of *ad credibility* is similar to the diversity found in previous studies of advertising research practice (Bergkvist and Langner 2017; Bruner 1998). A consequence of this diversity is that the comparability between studies is threatened since it cannot be safely assumed that measures with different items will yield comparable results.

Same Construct Content but Different Name

The search for constructs appearing under different names and measures whose items overlapped found several instances of both. There were three constructs whose item operationalizations suggest that they are identical with ad credibility. These are *claim believability, message believability*, and *trustworthiness of the ad* (Table A2). *Claim believability* was measured with three items, all of which were included in at least one of the *ad credibility* measures in Table A1; two out of three items in *message believability* were included in at least one *ad credibility* measure; and three out of four items in the measure of *trustworthiness of the ad* had an equivalent in at least one *ad credibility* measure. Although none of the studies that measured these constructs defined it, the item overlap clearly suggests that the constructs for all intents and purposes are the same as *ad credibility*.

The analysis also identified three constructs with different names but overlapping content, namely *involvement in the ad, message involvement*, and *cognitive engagement* (Table A3). All measures of these constructs, except the one used by Lawrence et al. (2013), included items relating to the "involvement" or "relevance" of the ad. Moreover, the two studies that defined the construct defined it as either a "motivational construct" or "mental state" that affects individuals' information processing (Lawrence et al. 2013; Wang and Muehling 2012), and two studies (Banks and De Pelsmacker 2014; Maslowska et al. 2013) used the same measurement scale (the revised personal involvement inventory; Zaichkowsky 1994). In addition, there was item overlap between three studies that measured "attention" and three studies that measured whether the ad was perceived as "interesting."

Inconsistencies in the naming of constructs increase the risk that studies and results are overlooked in literature reviews and meta-analyses, and that research efforts are duplicated because previous studies are overlooked. Naturally, it is in the interest of everyone in the field that advertising research constructs are consistently named.

Overlap in Items Between Measures of A_{Ad} and Other Constructs

The most common way to measure A_{Ad} is to use a multiple-item measure with three or four items (Bergkvist and Langner 2017). Over time, marketing academics have used many different items in their A_{Ad} measures. For example, Bruner (1998) lists 53 different A_{Ad} items and Bergkvist and Langner (2017) list 25. This item proliferation not only means that A_{Ad} measures come in many different versions but also that there is a high likelihood that A_{Ad} items appear in multiple-item measures of other constructs.

Several of the items included in the measures of *ad credibility* (Table A1) have previously been used to measure A_{Ad}. Specifically, the items "believable," "trustworthy," "convincing," and "honest" have all been included in A_{Ad} measures at some point (see the Appendix in Bergkvist and Langner 2017, p. 140; and Appendix 1 in Bruner 1998, p. 14). There is also overlap between A_{Ad} and the revised personal involvement inventory (Zaichkowsky 1994) used in two studies to measure *involvement in the ad* or *message involvement* (Banks and De Pelsmacker 2014; Maslowska et al. 2013): Four involvement items, "important," "interesting," "appealing," and "valuable," are commonly found in measures of A_{Ad}.

In measures of other constructs there was complete or near-complete overlap with A_{Ad}. The measure of *ad persuasions* in Sheehan et al. (2012) was made up of five items. Three of these items, "believable," "effective," and "important to me," have previously been used to measure A_{Ad}. Two items, "interesting" and "informative," out of a total of three items in the operationalization of *cognitive engagement* in Lawrence et al. (2013) have also been used to measure A_{Ad}. The operationalization of the construct *ad meaningfulness* in Lehnert et al. (2014) overlaps completely with A_{Ad}. The measure is made up of four items, "appropriate," "meaningful," "valuable," and "useful," which have all been previously used to measure A_{Ad}. Similarly, the operationalization of the construct *visual appeal* in Banks and De Pelsmacker (2014) is made up of three items commonly used to measure A_{Ad} ("good," "pleasant," "likeable").

The overlap between A_{Ad} and other advertising constructs leads to problems with discriminant validity. If two measures have several items in common, they will to a certain extent measure the same underlying phenomenon and arguments to the effect that they are measuring two different constructs are likely to become tenuous. It is also likely that statistical tests of discriminant validity (e.g., Fornell and Larcker 1981) would find them lacking if both measures were included in the same study. If there is complete, or near-complete, overlap in the items of two measures there definitely is a problem with discriminant validity. Why would it be acceptable, say, to refer to two identical measures as a measure of A_{Ad} in one study and as a measure of *ad meaningfulness* in another study?

4 Discussion

The present analysis of the operationalizations of the construct ad credibility has provided several examples of three problems in construct measurement in advertising research: Heterogeneity in the operationalizations of the same construct, lacking consistency in the naming of constructs, and complete or near-complete overlap in items between operationalizations of A_{Ad} and other constructs. These problems all contribute to hamper the accumulation of knowledge and progress in advertising research.

If there are substantial differences in the measures of the same construct, as was the case for *ad credibility* in the present analysis, it is highly likely that the convergent validity of the different measures is, at best, moderate. And moderate, or low, convergent validity means that the results from studies with different measures are not comparable as their correlations with measures of other constructs will be significantly different (Carlson and Herdman 2012; Rossiter 2016). Thus, results in one study may not replicate in another because the measures of key constructs were not the same. In addition, results in meta-analyses may be diluted because of differences in measurement that obscure substantial research results.

When the same construct appears under different names there is a risk that research efforts are duplicated, and that extant research is overlooked in literature reviews and meta-analyses. For example, the present study found four names for one construct (*ad credibility, claim believability, message believability,* and *trustworthiness of the ad*), which suggests a high risk that literature searches overlook relevant search terms. It follows from this that research resources are wasted, and the accumulation of knowledge is hampered.

The overlap in items between measures of A_{Ad} and other constructs raises issues of discriminant validity, the stringency of construct definitions, and the content validity of measure items. It is, of course, not tenable to argue that two identical (or near-identical) sets of items preceded by the same question measures two different constructs, so there is clearly a problem of lacking discriminant validity. There also appears to be a problem with how A_{Ad} is defined, since there are more than 50 items that have been included in measures of A_{Ad} in published research. This suggests that current definitions are lacking in stringency permitting a too wide range of items in current operationalizations, or that the extent to which definitions guide the research process is limited. Another likely contributing factor is that a substantial share of A_{Ad} studies do not define the construct (Bergkvist and Langner 2017). In addition, the definitions of the constructs that have item overlap with A_{Ad} could either be too close to A_{Ad} or lack in stringency. There is also a high likelihood that measures of A_{Ad} and similar constructs include items with low content validity.

An interesting observation is that all the reviewed operationalizations, except for the two measures based on the revised personal involvement inventory, were either ad hoc measures put together for the study at hand or measures used in previous research but that did not come out of a measurement development study. This suggests a widespread willingness among authors and reviewers to accept unvalidated measures.

One question that arises from the present study is how to weed out the reported weaknesses in measurement practice. One way is to move towards standard measures of frequently measured constructs (Rossiter 2016). This would require that measure development studies are carried out and that scholars agree to use what is generally considered to be the optimal measures. It also requires that reviewers and editors make sure standard measures are used (or, at a minimum, make sure that use of non-standard measures is noted in the limitations section of the paper). Furthermore, construct naming has to be precise and consistent, and item overlap between different constructs should be avoided. To solve these issues, editors and reviewers should be more sensitive to measurement issues in the first place. They should ensure that authors do their homework. Often, researchers do not define their constructs properly, do not report measures in their entirety, or are careless in reporting adaptations they have made in the measures sourced from literature (Bergkvist and Langner 2017). Furthermore, reviewers should examine the consistency of construct definitions and construct operationalizations. In the second place, advertising research as discipline should head towards the development of standard measures. Ideally, constructs frequently used in advertising research should be operationalized with the same measure across all studies.

An expedient way of ensuring greater transparency and reducing the problems highlighted in the present study would be to require advertising researchers to report definitions and measures of all constructs in one table when empirical work is submitted to a journal. This table should also include sources for the measures and information about any adaptations of the measures. Not only would a table make relevant information easily accessible to reviewers and editors but it would also bring definitions and measurement to the attention of the researchers reporting the study.

Tables

Table A1 Operationalizations of ad credibility

Study	Answer Scale Type	Answer Scale Length	Items
Aguirre-Rodriguez (2013)	S-D	9	1. Believable/Unbelievable 2. Biased/Unbiased 3. Convincing/Unconvincing
Bui et al. (2012)	L-T	7	1. "The claims in the advertisement are true" 2. "I believe the claims in the advertisement" 3. "The advertisement is sincere"
Chang (2014)	L-T	7	1. Authentic 2. Believable 3. Convincing 4. Reasonable
Eisend et al. (2014)	S-D	7	1. Believable/Unbelievable 2. Convincing/Unconvincing 3. Honest/Dishonest
Kim et al. (2012)	S-D	7	1. Believable/Unbelievable 2. Convincing/Unconvincing
Okazaki et al. (2013)	S-D	7	1. Acceptable/Unacceptable 2. Believable/Unbelievable 3. Convincing/Unconvincing 4. Credible/Not credible 5. Truthful/Untruthful
Tucker et al. (2012)	S-D	n.a.	1. Authentic/Not authentic 2. Believable/Unbelievable 3. Conclusive/Inconclusive 4. Convincing/Not convincing 5. Credible/Not credible 6. Honest/Dishonest 7. Reasonable/Unreasonable 8. Trustworthy/Untrustworthy 9. Unquestionable/Questionable

Notes
S-D – Semantic differential type of answer scale
L–T – Likert type of answer scale

Table A2 Constructs overlapping with ad credibility

Study	Items
Claim Believability	
Choi et al. (2012)	1. Believable 2. Credible 3. Trustworthy
Message Believability	
Wang and Muehling (2012)	1. Believable 2. Convincing 3. Informative
Trustworthiness of the Ad	
Lawrence et al. (2013)	1. "I trust what the ad has to say" 2. "The ad is trustworthy" 3. "The claims made in this ad are credible" 4. "The ad felt authentic"

Table A3 Overlapping involvement constructs

Study	Items
Involvement in the Ad	
Banks and De Pelsmacker (2014)	1. Appealing 2. Exciting 3. Fascinating 4. Important 5. Interesting 6. Involving 7. Means a lot to me 8. Needed 9. Relevant 10. Valuable
Puzakova et al. (2013)	1. Concentrated very hard 2. Paid a lot of attention 3. To what extent the ad is unusual 4. Very involved
Message involvement	
Maslowska et al. (2013)	1. Appealing 2. Exciting 3. Fascinating 4. Important 5. Interesting 6. Involving 7. Means a lot to me 8. Needed 9. Relevant 10. Valuable
Wang and Muehling (2012)	1. Overall attention paid to the messages 2. Perceived engagement with the messages 3. Perceived relevance of the messages 4. Self-reported attention to the message claims
Cognitive engagement	
Lawrence et al. (2013)	1. "The ad kept my attention" 2. "The ad was informative" 3. "The ad was interesting"

References

Aguirre-Rodriguez, A. (2013). The effect of consumer persuasion knowledge on scarcity appeal persuasiveness. *Journal of Advertising, 42*(October), 371–379.

Banks, I. B., & De Pelsmacker, P. (2014). Involvement, tolerance for ambiguity, and type of service moderate the effectiveness of probability marker usage in service advertising. *Journal of Advertising, 43*(June), 196–209.

Bergkvist, L., & Langner, T. (2017). Construct measurement in advertising research. *Journal of Advertising, 46*(1), 129–140.

Bruner, G. C., II. (1998). Standardization & justification: Do A_{ad} scales measure up? *Journal of Current Issues and Research in Advertising, 20*(Spring), 1–18.

Bui, My., Krishen, A. S., & LaTour, M. S. (2012). When Kiosk retailing intimidates shoppers: How gender-focused advertising can mitigate the perceived risks of the unfamiliar. *Journal of Advertising Research, 52*(September), 346–363.

Carlson, K. D., & Herdman, A. O. (2012). Understanding the impact of convergent validity on research results. *Organizational Research Methods, 15*(January), 17–32.

Chang, C. (2014). Why do caucasian advertising models appeal to consumers in Taiwan? A cue-triggered value-expressive framework. *International Journal of Advertising, 33*(February), 155–177.

Choi, H., Paek, H.-J., & King, K. W. (2012). Are nutrient-content claims always effective? Match-up effects between product type and claim type in food advertising. *International Journal of Advertising, 31*(May), 421–443.

Eisend, M., Plagemann, J., & Sollwedel, J. (2014). Gender roles and humor in advertising: The occurrence of stereotyping in humorous and nonhumorous advertising and its consequences for advertising effectiveness. *Journal of Advertising, 43*(September), 256–273.

Fornell, C., & Larcker, D. F. (1981). Evaluating structural equation models with unobservable variables and measurement error. *Journal of Marketing Research, 18*(February), 39–50.

Kim, J., Baek, Y., & Choi, Y. H. (2012). The Structural effects of metaphor-elicited cognitive and affective elaboration levels on attitude toward the Ad. *Journal of Advertising, 41*(June), 77–96.

Lawrence, B., Fournier, S., & Brunel, F. (2013). When companies don't make the Ad: A Multimethod inquiry into the differential effectiveness of consumer-generated advertising. *Journal of Advertising, 42*(October), 292–307.

Lehnert, K., Till, B. D., & Ospina, J. M. (2014). Advertising creativity: The role of divergence versus meaningfulness. *Journal of Advertising, 43*(September), 274–285.

Maslowska, E., Smit, E. G., & van den Putte, B. (2013). Assessing the cross-cultural applicability of tailored advertising: A comparative study between the Netherlands and Poland. *International Journal of Advertising, 32*(November), 487–511.

Okazaki, S., Mueller, B., & Diehl, S. (2013). A multi-country examination of hard-sell and soft-sell advertising comparing global consumer positioning in holistic and analytic-thinking cultures. *Journal of Advertising Research, 53*(September), 258–272.

Puzakova, M., Rocereto, J. F., & Kwak, H. (2013). Ads are watching me: A view from the interplay between anthropomorphism and customisation. *International Journal of Advertising, 32*(November), 513–538.

Rossiter, J. R. (2016). How to use C-OAR-SE to design optimal standard measures. *European Journal of Marketing, 50*(11), 1924–1941.

Sheehan, B., Tsao, J., & Pokrywczynski, J. (2012). Stop the music! How advertising can help stop college students from downloading music illegally. *Journal of Advertising Research, 52*(September), 309–321.

Tucker, E. M., Rifon, N. J., Lee, E. M., & Reece, B. B. (2012). Consumer receptivity to green Ads: A test of green claim types and the role of individual consumer characteristics for green Ad response. *Journal of Advertising, 41*(December), 9–23.

Wang, A., & Muehling, D. D. (2012). The moderating influence of brand status and source confirmation on third-party endorsement effects in advertising. *International Journal of Advertising, 31*(August), 605–622.

Zaichkowsky, J. L. (1994). The Personal involvement inventory: Reduction, revision, and application to advertising. *Journal of Advertising, 23*(December), 59–70.

Does a Lack of Control Alter Associative Structure of Brands? The Effects for Positioning Familiar and Unfamiliar Brands

Alicja Grochowska, Magdalena Gąsiorowska, and Piotr Hajda

1   Introduction

A brand's position in the market reflects its position in the minds of consumers (Kotler and Keller 2012; Keller 2013). In marketing communication marketers strive to build such a network of associations in consumers' minds that will differentiate their brand from the competition. As marketers are outdoing themselves in presenting various strategies, the market is overflowing with offers. The abundance of brands and products on the market and their accompanying marketing communication quite often result in consumers experiencing a state of mind defined as a lack of control (Whitson and Galinsky 2008; Cutright et al. 2013) or consumer confusion (Wang and Shukla 2013; Landau et al. 2015). Edward and Sahadev (2012) define consumer confusion as 'an uncomfortable psychological state consumers experience when exposed to an overload of marketing information which are often very similar, misleading, ambiguous and inadequate in nature'. The authors point to such psychological consequences of this state as a negative affect, decision postponement, evaluation costs. Similarly, other authors argue that the multiplicity, contradiction and similarity of stimuli may lead to the state of the lack of control over the situation. This state manifests itself in decline

A. Grochowska (✉) · M. Gąsiorowska · P. Hajda
SWPS University of Social Sciences and Humanities, Warszawa, Poland
E-Mail: agrochowska@swps.edu.pl

M. Gąsiorowska
E-Mail: mgasiorowska@swps.edu.pl

P. Hajda
E-Mail: phajda@st.swps.edu.pl

in motivation to solve a problem (motivational deficit), depressed mood, negative emotions (emotional deficit), and finally, difficulties in learning effective reactions (cognitive deficits) (e.g., Whitson and Galinsky 2008; Cutright et al. 2013; Maier and Seligman 2016).

Thus, concepts of a lack of control and consumer confusion refer to similar psychological mechanisms in terms of cognitive, emotional and motivational outcomes for individuals. In the current paper we refer to both concepts and, for clarity, we decided to use one term: 'lack of control' (over the situation).

The purpose of the current study is to show that lack of control alters associative structure of the positioned brands in consumers' minds. We show that these changes relate to different levels of product and brand, and we indicate possible practical implications. We expect that the effects of changes in associative structures of brands will differ between familiar and unfamiliar brands.

It is worth noting that the essence and the very beginning of the position of a brand on the market and brand equity is built in consumers' minds, in their memory, particularly in a network of associations to the brand which are favorable, strong and unique (Keller 1993). Thus, in our study we explore structures of associations which reflect the position of a number of brands in consumer's memory.

Nowadays the methods of demographic as well as psychographic segmentation of the market become more and more sophisticated. The use of big data sets and algorithms provides information on various consumer characteristics and makes it possible to segment them along selected features, and then to create brand communication targeted at specific consumer segments. In our study, we focused on the state of lack of control because it may influence consumers' behavior in today's market.

1.1 Consequences of Lack of Control for Consumer Behavior

The need to feel in control is a fundamental human motive (see: Cutright et al. 2013). Three groups of factors play an important role in the loss of control: information overload, ambiguous information, and similarity of products and brands (Mitchell et al. 2005). Regarding the purpose of the current study, we are going to focus on similarity because associative structure of positioned brands is based on similarity. Mitchell et al. (2005) define brand similarity confusion as: 'a lack of understanding and potential alteration of a consumer's choice or an incorrect brand evaluation caused by the perceived physical similarity of products or services'. Similar messages require increased cognitive effort on the part of consumers (Schwarz 2004), hence increase evaluation costs. Similarity of brands and products can cause memory errors (Wang and Shukla 2013).

Previous studies show that similarity of products and brands could confuse consumers. We go a step further, turning this relationship around and asking the question: How do confused consumers perceive similarity between brands? Many consumers remain in 'a vicious circle': profusion of products to choose between and their similarity result in confusion, and in the state of confusion, cognitive processes become impaired. The current study fills the gap in research on the relationships between consumer confusion (lack of control) and perceived similarity of brands. We examine whether this state determines the associative structure of positioned brands in terms of perceived similarity and whether it modifies the character of associations. A lack of control results in inferior, superficial, global and chaotic processing of information; in this state cognitive functions are impaired, and the perception of similarity is disrupted (Whitson and Galinsky 2008; Cutright et al. 2013).

1.2 Associative Structure of the Mind in Brands' Positioning

The position of a brand in the marketplace is determined by associations it evokes in consumers' minds. Within the framework of the theory of associative network of memory (Anderson 1983; McClelland 1995; Verhellen et al. 2016) it can be argued that knowledge about brands creates associations between elements of information which are organized in a network. This network of associations constitutes a brand's image. Understanding brand equity involves identifying the network of strong, favorable, and unique brand associations in consumers' memory (Keller 1993).

The concept of a brand and product is defined by Kotler and Keller (2012) around following five levels: 1) Core benefit which is the fundamental level of product or benefit that induces consumers to actually buy it. 2) Generic product level is a core benefit changed into a basic product (points-of-parity). 3) Expected product level defines a set of characteristics that consumers expect when considering purchasing a product or use a service. 4) Augmented product level differentiates the product from its competitors (points-of-difference). Brand-related associations and personal associations appear at this level. 5) Potential product level includes all the future transformations and extensions of the product.

Because points-of-parity and points-of-difference are essential for brand positioning, the current study includes generic as well as brand-related and personal associations.

The associative structure of a brand can be presented in the form of a mental representation map, and such a map can be interpreted in the context of brand positioning (see: a brand concept map, John et al. 2006; also: Coulter et al. 2001). Important ideas and techniques have been suggested by John et al. (2006), and by Henderson et al. (1998), who pioneered quantitative mapping techniques and showed the link to brand equity. The current study follows this research and adds one more aspect: segmentation of the market (in terms of consumers in the state of the lack of control vs. in control). Since the loss of control impairs cognitive processes we can expect that the associative structures of positioned brands will vary between consumers in a state of control as opposed to the lack of control.

1.3 Brand Familiarity and an Associative Structure of the Mind

Mental representations for familiar brands are more finely differentiated as compared to unfamiliar ones (Dube and Schmitt 1999). Memory structures for familiar brands, as compared to unfamiliar ones, are better developed and more stable in memory and offer greater resistance to contextual information (Campbell and Keller 2003; Saenger et al. 2017). Depending on their experience with the brand, consumers perceive brand images quite differently (Brandt et al. 2011). Greater knowledge fosters greater resistance to contextual information (Wänke et al. 1998; Bei et al. 2011). Thus, in the case of familiar brands differentiation is 'readily available' in consumer's mind, and the consumer does not have to make an effort, but loses vigilance in the selection of information. Unfamiliar brands arouse greater vigilance and differentiation between them requires a greater effort on the part of consumer. It can therefore be expected that the mental structure of unfamiliar brands, compared to the familiar ones, will be more susceptible to changes under the influence of such factors as the lack of control analyzed in the current study.

1.4 Hypotheses and Research Question

H 1: There will be differences between individuals in a state of lack of control and in control in the perceived similarity between positioned brands: Individuals in the state of lack of control will perform poorer at differentiating between brands (i.e. they will perceive a greater similarity between brands) compared to the controls. Stronger effects are expected for familiar rather than unfamiliar brands.

H 2: *There will be differences in the perception of similarity between positioned familiar and unfamiliar brands: Lower level of differentiation (i.e. perceived greater similarity) is expected for familiar brands than for unfamiliar ones.*

We can expect that not only the strength of links in an associative structure (perceived similarity) but also the nature of associations varies with the state of control and brand familiarity. Thus, we put forward a research question about the nature of these associations.

RQ 1: *What type of associations (brand-related, generic, personal) is specific for the state of a lack of control versus control, and for familiar versus unfamiliar brands?*

2 METHOD

2.1 Participants and Design

Eighty four undergraduates, volunteers (47 women, 37 men; $M_{age} = 21.75$; $SD = 2.13$) participated in the study. The basic material of the analyses were associations. The total number of associations produced by the participants was $N = 2596$. The experiment was designed in 2×2 between-subject conditions: in control vs. lack of control x familiar vs. unfamiliar brand.

2.2 Materials and Procedure

Control Manipulation
Participants in the lack of control (in control) condition were asked to recall and describe an important situation of their life in which they had a feeling of complete lack of control (a feeling of complete control) over the situation (see: Whitson and Galinsky, 2008; Friesen et al. 2014). The state of control vs. lack of control was the context in which the participants were placed to perceive selected beer brands and their similarities.
Stimuli – Products of Familiar and Unfamiliar Brands
A team of judges selected several well-known and not very well-known beer brands. Thirteen familiar and 13 unfamiliar brands of beer were selected for the

pilot study. Eventually, five familiar brands of beer and five unfamiliar ones were used in the study. Products were presented to the participants in the form of photographs in A4 size, each bottle on a separate chart.

Participants were randomly assigned to one of the experimental groups. After having described the situation regarding their being in control or lack of control, the participants received charts with photographs of five brands of beer (familiar or unfamiliar) and were asked to write out all associations that came to their mind, to each beer brand. Then, they were asked to evaluate the quality of each brand on a 10-point scale. Next, they were asked to evaluate the similarity of pairs of beer brands on a 10-point scale. Finally control questions referring to brand familiarity and purchase intention were asked.

2.3 The Affinity Index as a Measure of Similarity Derived from Associations

Kleine and Kernan's (1988) methodology of measuring 'consumption objects meaning' was applied to the analysis of the similarity between brands of beer. To establish the similarity, the strength of associations between pairs of brands was measured. The index value is arrived at by dividing the number of associations (dominance scores) two objects have in common by the number of all associations evoked by these objects. The index values vary between 0 and 1 and increase in value as inter-object affinity increases. The indices of similarity we obtained that way were placed in matrices (Fig. 1). These matrices included input data for multidimensional scaling MINISSA. Additionally, the mean of the similarities for each of the ten pairs of beer brands was taken to serve as a general index of similarity. Means were used in further analyses in the nonparametric Kruskal–Wallis test.

2.4 The Measurement of Similarity Based on Scales

The measurement of the similarity between pairs of beer brands evaluated on the 10-point scales allowed to obtain similarity indices for each pair of beer brands. This data was used in the analysis of variance. Whereas the means of the similarity of each pair of brands, in each of the experimental conditions, allowed for the creation of matrices of similarities that constituted the input data for the multidimensional scaling MINISSA (Fig. 5).

2.5 Criteria for the Qualitative Analysis of Associations

Associations generated to each brand of beer were subject to qualitative analysis. According to the product and brand level classification (Kotler and Keller 2012; Keller 2013), three judges divided the individual associations into three categories: generic, brand-related and personal associations. The frequency of associations of a given category and their dominance scores (affinity index methodology) were considered. Generic associations refer to any brand, for example, chilled beer, a slender bottle. Brand-related associations refer to characteristics specific for a given brand, for example, tradition, local brewery. Personal associations relate to consumers' individual experiences with a given beer, for example, holidays, party.

3 Results

3.1 Similarity Derived from Associations

Based on the associations generated for each brand, affinity indices were calculated for each experimental condition (Fig. 1).

Indices of similarity (10 indices for each condition) were used to calculate differences in the perceived similarity between experimental groups (Fig. 2). The nonparametric Kruskal–Wallis test was used. The main effect of the factor 'control' was not significant: there were no differences in terms of perceived similarity of beer brands. However, such differences were revealed for unfamiliar brands:

Familiar brands, in control

	Zywiec	Lech	Tyskie	Zubr
Zywiec	0			
Lech	0.290	0		
Tyskie	0.440	0.270	0	
Zubr	0.330	0.160	0.300	0
Warka	0.380	0.250	0.290	0.300

Familiar brands, lack of control

	Zywiec	Lech	Tyskie	Zubr
Zywiec	0			
Lech	0.330	0		
Tyskie	0.400	0.310	0	
Zubr	0.450	0.320	0.450	0
Warka	0.210	0.160	0.360	0.330

Unfamiliar brands, in control

	Rybnicki	Legion	Darlowiak	Fabryczne
Rybnicki	0			
Legion	0.230	0		
Darlowiak	0.240	0.210	0	
Fabryczne	0.300	0.240	0.370	0
Zdunskie	0.200	0.170	0.230	0.290

Unfamiliar brands, lack of control

	Rybnicki	Legion	Darlowiak	Fabryczne
Rybnicki	0			
Legion	0.140	0		
Darlowiak	0.250	0.180	0	
Fabryczne	0.120	0.130	0.280	0
Zdunskie	0.180	0.130	0.150	0.090

Fig. 1 Matrices of similarity derived from associations

$chi^2 = 7.2$; $df = 1$; $p < 0.01$. Individuals who lose control perceive a lower similarity between brands at the level of associations than those in the control group. This result is opposite to the hypothesis 1. We explain this result in terms of an increased alertness to new stimuli in the participants who lose control: In an unknown situation (unfamiliar brands) individuals in the state of the lack of control activate excessive vigilance, which may be related to the activation of anxiety over a new situation that is characteristic for the state of a lack of control. It is worth noting that this effect became apparent at the semantic level – in the associative structure.

It was found that there were differences in the perceived similarity between familiar and unfamiliar brands: $chi^2 = 14.4$; $df = 1$; $p < 0.0001$. More similar associations occurred between familiar brands than between the unfamiliar ones. The result supports hypothesis 2. This means that in the case of unfamiliar brands, consumers are more alert and more carefully analyze the products presented to them.

Analysis of the Similarity of Structures Obtained in Multidimensional Scaling, Data Derived from Associations

The obtained similarity matrices were subject to the multidimensional scaling MINISSA. Coefficients of fit (stress and alienation) for all structures were very high: $S < 0.00001$. The image of mental maps is presented in Fig. 3.

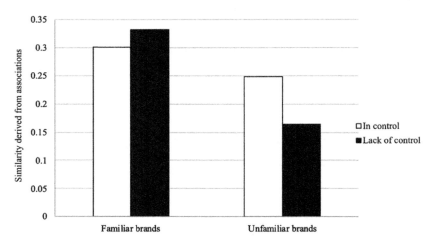

Fig. 2 Similarity between brands, derived from associations

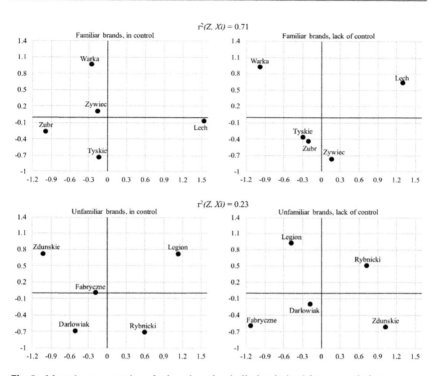

Fig. 3 Mental representations for beer brands, similarity derived from associations

Then, the PINDIS procedure (Lingoes and Borg 1978) was carried out. Using the method of centroid configuration, we compared the extent to which the structures are similar to each other in the situation of in control and the lack of control, for familiar and unfamiliar brands respectively. For familiar brands the structures of mental representations of individuals in conditions of a lack of control and in the situation of control are similar in 71% $[r^2 (Z, Xi) = 0.71]$. For unfamiliar brands this similarity is much lower and is equal to 23% $[r^2 (Z, Xi) = 0.23]$. These results are consistent with the Kruskal–Wallis tests for similarity derived from associations. In the case of familiar brands, consumers perceive the similarity between brands as high, regardless of the state of control. When brands are unfamiliar, vigilance and attention increase, particularly in the state of the lack of control. Thus, the mental maps of positioned brands are different for those in the situation of control and those with loss of control. This means that various marketing messages should be directed at these two groups of consumers.

3.2 Similarity Evaluated on Scales

The sums of perceived similarity between all analyzed beer brands were calculated. Means of these sums served as indices of similarity based on scales. Two-way ANOVA for the dependent variable 'similarity', and factors 'control' and 'brand familiarity' revealed the following effects: The main effect of the factor 'control' was statistically insignificant: the similarity between brands measured with the scales did not differ in terms of a lack of control and in control. However, there was a significant main effect of brand familiarity, $F(1, 79) = 17.14; p < 0.0001$, $eta^2 = 0.18$. The similarity between familiar brands ($M = 5.38$) was rated on the scales as higher than similarity between unfamiliar brands ($M = 4.33$) (Fig. 4). This result supports hypothesis 2. A similar effect was obtained in the study using associations. Further analysis showed that 'in control' participants clearly perceived differences in the similarity between familiar and unfamiliar brands $F(1, 39) = 14.808; p < 0.001; eta^2 = 0.275$ (H1 supported). However, in the case of the lack of control, this differentiation was weaker: $F(1, 39) = 4.403; p = 0.042$;

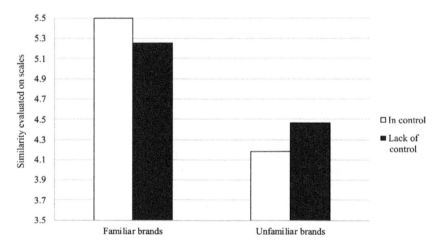

Fig. 4 Similarity between brands, evaluated on scales

$eta^2 = 0.101$ (Fig. 4). This means that in the case of the lack of control, similarity between unfamiliar brands is closer to the similarity between familiar brands as compared to the situation of control. The reverse effect emerged from the analysis of associations. Measurement on scales induces a situation of forced search for similarity ('since I have to ...') which is particularly evident in the situation of the lack of control. This effect was not revealed when analyzing deeper level of information processing (associations).

Analysis of the Similarity of Structures Obtained in Multidimensional Scaling, Data Based on the Scales

Data obtained on the basis of scales allowed us to prepare matrices (Fig. 5), which constituted input data for multidimensional scaling MINISSA.

Fit coefficients (stress and alienation) for all structures were very high: $S < 0.00001$. As in the procedure for associations, we compared the extent of similarity between structures (PINDIS procedure) in conditions of a lack of control and of being in control, for familiar and unfamiliar brands, respectively (Fig. 6). In the case of familiar brands, the structures of mental representation in the conditions of lack of control and of being in control are similar in 86% $[r^2 (Z, Xi) = 0.86]$. For unfamiliar brands the similarity of these structures is lower and amounts to 59% $[r^2 (Z, Xi) = 0.59]$. These results are consistent with those for similarity derived from associations. The similarity of structures in the condition of being in control compared to the lack of control is greater for familiar brands than for unfamiliar: individuals deprived of control position unfamiliar brands differently than those who are in control. The effect is revealed in both measurements: associations and scales. We explain the nature of the differences in the positioning of brands in qualitative analysis.

Familiar brands, in control				
	Zywiec	Lech	Tyskie	Zubr
Zywiec	0			
Lech	4.333	0		
Tyskie	7.429	5.048	0	
Zubr	5.333	4.619	5.191	0
Warka	6.429	4.619	6.619	5.400

Familiar brands, lack of control				
	Zywiec	Lech	Tyskie	Zubr
Zywiec	0			
Lech	4.619	0		
Tyskie	6.429	5.286	0	
Zubr	4.333	4.905	5.333	0
Warka	5.857	4.191	6.238	5.381

Unfamiliar brands, in control				
	Rybnicki	Legion	Darlowiak	Fabryczne
Rybnicki	0			
Legion	2.905	0		
Darlowiak	5.905	3.048	0	
Fabryczne	4.714	3.381	4.571	0
Zdunskie	4.810	3.857	4.762	3.850

Unfamiliar brands, lack of control				
	Rybnicki	Legion	Darlowiak	Fabryczne
Rybnicki	0			
Legion	3.714	0		
Darlowiak	6.000	2.857	0	
Fabryczne	4.571	5.333	4.095	0
Zdunskie	5.095	2.650	6.810	3.524

Fig. 5 Matrices of similarity, data obtained on the basis of scales

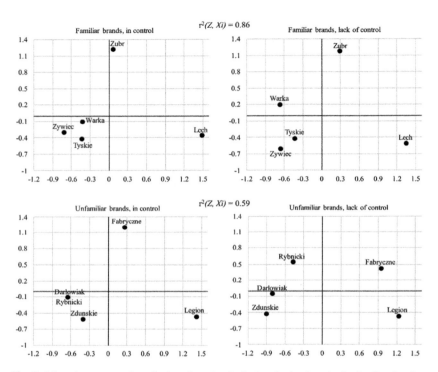

Fig. 6 Mental representations for beer brands, similarity obtained on the basis of scales data

3.3 Qualitative Analysis of Associations

To answer the research question the associations produced by the participants were assigned to one of three categories: brand-related, generic and personal. Then they were presented in the form of ratios calculated as follows: The sum of the dominance scores for a given category was divided by the sum of the dominance scores of all associations in a given experimental group, for a total of five brands of beer (Fig. 7).

Activation of generic features seems to be stronger in a situation of the lack of control ($M = 0.458$) than in control ($M = 0.382$): individuals in the state of lack of control tend to stick to what they see (generic features usually refer to perceptual properties of a product, e.g. a green bottle, chilled beer), they do not produce deeper (semantic) associative structures. Proportions of brand-related

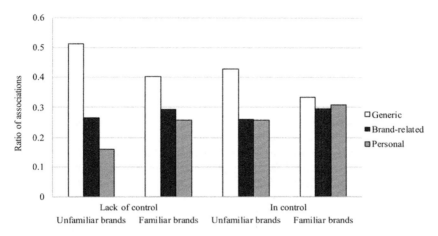

Fig. 7 Ratios for brand-related, generic and personal associations, considering control and brand familiarity

associations in the conditions of the lack of control and in control seem to be similar and, in general, are lower than proportions of generic associations. The role of personal associations is interesting here: personal associations relate to autobiographical memory, they are easier to connect to memory, but they also differ from person to person. Therefore, personal associations are worth taking into consideration when building marketing strategies but keeping in mind that a successful strategy needs to be built on more common associations (map of consensus: Zaltman 2003; John et al. 2006). A smaller activation of personal associations was in a situation of the lack of control ($M = 0.209$) compared to in control ($M = 0.283$). The effect for unfamiliar brands is particularly pronounced (respectively: $M = 0.160$ and $M = 0.258$). Recalling personal associations may be conducive to remembering the product of a given brand better, but in a situation of the lack of control, the chances of including information about the brand in the associative network are lower.

4 Conclusions

The aim of the study was to explore the role of (a lack of) control in an associative structure of the positioned brands, considering brand familiarity.

Referring our study to the theoretical concepts of lack of control in relations to the perception of similarity, it can be noted that previous studies have shown how perceived similarity affects the loss of control (e.g., Schwarz 2004; Wang and Shukla 2013). In our research we went a step further and showed how lack of control affects the perception of similarity.

Our study showed that the state of a lack of control, compared to the control, facilitated the perception of greater differences between the positioned brands at the level of associations, i.e. at the deeper level of information processing. The opposite effects were obtained when similarity was measured on scales – that is, at a shallower level of information processing. Moreover, there were more similar associations between familiar rather than unfamiliar brands of beer. Thus, when encountering unfamiliar brands, consumers are more vigilant, and they perceive more differences between products' properties. Paradoxically, this may lead consumers to confuse well-known products more often than the unknown ones. Our results indicate which marketing strategies should be adopted: for unfamiliar brands customers should be provided with good quality and positive presentation of product attributes; while in communication about familiar brands messages should focus on differentiation, because less vigilant consumers poorly differentiate between products of a given category. A qualitative analysis showed that in the situation of lack of control, compared to in control, there is a greater activation of generic properties and a lower activation of personal associations. By carefully analyzing consumers' associations with their brands, marketers can focus on strengthening selected features of their product and thus facilitate consumer decisions.

Some limitations of our study and implications to further research should be noted here.

In our study, we analyzed the perception of similarity between low-involvement products (beer), in the conditions of control vs. lack of control. The conclusions of our research are applicable to low-involvement products because the information about highly involving products is processed differently. Purchase of highly involving products, compared to low involving ones, engages a greater financial, social and psychological risk. Data concerning high-involvement products is usually actively searched and critically evaluated and processed more carefully, with greater vigilance (Boriboon et al. 2010; Chen and Wang 2010). Furthermore, people in a state of loss of control may face greater difficulties in processing information about high-involvement products (greater cognitive load) compared to low-involvement ones. That is why research on the perception of similarities between high-involvement products may offer some valuable insights.

Qualitative data obtained in this study (in the form of associations) offer many interpretative possibilities. From the point of view of building marketing strategies, one of the interesting interpretations of multidimensional scaling results is to take into account perceived similarities and differences between brands. Strengthening brand-specific associations, and neutralizing associations similar to other brands, is one of the most effective strategies of strengthening the brand's position in the competitive market.

Finally, our study has shown that individual differences—a state of lack of control vs. in control—modify the perception of similarity. On the one hand, it is worth developing research on the effects of individual differences in perception of similarity. In the classical theories of similarity this aspect has not been taken into account (see: Tversky 1977), however, there is a stream of current research indicating that such studies are justified (Carroll and Chang 1970; Simmons and Estes 2008; Day et al. 2010). On the other hand, our data suggest that it may be well worth to consider individual differences in perceived similarities between brands (i.e. brand positioning) in micro-targeting processes using big data sets and algorithms.

References

Anderson, J. R. (1983). *The architecture of cognition*. Cambridge: Harvard University Press.
Bei, L. T., Chu, C. H., & Shen, Y. C. (2011). Positioning brand extensions in comparative advertising: An assessment of the roles of comparative brand similarity, comparative claims, and consumer product knowledge. *Journal of Marketing Communications, 17*(4), 229–244. https://doi.org/10.1080/13527260903478367.
Brandt, C., Mortanges, De., Charles, P., Bluemelhuber, C., Riel, V., & Allard, C. R. (2011). Associative networks: A new approach to market segmentation. *International Journal of Market Research, 53*(2), 187–207. https://doi.org/10.2501/IJMR-53-2-187-208.
Boriboon, N., Alsua, C. J., & Suvanujasiri, A. (2010). High and low involvement products and their relationship with purchase intentions of thai consumers. *Journal of International Business and Economics, 10*(2), 37–54.
Campbell, M. C., & Keller, K. L. (2003). Brand familiarity and advertising repetition effects. *Journal of Consumer Research, 30*(2), 292–304. https://doi.org/10.1086/376800.
Carroll, J. D.; Chang, J. J . (1970). Analysis of individual differences in multidimensional scaling via an N-way generalization of "Eckart-Young" decomposition. *Psychometrika, 35*(3), 283–319. https://doi.org/10.1007/BF02310791.
Chen, Y. F., & Wang, Y. J. (2010). Effect of herd cues and product involvement on bidder online choices. *Cyberpsychology, Behavior, and Social Networking, 13*, 423–428.
Coulter, R. A., Zaltman, G., & Coulter, K. S. (2001). Interpreting consumer perceptions of advertising: An application of the Zaltman metaphor elicitation technique. *Journal of Advertising, 30*(4), 1–21. https://doi.org/10.1080/00913367.2001.10673648.

Cutright, K. M; Bettman, J. R., Fitzsimons, G. J. (2013). Putting brands in their place: How a lack of control keeps brands contained. *Journal of Marketing Research, 50*(3), 365–377. https://doi.org/10.1509/jmr.10.0202.

Day, S.; Goldstone, R. L.; Hills, T. (2010): The Effects of Similarity and Individual Differences on Comparison and Transfer. In: *Proceedings of the 32nd Annual Conference of the Cognitive Science Society*. Austin, S. 465–470.

Dube, L., & Schmitt, B. (1999). The effect of a similarity versus dissimilarity focus in positioning strategy: The moderating role of consumer familiarity and product category. *Psychology & Marketing, 16*(3), 211–224. https://doi.org/10.1002/(SICI)1520-6793(199 905)16:3%3c211::AID-MAR2%3e3.0.CO;2-C.

Edward, M., & Sahadev, S. (2012). Modeling the consequences of customer confusion in a service marketing context: An empirical study. *Journal of Services Research, 12*(2), 127–146.

Friesen, J. P., Kay, A. C., Eibach, R. P., & Galinsky, A. D. (2014). Seeking structure in social organization: Compensatory control and the psychological advantages of hierarchy. *Journal of Personality & Social Psychology, 106*(4), 590–609. https://doi.org/10.1037/a00 35620.

Henderson, G. R., Iacobucci, D., & Calder, B. J. (1998). Brand diagnostics: Mapping branding effects using consumer associative networks. *European Journal of Operational Research, 111*(2), 306–327. https://doi.org/10.1016/S0377-2217(98)00151-9.

John, D. R., Loken, B., Kim, K., & Monga, A. B. (2006). Brand concept maps: A methodology for identifying brand association networks. *Journal of Marketing Research, 43*, 549–563. https://doi.org/10.1509/jmkr.43.4.549.

Keller, K. L. (1993). Conceptualizing, measuring, and managing customer-based brand equity. *Journal of Marketing, 57*(1), 1–22. https://doi.org/10.2307/1252054.

Keller, K. L. (2013). *Strategic brand management. Building, measuring and managing brand equity*. New Jersey: Prentice Hall.

Kleine, R. E., & Kernan, J. B. (1988). Measuring the meaning of consumption object's: An empirical investigation. *Advances in Consumer Research, 15*, 498–504.

Kotler, P., & Keller, K. L. (2012). *Marketing management*. Upper Saddle River: Prentice Hall.

Landau, M. J., Aaron, C., & Whitson, J. A. (2015). Compensatory control and the appeal of a structured world. *Psychological Bulletin, 141*(3), 694–722. https://doi.org/10.1037/a00 38703.

Lingoes, J. C., & Borg, I. (1978). A Direct approach to individual differences scaling using increasingly complex transformations. *Psychometrika, 43*(4), 491–519.

Maier, S. F., & Seligman, M. (2016). Learned helplessness at fifty: Insights from neuroscience. *Psychological Review, 123*(4), 349–367.

McClelland, J. L. (1995). Constructive memory and memory distortions: A parallel distributed processing approach. In M. Distortion (Ed.), *Daniel Schacter* (pp. 69–90). Cambridge: Harvard University Press.

Mitchell, V. W., Walsh, G., & Yamin, M. (2005). Towards a conceptual model of consumer confusion. *Advances in Consumer Research, 32*(1), 143–150.

Saenger, C., Jewell, R. D., & Grigsby, J. L. (2017). The strategic use of contextual and competitive interference to influence brand-attribute associations. *Journal of Advertising, 46*(3), 424–439. https://doi.org/10.1080/00913367.2017.1281776.

Schwarz, N. (2004). Metacognitive experiences in consumer judgment and decision making. *Journal of Consumer Psychology, 14*(4), 332–348. https://doi.org/10.1207/s15327663jcp1404_2.

Simmons, S., & Estes, Z. (2008). Individual differences in the perception of similarity and difference. *Cognition, 108,* 781–795. https://doi.org/10.1016/j.cognition.2008.07.003.

Tversky, A. (1977). Features of similarity. *Psychological Review,* 84 (4):327–352.

Verhellen, Y., Dens, N., De Pelsmacker, Patrick. (2016). Do I know you? How brand familiarity and perceived fit affect consumers' attitudes towards brands placed in movies. *Marketing Letters, 27,* 461–471. https://doi.org/10.1007/s11002-015-9347-0.

Wang, Q., & Shukla, P. (2013). Linking sources of consumer confusion to decision satisfaction: The role of choice goals. *Psychology & Marketing, 30*(4), 295–304. https://doi.org/10.1002/mar.20606.

Wänke, M., Bless, H., & Schwarz, N. (1998). Context effects in product line extensions: Context is not destiny. *Journal of Consumer Psychology, 7*(4), 299–322. https://doi.org/10.1207/s15327663jcp0704_01.

Whitson, J. A., & Galinsky, A. D. (2008). Lacking control increases illusory pattern perception. *Science, 322,* 115–117. https://doi.org/10.1126/science.1159845.

Zaltman, G. (2003). *How consumers think: Essential insights into the mind of the market.* Boston: Harvard Business School Press.

Which Message Frames and Forms Best Promote Political Campaigns via Social Media?

Meily Mei Fung Cheung, Wai Han Lo, and Benson Shu Yan Lam

1   Introduction

With the increasing popularity and convenience of social media platforms, increasing numbers of politicians are bypassing traditional news gatekeepers and interacting directly with the public through social media posts, with the flexibility to select and package their messages via a strategy frame or an policy frame [Consider defining these terms on their first usage.]. Previous studies examining how differences between social media posts affect users' responses have focused on either the content (e.g., Brewer et al. 2016; Fernandes et al 2010; Lee and Shin 2012) or the form (Ksiazek et al. 2016; Ross et al. 2015) of such posts. Few have simultaneously examined the effects of the content and form of posts on the responses of social media users. To fill this research gap and contribute to the literature on social media and political communication, this study explored the differences in online responses to social media posts with various message frames and forms. The specific objectives were as follows.

M. M. F. Cheung (✉) · B. S. Y. Lam
The Hang Seng University of Hong Kong, Siu Lek Yuen, Hong Kong
E-Mail: cheungmeily@hotmail.com

B. S. Y. Lam
E-Mail: besonlam@hsu.edu.hk

W. H. Lo
Hong Kong Baptist University, Kowloon Tong, Hong Kong
E-Mail: janetlo@hkbu.edu.hk

1. To expand the scope of frame study, which has focused mainly on traditional media, to social media platforms. This study focused on election candidate posts on social media.
2. To gain insights into the effectiveness of message strategies by analyzing the influence of both the content and the form of social media posts on user responses, in contrast with past research, which has generally examined only content or form as an independent variable.
3. To determine how the quality of user engagement is affected by the length of user comments and the salience of policy keywords. This involved assessing the cognitive dimensions of user responses, whereas past research measured only the number of likes, shares and comments.
4. To conduct the first empirical analysis of the quality of Facebook responses during a political election, combining computational and traditional approaches and "big data" analysis.

2 Literature Review

During election campaigns, many politicians have started to take advantage of social media platforms to deliver their messages to the public instead of relying on traditional media (Enli 2017; Kalsnes 2016; Strandberg 2013). For election candidates, social media offer a foundational means of framing and underscoring campaign-based content, but the potential of policy frames as a tool to advocate relevant policies via social media has yet to be fully exploited. Empirical studies have shown that candidates prefer to post personal stories and details of campaign events than to explicate social issues or their proposed policies on social media (McGregor et al. 2017; Ross and Comrie 2015). This may be because audiences are more receptive to strategy-framed and personal-framed content (Iyengar et al. 2004; McGregor et al. 2015). The body of literature on framing is enormous and covers multiple disciplines (Entman 1993), such as business (e.g., Le Ber and Branzei 2010; Roy and Sharma 2015), health communication (e.g. Donovan and Jalleh 2000; Underhill et al. 2016), information technology (e.g. Seo and Park 2019) and environmental studies (e.g. Ekayani et al. 2016; Hoffman 2011).

Frames can be defined as the schemas used by viewers to identify, understand, and perceive information (Goffman 1974). "Framing" refers to the presentation of information in such a way as to resonate with these schemas underlying public perception (Scheufele and Tewksbury 2007). When frames are deployed in messages, they highlight certain aspects of the information conveyed, telling the audience what is important and people's perceptions of or beliefs about this information (Ferree et al. 2002; Nisbet and Huge 2006) and thus changing people's perceptions of or beliefs about reality (Entman 1993).

Frames with different discourse properties may elicit different interpretation strategies (Rhee 1997). Two types of message frames are commonly used in political campaigns. The first, strategy frames, are primarily related to campaign strategies and candidate performance, and focus on the results of elections (Iyengar 1991; Bennett 1988; Rhee 1997). The second, policy frames, are more concerned with the policies proposed by election candidates to solve existing societal problems (Graber 1993; Jamieson 1992; Patterson 1993; D'Angelo et al. 2005). Compared with policy frames, strategy frames are more event-oriented and person-centered (Iyengar 1991; Bennett 1988; Rhee 1997).

Different writers deliver their messages differently. A strategy-framed news story on an election written by a reporter is not expected to be identical to a strategy-framed social media post written by an election candidate. The difference between a news story and a social media post is determined by many factors. One of the difference is a reporter writing election-related news stories in the grammatical third person and emphasizes how the candidates are performing and how likely each candidate is to win the election. In contrast, a candidate shapes his/her messages and posts, which are very often filtered by mainstream media, around strategic elements of the election, including the candidate's background, leadership ability, polls, and fundraising efforts (Druckman, 2004), to build a positive image in the eyes of the public. Iyengar et al. (2004) suggested that messages adopting a strategy or game frame are more attractive to readers. We therefore hypothesized the following.

H1: Compared with those using an policy frame, candidate posts adopting a strategy frame on Facebook tend to a) receive more positive Facebook responses ("likes," "loves," and "hahas") and b) be shared more frequently.

Comments, whether simple or complex, reflect commenters' thinking, and are therefore considered a mode of cognitive engagement. Commenting on a post on social media generally delivers greater value than simply "liking" the post (Kim and Yang 2017; John et al. 2017; Srivastava et al. 2018), and is believed to be more representative of the quality of the feedback given to politicians in their election campaigns online. For example, the length of a comment could be used to determine the quality of the commenter's cognitive engagement with the original post (Sweetser and Lariscy 2008). This may also offer insights into how social media act as a public sphere.

Compared with policy frames, strategy frames offer readers a different perspective. A strategy frame guides readers through the process instead of the content (De Vreese 2012). The use of strategy frames has been found to reduce political trust, participation, and engagement (Borah 2013; de Vreese 2005; Pedersen 2012; Shehata 2014; Valentino et al. 2001). Policy frames, in contrast, foster political participation and substantive deliberation by focusing on the policy content proposed by the candidates (Ball-Rokeach and Loges 1996; Borah 2013; Lawrence 2000; Shehata 2014). Based on the literature, however, strategy-framed stories are more appealing to the public than issue-framed messages (De Vreese 2012). Discrepancies have also been noted between strategy-framed social media messages posted by election candidates and strategy-framed news stories from traditional media. It is therefore logical to question whether policy or strategy framing can better promote substantive deliberation, leading to the following research question.

RQ1: What kind of content on Facebook—either strategy-framed or policy-framed—receives a) more general comments and b) a larger number of long comments?

Research has shown that individuals who repeatedly read election-related news stories with a strategy or a policy frame are inclined to use ideas corresponding to that particular frame when they are asked to describe the election campaign (D'Angelo et al. 2005; Rhee 1997). Accordingly, we expected policies or policies to be mentioned more frequently in user comments on policy-framed than strategy-framed social media posts, leading to Hypothesis 2.

H2: Candidate posts on Facebook that adopt an policy frame include more salient policy-related keywords than those adopting a strategy frame.

Users' responses to messages depend not only on the messages' content, but also on their form. Research has found that media users hold more positive attitudes toward more vivid messages (Cheng and Lo 2015; Lo and Cheng 2015). Video-based posts with moving images and sound are more vivid than posts containing only text and/or pictures (Steuer 1994). Runs and Cameron (2006) also reported that the use of imagery in social media posts can predict user engagement. In addition, Kite et al. (2016) reported that social media posts including videos received more likes, comments, and shares than posts featuring photos and text only. Therefore, we proposed the following two hypotheses.

H3: Differences in the number of a) positive responses (likes, loves, and hahas) and b) shares are associated with differences in message form (e.g., text, photo, and/or video).

H4: Differences in the number of a) general comments and b) long comments are associated with differences in message form (e.g., text, photo, and/or video).

3 Methodology

We analyzed posts and user comments published on the Facebook campaign pages of the three candidates in the 2017 Hong Kong Chief Executive election, namely Carrie Lam, John Tsang, and Kwok-hing Woo, between January 1, 2017 (when Carrie Lam, the candidate last launched her election campaign among three candidates) and March 31, 2017 (the fourth day after the election). We extracted 509 candidate posts (excluding outliers) and 379,880 user comments (excluding null comments, i.e., picture icons) were extracted from the official Facebook pages of the three candidates using Facepager during the three-month election period.

Two human coders coded the message frames and forms of the posts of the three candidates. One coder was responsible for coding all of the posts, and the other coded a random sample of 30% of the posts. Cohen's kappa test yielded an overall intercoder reliability of 0.88. In addition, we [As per the above note, it is not clear whether, and if so, how, the researchers ("we") differed from the "human coders" mentioned above.]used a computational method to count user responses and code all of the comments. We examined a large number of comments (379,880) to improve the reliability and accuracy of the data analysis. We examined 379,880 comments to improve the reliability and accuracy of the data analysis.

We implemented a keyword search approach to measure the number of policy-related keywords in the user comments to determine whether the user comments on policy-framed posts showed greater policy salience than those on strategy-related posts. A dictionary was created to select keywords relevant to the election campaigns. We used term frequency-inverse document frequency (tf-idf) analysis, a text mining technique for the identification of keywords via an online search engine (Rahman et al. 2011) and document retrieval (Sachan et al. 2015), to automatically extract the most relevant keywords. Next, using keyword harvesting and expansion techniques, we semi-automatically obtained policy- related terms and phrases. In this semi-automatic procedure, one researcher was responsible for manually selecting relevant terms from the extracted tf-idf data. Two hundred and ten terms, including closely related ones (such as synonyms), were chosen.

Expansion was then performed using a deep learning tool (Word2vec; Mikolov et al. 2013). The final editing and verification were performed by the two other researchers, and the keywords constituting the dictionary were finalized. The unit of analysis in this study was an individual Facebook comment, and policy salience was automatically measured for 379,880 comments on strategy-framed and policy-framed posts.

We defined the independent variables as the message frames and message forms of the 509 sampled posts uploaded by the 3 candidates. The coders were trained to classify the message frames adopted in the candidate posts into three categories: "strategy frame," "policy frame," or "off-topic." Strategy-framed posts were event-oriented and candidate-centered. They emphasized campaign strategies, endorsement, volunteers, and candidates' personalities and performance (Bennett 1988; Enli 2017; Iyengar 1991; McGregor et al. 2017; Rhee 1997; Ross et al. 2015). Policy-framed posts dealt with societal problems and the policy solutions proposed by the candidates (Graber 1993; Jamieson 1992; Patterson 1993; D'Angelo et al. 2005). To ensure that all categories were represented, the off-topic category comprised irrelevant posts (such as those wishing readers a happy Valentine's Day; McGregor et al. 2017). Cohen's kappa test yielded an intercoder reliability of 0.84. We coded message form in terms of format type (text, photo and video) and variation in format (present or absent). We later recoded these items to give a single form indicator (message form) that classified candidates' posts as "text only," "text and photo," "text and video," or "other."

Next, we examined the association between the two sets of independent variables established in the two pairs of hypotheses (H1 and H2; H3 and H4), namely message frame and message form. A weak or no association between these two sets of variables meant that the hypotheses addressed the posts from two distinct perspectives. As these two sets of independent variables were mainly indicator variables, we calculated the phi coefficient instead of the correlation coefficient. Similar to the correlation coefficient, the phi coefficient is a number between -1 and 1. A larger positive or negative value denotes a stronger positive or negative association, respectively, between two variables. The phi coefficients for the two sets of independent variables are shown in Table 1.

When testing the two pairs of hypotheses, we ignored the "off-topic" category for message frame and the "other" category for message form. According to the general rule of correlation coefficients, the two sets of variables had either a weak association or no association. Thus, the two pairs of hypotheses (H1 and H2; H3 and H4) took different perspectives on the posts. We used computer-assisted content analysis to measure user responses by counting the number of positive Facebook responses, including likes, loves, and hahas, and the number of shares

Table 1 Phi Coefficients for the Two Sets of Independent Variables

		Message Frame	
		Strategy Frame	Issue Frame
Message Form	Text	0.396784	−0.32648
	Text and Photo	0.276454	−0.180764
	Text and Video	−0.0241912	0.12648

through the Facebook application programming interface. We also recorded the number of user comments, including general comments (all of the user comments on a particular post) and long comments (comments of 30 words or more). The iPolicy-related keyword salience of user responses was also investigated as an additional indicator of users' cognitive involvement. In addition, we measured the frequency of keywords featured in the dictionary created for this study (as previously described) in the comments on each of the posts.

4 Results

The findings of the t-test assessing H1 are summarized in Table 2. Candidate posts on Facebook adopting a strategy frame were found to receive more positive Facebook responses and shares than those adopting an policy frame. Therefore, H1 was supported (Table 2) and RQ1 was answered (Table 3). Compared with posts with a policy frame, Facebook posts with a strategy frame generated more positive Facebook responses, including more general comments and long comments. The results of an independent t-test assessing H2 are shown in Table 4. H2 was not supported according to the findings of another independent t-test of the difference in policy-related keyword salience between strategy-framed posts and policy-framed posts. This difference was found not to be statistically significant.

H3 and H4 concerned the potential variation in user responses to posts with different forms. Based on the findings of one-way analysis of variance (ANOVA), summarized in Table 5, H3 was supported. Posts containing both textual and video content (text-video posts) generally received more positive Facebook responses and shares than text-only posts and posts containing text and photos (text-photo posts). Another one-way ANOVA test was conducted to examine the potential variation in general comments and long comments. The results (shown in Table 6) supported H4. On average, text-video posts were found to receive more general comments and long comments than text-photo posts.

Table 2 Results of t-test and Descriptive Statistics for Facebook reactions and shares

	Strategic Frame			Policy Frame			Mean Difference		
	M	SD	N	M	SD	n		t	df
Likes	8137.89	9987.05	352	3379.98	3770.78	112	4757.90	7.43***	450.21
Loves	664.36	1037.93	352	223.06	291.73	112	441.30	7.14***	457.71
Hahas	159.79	414.70	352	26.23	36.99	112	133.56	5.97***	368.05
Shares	456.13	1346.69	352	130.29	198.05	112	325.85	4.39***	394.57

Notes. $*p<0.05; **p<0.01; ***p<0.001$

Table 3 Results of t-test and Descriptive Statistics for Facebook comments

	Strategic Frame		Policy Frame			Mean Difference	t	df
	M	SD	N	M	SD	n		
General comments	714.66	1028.11	346	200.36	339.74	111	63.990	8.04***	454.63
Long comments	159.82	262.30	346	56.31	60.60	111	103.51	6.80***	431.86

Notes. $*p<0.05$; $**p<0.01$; $***p<0.001$

Table 4 Results of t-test and Descriptive Statistics for Facebook comments

	Strategic Frame			Policy Frame			Mean Difference	t	df
	M	SD	N	M	SD	n			
Policy keyword related salience	73.55	164.8	346	90.17	14.01	111	−16.62	−0.948	455

Notes. *$p<0.05$; **$p<0.01$; ***$p<0.001$

Table 5 Results of ANOVA for Facebook reactions and shares

	Mean				Df			F
	Text only	Text + Photo	Text + Video	Total	Between Groups	Within Groups	Total	
Likes	2934.81	6517.36	8091.37	6906.14	2	469	471	3.16*
Loves	168.06	446.29	809.23	554.51	2	469	471	9.42***
Hahas	40.88	97.24	201.45	129.11	2	469	471	4.07*
Shares	54.44	213.70	717.63	371.65	2	469	471	10.32***

Notes. $*p < 0.05$; $**p < 0.01$; $***p < 0.001$

Table 6 Results of ANOVA for Facebook comments

	Mean				Df			F
	Text only	Text + Photo	Text + Video	Total	Between Groups	Within Groups	Total	
General Comments	622.63	390.87	984.61	592.93	2	462	464	21.62***
Long Comments	136.63	98.98	199.78	133.23	2	462	464	9.71***

Notes. $*p < 0.05$; $**p < 0.01$; $***p < 0.001$

5 Discussion

Given the widespread use of social media in political campaigns around the world, it is important to examine how different message strategies elicit different user responses on social media platforms. We suggest that important insights can be afforded by examining message frames and forms in relation to the quantity and quality of responses. This study found that compared with posts with an policy frame, Facebook posts with a strategy frame generated more positive Facebook responses, including likes, loves, and hahas, more shares, and more general comments and long comments. This suggests that the readers of posts with strategy frames on social media are more politically responsive and engaged than the readers of posts with policy frames.

Do social media provide an ideal public setting for the meaningful expression and exchange of political ideas? The findings of this study are not optimistic in this regard. They thus differ from the finding of several previous studies that policy-framed posts are better able than strategy-framed posts to encourage political engagement and deliberation (Borah 2013; Shehata 2014). The different perspectives of strategy-framed news reports and strategy-framed social media posts may account for this discrepancy. This study's findings suggest that compared with the strategy-framed news reports examined in previous studies, strategy-framed social media posts by election candidates may be better able to deliver a favorable image of the candidates.

This study also enhances understanding of the influence of information richness and message form on audience responses on social media. Its findings confirm that videos help to attract user responses (Kite et al. 2016). The use of videos on social media platforms may thus be a promising strategy for securing success in online election campaigns in the future. Text-video posts may also be better able than posts containing text only or than posts with textual and photographic content to elicit both affective responses and cognitive feedback. from social media users, as in this study, they received more positive Facebook responses, shares, general comments, and long comments. Compared with text-video posts, text-only posts were less able to generate affective responses, and text-photo posts received fewer and shorter comments. Similar to Kim and Yang's (2017) finding that the use of photos in posts was negatively related to the number of comments received, this study revealed that the use of photos in election campaigns on social media may not be very effective in generating cognitive feedback.

References

Ball-Rokeach, S., & Loges, W. (1996). Making choices: Media roles in the construction of value choices. In C. Seligman, J. M. Olson, & M. P. Zanna (Eds.), *The psychology of values: The Ontario symposium* (Vol. 8, pp. 277–298). Mahwah: Lawrence Erlbaum.
Bennett, W. L. (1988). *News: The politics of illusion* (2nd ed.). New York: Longman.
Borah, P. (2013). Interactions of news frames and incivility in the political blogosphere: Examining perceptual outcomes. *Political Communication, 30*(3), 456–473.
Brewer, P. R., Habegger, M., Harrington, R., Hoffman, L. H., Jones, P. E., & Lambe, J. L. (2016). Interactivity between candidates and citizens on a social networking site: Effects on perceptions and vote intentions. *Journal of Experimental Political Science, 3*(1), 84–96.
Cheng, B. K. L., & Lo, W. H. (2015). The effects of melodramatic animation in crime-related news. *Journalism and Mass Communication Quarterly., 92*(3), 559–579.
D'Angelo, P., Calderone, M., & Territola, A. (2005). Strategy and issue framing: An exploratory analysis of topics and frames in campaign 2004 print news. *Atlantic Journal of Communication, 13*(4), 199–219.
de Vreese, C. H. (2005). News framing: Theory and typology. *Information Design Journal & Document Design, 13*(1), 51–62

Donovan, R. J., & Jalleh, G. (2000). Positive versus negative framing of a hypothetical infant immunization: The influence of involvement. *Health Education & Behavior, 27*(1), 82–95.

Druckman, J. N. (2004). Priming the vote: Campaign effects in a U.S. Senate Election. *Political Psychology, 25*(4), 577–594.

Ekayani, M., Nurrochmat, D. R., & Darusman, D. (2016). The role of scientists in forest fire media discourse and its potential influence for policy-agenda setting in Indonesia. *Forest Policy and Economics, 68,* 22–29.

Enli, G. (2017). Twitter as arena for the authentic outsider: Exploring the social media campaigns of Trump and Clinton in the 2016 US presidential election. *European Journal of Communication, 32*(1), 50–61.

Entman, R. M. (1993). Framing: Toward clarification of a fractured paradigm. *Journal of Communication, 43*(4), 51–58.

Ferree, M. M., Gamson, W. A., Gerhards, J., et al. (2002). *Shaping Abortion Discourse: Democracy and the Public Sphere in Germany and the United States.* New York: Cambridge University Press.

Fernandes, J., Giurcanu, M., Bowers, K. W., & Neely, J. C. (2010). The writing on the wall: A content analysis of college students' Facebook groups for the 2008 presidential election. *Mass Communication and Society, 13*(5), 653–675.

Goffman, E. (1974). *Frame analysis: An essay on the organization of experience.* Cambridge: Harvard University Press.

Graber, D. A. (1993). *Mass media and American politics* (4th ed.). Washington, DC: CQ Press.

Hoffman, A. J. (2011). Talking past each other? Cultural framing of skeptical and convinced logics in the climate change debate. *Organization & Environment, 24*(1), 3–33.

Iyengar, S. (1991). *Is anyone responsible? How television frames political issues.* Chicago: University of Chicago Press.

Jamieson, K. H. (1992). *Dirty politics.* New York: Oxford University Press.

John, L., Mochon, D., Emrich, O., & Schwartz, J. (2017). What's the value of a Like? Harvard Business Review, March–April 2017 Issue. https://hbr.org/2017/03/whats-the-value-of-a-like.

Kalsnes, B. (2016). The social media paradox explained: comparing political parties' Facebook strategy versus practice. *Social Media+ Society, 2*(2), 2056305116644616.

Kim, C., & Yang, S. U. (2017). Like, comment, and share on Facebook: How each behavior differs from the other. *Public Relations Review, 43*(2), 441–449.

Kite, J., Foley, B. C., Grunseit, A. C., & Freeman, B. (2016). Please like me: Facebook and public health communication. *PloS one, 11*(9), e0162765. https://dx.doi.org/10.1371/journal.pone.0162765.

Ksiazek, T. B., Peer, L., & Lessard, K. (2016). User engagement with online news: Conceptualizing interactivity and exploring the relationship between online news videos and user comments. *New Media & Society, 18*(3), 502–520.

Lawrence, R. G. (2000). *The politics of force: Media and the construction of police brutality.* London: University of California Press.

Le Ber, M. J., & Branzei, O. (2010). Value frame fusion in cross sector interactions. *Journal of Business Ethics, 94*(1), 163–195.

Lee, E. J., & Shin, S. Y. (2012). Are they talking to me? Cognitive and affective effects of interactivity in politicians' Twitter communication. *Cyberpsychology, Behavior, and Social Networking, 15*(10), 515–520.

Lo, W. H., & Cheng, B. K. L. (2015). The use of melodramatic animation in news, presence and news credibility: A Path model. *Journalism Studies*. http://www.tandfonline.com/doi/abs/10.1080/1461670X.2015.1087814?journalCode=rjos20.

McGregor, S. C., Lawrence, R. G., & Cardona, A. (2017). Personalization, gender, and social media: Gubernatorial candidates' social media strategies. *Information, Communication & Society, 20*(2), 264–283.

Mikolov, T., Chen, K., Corrado, G.S and Dean, J. (2013). Efficient Estimation of Word Representations in Vector Space. In Proceedings of Workshop at ICLR.

Nisbet, M. C., & Huge, M. (2006). Attention cycles and frames in the plant biotechnology debate – Managing power and participation through the press/policy connection. *Harvard International Journal of Press-Politics, 11,* 3–40.

Patterson, T. E. (1993). *Out of order*. New York: Knopf.

Pedersen, R. (2012). The game frame and political efficacy: Beyond the spiral of cynicism. *European Journal of Communication, 27*(3), 225–240. https://doi.org/10.1177/0267323112454089.

Rahman, M. M., Karmaker, A., & Hasan, M. M. (2011). HCPR multiplied with TFIDF for effective search method: For effective web ranking. LAP LAMBERT Academic Publishing.

Rhee, J. W. (1997). Strategy and issue frames in election campaign coverage: A social cognitive account of framing effects. *Journal of Communication, 47*(3), 26–48.

Ross, K., Fountaine, S., & Comrie, M. (2015). Facing up to Facebook: Politicians, publics and the social media (ted) turn in New Zealand. *Media, Culture & Society, 37*(2), 251–269. https://doi.org/10.1177/0163443714557983.

Roy, R., & Sharma, P. (2015). Scarcity appeal in advertising: Exploring the moderating roles of need for uniqueness and message framing. *Journal of Advertising, 44*(4), 349–359.

Sachan, D. & Kumar, S. (2015) "Class Vectors: Embedding representation of Document Classes", Computation and language. https://arxiv.org/abs/1508.00189

Scheufele, D. A., & Tewksbury, D. (2007). Framing, agenda setting, and priming: The evolution of three media effects models. *Journal of Communication, 57*(1), 9–20. https://doi.org/10.1111/j.1460-2466.2006.00326.x.

Seo, B. G., & Park, D. H. (2019). The effect of message framing on security behavior in online services: Focusing on the shift of time orientation via psychological ownership. *Computers in Human Behavior, 93:* 357–369.

Shehata, A. (2014). Game frames, issue frames, and mobilization: Disentangling the effects of frame exposure and motivated news attention on political cynicism and engagement. *International Journal of Public Opinion Research, 26*(2), 157–177.

Srivastava, J., Saks, J., Weed, A. J., & Atkins, A. (2018). Engaging audiences on social media: Identifying relationships between message factors and user engagement on the American Cancer Society's Facebook page. *Telematics and Informatic, 35,* 1832–1844.

Steuer, J. (1994). *Vividness and source of evaluation as determinants of social responses toward mediated representation of agency*. Unpublished doctoral dissertation, Standford University.

Strandberg, K. (2013). A social media revolution or just a case of history repeating itself? The use of social media in the 2011 finnish parliamentary elections. *New Media & Society, 15*(8), 1329–1347.

Sweetser, K. D., & Lariscy, R. W. (2008). Candidates make good friends: An analysis of candidates' uses of Facebook. *International Journal of Strategic Communication, 2*(3), 175–198.

Underhill, K., Morrow, K. M., Colleran, C., Calabrese, S. K., Operario, D., Salovey, P., & Mayer, K. H. (2016). Explaining the efficacy of pre-exposure prophylaxis (PrEP) for HIV prevention: A qualitative study of message framing and messaging preferences among US men who have sex with men. *AIDS and Behavior, 20*(7), 1514–1526.

Valentino, N., Beckmann, M., & Buhr, T. (2001). A spiral of cynicism for some: The contingent effects of campaign news frames on participation and confidence in government. *Political Communication, 18,* 347–367.

Can It Hurt to Be Honest About Nudging? the Impact of a (Disclosed) Social Norm Nudge on Food Preferences and Choice

Lotte Hallez, Rob Van Roy, Bieke Zaman, and Tim Smits

1   Introduction

Health interventions have often focused on changing consumers' knowledge, attitudes and perceptions towards healthy eating. Over the last decades, consumers have become more concerned with healthy eating and they are increasingly interested in their general health and wellbeing (Nielsen 2018). And yet, they are also increasingly overweight or obese (The GBD Obesity Collaborators 2017; World Health Organisation 2018). There seems to be a gap between people's knowledge and intentions on the one hand and their behaviours on the other (cf. the attitude-behaviour gap; Vermeir and Verbeke 2006), which can be explained by insights from behavioural economics. Food choices are generally made quickly and automatically (Moldovan and David 2012), and are highly dependent on the social and physical context. The smallest change in these contexts could lead to changes in people's eating behaviours (Thaler and Sunstein 2009). This leaves people vulnerable to all sorts of (marketing) influences, but it also paves the way for policymakers to steer people's health in a positive manner. Over the last decade, insights from behavioural economics have caused a shift in the public policy landscape (Whitehead et al. 2014). Policymakers are not just educating consumers, they are increasingly steering their behaviours with *nudging* interventions. These interventions are especially useful within the realm of health communication, because this is a domain where freedom of choice is considered particularly important and where regulations and penalties are not always appropriate (Ly and Soman 2013).

There has been much enthusiasm about the possibilities of nudging, but it has also raised concerns. Nudges that target people's automatic responses fly under the radar of our conscious thoughts and are therefore often considered manipulative and threatening to people's individual autonomy (Baldwin 2014; Chater 2015; Evans 2012). This contrasts with more overt types of persuasive communication, such as traditional advertising or public service announcements. People are generally able to recognize the persuasive intent of those messages, which enables them to activate their persuasion knowledge. This knowledge provides them with the necessary skill set to reject the persuasive attempt should they wish to do so (Friestad and Wright 1994). Covert persuasion like nudges, however, hinders the activation of persuasion knowledge, which renders people 'defenceless' to their influence. This chapter will focus on how the effect of subtle nudging interventions is affected by an upfront disclosure of this persuasive technique.

Authors have proposed that nudges need to be sufficiently transparent to lose their manipulative character (Chater 2015; Fischer and Lotz 2014; Sunstein 2015). Transparency has already become a standard requirement for policymakers in most democratic countries that apply nudging. It has been suggested by some, however, that transparency could decrease or even completely eliminate the effectiveness of a nudge (Bovens 2009; Bruns et al. 2018). Drawing attention to the persuasive intent of a message could possibly lead to resistance or *reactance* (Brehm 1989). To date, however, not many studies have considered the consequences of disclosing the persuasive intent of a nudge (Marchiori et al. 2017). In a lab setting, we investigate the influence of a *social norm nudge* on people's food preferences and choices, and examine whether changes occur when the persuasive intent of the nudge is explicitly disclosed.

2 Literature Review and Hypotheses

2.1 Social norm nudge

It is well established in social research that human behaviour is driven by social norms. People are members of different social groups, and have an internal desire to fit in to make sure they maintain their membership status. To achieve this, they align their behaviours with the standards and expectations of the groups. This is the underlying idea of *The Focus Theory of Normative Conduct* (Cialdini et al. 1990), and has led to the assumption that people are more likely to act out a behaviour if they perceive that this behaviour is common in their social group (i.e. descriptive norm). This means that people's behaviours could be *nudged* into a desired direction by drawing attention to a descriptive social norm (i.e., a message suggesting a high or majority prevalence of a behaviour) about a relevant social group. As such, studies have indicated that social norm nudges in which a descriptive norm is made salient have the potential to steer people into a variety of behaviours, such as obtaining higher test scores (Heap et al. 2017), donating money (Bartke et al. 2017), saving energy (Wong-Parodi et al. 2019), and making more frequent use of public transport (Kormos et al. 2015). A stream of research has investigated the potential of social norm nudges in the domain of healthy eating. A number of studies have found that social norm nudges can shift people's eating behaviours into a healthier direction (e.g. Burger et al. 2010; Collins et al. 2019; Mollen et al. 2013; Robinson et al. 2013; Robinson and Higgs 2013). Social norm effects also cause people to adapt their consumption to portion sizes (Aerts and Smits 2017; Zlatevska et al. 2014), including young consumers (McGale et al. 2019; Neyens et al. 2015). We therefore hypothesize the following:

H1: A social norm nudge leads people to conform to the descriptive norm that is made salient

Normative messages are said to be more effective when they correspond with the opinions and values of the recipient (White and Simpson 2013). We therefore explore whether a social norm nudge that tries to steer people towards a healthier behaviour is more effective for people who are already interested in maintaining good general health.

2.2 Disclosure

In the field of advertising, several studies have uncovered that disclosing the persuasive intent of a covert message can lead to resistance or *reactance*. Covert messages that conceal their commercial or persuasive intent hinder the activation of people's *persuasion knowledge* (Friestad and Wright 1994), a concept related to *advertising literacy* which develops from childhood to adulthood (Hudders et al. 2017; Rozendaal et al. 2011). Disclosing the persuasive intent can trigger the persuasion knowledge that would provide people with the necessary skill set to reject (some aspects of) the message. Previous research has indicated that covert messages such as sponsorships (Boerman et al. 2014a), native ads (Lee 2010), and product placements (Boerman et al. 2014b) become less effective when their persuasive nature is disclosed.

Many nudges are also considered covert, as their persuasive intent is not always clear to the recipients. However, people may react differently when the persuasive intent of a nudge is disclosed. To our knowledge, four studies have examined the influence of a disclosed *default nudge* (Bruns et al. 2016; Loewenstein et al. 2015; Paunov et al. 2018; Steffel et al. 2016) and one study has examined the influence of a disclosed *repositioning nudge* (Kroese et al. 2016). A default nudge refers to a situation where the default option is changed towards the more desirable behaviour, for instance when a country decides that people are automatically enrolled in an organ donation program (with opt-out) versus a system where people have to opt in. A repositioning nudge refers to a situation where choices are laid out differently (repositioned) in the physical context such that it is easier to opt for the desirable choice (e.g. shelving healthy foods rather than candy at the supermarket check-out). In each of these studies, the nudge significantly influenced people's behaviours and disclosure did not reduce this influence. One of these studies provided initial evidence that disclosure could even strengthen the intended effect of a nudge (Paunov et al. 2018). The reason for this may be that these nudges aimed to steer people's behaviours into a better or healthier direction, which means that the recipients may have felt that the end justifies the means (Reisch and Sunstein 2016). This leads to the following hypothesis:

> H2: Even when the persuasive intent is disclosed, the nudge leads people to conform to the descriptive norm

> RQ1: How does the effect of the nudge differ when the persuasive intent is disclosed in advance?

However, according to Sunstein (2018), drawing attention to the nudge by disclosing its persuasive intent may produce reactance in *some* people. People differ in the extent to which they are prone to experiencing psychological reactance, a concept referred to as *trait reactance* (Brehm 1989). People with high levels of trait reactance are more likely to consider persuasive messages as a threat to their individual autonomy (Quick and Stephenson 2008; Quick et al. 2011) and to reject those messages to restore their sense of freedom (Brehm 1989). We therefore hypothesize the following:

> *H3: The more people show trait reactance, the more disclosure of persuasive intent will block the social norm effect of the nudge*

3 Method

3.1 Participants

Participants were 99 undergraduate students enrolled in a Flemish university. The sample size of this study is similar to other studies that have used a between-subjects design to investigate the influence of normative information on people's food choices (e.g., Staunton et al. 2014; Tarrant et al. 2015). All participants were between the age of 18 and 24 ($M = 20.96$, $SD = 1.54$) and the majority was female (71.30%). A small majority of participants (54%) were invited to participate via social media. The remaining participants were randomly approached for recruitment on the university campus.

3.2 Procedure

We placed participants in a situation where they had to choose between a healthy and an unhealthy snack. Participants were invited to come to a classroom and were alone except for one researcher. After giving initial instructions, the researcher turned away from the participant to avoid influencing their food choice. The first instruction was to complete a language task on paper. This was a filler task to conceal the true objective of the experiment. On the last page, participants were informed that they could choose one snack from two different bowls as a 'reward' for completing the language task. One bowl was filled with healthy snacks, more specifically eight identical pieces of fruit (mandarin oranges; 47 cal

Table 1 Overview of experimental groups and design with stimulus material

Experimental group	Procedure		
Nudge	filler task <		< survey
Nudge + Disclosure	filler task < Disclosure <		< survey
Control	filler task <		< survey

per serving) and the other bowl was filled with unhealthy snacks, more specifically eight regular-sized Mars chocolate bars (234 cal per serving). Participants later indicated that they considered the pieces of fruit to be healthier (7-point scale; $Med = 7.00$) than the chocolate bars (7-point scale, $Med = 1.00$), *Wilcoxon T* $= 0.00$, $p < 0.0001$, $r = -0.88$ (Urala and Lähteenmäki 2006). There were signs in front of the bowls. In the nudge condition, the signs stated that the majority of participants (73%) had previously chosen the healthy snack. In the nudge + disclosure condition, participants saw the same signs, but the persuasive intent of those signs was disclosed in advance. Participants received written information at the end of the language task stating that "the signs were there to influence their snack choice". In a control condition, the signs simply mentioned the names of the snacks. After choosing a healthy or unhealthy snack, participants filled in a paper-based survey (Table 1).

3.3 Measures

Food wanting. We measured to what extent participants wanted the healthy and unhealthy snack with two items ('I want to eat the chocolate bar' and 'I want to eat the piece of fruit') on a 7-point scale (Finlayson, King, and Blundell 2008). We later transformed these items into a relative measure, by subtracting participants' score on the unhealthy snack item from their score on the healthy snack item. Thus, the relative score indicated how much participants wanted the healthy snack relative to the unhealthy snack.

Food Liking. We also gauged to what extent participants liked both snacks with two items ('I like the chocolate bar' and 'I like the piece of fruit') on a 7-point scale (Urala and Lähteenmäki 2006). Again, we transformed the two items into a relative measure, which indicated how much participants liked the healthy snack relative to the unhealthy snack.

Food Choice. After each participant had left the classroom, the researcher counted the bowls to check whether participants had chosen either the healthy or the unhealthy snack.

Trait Reactance. We gauged to what extent participants were prone to experiencing psychological reactance with fourteen items (e.g. 'Regulations trigger a sense of resistance in me', 'I find contradicting others stimulating', etc.) on a 5-point scale ($\alpha = 0.84$; Hong and Faedda 1996).

General Health Interest. We measured participants' interest in maintaining a healthy diet with eight items (e.g. 'It is important to me that my diet is low in fats', 'I always follow a healthy and balanced diet', etc.) on a 7-point scale ($\alpha = 0.89$; Roininen et al. 2001). This measure was added for exploratory purposes.

Reason for Food Choice. Participants reported their motives for choosing the healthy or unhealthy snack by indicating their agreement with six independent statements on a 5-point scale. More specifically, participants were asked to what extent they chose their snack because that option was most *attractive, healthy, impulsive, popular, accessible* and *sustainable*. This measure was added for exploratory purposes.

4 Results

Five participants were excluded from the analyses, because they indicated that they disliked one of the snacks. The analyses were thus performed on 94 participants, nearly equally divided over the nudge condition ($n = 33$), the nudge +

disclosure condition ($n = 31$) and the control condition ($n = 30$). In general, participants were somewhat interested in healthy eating (7-point scale; $M = 4.30$, $SD = 1.12$) and they were moderately prone to experiencing psychological reactance (5-point scale; $M = 2.84$, $SD = 0.55$).

4.1 Food Preferences

We conducted a MANOVA to investigate whether the (disclosed) social norm nudge influenced participants' internal food preferences. More specifically, we investigated whether the (disclosed) nudge led them to like and want the healthy snack more than the unhealthy snack, when controlling for their general health interest and level of trait reactance. Using Pillai's trace, the analysis indicated no significant differences between the three experimental groups on people's relative food liking and wanting ($V = 0.07$, $F(4,178) = 1.56$, $p = 0.19$). We were also interested to see whether the presence of a nudge (with or without disclosure) influenced food wanting and liking compared to the control situation. We combined the two nudging groups, and conducted two independent t-tests to compare the nudging groups on the one hand and the control group on the other. The tests indicated that the presence of a nudge significantly influenced people's food liking, such that they liked the healthy snack more than the unhealthy snack ($M = 0.25$), whereas people who were not nudged actually liked the unhealthy snack more ($M = -0.17$; $t(92) = 2.02$, $p < 0.05$). The nudge had no significant influence on people's food wanting ($t(92) = 0.09$, $p = 0.93$). This partly confirms H1 and H2. To gain more insight into our research question, we conducted an independent t-test to investigate how the two nudging conditions (with vs. without disclosure) differed from each other on these two variables. The analysis indicated that the two groups did not significantly differ from each other for both relative food liking ($t(62) = -0.07$, $p = 0.95$) and food wanting ($t(62) = -0.88$, $p = 0.38$) (Fig. 1).

To test our third hypothesis, which states that people with higher levels of trait reactance are more resistant towards a nudge of which the persuasive intent is disclosed, we calculated the Pearson correlation between trait reactance on the one hand and relative food liking / relative food wanting on the other. Within the nudge + disclosure group, the analysis indicated no significant relationship between participants' level of trait reactance and their food liking ($r = -0.02$, $p = 0.45$) or food wanting ($r = -0.09$, $p = 0.32$). This leads us to partly reject H3.

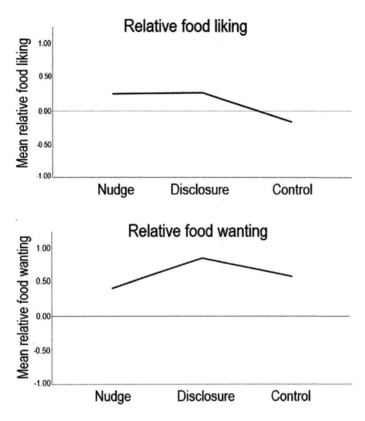

Fig. 1 Mean relative food liking and mean relative food wanting among the three experimental groups

4.2 Food choice

The majority of participants in the nudge condition chose the healthy snack (i.e. 20/33, 60.6%) over the unhealthy snack. In comparison, within the control condition, an equal amount of participants chose the healthy snack (i.e. 15/15, 50.0%) as the unhealthy snack. We conducted a binary logistic regression analysis to check whether the social norm nudge influenced participants' food choice, when controlling for their general health interest and their level of trait reactance. According to the analysis, even though more people chose a healthy snack when nudged compared to when there was no nudge (60.6% vs. 50.0%), this difference was not significant ($p = 0.40$, $OR = 1.54$, $95\% CI = [0.55; 4.34]$). So, contrary to our expectation written out in H1, the social norm nudge did not lead people to conform their behaviour to the descriptive norm.

Furthermore, within the nudge + disclosure condition, fewer participants chose the healthy snack (i.e. 15/31, 48.8%) compared to the unhealthy snack. This is close to the proportion of participants who chose the healthy snack in the control condition (i.e. 50.0%), and the regression analysis indicated that indeed there were no significant differences between these two conditions ($p = 0.86$, $OR = 0.96$, $95\% CI = [0.58, 1.60]$). This leads us to partly reject H2, which states that a disclosed nudge would lead people to conform to the descriptive norm. Moreover, the regression analysis provided more insight into our research question. Even though participants in the nudge + disclosure condition chose the healthy snack less often than participants in the nudge condition (48.8% vs. 60.6%), the analysis indicated no significant difference between these two nudging groups ($p = 0.41$, $OR = 0.64$, $95\% CI = [0.23; 1.84]$).

Lastly, we tested the third hypothesis by investigating the Spearman correlation between level of trait reactance and food choice among participants who were informed about the persuasive intent of the nudge. The analysis indicated that their level of trait reactance was not significantly correlated to their food choice ($r = -0.15$, $p = 0.43$). This leads us to reject H3.

4.3 Exploratory results

According to the MANOVA and the regression analysis, participants' preferences ($V = 0.09$, $F(2,88) = 4.32$, $p < 0.05$) and food choice ($p < 0.05$, $OR = 1.56$, $95\% CI = [1.05, 2.33]$) were directly influenced by their general health interest, such that lower interests in healthy eating decreased the likelihood of a healthy food choice. Moreover, we were interested to see whether the nudge had a stronger behavioural effect on people who were more concerned with their general health. When adding an interaction term between general health interest and condition to the logistic regression analysis, we found that this was not the case ($p = 0.73$, $OR = 0.91$, $95\% CI = [0.57, 1.47]$).

We also measured participants' self-reported motives for choosing a certain snack. For each motive, participants could indicate to what extent they believed that reason was true for them. A Mann–Whitney test indicated that participants who had chosen the unhealthy snack (5-point scale; $M = 3.11$, $SD = 2.38$) agreed more strongly that they had made an impulsive choice than participants who had chosen the healthy snack ($M = 2.38$, $SD = 1.28$), $U = 1464.00$, $z = 2.86$, $p < 0.0001$, $r = 0.29$. Another proposed motive was that participants had chosen their snack because it was the most popular option. Participants who had chosen a healthy snack following exposure to the nudge, and who thus conformed to the group norm, disagreed with this statement (5-point scale; $M = 2.20$, $SD = 1.28$). When the nudge was disclosed in advance, there was less disagreement with this statement ($M = 3.07$, $SD = 1.62$). A Kruskal–Wallis test indicated, however, that this difference was not significant ($U = 193.00$, $z = 1.49$, $p = 0.16$, $r = 0.15$).

5 Discussion

The results of this experiment contribute to the literature concerning social norm effects on food preferences and eating behaviours. The current study adds to this field by investigating actual choice behaviours following a social norm manipulation. The results of this study are not in line with previous studies concerning normative influence. Many studies have shown that descriptive norms can nudge people to adopt healthier eating behaviours (e.g. Burger et al. 2010; Collins et al. 2019; Mollen et al. 2013; Robinson et al. 2013; Robinson and Higgs 2013). In this study, the social norm nudge had no significant impact on people's food choices, although the results pointed in the expected direction. However, we did find that the nudge impacted people's snack liking, such that they liked the healthy snack more than the unhealthy snack following exposure to the descriptive norm message. In contrast, people who were not exposed to any nudge had higher liking for the unhealthy snack. The nudge thus seemed to have an impact on people's attitudes, but this did not translate to their behavioural choices. This might be due to the artificial nature of the experiment. Although people's food choices are usually quick and automatic in real life (Moldovan and David 2012), a lab setting could lead people to think more consciously about their decisions (Urala and Lähteenmaki 2006). If people's food choice was rather conscious, then this could explain the ineffectiveness of a nudge that is supposed to influence people's automatic thought processes.

Moreover, the results of this experiment contribute to the limited literature on the effectiveness of disclosed nudges. To our knowledge, this study is the first to investigate the effectiveness of a social norm nudge of which the persuasive intent is explicitly disclosed. Other studies that have investigated the influence of a disclosed *default option* or of a disclosed *repositioning nudge* provided evidence that a nudge can influence people's (health) behaviours, even when its persuasive intent is disclosed. The results of this study are not entirely in line with those findings. We found that a disclosed nudge influenced people's food liking, but again this effect did not transfer to their behaviour. A possible reason could be that the social norm nudge was already transparent, even without disclosure. According to Hansen and Jespersen (2013), a nudge is transparent when people can figure out its intent. It is probable that, even without explicit disclosure, the participants in this study interpreted the signs in front of the snacks as having been placed there to influence their food choice. If people think they are being influenced, then disclosure may not make much difference (Sagarin and Henningsen 2017).

6 Limitations and Suggestions for Future Research

This study has a few limitations. The first is that our sample was rather small and consisted solely of undergraduate students, meaning that participants were young and highly educated. This limits the generalizability of the study, as younger people are more prone to experiencing psychological reactance (Goldsmith, Clark, and Lafferty 2005) and can experience more anger when exposed to a nudge (Bruns et al. 2016). Moreover, it is possible that participants' food choices were influenced by the artificial nature of the experiment. In reality, people make quick and automatic food choices, but the setting of the experiment could have led people to think more consciously about their choice behaviour. To gain more insight into these food choices, we asked participants to report their motives for choosing either the healthy or unhealthy snack. However, people lack insight into their own behaviour and often improvise when asked to explain their food choices (Moldovan and David 2012). Moreover, we excluded participants if they disliked one of the snacks, but we did not investigate if there were cases of allergies. Another limitation is that the nudge may not have been sufficiently covert and that participants were probably already able to figure out its persuasive intent. The challenges for future studies are to set up similar experiments where the intent of the nudge is more covert, which may be achieved by setting up field experiments. Moreover, future studies could investigate other types of disclosure, such as disclosure of the source of the nudge, of the persuasive tactics at work or of the underlying automatic processes (Marchiori et al. 2017).

References

Aerts, G., & Smits, T. (2017). The package size effect: How package size affects young children's consumption of snacks differing in sweetness. *Food Quality and Preference, 60*(C), 72–80.

Baldwin, R. (2014). From regulation to behaviour change: Giving nudge the third degree. *Modern Law Review, 77*(6), 831–857.

Bartke, S., Friedl, A, Gelhaar, F, & Reh, L. (2017). Social comparison nudges—Guessing the norm increases charitable giving. *Economics Letters, 152*(c), 73–75.

Boerman, S., Reijmersdal, E., & Neijens, P. (2014). Effects of sponsorship disclosure timing on the processing of sponsored content: A study on the effectiveness of european disclosure regulations. *Psychology & Marketing, 31*(3), 214–224.

Boerman, S., Reijmersdal, E., & Neijens, P. (2014). Using eye tracking to understand the effects of brand placement disclosure types in television programs. *Journal of Advertising, 44*(3), 1–12.

Bovens, L. (2009). The ethics of nudge. In T Grüne-Yanoff & Sven Hansson (eds.), *Preference change: approaches from philosophy, economics and psychology.* pp. 207–219.

Brehm, J. (1989). Psychological reactance: Theory and applications. *Advances in Consumer Research, 16,* 72–75.

Bruns, H., Kantorowicz-Reznichenko, E., Klement, K., Jonsson, M., & Rahali, B. (2018). Can nudges be transparent and yet effective? *Journal of Economic Psychology, 65,* 41–59.

Burger, J., Bell, H., Harvey, K., Johnson, J., Stewart, C., Dorian, K., & Swedroe, M. (2010). Nutritious or delicious? The effect of descriptive norm information on food choice. *Journal of Social and Clinical Psychology, 29*(2), 228–242.

Chater, N. (2015). The nudge theory and beyond: How people can play with your mind. *The Guardian,* September 12, https://www.theguardian.com/theobserver/2015/sep/12/nudge-theory-mental-manipulation-wrong.

Cialdini, R., Reno, R., & Kallgren, C. (1990). A focus theory of normative conduct: Recycling the concept of norms to reduce littering in public places. *Journal of Personality and Social Psychology, 58*(6), 1015–1026.

Collins, E., Thomas, J., Robinson, E., Aveyard, P., Jebb, S., Herman, P., & Higgs, S. (2019). Two observational studies examining the effect of a social norm and a health message on the purchase of vegetables in student canteen settings. *Appetite, 132,* 122–130.

Evans, N. (2012). A 'Nudge' in the Wrong Direction. *Institute of Public Affairs, 64*(4), 16–19.

Finlayson, G., King, N., & Blundell, J. (2008). The role of implicit wanting in relation to explicit liking and wanting for food: Implications for appetite control. *Appetite, 50*(1), 120–127.

Fischer, M., & Lotz, S. (2014). Is soft paternalism ethically legitimate?—The relevance of psychological processes for the assessment of nudge-based policies. In: *CGS Working Paper,* 5, Cologne Graduate School in Management, Economics and Social Sciences, University of Cologne.

Friestad, M., & Wright, P. (1994). The persuasion knowledge model: How people cope with persuasion attempts. *Journal of Consumer Research, 21*(1), 1–31.

Goldsmith, R., Clark, R., & Lafferty, B. (2005). Tendency to conform: A new measure and its relationship to psychological reactance. *Psychological Reports, 96*(3), 591–594.

Hansen, P., & Jespersen, R. (2013). Nudge and the manipulation of choice. *European Journal of Risk Regulation, 1,* 3–28.

Heap, S., Ramalingam, A., & Arjona, D. (2017). Social information "Nudges": An experiment with multiple group references. *Southern Economic Journal, 84*(1), 348–365.

Hong, S.-M., & Faedda, S. (1996). Refinement of the hong psychological reactance scale. *Educational and Psychological Measurement, 56*(1), 173–182.

Hudders, L., De Pauw, P., Cauberghe, V., Panic, K., Zarouali, B., & Rozendaal, E. (2017). Shedding new light on how advertising literacy can affect children's processing of embedded advertising formats: A future research agenda. *Journal of Advertising, 46*(2), 333–349.

Kormos, C., Gifford, R., & Brown, E. (2015). The influence of descriptive social norm information on sustainable transportation behavior. *Environment and Behavior, 47*(5), 479–501.

Kroese, F., Marchiori, & D., De Ridder, D. (2016). Nudging healthy food choices: A field experiment at the train station. *Journal of Public Health, 38*(2), e133–e137.

Lee, S. (2010). Ad-induced affect: The effects of forewarning, affect intensity, and prior brand attitude. *Journal of Marketing Communications, 16*(4), 225–237.

Ly, K., & Soman, D. (2013). Nudging around the world. https://www.um.es/documents/1922922/1973600/Nudging+Around+The+World.pdf/3af04386-ba8b-4742-b339-73626bf2be94.

Marchiori, D., Adriaanse, M., & De Ridder, D. (2017). Unresolved questions in nudging research: Putting the psychology back in nudging. *Social and Personality Psychology Compass, 11*(1), e12297

McGale, L., Smits, T., Halford, J., Harrold, J., & Boyland, E. (2019). The influence of front-of pack portion size images on children's serving and intake of cereal. *Pediatric Obesity,* e12583

Moldovan, A., & David, D. (2012). Features of automaticity in eating behavior. *Eating Behaviors, 13*(1), 46–48.

Mollen, S., Rimal, R., Ruiter, R., & Kok, G. (2013). Healthy and unhealthy social norms and food selection Findings from a Field-Experiment. *Appetite, 65,* 83–89.

Neyens, E., Aerts, G., & Smits, T. (2015). The impact of image-size manipulation and sugar content on children's cereal consumption. *Appetite, 95,* 152–157.

Nielsen. (2018). The database: Episode 4, a look at what's driving modern health and well-being. https://www.nielsen.com/us/en/insights/news/2018/episode-4-a-look-at-whats-driving-modern-health-and-wellness.html.

Paunov, Y., Wänke, M., & Vogel, T. (2018). Transparency effects on policy compliance: disclosing how defaults work can enhance their effectiveness. *Behavioural Public Policy,* 1–22.

Quick, B., & Stephenson, M. (2008). Examining the role of trait reactance and sensation seeking on perceived threat, state reactance, and reactance restoration. *Human Communication Research, 34*(3), 448–476.

Quick, B., Scott, A., & Ledbetter, A. (2011). A close examination of trait reactance and issue involvement as moderators of psychological reactance theory. *Journal of Health Communication, 16*(6), 660–679.

Reisch, L., & Sunstein, C. (2016). Do Europeans like nudges? *Judgment and Decision Making, 11*(4), 310–325.

Robinson, E., Benwell, H., & Higgs, S. (2013). Food intake norms can increase and decrease snack food intake in a remote confederate study. *Appetite, 65,* 20–24.

Robinson, E., & Higgs, S. (2013). Eat as they eat, not as they think. Descriptive but not injunctive social norm messages can increase fruit and vegetable intake. *Appetite, 71,* 484–484.

Roininen, K., Tuorila, H., Zandstra, E., De Graaf, C., Vehkalahti, K., Stubenitsky, K., & Mela, D. (2001). Differences in health and taste attitudes and reported behaviour among Finnish, Dutch and British consumers: A cross-national validation of the Health and Taste Attitude Scales (HTAS). *Appetite, 37*(1), 33–45.

Rozendaal, E., Lapierre, M., van Reijmersdal, E., & Buijzen, M. (2011). Reconsidering advertising literacy as a defense against advertising effects. *Media Psychology, 14*(4), 333–354.

Sagarin, B., & Henningsen, M. L. (2017). Resistance to influence. In S. Harkins, K. Williams, & Jerry Burger (eds.), *The oxford handbook of social influence.* Oxford: University Press.

Staunton, M., Louis, W., Smith, J., Terry, D., & Mcdonald, R. (2014). How negative descriptive norms for healthy eating undermine the effects of positive injunctive norms. *Journal of Applied Social Psychology, 44*(4), 319–330.

Sunstein, C. (2015). Nudging and choice architecture: Ethical considerations. *Yale Journal on Regulation,* 809.

Sunstein, C. (2018). Misconceptions about nudges. *Journal of Behavioral Economics for Policy, 2*(1), 61–67.

Tarrant, M., Khan, S., & Qin, Qi. (2015). Effects of norm referent salience on young people's dietary orientation. *Appetite, 85,* 160–164.

Thaler, R., & Sunstein, C. (2009). *Nudge: Improving decisions on health, wealth, and happiness.* London: Penguin.

The GBD Obesity Collaborators. (2017). Health effects of overweight and obesity in 195 countries over 25 years. *the New England Journal of Medicine, 377*(15), 13–27.

Urala, N., & Lähteenmäki, L. (2006). Hedonic ratings and perceived healthiness in experimental functional food choices. *Appetite, 47*(3), 302–314.

Vermeir, I., & Verbeke, W. (2006). Sustainable food consumption: Exploring the consumer "attitude–behavioral intention" gap. *Journal of Agricultural and Environmental Ethics, 19*(2), 169–194.

White, K., & Simpson, B. (2013). When do (and don't) normative appeals influence sustainable consumer behaviors? *Journal of Marketing, 77*(2), 78–95.

Whitehead, M., Jones, R., Howell, R., Lilley, R., & Pykett, J. (2014). Nudging all over the world: Assessing the global impact of the behavioural sciences on public policy. https://changingbehaviours.files.wordpress.com/2014/09/nudgedesignfinal.pdf.

Wong-Parodi, G., Krishnamurti, T., Gluck, J., & Agarwal, Y. (2019). Encouraging energy conservation at work: A field study testing social norm feedback and awareness of monitoring. *Energy Policy, 130,* 197–205.

World Health Organisation. (2018) Obesity and overweight. https://www.who.int/news-room/fact-sheets/detail/obesity-and-overweight.

Zlatevska, N., Dubelaar, C., & Holden, S. (2014). Sizing up the effect of portion size on consumption: A meta-analytic review. *Journal of Marketing, 78*(3), 140–154.

The Impact of Source Credibility on Irish Millennials' Brand Attitudes and Perceptions of Brand Credibility: A Study of Instagram Influencers' Health and Fitness Endorsements

Andrea Manning and Laurent Muzellec

1 Introduction

Abidin (2016, p.3) defines influencers as micro-celebrities who gain large online followings by sharing "textual and visual narrations of their personal, everyday lives, upon which paid advertorials…are premised". In 2016, Djafarova and Rushworth found that consumers deem influencers as more credible endorsers than celebrities due to their relatable and genuine nature. Furthermore, Booth and Matic (2011) claim that influencers are effective endorsers as they combine the glamour and recognition of celebrities with the sincerity and similarity of peers.

Thus, advertisers are projected to spend €2.06 billion in 2019 in order to have influencers disseminate positive word-of-mouth to their large online followings (Asano 2018). The present research will examine fitness influencers due to their prevalence in the influencer marketing space. This study aims to contribute to the limited body of research on digital marketing for the fitness industry through

---

Laurent Muzellec, Trinity Centre for Digital Business, Trinity College Dublin, laurent.muzellec@tcd.ie
Andrea Manning, Trinity College Dublin, manninan@tcd.ie

A. Manning (✉) · L. Muzellec
Trinity College Dublin/Trinity Centre for Digital Business, Dublin, Ireland
E-Mail: manninan@tcd.ie

L. Muzellec
E-Mail: laurent.muzellec@tcd.ie

a quantitative investigation of the impact of source credibility upon consumer attitudes.

2 The Relationship Between Source Credibility and Brand Attitudes and Credibility

This study provides a quantitative summary of the relationships between influencer source credibility, brand attitudes and brand credibility within the context of influencer marketing for the fitness industry on Instagram. Through an improved understanding of source credibility's impact upon consumer attitudes, marketing practitioners can better identify appropriate endorsers for their brands.

The findings reveal that out of the three constructs of source credibility, only source trustworthiness, and neither source attractiveness nor source expertise, significantly and positively impacts brand attitudes and brand credibility. These findings suggest, therefore, that brands should select influencer endorsers who are perceived as highly trustworthy by the target market.

2.1 Source Credibility Theory

The source credibility model is related to social effect and influence theories which indicate that a communicator's characteristics can impact the effectiveness and acceptance of the advertising message (Kelman 1961; Erdogan 1999). In 1990, Ohanian developed a new fifteen-point tri-component source credibility scale comprising of source trustworthiness, attractiveness and expertise (Erdogan 1999). This scale has previously been adopted to examine celebrity print endorsements and found source credibility to significantly impact consumer attitudes (Till and Busler 1998; 2000; Pornpitakpan 2003; Close Scheinbaum and Wang 2016). Therefore, the researcher predicts that influencer credibility will significantly impact consumer attitudes regarding brand attitudes and brand credibility within this study.

> *H1: An influencer's source credibility positively impacts brand attitudes*
>
> *H2: An influencer's source credibility positively impacts brand credibility*

2.2 Source Credibility Constructs: Trustworthiness, Expertise and Attractiveness

Amos, Holmes and Strutton define trustworthiness as "the degree of confidence consumers place in a communicator's intent to convey the assertions s/he considers most valid" (2008, p. 215). Ohanian's source credibility model (1990), states that trustworthiness consists of the constructs of trustworthy, dependable, honest, reliable, and sincere. Rossiter and Smidts (2012) argue that source trustworthiness does not impact endorsement effectiveness as consumers know that celebrities are paid to be endorsers. Others claim, however, that source trustworthiness is a greater predictor of brand attitudes and brand credibility than expertise or attractiveness (McGinnies and Ward 1980; Close Scheinbaum and Wang 2016). Existing research is, however, limited to celebrity print ads and thus, findings may vary in the digital context.

Expertise refers to "the extent to which a communicator is perceived to be a source of valid assertions" based upon the endorser's perceived "knowledge, experience and skills" (Erdogan 1999, p. 298). Expertise has been found to positively impact brand attitudes in celebrity print ads (Till and Busler 2000). Furthermore, industry-expert endorsers are thought to be more persuasive and can heighten the perception of product quality (Erdogan 1999). Ohanian's (1990) source credibility model claims that expertise consists of the constructs of expert, experienced, knowledgeable, qualified and skilled. Till and Busler (1998) found that expertise is a greater predictor of endorsement effectiveness than attractiveness. Close Scheinbaum and Wang (2016), however, found that expertise, unlike trustworthiness or attractiveness, did not impact consumer attitudes in celebrity airline endorsements. This may be linked to Erdogan's (1999) claim that expertise is only significant when consumers perceive it to be so with regards to the industry. It is likely, however, that consumers will value expertise for the fitness industry.

Erdogan (1999) notes that physically attractive endorsers are typically viewed as more competent individuals and, consequently, more credible sources of information. Erdogan deems this "the halo effect", referring to the idea that those who excel in one way are presumed to excel in all other ways (1999, p. 301). Ohanian's (1990) source credibility model states that source attractiveness consists of being attractive, classy, beautiful, elegant and sexy. Previous studies indicate that source attractiveness positively impacts brand attitudes, yet found that it may only impact endorsement effectiveness when the endorsed product is directly linked to enhancing one's physical attractiveness (Joseph 1982; Kahle and Homer 1985; Till and Busler 1998). Close Scheinbaum and Wang (2016), however, also identified a positive correlation between source attractiveness, brand credibility and brand attitudes regarding airline endorsements. This study will re-examine these relationships within the context of social media influencer marketing for the fitness industry.

2.3 Brand Attitude and Brand Credibility

Brand attitude may be defined as "a predisposition to respond in a favourable or unfavourable manner to a particular brand after the advertising stimulus has been shown to the individual" (Phelps and Hoy 1996, p. 90). Positive brand attitudes have been proven to influence consumer behaviour such as purchase intentions (Ghorban 2012; Close Scheinbaum and Wang 2016).

According to Spears and Singh (2004), a positive brand attitude refers to one's feelings towards a brand being appealing, good, pleasant, favourable, and likeable. Existing studies of celebrity print endorsements revealed that source credibility and its elements significantly impact brand attitudes (McGinnies and Ward 1980; Till and Busler 2000; Close Scheinbaum and Wang 2016). Thus, this study will re-examine these findings in the digital context of influencer marketing.

Erdem and Swait (2004, p. 192) define brand credibility as the "believability of the information conveyed by a brand, which requires that consumers perceive that the brand has the ability and willingness to continuously deliver what has been promised". Brand credibility has been linked to brand choice as it reduces one's risk or uncertainty when choosing a brand (Erdem and Swait, 1998). Furthermore, researchers have identified a link between brand credibility and purchase intentions (Erdem and Swait 2004; Wang and Yang 2010) and brand loyalty (Sweeney and Swait 2008; Alam et al. 2012). Research has also found that the constructs of source credibility significantly impact brand credibility in the context of celebrity print endorsements (Spry et al. 2011; Close Scheinbaum and Wang 2016). This study will re-examine these findings within the context of social media influencer marketing.

> *H3: An influencer endorser's trustworthiness positively impacts brand attitudes*
>
> *H4: An influencer endorser's expertise positively impacts brand attitudes*
>
> *H5: An influencer endorser's attractiveness positively impacts brand attitudes*
>
> *H6: An influencer endorser's trustworthiness positively impacts brand credibility*
>
> *H7: An influencer endorser's expertise positively impacts brand credibility*
>
> *H8: An influencer endorser's attractiveness positively impacts brand credibility*

2.4 Endorser and Consumer Gender

Ferebee (2008) states that it is necessary to understand how both genders perceive source credibility as advertisers often target consumers by gender. Ohanian (1991) argues that gender does not affect the impact of source credibility on consumer attitudes. This claim, however, appears to be lacking in additional research and thus, will be re-investigated within this study.

> H9: *Consumer gender does not significantly impact which source credibility constructs predict brand attitudes.*
>
> H10: *Consumer gender does not significantly impact which source credibility constructs predict brand credibility.*

3 Research Methodology

3.1 Study Sampling

This study employs a non-probabilistic sampling method. Due to the niche nature of the fitness product market, a homogeneous sampling technique was employed to provide insights into a group of similar subjects. This study examined millennials as by 2018, 61% of Instagram users were aged 18–34 (Statista 2018a). Moreover, McCormick (2016, p.40) asserts that millennials identify more with brands and are more influenced by celebrity endorsements than earlier generations (ibid). In addition, as of April 2018, 50.7% of active Instagram users were female and 49.3% were male (Statista 2018b). The fitness industry is also popular among males and females and thus, both genders were examined. Data was analysed solely from fitness enthusiasts who are active Instagram users who follow at least one fitness influencer, since only subjects fitting such criteria are likely to be exposed to fitness influencer marketing strategies. Finally, all subjects were Irish due to the researcher's country of residence.

3.2 Research Strategy and Subject Participation

A questionnaire technique was employed for data collection which allowed the researcher to explore specific relationships between variables and to compare the relationships by participant gender. Following a pilot test, the final questionnaire was built and distributed using Qualtrics. Data collection took place from May 27th to June 10th, 2018. Respondents were recruited in two ways. Firstly, to improve participation from subjects meeting the sampling criteria, a survey link was sent to Irish Instagram users who followed fitness-related accounts. Secondly, students were approached on a university campus and invited to complete the survey.

3.3 Operationalisation and Survey Design

To operationalise the impact of source credibility upon brand attitudes and brand credibility, three scales were used (see Figs. 1, 2, 3). To measure source credibility, fifteen items were adapted from Ohanian's (1990) source credibility scale. To measure brand attitude, three items were adapted from Sengupta and Johar's (2002) brand attitude scale. Finally, to measure brand credibility, seven items were adapted from Erdem and Swait's (2004) brand credibility scale.

Categorical questions ensured that subjects met the sampling criteria. Source credibility, brand attitudes and brand credibility were then examined with selected stimuli comprising of protein powder Instagram endorsements by four fitness influencers. Brief descriptions including the influencer's name, profession, endorsed brand and product were provided. Subjects identified the most credible endorser based on the stimuli and answered Likert scale questions measuring source credibility, brand attitude and brand credibility.

4 Analysis and Results

4.1 Data Preparation and Outlier Identification

238 subjects participated in the survey. Initial data cleaning occurred in Excel whereby cases that did not meet the sampling criteria were deleted. SPSS was then used for further data cleansing and normality and hypothesis testing. Normality was tested with descriptive statistics including skewness, kurtosis, visual examination of histograms, Q-Q plots, boxplots, and a Kolmogorov–Smirnov test of normality. The final sample (N = 123, 70 female, 53 male) had no missing values. As the 1–7 Likert scale items included a neutral option of '4', it was not possible to compute a valid mean. Thus, all '4' responses were recoded as missing values, enabling the computation of summary scales by averaging participant scores on the raw items in each scale.

4.2 Results: Gender Differences in Source Credibility, Brand Attitudes, Brand Credibility

Gender differences in the mean scores on all constructs were tested using independent samples t-test for source credibility and its elements, brand attitudes and brand credibility (see Fig. 4). This analysis found that females had higher trustworthiness scores (M = 5.33, SD = 0.77) than males (M = 4.94, SD = 1.18), t(80.106) = −1.989, p = 0.050. Mean scores on source credibility, attractiveness, expertise, brand attitudes and credibility did not differ greatly between genders.

5 Correlation Analysis Pearson

Correlation analysis (two-tailed) studied the relationships between source credibility elements (expertise, trustworthiness, attractiveness), brand attitudes and brand credibility (see Fig. 5). Cohen (1988, cited in Pallant 2005) classified the size of a correlation coefficients as: small – r = 0.10 to 0.29; medium – r = 0.30 to 0.49; or large – r = 0.50 to 1.0. Thus, source credibility correlated positively and moderately with brand credibility (r(123) = 0.473, p = 0.001), and brand attitudes (r(109) = 0.384, p = 0.001). The source credibility elements also correlated positively with brand credibility, of these, trustworthiness had the strongest relationship (r(113) = 0.633, p = 0.001), followed by expertise (r(120) = 0.242, p = 0.008), and then attractiveness r(116) = 0.201, p = 0.031). Trustworthiness correlated positively and moderately with brand attitudes (r(102) = 0.565, p = 0.001). Both expertise and attractiveness were uncorrelated with brand attitudes.

6 Linear and Multiple Regression

Regression analyses modelled source credibility and its constructs' impacts on brand attitudes and credibility (see Fig. 6). The data met the adequate sample size of 15–20 subjects per predictor variable (Tabachnick and Fidell 2001) and showed normality, linearity, independence of errors with no issues of multicollinearity as all inter-correlations were below 0.8 (Field 1999).

Linear regression analysis revealed that influencer source credibility positively impacts brand attitudes, R2 = 0.147, B = 0.541, Beta = 0.384, t = 4.298, p = 0.001, supporting H1. A multiple regression model with the source credibility elements predicting brand attitudes scores was significant, R2 = 0.379, F(3, 91) = 18.496, p = 0.001. Trustworthiness significantly and positively impacts brand attitudes (B = 0.662, Beta = 0.616, t = 6.842, p = 0.001), supporting H3. Attractiveness and expertise did not impact brand attitudes, thus, H4 and H5 are not supported. The multiple regression model was rerun to compare genders. The male model was significant, R^2 = 0.756, F(3,42) = 43.308, p = 0.0001. Trustworthiness was the sole predictor of male brand attitudes (B = 0.950, Beta = 0.871, t = 10.832, p = 0.001). The female model was non-significant, R^2 = 0.047, F(3,45) = 0.746. Thus, H9 is not supported.

Linear regression proved that source credibility significantly impacts brand credibility, supporting H2, R^2 = 0.223, B = 0.607, Beta = 0.473, t = 5.898, p = 0.001. Multiple regression showed that source credibility elements significantly impact brand credibility scores, R^2 = 0.438, F(3, 99) = 25.673, p = 0.001. Trustworthiness predicted brand credibility, supporting H6 (B = 0.666, Beta = 0.625, t = 7.656, p = 0.001). H7 and H8 are not supported as expertise and attractiveness did not predict brand credibility. This model was rerun to compare genders and found source credibility elements significantly impact brand credibility for males, R^2 = 0.542, F(3,44) = 17.364, p = 0.001, and females, R^2 = 0.423, F(3,51) = 12.452, p = 0.001. Trustworthiness positively impacted brand credibility for males (B = 0.660, Beta = 0.741, t = 6.850, p = 0.001) and females (B = 0.765, Beta = 0.552, t = 4.608, p = 0.001). Attractiveness and expertise did not impact either gender's brand credibility scores, which supports H10.

7   Discussion

Researchers have identified gaps in celebrity endorsement literature regarding online environments (Matthes and Knoll 2017) and the source credibility of different types of celebrities (Spry et al. 2011). Moreover, it is essential to understand the impact of source credibility in Instagram influencer strategies as this market has a projected value of $2.38B by 2019 (Statista 2019). Thus, this study aimed to contribute to this limited body of research through an examination of the impact of source credibility upon brand attitudes and brand credibility in the context of fitness influencer marketing on Instagram. Findings revealed that influencer credibility significantly impacts consumer attitudes which is consistent with the findings of existing source credibility research on celebrity print ads (Till and Busler 2000; Spry et al. 2011; Close Scheinbaum and Wang 2016). Thus, these results indicate that existing theories on source credibility maintain their validity within the digital context.

As Erdogan (1999) notes, source expertise is only a predictor of consumer attitudes when the audience perceives expertise as being important. Source expertise was not a predictor of brand attitudes or brand credibility in this study. This may be attributed to the sample used. Perhaps as millennials are digital natives accustomed to having unprecedented access to information online, true expertise derived from experience and qualifications is meeting its devaluation.

Source attractiveness did not predict brand attitudes or brand credibility in this study. It has been noted, however, that source attractiveness may only predict consumer attitudes when the product is linked to physical attractiveness (Joseph 1982; Kahle and Homer 1985; Till and Busler 1998). Protein powder is not explicitly linked to enhancing attractiveness which could explain why source attractiveness did not predict brand attitudes or brand credibility in this study.

Source trustworthiness predicted brand attitudes and brand credibility in this study. Consumers often consider trust as essential online due to the perceived risks associated with digital environments (Van der Heijden et al. 2003). Furthermore, trust has also been found to influence consumer attitudes in online business environments (Wang and Emurian 2005). Therefore, as influencer endorsements are often for e-commerce businesses, the significance of trust as an antidote to a heightened perception of risk online may, in part, explain the impact of source trustworthiness on consumer attitudes in this study.

Finally, a recent study claimed that 84% of millennials distrust traditional advertising, which may explain why millennials value trustworthiness above all else (Conlon 2017). Moreover, as consumers have access to unprecedented information nowadays such as online reviews and price comparisons, consumers place their greatest trust in sources which they deem as being authentic (Lobaugh et al. 2015). Influencer marketing is effective in establishing trust as the endorsements typically emulate the existing editorial content on the endorser's account, thus creating an air of authenticity (De Veirman et al. 2017). Therefore, when employing influencer marketing strategies, brands should select influencer endorsers who are, primarily, perceived as trustworthy by the target market.

8   Figures

8.1   Source Credibility Scale (Ohanian 1990)

Attractiveness	Trustworthiness	Expertise
Attractive- Unattractive	Trustworthy- Untrustworthy	Expert- Not Expert
Classy- Not Classy	Dependable- Undependable	Experienced- Inexperienced
Beautiful- Ugly	Honest- Dishonest	Knowledgeable- Unknowledgeable
Elegant- Plain	Reliable- Unreliable	Qualified- Unqualified
Sexy- Not Sexy	Sincere- Insincere	Skilled-Unskilled

8.2   Brand Attitude Scale (Sengupta et al. 2002)

I think the (brand name) is a very good (product category name)
I think the (brand name) is a very useful (product category name)
My opinion of the (brand name) is very favourable

8.3   Brand Credibility Scale (Erdem and Swait 2004)

This brand reminds me of someone who's competent and knows what he/ she is doing
This brand has the ability to deliver what it promises
This brand delivers what it promises
promises This brand's product claims are believable
Over time, my experiences with this brand have led me to expect it to keep its promises, no more and no less
This brand has a name you can trust
This brand doesn't pretend to be something it isn't

8.4 Independent T-Test Comparing Gender Differences in Mean Scores on Constructs

Variables	Gender	N	Mean	SD	t-value	p-value
Source Credibility	M	53	5.03	0.83	-0.998	0.320
	F	70	5.17	0.77		
Attractiveness	M	53	4.21	1.43	0.718	0.474
	F	63	4.01	1.52		
Trustworthiness	M	50	4.94	1.18	-1.989	0.050
	F	63	5.53	0.77		
Expertise	M	51	5.62	1.19	-1.250	0.215
	F	69	5.86	0.73		
Brand Attitude	M	48	5.15	1.28	-0.390	0.697
	F	61	5.23	0.94		
Brand Credibility	M	53	5.17	1.04	-0.007	0.994
	F	70	5.17	1.02		

SD = Standard Deviation, M = Male, F = Female

8.5 Pearson Correlation Between Constructs

Variables		Brand Credibility	Brand Attitude	Credibility	Expertise	Trustworthiness
Source Credibility	Pearson Correlation	0.473	0.384			
	Sig. (2-tailed)	0.000	0.000			
	N	123	109			
Expertise	Pearson Correlation	0.242	0.180	0.612		
	Sig. (2-tailed)	0.008	0.062	0.000		
	N	120	109	120		
Trustworthiness	Pearson Correlation	0.633	0.565	0.633	0.357	

Variables		Brand Credibility	Brand Attitude	Credibility	Expertise	Trustworthiness
	Sig. (2-tailed)	0.000	0.000	0.000	0.000	
	N	113	102	113	110	
Attractiveness	Pearson Correlation	0.201	0.162	0.686	−0.006	0.168
	Sig. (2-tailed)	0.031	0.103	0.000	0.951	0.086
	N	116	102	116	113	106

8.6 Summary of All Linear and Multiple Regression Results

	Brand Attitudes	Brand Credibility
Model 1		
Influencer source credibility (β)	0.384*** (4.298)	0.473*** (5.898)
R^2	0.147	0.223
Adj. - R^2	0.139	0.217
F-ratio	18.476***	34.786***
Model 2		
Attractiveness (β)	0.027 (0.318)	0.122 (1.605)
Trustworthiness (β)	0.616*** (6.842)	0.625*** (7.656)
Expertise (β)	-0.018 (-0.205)	0.018 (0.224)
R^2	0.379	0.438
Adj. - R^2	0.358	0.421
F-ratio	18.496***	25.673***

Significance levels: *$p<0.05$, **$p<0.01$, ***$p<0.001$

References

Abidin, C. (2016). "Aren't these just young, rich women doing vain things online?" Influencer selfies as subversive frivolity. *Social Media + Society*, 2(2), 1–17.

Alam, A., Arshad, M. U., & Shabbir, S. A. (2012). Brand credibility, customer loyalty and the role of religious orientation. *Asia Pacific Journal of Marketing and Logistics, 24*(4), 583598.

Amos, C., Holmes, G., & Strutton, D. (2008). Exploring the relationship between celebrity endorser effects and advertising effectiveness. *International Journal of Advertising, 27*(2), 209–234.

Asano, E. (2018). Instagram influencer marketing is now a $1 billion Industry. https://mediakix.com/2017/03/instagram-influencer-marketing-industry-sizehowbig/. Accessed: 19. June 2018.

Booth, N., & Matic, J. (2011). Mapping and leveraging influencers in social media to shape corporate brand perceptions. *Journal of Corporate Communications, 16*(3), 184–191.

Close Scheinbaum, A., & Wang, S. W. (2018). Enhancing brand credibility via celebrity endorsement: Trustworthiness trumps attractiveness and expertise. *Journal of Advertising, 58*(1), 16–31.

Conlon, K. (2017). The irish social media landscape. https://www.juvo.ie/the-irish-social-media-landscape/. Accessed: 17. May 2018.

De Veirman, M., Cauberghe, V., & Hudders, L. (2017). Marketing through Instagram influencers: The impact of number of followers and product divergence on brand attitude. *International Journal of Advertising, 36*(5), 798–828.

Djafarova, E., & Rushworth, C. (2017). Exploring the credibility of online celebrities' Instagram profiles in influencing the purchase decisions of young female users. *Computers In Human Behavior, 68,* pp. 1–7, ScienceDirect, EBSCOhost

Erdem, T., & Swait, J. (2004). Brand credibility, brand consideration, and choice. *Journal of Consumer Research, 31*(1), 191–198.

Erdem, T., & Swait and Joffre, . (1998). Brand equity as a signaling phenomenon. *Journal of Consumer Psychology, 7*(2), 131–157.

Erdogan, B. Z. (1999). Celebrity endorsement: A literature review. *Journal of Marketing Management, 41*(3), 291–314.

Ferebee, S. (2008). The influence of gender and involvement level on the perceived credibility of web sites. Persuasive Technology (pp. 279–282).

Field, A. (1999). Discovering Statistics Using SPSS. (4. ed.) London: Sage Publications Ltd.

Ghorban, Z. S. (2012). Brand attitude, its antecedents and consequences. Investigation into smartphone brands in Malaysia. *Journal of Business and Management, 2*(3), 31–35.

Joseph, W. B. (1982). The credibility of physically attractive communicators: A review. *Journal of Advertising, 11*(3), 15–24.

Kahle, L. R., & Homer, P. M. (1985). Physical attractiveness of the celebrity endorser: A social adaptation perspective. *Journal of Consumer Research, 11*(4), 954–961.

Kelman, H. C. (1961). Processes of opinion change. *Public Opinion Quarterly, 25*(1), 57–78.

Knoll, J., & Matthes, J. (2017). The effectiveness of celebrity endorsements: A meta-analysis. *Journal of the Academy of Marketing Science, 45*(1), 55–75.

Lobaugh, K., Simpson, J., & Ohri, L. (2015). *Navigating the new digital divide: Capitalizing on digital influence in retail.* s.l.: Deloitte Development LLC.

McCormick, K. (2016). Celebrity endorsements: Influence of a product-endorser match on Millennials attitudes and purchase intentions. *Journal of Retail and Consumer Services., 32,* 39–45.

McGinnies, E., & Ward, C. D. (1980). Better liked than right trustworthiness and expertise as factors of credibility. *Personality and Social Psychology Bulletin, 6*(3), 467–472.

Ohanian, R. (1990). Construction and validation of a scale to measure celebrity endorsers' perceived expertise, trustworthiness, and attractiveness. *Journal of Advertising, 19*(3), 39–52.

Ohanian, R. (1991). The impact of celebrity spokesperson's perceived image on consumers' intention to purchase. *Journal of Advertising Research., 31*(1), 46–52.

Pallant, J. (2005). *SPSS survival manual. A step by step guide to data analysis using SPSS for windows* (2nd ed.). New York: Open University Press.

Phelps, J. E., & Hoy, M. G. (1996). The Aad-Ab-PI relationship in children: The impact of brand familiarity and measurement timing. *Psychology and Marketing, 13*(1), 77–105.

Pornpitakpan, C. (2003). The effect of celebrity endorsers' perceived credibility on product purchase intention. *Journal of International Consumer Marketing, 16*(2), 55–74.

Rossiter, J. R., & Smidts, A. (2012). Print advertising: Celebrity presenters. *Journal of Business Research, 65*(6), 874–879.

Sengupta, J., & Johar, G. V. (2002). Effects of inconsistent attribute information on the predictive value of product attitudes: Toward a resolution of opposing perspectives. *Journal of Consumer Research, 29*(1), 39–56.

Spears, N., & Singh, S. N. (2004). Measuring attitude toward the brand and purchase intentions. *Journal of Current Issues and Research in Marketing, 26*(2), 53–66.

Spry, A., Pappu, R., & Cornwell, T. B. (2011). Celebrity endorsement, brand credibility and brand equity. *European Journal of Marketing, 45*(6), 882–909.

Statista. (2018b). Distribution of global Instagram users as of April 2018, by age and gender. https://www.statista.com/statistics/248769/age-distribution-of-worldwide-instagram-users/. Accessed: 19. May 2018.

Statista. (2018a). Distribution of Instagram users worldwide as of January 2018, by age group. https://www.statista.com/statistics/325587/instagram-global-age-group/. Accessed: 19. May 2018.

Statista. (2019). Global Instagram influencer market size from 2017 to 2019 (in billion U.S. dollars) https://www.statista.com/statistics/748630/global-instagram-influencer-market-value/. Accessed: 18. June 2018.

Sweeney, J., & Swait, J. (2008). The effects of brand credibility on customer loyalty. *Journal of Retailing and Consumer Services, 15*(3), 179–193.

Tabachnick, B., & Fidell, L. (2001). *Using multivariate statistics* (4th ed.). Boston: Allyn and Bacon.

Till, B. D., & Busler, M. (1998). Matching products with endorsers: Attractiveness versus expertise. *Journal of Consumer Marketing, 15*(6), 576–586.

Till, B. D., & Busler, M. (2000). The match-up hypothesis: Physical attractiveness, expertise, and the role of fit on brand attitude, purchase intent and brand beliefs. *Journal of Advertising, 29*(3), 1–13.

Van der Heijden, H., Verhagen, T., & Creemers, M. (2003). Understanding online purchase intentions: Contributions from technology and trust perspectives. *European Journal of Information Systems, 3*(1), 41–48.

Wang, Y. D., & Emurian, H. H. (2005). An overview of online trust: Concepts, elements, and implications. *Computers in Human Behaviour, 21*(1), 105–125.

Wang, X., & Yang, Z. (2010). The effect of brand credibility on consumers' brand purchase intention in emerging economies: The moderating role of brand awareness and brand image. *Journal of Global Marketing, 23*(3), 177–188.

General Language Use, Language Proficiency and Language Attitudes as Predictors of Consumer Response to the Use of Spanish and English in Advertising in Chile and Mexico

Andreu van Hooft, Frank van Meurs, and Qudsiyah Braaf

1 Introduction

English is widely used in advertising in countries all over the world where English is not an official language (Piller 2003), including countries in Hispanic America (e.g. Chile: Gerding and Morrison and Kotz 2012, p. 142; Instituto Chileno 2016, pp. 13–14; Mexico: Baumgardner 2008). To date, consumers' response to the use of English in advertising in countries where English is not an official language has been measured by exposing young highly educated consumers to ads in the national language (the consumers' mother tongue), and the same ads with English. Some studies found partial evidence that English led to better response than the consumers' native language, for instance for ads from multinational companies (versus local companies) and for ads promoting luxury products (versus necessity products) (e.g. Taiwan: Lin and Wang 2016; Romania: Micu and Coulter 2010) effect. However, several experiments conducted in Europe (Gerritsen et al. 2007, 2010; Planken et al. 2010), Arab countries (Nickerson and Camiciottoli 2013); and Hispanic America (Chile and Mexico: Alonso García et al. 2013; Álvarez

A. van Hooft (✉) · F. van Meurs · Q. Braaf
Faculty of Arts, Nijmegen, Netherlands
E-Mail: a.v.hooft@let.ru.nl

F. van Meurs
E-Mail: F.v.Meurs@let.ru.nl

Q. Braaf
E-Mail: qubraaf995@hotmail.com

et al. 2017; Ueltschy and Ryans 1997) found hardly any or no differences in consumers' response depending on the language used in the ads (mother tongue versus English). A relevant question is what predicts consumers' response to ads using English as foreign language or the consumers' mother tongue.

2 Theoretical Rramework: Predictors of Consumer Response to Ads Using English or Consumer's Native Language

Attitudes to languages in advertising are likely to be manifestations of more general language attitudes. This is suggested by Luna and Peracchio's (2005a; b) findings that Hispanic consumer response to code-switching between Spanish and English in advertising was influenced by manipulations of general attitude towards the importance of the first language and second language, and of general attitude towards code-switching. Only two studies investigating the effect of English versus the mother tongue in non-English-speaking countries would appear to have taken into consideration how consumers' response to ads with English or ads with their mother tongue could be influenced by consumers' general use and perception of these two languages. Van Hooft et al. (2017b) found that, for ads in English, general language attitudes towards English were a predictor of Egyptian consumers' ad and product evaluation. In their research with Ecuadorian, Mexican and Chilean young consumers, Álvarez et al. (2017) found that the variable attitude towards speakers of English and speakers that code-mixed Spanish and English—which could be seen as a proxy measure for general language attitudes—to a limited extent influenced ad evaluations: attitudes to English speakers did not predict ad evaluation, and only for Chilean consumers was attitude to code-switchers found to be a predictor for ad evaluation.

Another possible predictor of consumer response to ads in English and the mother tongue is the extent to which they use and are exposed to these two languages. On the basis of the Mere Exposure Effect Theory (Zajonc 1968), it could be assumed that Spanish-speaking consumers have a preference for messages in Spanish merely because they are exposed to Spanish more than English, and because Spanish is therefore more familiar and closer to them than English. To date, however, this assumption would not appear to have been experimentally tested.

Finally, consumers' response to ads in English and their mother tongue may be affected by their proficiency in these two languages. More proficiency in a language is likely to lead to more fluency in processing an ad in that language, which in turn can be expected to lead to better ad evaluation (for the link between processing fluency and evaluation see e.g. Álvarez et al. 2017; Dragojevic and Giles 2016). The link between consumers' proficiency in their mother tongue and English, on the one hand, and their response to ads in these languages, on the other hand, would not appear to have been experimentally tested.

3   Research Questions

In view of the above considerations, the present study examines general use of English and Spanish, proficiency in English and Spanish, and attitudes towards the two languages as predictors of consumers' response to Spanish and English in advertising in Chile and Mexico. The predictive value of general language use and proficiency has not been investigated before, and the predictive value of general language attitudes has only been investigated in a limited number of studies. The aim of the current experiment, therefore, was to answer the following research questions:

> *RQ1: To what extent do Chileans and Mexican consumers' general use of Spanish, proficiency in Spanish and attitudes to Spanish predict their Consumer Response to Spanish advertising?*
>
> *RQ2: To what extent do Chileans and Mexican consumers' general use of English, proficiency in English and attitudes to English predict their Consumer Response to English advertising?*

4   Method

4.1   Design and Materials

The experiment in this study had a between-within-subjects post-test-only design, with language version of the advertisement (English and Spanish) and product type category (high/low involvement, based on Rossiter et al. 1991) as within-subjects factors to control for the effect of product type and to increase generalizability.

The stimuli were taken from Van Hooft et al. (2017a). In order to increase the experiment's ecological validity, the stimuli were based on real product ads. We replaced the original text of the ads with new English text and slogans. In order to prevent brand associations, we replaced the original two brand names with fictitious brand names. A native speaker of Spanish afterwards translated the English text and the slogans of the two ads into Spanish. The first advertisement depicted a low-involvement product, an adhesive paper note, with the brand name "Sticker" and the slogan "When people count on you, count on Sticker notes". The second advertisement showed a high-involvement product, a photo camera, with the brand name "Magnus" and the slogan "Capture every moment". Brand names and all visual elements were identical in the two language versions (see Fig. 1 for all advertisements used in the experiment).

4.2 Participants and Procedure

A sample of 176 participants (71 Chilean and 105 Mexican) took part in the experiment. We selected only participants who indicated that Spanish was their mother tongue, and all participants were university students, as was the case in earlier studies in the same countries (Alonso García et al. 2013; Álvarez et al. 2017; Ueltschy and Ryans 1997).

The sample consisted of 63.1% women (mean age: 25.87 years, SD = 7.3). Participants' mean self-assessed Spanish proficiency was 6.86 (SD = 0.38) and self-assessed English proficiency was 4.60 (SD = 1.47) (1 = very low proficiency, 7 = very high proficiency). A paired sample t test showed that participants' self-assessed Spanish language proficiency was significantly higher than their self-assessed English language proficiency (t(175) = 21.172; p < .001, CI 2.05 − 2.47). In addition, participants reported using Spanish (M = 4.94, SD = 1.08) significantly more than English (M = 0.87, SD = 0.95) (t(175) = 27.58, p < .001, CI 3.78 − 4.37).

The homogeneity of distribution of participant characteristics between the two groups that saw different language versions of the ads (English or Spanish) was assessed with a series of Chi-square tests between language version and participant characteristics (nationality, gender, language use of English and Spanish at home, at university, with friends, with fellow students, with professor). These tests showed no significant relations between language version and the participant characteristics that were measured (all p's > .223). Therefore, the two groups were similar and comparable in these respects.

Fig. 1 Advertisements used in the experiment

4.3 Dependent and Control Variables

The criterion variable Consumer Response was measured with ten 7-point semantic differential scales that included Ad Attitude (interesting—boring, original—ordinary, attractive—unattractive, international—local), Product Attitude (nice—not nice, very good—very bad, innovative—conventional, old-fashioned—modern, reliable—not reliable), and Purchase intention (Yes, I would buy the product—No, I would not buy the product), partly based on Hornikx et al. (2013, p. 158), Maes et al.(1996, p. 209), and Van Hooft and Truong (2012, pp. 185–186). After recoding, α was .832 for the low-involvement product, and for the high-involvement product α was .889.

The predictor variables general use of, proficiency in and attitudes to Spanish and English were composed of five aspects. Self-assessed Spanish and English proficiency was established using four 7-point scales which measured how fluent they thought they were in speaking, listening, reading and writing (1 = very low; 7 = like a native speaker; based on Luna et al. (2008, p. 291); α = .924 for English language proficiency; α = .774 for Spanish language proficiency). The participants' Self-assessed language use in six situations was determined with the question 'Which language do you normally use in the following situations?': at home, at university, with friends, with fellow students, with your professor, and when watching TV programs (partly based on Koslow et al. 1994, pp. 579–580; Krishna and Ahluwalia 2008, p. 695). Participants were invited to choose one of two language options: 'Spanish' or 'English'. By adding the individual scores for each item for each language separately, we transformed the original dichotomous variables into a scale on which 0 = no use of English and no use of Spanish and 6 = Use of English and Spanish in all situations. Participants' General language attitudes towards Spanish and English were measured with four seven-point semantic differential scales (pleasant—unpleasant, elegant—inelegant, beautiful—ugly, attractive—repellent; based on Schoel et al. 2012; after recoding, α = .812 for Spanish and α = .884 for English). Perceived Symbolic value of Spanish and English was determined with seven items on seven-point semantic differentials (modern- outdated; international-local, youthful—outdated, dynamic—passive, marks prestige—marks lack of prestige, a symbol of urban growth—not a symbol of urban growth, a symbol of technological superiority—not a symbol of technological superiority; based on Van Hooft et al. 2017b, p. 145; after recoding, α = .808 for Spanish and α = .873 for English). Finally, Perceived International importance of Spanish and English was measured with one 7-point Likert scale for each language (Spanish is an important world language; English is an important world language; 1 = completely disagree and 7 = completely agree).

The experiment was administered both online (through Qualtrics) and on paper. The Chilean sample consisted of a number of different student seminar groups at one university (Universidad Católica de Valparaíso). The Mexican sample was recruited through snowball sampling at different universities. Mexican students were either approached through messages on social media platforms, such as Facebook, Instagram and Snapchat, or received an invitation to participate in the experiment at the end of a lecture, in both cases with a link to the online questionnaire. Furthermore, Mexican students were asked to forward the invitation to other potential participants. All participants were randomly assigned to one of the two language conditions. Participation was voluntary and anonymous. Participants received no reward for their participation. On average, completing the questionnaire took fifteen minutes.

5 Results

In order to establish to what extent the general use of, proficiency in and attitudes towards of Spanish and English were predictors of Consumer Response to Spanish and English ads (criterions), five predictors were included in the model for each language (Spanish, English) separately and for the two ads (post-it Sticker and photo camera Magnus) combined. The five predictors were (1) Self-assessed Spanish/English proficiency, (2) Participants' self-assessed Spanish/English language use, (3) Participants' general language attitudes towards Spanish/English, (4) Perceived Symbolic value of Spanish/ English, and (5) Perceived International Importance of Spanish/English.

5.1 General use of Spanish, Proficiency in Spanish and Attitudes to Spanish as Predictors of Consumer Response to Spanish Ads

Multiple regression analysis was used to test if general use of Spanish, proficiency in Spanish and attitudes to Spanish significantly predicted Chilean and Mexican participants' ratings for Consumer response to the Spanish version of the two ads (Sticker and Magnus, n = 89). Preliminary analyses showed no violation of the assumptions of normality, linearity, multicollinearity and homoscedasticity. The results of the regression indicated that the model with the five predictors explained

Table 1 Summary of descriptives and multiple regression analyses for the predictor variables on Consumer response to the Spanish ad versions (N = 89)

Variable	Mean	SD	B	SE B	β
Constant			3.068	1.778	
Symbolic Value of Spanish	4.53	1.09	0.31	0.09	.380*
Language use of Spanish	4.87	1.27	0.19	0.07	.272*
General Language Attitude Spanish	5.83	1.07	−0.16	0.09	−.189
Participants' Fluency Spanish	6.86	0.37	−0.08	0.24	−.034
Importance of Spanish	5.62	1.41	0.00	0.07	.006
Ad Response	3.95	0.88			
R^2	.200				
F	4.152*				

*p<.01

20% of the variance (R^2 = .200, F(5,83) = 4.152, p<.01). It was found that Perceived Symbolic Value of Spanish significantly predicted Consumer Response to the Spanish versions of the ads (β = .380, p<.01, CI .125− .491), as did Self-assessed Spanish Language use (β = .272, p<. 1, CI .048− .329). However, participants' Self-assessed Proficiency in Spanish (β = -.034, p = .738, CI −.558− .397), General Language Attitude towards Spanish (β = −.189, p = .099, CI −.340− .030), and Perceived International Importance of Spanish (β = −.006, p = .926, CI −.135− .143) were not significant predictors. The more participants reported they used Spanish, the more positive was their response to the Spanish ads. Furthermore, the higher participants' perception of Symbolic value of the Spanish Language, the better was their response to the Spanish ads.

Table 1 shows a summary of descriptives and the multiple regression analyses for the predictor variables on Consumer response to the Spanish versions of the ads.

5.2 General Use of English, Proficiency in English and Attitudes to English as Predictors of Consumer Response to English Ads

Multiple regression analysis showed that General use of English, proficiency in English and attitudes to English did not significantly predict Chilean and Mexican

Table 2 Summary of descriptives and multiple regression analyses for the predictor variables on Consumer response to the English ad versions (N = 87)

Variable	Mean	SD	B	SE B	β
Constant			3.314	0.889	
Symbolic Value of English	5.56	1.00	−0.04	0.11	−.042
Language use of English	0.86	0.84	0.12	0.13	.104
General Language Attitude English	5.18	1.33	0.03	0.08	.046
Participants' Fluency English	4.78	1.33	−0.11	0.08	−.152
Importance of English	6.43	1.12	0.17	0.09	.204
Ad Response	3.96	0.94			
R^2	0.07				
F	1.14				

participants' Consumer Response to the English versions of the two ads (Sticker and Magnus, n = 87). The results of the regression indicated that the model was not significant (R^2 = .066, F(5,86) = 1.14 p = .345). Furthermore, none of the five predictors was significant (all p's > .071). Table 2 shows a summary of descriptives and the multiple regression analyses for the predictor variables on Consumer response to the English versions of the ads.

6 Conclusion and Discussion

This study aimed to investigate to what extent Mexican and Chilean consumers' general use of Spanish and English, proficiency in the two languages and attitudes to the two languages predict Consumer response to Spanish or English ads, respectively. The findings showed that general language use and perception of Spanish were predictors of Consumer response. More specifically, self-assessed Spanish Language use and Perceived symbolic value of Spanish (and aspect of general language attitudes) were found to be predictors of Consumer response to the Spanish versions of the two ads evaluated by participants in the current study (RQ1). The other predictors tested (Self-assessed Proficiency in Spanish, General Language Attitude towards Spanish, and Perceived International Importance of Spanish) did not influence consumer response. For the two English versions of the ads, none of the predictors that were tested influenced Consumer Response (RQ2).

The findings indicated that consumer response to language choice in advertisements is, at least to some extent, influenced by more general language attitudes and language use. This general finding confirms and extends results from a thus far limited set of earlier studies (Álvarez et al. 2017; Van Hooft et al. 2017b), which investigated the predictive value of general language attitudes but not of general language use. The two significant predictors in the current study, self-assessed language use and perceived symbolic value, only related to the participants' mother tongue, Spanish, in relation to evaluation of Spanish language ads, and not to English as a foreign language in relation to the evaluation of English ads. The predictive value of Spanish Language Use could be explained by the dominant presence of Spanish in Chile and Mexico as a manifestation of the Mere Exposure Effect (Zajonc 1968), since participants' exposure to Spanish was higher than to English. The finding that consumer response was predicted by the Symbolic value of the participants' mother tongue and not by the symbolic value of English a foreign language could be explained by the greater emotional closeness that people in general feel to their first language in comparison to other languages (see e.g. Dewaele 2013; Puntoni et al. 2009), which may mean that symbolic values of the mother tongue have more impact than those of a foreign language. However, the current study did not measure the perceived emotionality of participants' first language and of English as foreign language. Future studies should therefore include explicit measures of the perceived emotionality of the language used in the advertisements as well as of the participants' mother tongue and the English language in general.

The present study did not find that proficiency in English or Spanish predicted consumers' response to ads containing these languages. The underlining motivation for investigating the link between language proficiency and consumer response was that proficiency would be an indicator of the ease with which advertisements are processed, based on the importance of processing fluency in evaluations (Dragojevic and Giles 2016). However, language proficiency may be too indirect measure of processing fluency. What matters may not be consumers' general language proficiency but the ease with which they process the specific advertising message in English as a foreign language or in their own language. It is therefore suggested that processing fluency should be measured explicitly in future studies exploring factors that could determine the effects of language choice in advertising.

Another limitation of the current study is that, like in the majority of earlier studies on the effects of English versus the participants' mother tongue in non-English-speaking countries, the participants in the experiment were all young and highly educated. This means that the findings cannot be extrapolated to other populations. Therefore, more research is needed with older and less highly educated groups.

A practical implication of the findings of our study is that they suggest advertisers should take into account differences in the extent to which consumers use their mother tongue and attach symbolic value to their mother tongue.

Acknowledgements We would like to thank the following people for their help and participation: Dr Giovanni Parodi Sweis, Dr Pedro Alfaro Faccio, Fernando Moncada (MA), Julio Cristobal (MA) and their students from the Universidad Católica de Valparaíso (Chile), and Dr Moisés Perales Escudero and his students from the Universidad de Quintana Roo (Mexico). We would also like to thank students from the Universidad de Aguascalientes, the Universidad de Guadalajara, the University de Guanajuato and Universidad Nacional de México (Mexico) for participating in the experimental study.

References

Alonso García, N., Chelminski, P., & González Hernández, E. (2013). The effects of language on attitudes toward advertisements and brands trust in Mexico. *Journal of Current Issues & Research in Advertising, 34*(1), 77–92.

Álvarez, C. M., Uribe, R., & León De-La-Torre, R. (2017). Should I say it in English? Exploring language effects on print advertising among Latin American bilinguals. *International Journal of Advertising, 36*(6), 975–993.

Baumgardner, R. J. (2008). The use of English in advertising in Mexican print media. *Journal of Creative Communications, 3*(1), 23–48.

Dewaele, J. M. (2013). *Emotions in multiple languages*. Basingstoke: Pelgrave Macmillan.

Dragojevic, M., & Giles, H. (2016). I don't like you because you're hard to understand: The role of processing fluency in the language attitudes process. *Human Communication Research, 42*(3), 396–420.

Gerding, C., Morrison, M. F., & Kotz, G. (2012). Anglicismos y aculturación en la sociedad chilena. *Onomázein: Revista de Lingüística, Filología y Traducción de la Pontificia Universidad Católica de Chile, 25*, 139–162.

Gerritsen, M., Nickerson, C., Van den Brandt, C., Crijns, R., Dominguez, N., Van Meurs, F., & Nederstigt, U. (2007). English in print advertising in Germany, Spain and the Netherlands: Frequency of occurrence, comprehensibility and the effect on corporate image. In G. Garzone & C. Ilie (Eds.), *The role of English in institutional and business settings: An intercultural perspective* (pp. 79–98). Bern: Lang.

Gerritsen, M., Nickerson, C., van Hooft, A., van Meurs, F., Korzilius, H., Nederstigt, N., et al. (2010). English in product advertisements in non-English-speaking countries in Western Europe: Product image and comprehension of the text. *Journal of Global Marketing, 23*(4), 349–365.

Hornikx, J., Van Meurs, F., & Hof, R. J. (2013). The effectiveness of foreign-language display in advertising for congruent versus incongruent products. *Journal of International Consumer Marketing, 25*(3), 152–165.

Instituto Chileno. (2016). Cuenta de las actividades efectuadas por el Instituto Chileno y sus Academias. Retrieved from https://www.institutodechile.cl/wp-content/uploads/2019/01/cuenta2016.pdf Accessed 27 Nov 2019.

Koslow, S., Shamdasani, P. N., & Touchstone, E. E. (1994). Exploring language effects in ethnic advertising: A sociolinguistic perspective. *Journal of Consumer Research, 20*(4), 575–585.

Krishna, A., & Ahluwalia, R. (2008). Language choice in advertising to bilinguals: Asymmetric effects for multinationals versus local firms. *Journal of Consumer Research, 35*(4), 692–705.

Lin, Y. C., & Wang, K. Y. (2016). Language choice in advertising for multinational corporations and local firms: A reinquiry focusing on monolinguals. *Journal of Advertising, 45*(1), 43–52.

Luna, D., & Peracchio, L. A. (2005a). Advertising to bilingual consumers: The impact of code-switching on persuasion. *Journal of Consumer Research, 31*(4), 760–765.

Luna, D., & Peracchio, L. A. (2005b). Sociolinguistic effects on code-switched ads targeting bilingual consumers. *Journal of Advertising, 34*(2), 43–56.

Luna, D., Ringberg, T., & Peracchio, L. A. (2008). One individual, two identities: Frame switching among biculturals. *Journal of Consumer Research, 35*(2), 279–293.

Maes, A., Ummelen, N., & Hoeken, H. (1996). *Instructieve teksten. Analyse, ontwerp en evaluatie*. Bussum: Coutinho.

Micu, C. C., & Coulter, R. A. (2010). Advertising in English in nonnative English-speaking markets: The effect of language and self-referencing in advertising in Romania on ad attitudes. *Journal of East-West Business, 16*, 67–84.

Nickerson, C., & Camiciottoli, B. C. (2013). Business English as a lingua franca in advertising texts in the Arabian Gulf: Analyzing the attitudes of the Emirati community. *Journal of Business and Technical Communication, 27*(3), 329–352.

Piller, I. (2003). Advertising as a site of language contact. *Annual Review of Applied Linguistics, 23*, 170–183.

Planken, B., Van Meurs, F., & Radlinska, A. (2010). The effects of the use of English in Polish product advertisements: Implications for english for business purposes. *English for Specific Purposes, 29*(4), 225–242.

Puntoni, S., De Langhe, B., & Van Osselaer, S. M. (2009). Bilingualism and the emotional intensity of advertising language. *Journal of Consumer Research, 35*(6), 1012–1025.

Rossiter, J. R., Percy, L., & Donovan, R. J. (1991). A better advertising planning grid. *Journal of Advertising Research, 31*(5), 11–21.

Schoel, C., Roessel, J., Eck, J., Janssen, B., Petrovic, A., ... & Stahlberg D. (2012). 'Attitudes Towards Languages' (AToL) scale: A global instrument. *Journal of Language and Social Psychology, 32*(1), 21–45.

Ueltschy, L. C., & Ryans, J. K., Jr. (1997). Employing standardized promotion strategies in Mexico: The impact of language and cultural differences. *the International Executive, 39*(4), 479–495.

Van Hooft, A., Van Meurs, F., & Schellekens, L. (2017a). The same or different? Spanish-speaking consumers' response to the use of English or Spanish in product advertisements in Spain and the USA. In V. Cauberghe & L. Hudders (Eds.), *Power to the consumers: How content becomes the message. The 16th International Conference on Research in Advertising (ICORIA)*. Ghent: European Advertising Academy/University of Ghent.

Van Hooft, A., Van Meurs, F., & Spierts, D. (2017b). In Arabic, English, or a mix? Egyptian consumers' response to language choice in product advertisements, and the role of language attitudes. In V. Zabkar & M. Eisend (Eds.), *Challenges in an age of dis-engagement. Advances in advertising research VIII* (pp. 139–153). Wiesbaden: Springer Gabler.

Van Hooft, A., & Truong, T. (2012). Language choice and persuasiveness: The effects of the use of English in product advertisements in Hong Kong. In P. Heynderickx, S. Dieltjens, G. Jacobs, P. Gillaerts, & E. de Groot (Eds.), *The language factor in international business: New perspectives on research, teaching and practice* (pp. 175–198). Bern: Lang.

Zajonc, R. B. (1968). Attitudinal effects of mere exposure. *Journal of Personality and Social Psychology, 9*(2), 1–27.

Disclaimers in Real Estate Print Advertisements

Emmanuel Mogaji

1   Introduction

Buying a home is considered a major financial decision and one of the most expensive purchases an individual can ever make (Mercadante 2017). Making an informed choice is, therefore, considered vitally important. While acknowledging the complex and multi-faceted due diligence that buyers usually invest before buying houses, the role of advertisements in marketing new-build homes cannot be overemphasised. Like in other regulated markets, advertisers are expected to put disclaimers in their advertisements to warn prospective buyers about what they are buying.

Disclaimers are 'statement or disclosure made with the purpose of clarifying or qualifying potentially misleading or deceptive statements made within an advertisement' (Stern and Harmon 1984, p;0.13), they are included to "limit and restrict unsubstantiated claims or misleading cues" (Veloso et al. 2017, p. 893), and there has been increasing advocacy around the world for the implementation of laws requiring disclaimer labels to be attached to media images that have been digitally altered (Bury et al. 2016), especially for fashion and cosmetics product advertisement.

While considerable empirical research on disclaimer advertisement has been conducted on direct-to-consumer prescription drug advertisements and food and dietary supplements, there is no evidence of empirical insight into disclaimers in real estate advertisement. While there may not be direct health implications

---

E. Mogaji (✉)
University of Greewich, London, UK
E-Mail: e.o.mogaji@greenwich.ac.uk

from misleading claims in prescription drug and food advertisements, there are possibilities for huge financial loss through misleading real estate advertisement, and this loss can also have an effect on physical and mental health as the consumer deals with the aftermath of the financial loss.

This was therefore considered important for this present study. This study focuses on real estate advertisements for *Off-the plan homes*. These are houses that are being sold in advance of their completion. Prospective buyers do not get to see the house until they are about to be completed. They rely on other things, such as marketing materials provided by the developers as an indication of how their house will look upon completion. This includes Computer Generated Images (CGI). Consumers are making decisions about unknown and unseen products.

With the divergent and sporadic nature of work in new-build homes, the overarching aim of this study is to reveal the disclaimers in advertising strategies being used to sell off-the-plan homes in London. This study offers theoretical contributions and opens a new avenue of research into disclaimers in marketing strategies. This study moves beyond advertising for children and drug and food supplements to consider a different high involving purchase. The study highlights the unique feature of print advertising as consumers have the ability to understand and process the disclaimers at their pace, unlike listening to it on TV. Finally, disclaimers in the new-build homes sector are still under research. Therefore, this study offers both theoretical and managerial implication on how the disclaimers are being presented.

2   Literature Review

Disclaimers are often presented as footnotes in advertisements to provide consumers with supplemental information and as a self-protective decision of the advertiser (Foxman, Muehling and Moore 1988). Although they do not play a prominent role in the marketing message, they represent an essential aspect which provides additional information, such as warnings, advice or clarifications for the customers (Petrescu et al. 2019). Disclaimers information are also presented to avoid lawsuits (Green and Armstrong 2012), and they can be mandatory for some industry like the Tobacco industry where 'Smoking seriously harms you and others around you' is used.

The growing creative possibilities of digital tools such as Photoshop for manipulating images for advertisement and growing consumer and regulator concerns about brand ethical practice (Petrescu et al. 2019; Herbst et al. 2013) as further necessitated the inclusion of disclaimers in advertisement to remind the consumers to be cautious of the marketing message, explain more prominent claims, stating significant limitations and qualifications (ASA 2014). This practice of digitally enhancing images has become an established and common practice among marketers (Cornelis and Peter 2017), especially for fashion ad cosmetics products and this has often been negatively received as the images were not accurately illustrating what could be achieved by using the products. In 2011, an advertisement featuring airbrushed images of actress Julia Roberts and model Christy Turlington were banned by the UK Advertising Regulatory body. The UK The Committee of Advertising Practice (CAP) had to issue guidance on the use of pre and post-production techniques in ads for cosmetics.

Advertisers are expected to communicate the limitations of their product or services to the customers. Green and Armstrong (2012) identified the economic rationale for the presentation of disclaimer information from both the seller's and consumers' perspective. The sellers' economic interests to provide the information in order not mislead the buyer, to avoid lawsuit, costs of dealing with unsatisfied customers and importantly building good long-term relationships with them and while the buyers may be faced with biased information, they are expected to process the information provided and possibly seek out out independent information and professional advice.

The review of literature has presented an extensive coverage of the use of disclaimer information in advertising to children (Stern and Harmon 1984; Veloso et al. 2017), direct-to-consumer prescription drug advertisements (Wilkes et al. 2000; Hoek et al. 2011), food and dietary supplements (Kesselheim et al. 2015) and a small but growing body of evidence on digitally altered images (Cornelis and Peter 2017), as well as fashion magazine shoots (Tiggemann et al. 2017). These studies highlight the need for brands to give consumers information about the products consumers are buying in order to make an informed decision and to avoid a side effect which may arise from the use of this product. These previous studies have actually focused more on the health implications and not necessarily on the financial implication with the exemption of Mercer et al. (2010) which examined the effectiveness of disclaimers in mutual fund advertisements. When prospective consumers are misled into buying a house which do not exists, they may lose their money, and this may as well affect their physical and mental wellbeing. This further highlight the interest in this research area and worthy of investigation.

In addition, research on disclaimers in advertising has predominantly been on broadcast media (television and radio). Print advertisements are seldom used and, when used, are usually fictitious advertisements except for fashion magazines

(Bury et al. 2016). The use of disclaimers in advertising on broadcast media has not been considered effective as there are doubts on how well the consumers are able to engage with the advertisement due to the pace and duration of the message.

Advertisers frequently have only 30 s to convey their message on broadcast media like TV and Radio. Due to the limited time for the advertisements and, in an effort to save media costs and with regulatory agencies sometimes demanding the inclusion of disclaimers, advertisers may want to read out the disclaimers as quickly as possible, maximizing the available time to convey the primary message whiles simultaneously glossing over undesirable product information (Herbst et al. 2012). Green and Armstrong (2012) found that those mandated messages were not only ineffective but also increased confusion for consumers.

Furthermore, Herbst et al. (2013) argued that fast disclaimers greatly reduce consumer comprehension of product risks and benefits, while Herbst et al. (2012) also noted that fastpaced speech could serve as a negative heuristic cue for the untrustworthiness of the advertiser. This further highlight a research agenda for disclaimers in print advertisements whereby readers can take their time to read the disclaimers. James and Kover (1992) suggested that reading advertisements in a newspaper are a matter of choice, unlike the intrusive nature of television advertisements, where the viewer has limited choices.

Smit (1999) believed that newspaper readers could get involved in the information and read the message at their own pace. In addition, television is considered entertaining but low-involving, while newspaper media is considered high-involving, as the reader's involvement in the search for information is not interrupted (Mogaji 2018). The degree of attention and how much energy is devoted to apprehending and understanding the messages (James and Kover 1992) is considered higher in the newspaper media. Print media is considered more factual and informative than television or radio (Haller 1974; Somasundaran and Light 1991). The disclaimer information provided in print media (newspaper and magazines) are not read out at fast-paced as in broadcast media, consumers have control over how they engage and process the information.

Moving beyond the research on disclaimers presented on food and advertisement targeted for children on broadcast media, this study specifically sought to understand the disclaimers presented in newspaper advertisements for new homes in London.

3 Methodology

The research method used for this study is a thematic and content analysis of the advertisement to establish key themes and numerical significance of the emerged themes. Braun and Clarke (2006, p. 79) considered thematic analysis as: "a method for identifying, analysing and reporting patterns within data". To this extent, patterns within the disclaimers that give an indication of how London developers are communicating with prospective buyers were derived from subsequent analyses of the advertisements. Content analysis is arguably one of the most suitable methods for analysing advertisements and is frequently used by researchers (Mogaji et al. 2018; Belch and Belch 2013).

Advertisements for new homes in London were collected over a period of two years — January 2016 and December 2017 — from two freely distributed newspapers in London, the London Metro and the London Evening Standard. 1645 advertisements were collected; 798 (48.5%) were from 2016 and 847 (51.5%) were from 2017. The disclaimers are often presented at the bottom of the advertisements. They are presented in small print and sometimes in capital letters. Asterisks (*) are also used around key messages around the advertisements (like prices and location) as a pointer to the disclaimers at the bottom of the page.

Thematic analysis of the disclaimers was initially carried out. The phases of analysis established by Braun and Clarke (2006) were adopted for the data analysis. Familiarisation and immersion with the data were achieved by reading the disclaimers repeatedly. This gave a better understanding of how the developers were communicating with prospective buyers. Six parent nodes (themes) underlying the key themes in the disclaimers were identified, highlighting efforts developers are making to ensure that prospective buyers are making an informed choice. These themes later formed part of the content analysis, which quantitatively explored their prevalence of these themes.

The coding protocol suggested by Krippendorff (2012) was followed. Two coders of different genders and residents of London served as the coders. Both the coders were trained in coding procedures for ten hours, which includes the concept and strategies of content analysis, using the codebook which contains the operational definitions of the variables and categories and the coding sheet. Independently of each other, they coded all the advertisements for this study. The different categories of the analysis were pre-tested and adjusted accordingly. This is the guideline-recommended by Kolbe and Burnett (1991) and adopted by Mogaji (2015). With regard to the London boundary, some of the advertisements featured developments just outside London (e.g. Chelmsford and Slough), but coders were trained to select only advertisements within the M25, as verified through the postcode (Farinloye et al. 2019). An intercoder reliability check was conducted and assessed by using Cohen's kappa (ranging from 0.948 to 1.00). After initial coding, the differences were discussed and collectively resolved with the author and the adjusted scores were analyzed.

4 Results

Developers are putting effort into place to make sure that prospective buyers are making an informed choice. Prospective buyers are warned that the information presented in the advertisements are believed to be correct at the time of distribution or placing of the advertisement, but its accuracy cannot be guaranteed and no such information forms part of any contract. After the thematic and content analysis, six key themes to summarise these disclaimers are presented below.

4.1 CGI

Developer relies on computer-generated images (CGIs) to provide an insight into the buildings that are still under construction. There are warnings with regard to the reliability and validity of these images. Of the advertisements analysed, 91.5% (n = 1505) made reference to the CGI, identifying the view in the image and advising prospective buyers that the images were for indicative and illustrative purposes only. This suggested that the images might not be a true reflection of what they have seen in the advertisements. There could be variations to the landscaping, the external and internal design, and some of the features in a CGI might only be available with an optional upgrade at additional cost.

4.2 Home Repossession

Understanding the highly involved nature of buying a house and the ongoing financial commitment, 65.0% (n = 1069) of the sampled advertisements warned prospective buyers that their homes might be repossessed if they do not keep up payments on their mortgage or secured debt. This warning is often provided in capital letters to indicate that it is different from other small-print warnings. This type of message is often associated with mortgage advertisements from banks, but perhaps it also stems from a sense of responsibility on the part of the developers to alert buyers to the implications of the decision they are making.

4.3 Price Change

Price is often considered as a rational appeal, one that allows potential buyers to compare and make an informed decision. The highly-involved nature of buying a house also necessitates providing information to prospective buyers. In the advertisements analysed, 91.8% (n = 1510) presented price indications. Exact figures are not often presented as there are always possibilities to upgrade and have additional features. When fixed prices are indicated on the advertisements, the developer says they are correct at the time of going to press, implying that by the next time the prospective buyer visits the site the price may have changed. Prospective buyers are advised to check the website and speak with a sales agent for details.

4.4 Incentives and Offers Are Not Guaranteed

Developers were organising first-time buyer events to share government initiatives and offer buyers incentives on stamp duty, legal fees and even furniture and kitchen fittings. However, this is also a disclaimer to this offer. Some developers expect some level of commitment before prospective buyers can receive incentives. This can sometimes include paying a deposit at the first-time buyer events. Prospective buyers are expected to make an instant decision, as the deal might not be available next time and, therefore, creating a sense of urgency in making this financial decision.

4.5 Purchase Not Guaranteed

In 51.8% (n = 852) of advertisements, prospective buyers were informed of terms and conditions that did not necessarily guarantee a purchase such as places are subject to availability and entry criteria which include affordability, eligibility and lender-requirement checks to see if the buyer is financially capable of buying a house. Offers such as London's Help to Buy scheme and paid stamp duty are also available on selected plots, developments and properties, and prospective buyers are advised to speak to their sales executives regarding tenure and offers of new homes.

4.6 Source of Information

To make sure they are providing accurate information, developers often include the sources of their information, especially with regard to the distance to train stations. Often, the distances to a train station are graphically presented in minutes to allow prospective buyers to imagine the proximity to Central London. They claim journey times, and distances are approximate and train times are taken from the National Rail, Transport for London and Google Maps websites while walking time is from the walkit.com website.

5 Discussion

The developers are marketing the unseen. These houses have not been built, and it is not ready for occupation. The Real Estate Agent has not accessed the building to take photographs and invite prospective buyers to have a tour around the house. There is a need to provide a reasonable amount of information about these unknown and unseen products for prospective buyers and importantly disclaimers for those who may be interested.

There is a huge reliance on CGI which can be emotionally appealing and presents an artistic impression of the houses. This, however, might not be enough to justify a purchase. It is recognized that in this digital age and advancement in software development, advertisement can use digitally enhanced images to obtain presentation-quality images like the CGIs and this could misrepresent the reality of the house even though consumers assume and expect basic honesty of the presented home over unreal effects of the advertised product (Petrescu et al. 2019; Cornelis and Peter 2017). Prospective buyers are expected to be aware of the small print; however, as the developers will claim they have suggested that the CGIs are not a real reflection of what the house will look like when completed.

Though the CGIs has been manipulated to enhance attributes of the house and its location, this creative decision cannot be classified under the umbrella of deceptive advertising as the images used is not a manipulation of an existing image, unlike the models) in Fashion advertisement in particular) who have been airbrushed to look thinner. These disclaimers are there presented advertising to highlight potentially deceptive features of the advertisements (Petrescu et al. 2019; Herbst et al. 2013) and therefore consumers will consider these in their decision-making process and possible seek professional advice if in doubt.

The technicalities regarding disclaimers on broadcast media are acknowledged. There is a concern about the visual presentation of the disclosure in the text on

TV (Fowler et al. 2010). This includes the legibility due to font size, background colour, distracting music and the position on the screen or the duration. For radio, the pace at which the disclaimer is being read and the accent could be a hindrance as consumers may not be able to process the provided information (Herbst and Allan 2006; Morgan and Stoltman 2002). However, is not the case of print advertising as the disclaimers are presented for the consumers to read and process the information at their own pace (Mogaji and Danbury 2017), though there could be concerns around the font size and legibility. It is easier for consumers to process the information compared to broadcast media.

The developer wants to sell their house off-plan, they have legitimate reasons to market the houses even though not ready yet. Disclaimer information has been included in the advertisements to provide additional information for consumers and to absorb the developers of some responsibilities regarding the claims and offer made available. While developers are aware that prospective buyers may make quick decisions based on the incentives that are being offered, they warned buyers that it is for a limited time and not everyone may benefit from it, a consumer who reads that should be able to proceed with caution and not rush to make an uninformed decision. Likewise, prospective buyers are warned about the possibilities of change in prices, they have been informed that the prices are correct at the time of going to press and this suggests the need for consumers to be mindful before making a commitment as they price they see on the advertisement may have changed by the time they want to make an offer. The Developer has further absorbed themselves of any responsibility by using data from Google Map and Travel for London to back up their claims with regards to location and travel time. They cannot be held responsible if the journey time (as indicated in the advertisement as at the time of going to press) changed upon the completion of the house.

This research makes several contributions to the literature of advertising and marketing communications of the property market, which is relevant for academic researchers, managers and policymakers.

Firstly, the present study contributes to the growing body of research on advertising disclaimers by specifically focusing on print advertisement as previous studies have been on radio and television. Drumwright and Murphy (2009, p. 86) noted that: "the traditional challenge of advertising is to create a commercial message that is both effective in selling and truthful". This has necessitated the need for disclaimers on advertisements, especially regarding computer-generated images, transport times, and the prices, as these are key advertising appeals for prospective customers. Previous studies on disclaimers on TV advertisements have shown that quickly read disclaimers greatly reduce consumer comprehension of product risks and benefits, creating implications for risks and benefits and social responsibility (Herbst et al. 2013), however with a print advertisement, and consumers are in control of how and when they process the information.

Second, the research in this study is believed to be the first to consider the disclaimers in high involving repurchases like property. While past research has focused on advertising food for children, health and beauty products, this study extends knowledge on property market advertising and the print media. The disclaimers on print advertisements allow developers to present warnings without any timeframe and allow consumers to read and understand the message at their own pace.

Thirdly, with the increased advocacy for the implementation of laws requiring disclaimer labels to be attached to media images that have been digitally altered (Bury et al. 2016), this study contributes to research on manipulated images used for advertisements. While the idea may predominantly be from fashion advertisements, presenting an unrealistic impression of a real person, computer-generated images present a realistic view of an unreal building. As at the time of presenting the CGI, the building is not existing. These images are used to show different views of and around the house, to make it more attractive and presentable to prospective buyers. This, however, cannot be deemed to be misleading, unlike the manipulated images in fashion advertisement.

In terms of practical implications, the present findings contribute to a better understanding of the declaimers which are relevant to the ASA and CAP codes. There was no indication that the inclusion of disclaimers was required by an outside regulatory agency such as the ASA, and more so, it was noted that not all the advertisements analyzed carried the disclaimers. This highlight implication for the policymakers which suggest the possibilities of regulating the disclaimer content and typographical elements. From the broadcast media point of view, there are regulations on percentage of advertisement duration that can be devoted to duration to the disclaimer, ranging from 13% (4 s in a 30-s spot) to 23% (7 s in a 30-s spot) (Herbst et al. 2011). Regulators might want to address details around the font size and the case. Should disclaimers be in fixed font or a percentage of the biggest font in the print advert? Should the disclaimers be printed in upper case for emphasis or simply capitalizing each word.

The use of misleading claims and manipulated images in advertisement could make consumer distrust the advertisement and the brand (Amyx and Lumpkin 2016; Czarnecka and Mogaji 2019).), and as developers market the unknown and unseen building, trust is essential. Though disclaimers are included, with the knowledge that the houses being marketed are off-plan and have not yet been built, there is a need to build trust and credibility in the developers continually. Consumers should feel assured that their deposit is safe, and they will get the houses as promised. It was not surprising to see developers include awards and accolades in their advertisements; however, testimonials and word of mouth can also be used to establish this trust and be a credible developer.

Advertising practitioners can make wise decisions in light of the different themes and update their disclaimers and be mindful of the wording of the disclaimers in order to protect their brand, follow the Advertising Code and offer relevant information to prospective buyers. As advised by Fowler et al. (2010), the disclosure should not contain language that the average consumer could not comprehend. Prospective buyers are also becoming better informed, more demanding and less tolerant of poor service and construction defects (Barlow and Ozaki 2003), highlighting a managerial implication for developers to ensure prospective buyers receive good value for money and excellent customer service before and after purchase.

6 Conclusion

Buying a house may not always be a straightforward process. The complex and multi-faceted due diligence that buyers usually invest before buying houses is acknowledged, and this highlight the value to be placed on disclaimers in advertisements. This is a high-involving decision and considering that many people believe that advertisers use deceitful tactics to manipulate consumers (Herbst et al. 2012), information gathered from different sources needs to be processed before making an informed choice.

While the developers have provided insight into the house and neighbourhood using formation using CGI, the location of the property, transport links, price and incentives have been presented as a key message to appeals to prospective buyers, and the developer absorbs themselves of any responsibility of misrepresentation. This aligns with the theoretical reasoning behind the recommended use of disclaimer labels as brands can advertise their products from a position of caveat emptor, "let the buyer beware" (Herbst et al. 2013). The prospective buyers are therefore expected to engage with these disclaimers at their pace and understanding and seek professional advice before deciding or committing to buy the house.

As with any study, there are limitations in this study, and therefore the results should be interpreted with that understanding. These limitations also highlight the direction of future work. Print advertising in London was considered over a fixed period. The disclaimers in new-build homes media are still under-researched, which illustrates many more gaps in existing research that can still be filled. Further research should explore other cities in the country (for example, Liverpool, Manchester or Edinburgh). To have a better understanding, a comparative study with other countries could be carried out.

Although disclaimer labels represent an attractive strategy that can be relatively easily implemented (Tiggemann et al. 2017), there has been little empirical evidence supporting their effectiveness, especially with regards to print advertising and new-build homes. Future studies should aim towards testing the effectiveness of this disclaimer, its influence of ad scepticism, advertising believability and brand trust. Further research can also seek to understand how prospective home buyers comprehend disclaimer messages and how it shapes their purchase intention.

References

Belch, G. E., & Belch, M. A. (2013). A content analysis study of the use of celebrity endorsers in magazine advertising. *International Journal of Advertising, 32*(3), 369–389.

Braun, V., & Clarke, V. (2006). Using thematic analysis in psychology. *Qualitative Research in Psychology, 3*(2), 77–101.

Cornelis, E., & Peter, P. C. (2017). The real campaign: The role of authenticity in the effectiveness of advertising disclaimers in digitally enhanced images. *Journal of Business Research, 77*, 102–112.

Czarnecka, B., & Mogaji, E. (2019). How are we tempted into debt? Emotional appeals in loan advertisements in UK newspapers. *International Journal of Bank Marketing, 38*(3), 756–776.

Drumwright, M. E., & Murphy, P. E. (2009). The current state of advertising ethics: Industry and academic perspectives. *Journal of Advertising, 38*(1), 83–108.

Farinloye, T., Mogaji, E., Aririguzoh, S., & Kieu, T. A. (2019). Qualitatively exploring the effect of change in the residential environment on travel behaviour. *Travel Behaviour and Society, 17*, 26–35.

Foxman, E. R., Muehling, D. D., & Moore, P. A. (1988). Disclaimer footnotes in ads: Discrepancies between purpose and performance. *Journal of Public Policy & Marketing, 7*(1), 127–137.

Herbst, K. C., & Allan, D. (2006). The effects of brand experience and an advertisement's disclaimer speed on purchase: Speak slowly or carry a big brand. *International Journal of Advertising, 25*(2), 213–222.

Herbst, K. C., Finkel, E. J., Allan, D., & Fitzsimons, G. M. (2012). On the dangers of pulling a fast one: Advertisement disclaimer speed, brand trust, and purchase intention. *Journal of Consumer Research, 38*(5), 909–919.

Herbst, K. C., Hannah, S. T., & Allan, D. (2013). Advertisement disclaimer speed and corporate social responsibility: "Costs" to consumer comprehension and effects on brand trust and purchase intention. *Journal of Business Ethics, 117*(2), 297–311.

James, W. L., & Kover, A. J. (1992). Do overall attitudes toward advertising affect involvement with specific advertisements? *Journal of Advertising Research., 32*(5), 78–83.

Krippendorff, K. (2012). *Content analysis: An introduction to its methodology*. Newbury Park: Sage.

Kieu, T. A., & Mogaji, E. (2018). Marketing communication strategies of off-plan homes. ANZMAC 2018 Conference Proceedings. 419–422.

Lawson, G. (2013). A rhetorical study of in-flight real estate advertisements as a potential site of ethical transformation in Chinese cities. *Cities, 31,* 85–95.

Mercadante, K. (2017). The truth? Your house is not an investment. https://www.moneyunder30.com/why-your-house-is-not-an-investment. Accessed: 8 Aug. 2018.

Mercer, M., Palmiter, A. R., & Taha, A. E. (2010). Worthless warnings? Testing the effectiveness of disclaimers in mutual fund advertisements. *Journal of Empirical Legal Studies, 7*(3), 429–459.

Mogaji, E. (2015). Reflecting a diversified country: A content analysis of newspaper advertisements in Great Britain. *Marketing Intelligence & Planning, 33*(6), 908–926.

Mogaji, E., & Danbury, A. (2017). Making the brand appealing: Advertising strategies and consumers' attitude towards UK retail bank brands. *Journal of Product & Brand Management., 26*(6), 531–544. https://doi.org/10.1108/JPBM-07-2016-1285.

Mogaji, E., Czarnecka, B., & Danbury, A. (2018). Emotional appeals in UK business-to-business financial services advertisements. *International Journal of Bank Marketing, 36*(1), 208–227.

Morgan, F. W., & Stoltman, J. J. (2002). Television advertising disclosures: An empirical assessment. *Journal of Business and Psychology, 16*(4), 515–535.

Petrescu, M., Mingione, M., Gironda, J., & Brotspies, H. (2019). Ad scepticism and retouch-free disclaimers: Are they worth it? *Journal of Marketing Communications, 25*(7), 738–762.

Smith, S., Munro, M., & Christie, H. (2006). Performing (housing) markets. *Urban Studies, 43*(1), 81–98.

Somasundaran, T. N., & Light, C. D. (1991). A cross-cultural and media specific analysis of student attitudes toward advertising. In Proceedings of the American Marketing Association's 1991 Educators' Conference (pp. 667–669).

Stern, B. L., & Harmon, R. R. (1984). The incidence and characteristics of disclaimers in children's television advertising. *Journal of Advertising, 13*(2), 12–16.

Tiggemann, M., Brown, Z., Zaccardo, M., & Thomas, N. (2017). "Warning: This image has been digitally altered": The effect of disclaimer labels added to fashion magazine shoots on women's body dissatisfaction. *Body Image, 21,* 107–113.

Veloso, A. R., Hildebrand, D., & Sresnewsky, K. B. (2017). Online advertising disclaimers in unregulated markets: Use of disclaimers by multinational and local companies in the Brazilian toy industry. *International Journal of Advertising, 36*(6), 893–909.

Wallace, A. (2008). Knowing the market? Understanding and performing York's housing. *Housing Studies, 23*(2), 253–270.

Wicks, J. L., Warren, R., Fosu, I., & Wicks, R. H. (2009). Dual-modality disclaimers, emotional appeals, and production techniques in food advertising airing during programs rated for children. *Journal of Advertising, 38*(4), 93–105.

"Trust Me, I'm an Advertiser". The Influence of Message Sidedness and Advertiser Credibility on Readers' Perceptions of Native Advertisements

Dr. Simone Krouwer, Prof. Dr. Karolien Poels, and Prof. Dr. Steve Paulussen

1 Introduction

News media and advertisers increasingly utilize advertising formats that mirror the editorial news in style and content: so-called 'native advertising' (Wojdynski 2016). Proponents reason that native advertising may be more effective than traditional online advertising formats (e.g. banner ads) because readers consider the editorial format to be more valuable and engaging (Campbell and Marks 2015; Harms et al. 2017). Critics, however, argue that native advertising mainly works because readers are deceived into thinking that they are looking at an actual news article (Einstein 2016). Following this criticism, a plethora of studies have investigated the relationship between readers' advertising recognition and evaluations. While the vast majority of these studies showed indeed a negative relationship between readers' advertising recognition and evaluations (Amazeen and Muddiman 2017; Wojdynski and Evans 2015), in some studies readers' advertising recognition did not result into more negative evaluations (Becker-Olsen 2003; Krouwer et al. 2018). This suggests that the extent to which readers' advertising recognition results into more negative evaluations can potentially be influenced

---

Dr. S. Krouwer (✉) · Prof. Dr. K. Poels · Prof. Dr. S. Paulussen
Department of Communication Studies, Universiteit Antwerpen, Antwerpen, Belgium
E-Mail: simone.krouwer@uantwerpen.be

Prof. Dr. K. Poels
E-Mail: karolien.poels@uantwerpen.be

Prof. Dr. S. Paulussen
E-Mail: steve.paulussen@uantwerpen.be

by other factors. We argue that it is important to identify these different factors, as native advertising is not a sustainable advertising technique if its effectiveness relies solely on misleading readers. After all, deceptive advertising practices may eventually erode readers' credibility perceptions of the news websites, and also result into more negative perceptions of native advertising in general (Darke and Ritchie 2007; Schauster et al. 2016). Therefore, there is a need for more research on factors that can help to maintain the credibility of native advertisements without misleading readers into thinking that they are looking at a news article. Some research has suggested that factors related to the content of the native ads, such as a low prominence of the advertising brand and high information utility, may help to suppress critical processing among readers who have recognized the advertisements as such (Krouwer et al. 2018; Sweetser et al. 2016). However, besides these studies, there is still little empirical knowledge available on other factors related to the content and context of native advertisements that can potentially suppress readers' critical processing when they are aware that they are viewing advertising. The present study aims to address this knowledge gap, by investigating two factors that can possibly influence readers' critical processing and subsequent evaluations when they recognize native advertisements as such: message sidedness and advertiser credibility.

2   Conceptual Framework

2.1   Advertiser Credibility

Most of the available research on native advertising centers around the Persuasion Knowledge Model (PKM). The PKM suggests that when readers recognize advertisements as such, they could become more critical of the message, as the message has changed from neutral (in this case: a news article) into one that potentially tries to influence them (content from an advertiser) (Brehm 1966; Friestad and Wright 1994). Consumers who view advertising also often infer 'manipulative intent', which means that they perceive that the advertiser is trying to influence them to benefit itself, which can increase their resistance to the message (Campbell 1995; Campbell and Kirmani 2000). Journalists, on the other hand, are expected to provide objective information to readers (Deuze 2005), and are therefore generally perceived as more credible than advertisers (Lord and Putrevu 1993). However, it should be noted that advertisers can also differ in their degree of credibility. Some advertisers are perceived as more credible because they are considered to be a well-known expert on a topic (i.e. high expertise), or because consumers perceive that the advertiser acts in their best interest (i.e. trustworthiness) (Lafferty and Goldsmith 1999; Metzger et al. 2003). Readers who recognize a native advertisement from a high-credibility advertiser might reason that the information in a native advertisement can still be trusted and is therefore still useful to them (Flanagin and Metzger 2007; Hovland and Weiss 1951; Pornpitakpan 2004). They may infer less manipulative intent when they consider the advertiser to be more credible, which likely results into less resistance and more positive evaluations (Fransen et al. 2015). Given the preceding arguments, we propose the following hypotheses:

> *H1. Readers who read a native advertisement from both a high- and low-credibility advertiser will (a) perceive higher inferences of manipulative intent, and (b) perceive the message to be less credible, compared to readers who view a news article.*
>
> *H2. The negative effect of readers' native advertising recognition on (a) inferences of manipulative intent, and (b) the credibility of the advertisement will be smaller when the advertisement is provided by a high-credibility company.*

2.2 Message Sidedness

Advertisers typically aim to influence consumers by using one-sided advertising messages that solely mention the positive characteristics of a subject or brand (Crowley and Hoyer 1994; Kamins and Assael 1987). However, when readers recognize a native ad, they may already infer manipulative intent. Reading a one-sided message may further increase inferences of manipulative intent, as a one-sided message confirms readers' expectation that the advertiser is mainly acting in its own interest (An et al. 2018; Eisend 2007). This likely results into more resistance and negative evaluations (Fransen et al. 2015). Conversely, research in traditional advertising contexts suggests that advertisers can increase their own credibility and subsequently decrease consumers' resistance by voluntarily providing some negative information, which is called 'two-sided advertising' (Eisend 2007). The attribution theory poses that when an advertiser provides some negative information in an advertisement, consumers are likely to attribute this (unexpected) behavior to an advertiser's desire to tell the truth, which could increase the credibility of the advertiser and its message (Crowley and Hoyer 1994). We therefore expect that the negative effect of readers' advertising recognition on their evaluations will be smaller when the advertisement contains two-sided information:

H3. Readers who view a two-sided (versus one-sided) native advertisement will (a) perceive lower manipulative intent, which will subsequently (b) increase the credibility of the advertiser, (c) increase the credibility of the native ad and (d) positively influence readers' evaluations of the advertiser.

2.3 The Joint Effect of Message Sidedness and Source Credibility

Using a two-sided message strategy for native advertising might be particularly beneficial when consumers already hold negative beliefs about an advertiser. Especially when a low-credibility advertiser provides a native ad, readers may be more likely to infer that the advertiser is mainly providing information in its own interest (Hastak and Jong-Won 1990; Jones and Davis 1965). Using a one-sided message will confirm this expectation, and in order to cope with the persuasive attempt, it is likely that readers will dismiss the credibility of the non-credible source and its message even further (Fransen et al. 2015). On the other hand, when a more credible advertiser provides only one-sided information in a native advertisement, readers could still rationalize that the information is correct and comprehensive (Flanagin and Metzger 2007; Hovland and Weiss 1951). We therefore expect the following interaction effect:

H4: The positive effect of using a two-sided native advertising strategy on (a) perceived manipulative intent, (b) the credibility of the advertiser, (c) the credibility of the advertisement and (d) attitudes towards the advertiser will be stronger for a low-credibility advertiser (compared to a high-credibility advertiser).

3 Methodology

The study used a native advertisement about the characteristics of the artificial sweetener stevia, a topic that could be of interest to both men and women of different ages. A pre-test (N = 39, 56.4% male, Mage = 27, SDage = 5.92) was performed to select a high- and low-credibility advertiser and to select positive and negative arguments for the message sidedness manipulation.

3.1 Pre-test

Perceived importance of the arguments. Past studies have shown that in order to make a two-sided message effective, the two-sided message needs to start with positive arguments (Eisend 2006; Igou and Bless 2003), the amount of negative arguments needs to be less than the amount of positive arguments (Crowley and Hoyer 1994; Eisend 2006), and the negative arguments should be of low to moderate importance to consumers (Eisend 2007). In order to select positive and negative arguments that differ in importance, participants of the pre-test rated the importance of nine positive and negative attributes of sweeteners. A seven-point scale ranging from "not important at all" to "extremely important" was used. Participants were asked: *"If you need to pick a sweetener as an alternative to sugar, how important would each of these attributes be to you?"* (Settle and Golden 1974). GLM repeated measures analysis (using the Greenhouse–Geisser correction) showed a significant difference in the importance of the positive and negative arguments $(F(6.00,228.15) = 10.75, p < .001)$. The post hoc comparisons analysis showed that the negative arguments *"The sweetener tastes differently than sugar"* $(M = 4.18, SD = 1.43)$ and *"There is a maximum acceptable daily intake of the sweetener, you cannot take unlimited amounts of it"* $(M = 3.97, SD = 1.39)$ were perceived as significantly less important $(p < .05)$ than the positive arguments *"the sweetener does not affect blood sugar levels"* $(M = 5.38, SD = 1.11)$, *"the sweetener contains little to no calories"* $(M = 5.59, SD = 1.51)$, *"the sweetener is tooth-friendly"* $(M = 5.49, SD = 1.30)$, and *"the sweetener is approved by the EU as a safe ingredient"* $(M = 5.79, SD = 1.33)$. Following these results, the researchers created the one-sided article with four positive arguments, and the two-sided article with four positive and two negative arguments.

Advertiser credibility. Next, in order to select a high- and low-credibility advertiser, participants rated the credibility of five (commercial and non-profit) organizations. Participants, who were asked to imagine they were looking for information about sweeteners, had to rate the credibility of the organization as an information provider on three 7-point scales *(not trustworthy/ trustworthy/, dishonest/honest, not credible/credible)*. GLM repeated measures analysis (using the Greenhouse–Geisser correction) showed a significant difference in the credibility of the companies $(F (3.06,116.36) = 23.86, p < .001)$. Based on the results of the pre-test, the soft drink brand "Coca-Cola" was selected as the low-credibility advertiser $(M = 3.66, SD = 1.80)$, and "Weight Watchers" $(M = 5.01, SD = 1.11)$ as the high-credibility advertiser. Results of the pairwise comparisons analysis showed that these organizations significantly differed in credibility $(p < .001)$.

3.2 Main Study

The main study was conducted on a well-known national news website that is perceived as credible among news readers (Newman et al. 2019). The study used a 2 (message sidedness: one-sided versus two-sided article) × 3 (source: journalist of the news website, high-credibility advertiser, low-credibility advertiser) between-subjects, experimental design. A total of 381 participants (50.9% male) were recruited via a market research company. Participants varied in age from 18 to 81 ($M_{age} = 40.78$, $SD_{age} = 13.87$). All participants were familiar with the national news website on which the native advertisement was inserted. The questionnaire started with briefing participants that they were about to view a [news article / native advertisement], provided by [a journalist / high-credibility organization / low-credibility organization] on a national news website. We briefed participants about what they were going to read, in order to measure the influence of advertiser credibility and message sidedness once readers have recognized that they are viewing content from an advertiser. Readers read either a one-sided or two-sided article about the sweetener stevia on the news website. When finished, they clicked to continue to the questionnaire. The button appeared after thirty seconds, to ensure that participants would not automatically click to continue.

Measures
Perceived message sidedness. In order to check whether the manipulation of message sidedness was successful, a single item measured perceived message sidedness on a seven-point semantic differential scale: *"this article only mentions advantages of stevia"* - *"this article mentions advantages and disadvantages of stevia"* (Eisend 2006).

Inferences of Manipulative Intent was measured on a six-item, seven-point scale developed by Campbell (1995) ($M = 3.02$, $SD = 1.09$, $\alpha = .87$).

The *credibility of the native advertisement* or *news article* was measured on a five-item, seven-point scale (Wojdynski and Evans 2015), ($M = 4.75$, $SD = 1.15$, $\alpha = .85$).

Attitude toward the source (i.e. the advertiser, or journalist in the control condition) was measured on a four-item, seven-point scale (Campbell 1995) ($M = 5.17$, $SD = 1.30$, $\alpha = .93$).

News website credibility was measured on the five-item, seven-point scale from Kiousis (2001), ($M = 4.80$, $SD = 1.13$, $\alpha = .87$).

Involvement. As it has been shown that consumers' involvement with the subject of an advertisement can influence the effectiveness of using a two-sided advertising strategy (Cornelis et al. 2014), participants' involvement with the subject (stevia) has been measured on a 5-item, 7-point scale and taken into account as a control factor ($M = 4.74$, $SD = 1.56$, $\alpha = .97$).

Analyses
The hypotheses were tested using ANCOVA analyses with message sidedness and source as factors, involvement as covariate, and the different dependent variables. Next, post hoc pairwise comparisons (using the Bonferroni correction) were performed to check which conditions differed significantly from each other. Second, the mediating role of readers' inferences of manipulative intent when explaining the effect of message sidedness on the dependent variables was tested using the PROCESS macro in SPSS (Model 4, with a bootstrap approach of 10,000 drawings; Hayes and Preacher 2014).

4 Results

Manipulation check. The manipulation of 'message sidedness' was successful. Readers perceived the two-sided message ($M = 5.65$, $SD = 1.54$) to be significantly more two-sided than the one-sided message ($M = 2.41$, $SD = 1.56$), $F(1, 379) = 330.29$, $p < .001$,

Effects of source
IMI. Results of the ANCOVA analysis showed a significant main effect of source on readers' IMI $F(2, 374) = 808.99$, $p < .001$. H1a predicted that readers' IMI would be significantly lower when they are reading a news article, compared to a native ad from both the high-credibility and low-credibility advertiser. The Bonferroni post-hoc test showed that readers indeed perceived significantly less manipulative intent when they were viewing the news article ($M = 2.75$, $SD = .91$), compared to when they were exposed to the native ad from the low-credibility advertiser ($M = 3.30$, $SD = 1.13$) ($p < .001$). However, the difference in perceived manipulative intent between the high-credibility advertiser ($M = 3.09$, $SD = 1.14$) and journalist was not significant. Thus, H1a was only partially confirmed. H2a was confirmed, as IMI was significantly lower among readers who read the native ad from the high-credibility advertiser, compared to readers who read the ad from the low-credibility advertiser ($p < .05$).

Credibility of the ad / article. Source also had a significant main effect on readers' credibility perceptions of the ad / article $F(2, 374) = 5.55$, $p = .004$. H1b was partially confirmed, as post hoc comparison analysis showed only a

Table 1 Effects of message sidedness and type of advertiser on IMI, ad credibility, source credibility and attitude towards the source

		IMI	Ad credibility	Source credibility	Attitude towards the advertiser
One-sided	Coca-Cola	3.99	4.40	4.41	4.80
	Weight-watchers	3.33	4.55	4.52	5.01
Two-sided	Coca-Cola	3.46	4.70	4.66	5.16
	Weight-Watchers	2.76	4.87	4.81	5.18

significant difference between the native ad from the low-credibility advertiser ($M = 4.55$, $SD = 1.17$) and journalist ($M = 5.17$, $SD = 1.04$), $p = .003$, but no significant difference in credibility between the native ad from the high-credibility advertiser ($M = 4.63$, $SD = 1.20$) and news article from the journalist. H2b was also rejected, as the native ads from the high-credibility advertiser and low-credibility advertiser did not significantly differ in credibility.

Effects of message sidedness
IMI. The results confirmed H3a. Readers' IMI was significantly higher in one-sided message conditions ($M = 3.17$, $SD = 1.15$) than in two-sided conditions ($M = 2.86$, SD $= 1.02$), $F(1, 374) = 7.48$, $p = .007$. This positive effect occurred for both the high- and low-credibility advertiser (see table 1).

Credibility of the ad / article. The results confirmed H3b: readers perceived a two-sided message as significantly more credible ($M = 4.93$, $SD = 1.11$), than a one-sided message ($M = 4.56$, $SD = 1.17$), $F(1, 374) = 9.55$, $p = .002$. This positive effect occurred for both the high- and low-credibility advertiser (see table 1). Results of the mediation analysis showed that the positive effect providing a two-sided message on credibility was mediated by the decrease in participants' inferences of manipulative intent (see table 2).

Credibility of the source. The results confirmed H3c, showing that readers perceived the advertiser as significantly more credible when a two-sided message was provided ($M = 4.98$, $SD = 1.09$), compared to when a one-sided message was provided ($M = 4.62$, $SD = 1.16$), $F(1, 374) = 8.94$, $p = .003$. This positive effect occurred for both the high- and low-credibility advertiser (see table 1). Results of the mediation analysis showed that this effect was mediated by the decrease in participants' inferences of manipulative intent (see table 2).

Table 2 Results of the Hayes Mediation analyses for the effect of message sidedness on the DV's through IMI

Mediation Model					
Dependent variable	*a* path	*b* path	*c'* path	Indirect effect	95% BC-CI
Credibility of the ad	.31**	−.83***	.11^{NS}	.27	.084 to .457
Credibility of the source	−.31**	−.87***	.08^{NS}	.27	.085 to .466
Attitude towards the source	−.31**	−.78***	.12^{NS}	.24	.073 to .416

Note. *a* path: relationship between a two-sided message and IMI; *b* path: relationship between IMI and the dependent variable; *c'* path: the direct effect of using a two-sided message on the dependent variable, when IMI is included as mediator. *$p < .05$; **$p < .01$; ***$p < .001'$; NS = non-significant

Attitude towards the source. The results confirmed H3d: readers' attitude towards the advertiser was significantly more positive when a two-sided message was used (M = 5.35, SD = 1.24), compared to a when a one-sided message was used (M = 4.99, SD = 1.34), F(1, 374) = 6.91, $p = .009$. Results of the mediation analysis showed that this positive effect was mediated by the decrease in participants' inferences of manipulative intent (see table 2).

Message sidedness x Source

The results showed no interaction effects between source and message sidedness for IMI ($F(2, 374) < 1$, $p = .757$). As displayed in table 1, readers' IMI decreased for all sources when a two-sided message was used. The strength of this effect did not significantly differ between the low-credibility advertiser and high-credibility advertiser. Using a two-sided message also had an equally strong (positive) effect on perceived credibility of the advertisement ($F(2, 374) < 1$, $p = .962$) source credibility $F(2, 374) < 1$, $p = .714$) and attitude towards the source $F(2, 374) < 1$, $p = .696$) for both advertisers (see table 1). Thus, H4a – H4d are rejected.

5 Discussion and conclusion

Many studies have investigated the potential negative effect of readers' native advertising recognition on their evaluations (e.g. Wojdynski and Evans 2015; Krouwer et al. 2018). However, in these studies readers' advertising recognition did not always result into more negative evaluations, which suggests that there are other factors that can influence the extent to which readers' advertising recognition results into more negative evaluations. Identifying these factors is important to help news media and advertisers to implement native advertising in an effective and sustainable manner, without deceiving readers about the fact that they are viewing advertising. This study shows two new factors that can influence the extent to which readers' advertising recognition leads to feelings of manipulation and lower credibility perceptions: (1) advertiser credibility and (2) message sidedness. Regarding the credibility of the advertiser, results suggest that a native ad from a high-credibility advertiser can be perceived to be just as credible as a news article. For low-credibility advertisers, there was a (small) negative effect of advertising recognition on readers' evaluations. Thus, low-credibility organizations might suffer more from a more transparent implementation of native advertising. However, the results also suggest that making a native advertisement two-sided can decrease feelings of manipulation, which in turn positively influences readers' credibility perceptions. In this study, a two-sided message from a low-credibility advertiser was perceived to be just as credible as a one-sided native advertisement from a high-credibility advertiser. Thus, using a two-sided native advertising strategy may help less credible organizations to implement native advertising in a transparent manner, while still minimizing readers' critical processing of the advertising message. Based on previous work, we also expected that the low-credibility organization would benefit the most from a two-sided message strategy. This was not the case. The positive effect of using a two-sided message was equally strong for both organizations. One possible explanation for this result is that in an experimental setting, participants often process the information more elaborately than they usually do. When readers process an advertisement elaborately, the influence of source cues (i.e. the type of advertiser) can decrease (Eisend 2006; Petty and Cacioppo 1981). Another possible explanation is that although the high- and low-credibility advertisers significantly differed in credibility, both were commercial organizations with a (potential) financial interest in the subject (stevia), and readers may therefore still question whether the high-credibility organization provides information that is in their best interest (Goldsmith et al. 2000). The differences in the main effects of source were also rather small. The positive effect of a high-credibility source on credibility perceptions might be larger when a non-profit organization (NPO) uses the native advertising format to provide its content, as non-profit organizations are often not only perceived as authoritative, but consumers are also more likely to infer that nonprofits provide information with the intention to benefit society (Szykman et al. 2004). It would therefore be interesting to replicate the study using other types of organizations, such as non-profit organizations.

In conclusion, while the study shows that readers' advertising recognition can indeed lead to more critical processing and subsequently more negative evaluations, the study also suggests two factors that news media and advertisers can take into account to decrease critical processing and evaluations among readers: message sidedness and advertiser credibility. The study furthermore suggests that readers' feelings of manipulation play an important role when explaining the effect of readers' advertising recognition on their evaluations. It seems that readers' advertising recognition does not always automatically result into more feelings of manipulation and a decrease in readers' credibility perceptions. Instead, this (partly) depends on readers' perceptions of the credibility of the advertiser, and perceived message sidedness. The findings encourage more research on factors that can help to maintain the effectiveness of native advertisements, without deceiving readers about the fact that they are reading commercial commercial content.

References

Amazeen, M. A., & Muddiman, A. R. (2017). Saving media or trading on trust? The effects of native advertising on audience perceptions of legacy and online news publishers. *Digital Journalism, 6*(2), 1–20. https://doi.org/10.1177/1464884918754829.

An, S., Kerr, G., & Jin, H. S. (2018). Recognizing native ads as advertising: Attitudinal and behavioral consequences. *Journal of Consumer Affairs, 0*(ja). https://doi.org/10.1111/joca.12235

Becker-Olsen, K. L. (2003). And now, a word from our sponsor - A look at the effects of sponsored content and banner advertising. *Journal of Advertising, 32*(2), 17–32.

Brehm, J. W. (1966). *A theory of psychological reactance.* Oxford: Academic.

Campbell, C., & Marks, L. J. (2015). Good native advertising isn't a secret. *Business Horizons, 58*(6), 599–606.

Campbell, M. C. (1995). When attention-getting advertising tactics elicit consumer inferences of manipulative intent: The importance of balancing benefits and investments. *Journal of Consumer Psychology, 4*(3), 225–254.

Campbell, M. C., & Kirmani, A. (2000). Consumers' Use of persuasion knowledge: The effects of accessibility and cognitive capacity on perceptions of an influence agent. *Journal of Consumer Research, 27*(1), 69–83. https://doi.org/10.1086/314309.

Cornelis, E., Cauberghe, V., & De Pelsmacker, P. (2014). The inoculating effect of message sidedness on adolescents' binge drinking intentions: The moderating role of issue involvement. *Journal of Drug Issues, 44*(3), 254–268. https://doi.org/10.1177/0022042613500053.

Crowley, A. E., & Hoyer, W. D. (1994). An integrative framework for understanding two-sided persuasion. *Journal of Consumer Research, 20*(4), 561–574.

Darke, P. R., & Ritchie, R. J. (2007). The defensive consumer: Advertising deception, defensive processing, and distrust. *Journal of Marketing Research, 44*(1), 114–127.

Deuze, M. (2005). What is journalism?: Professional identity and ideology of journalists reconsidered. *Journalism, 6*(4), 442–464.

Einstein, M. (2016). *Black ops advertising*. New York: OR Books LLC.

Eisend, M. (2006). Two-sided advertising: A meta-analysis. *International Journal of Research in Marketing, 23*(2), 187–198.

Eisend, M. (2007). Understanding two-sided persuasion: An empirical assessment of theoretical approaches. *Psychology and Marketing, 24*(7), 615–640.

Flanagin, A. J., & Metzger, M. J. (2007). The role of site features, user attributes, and information verification behaviors on the perceived credibility of web-based information. *New Media & Society, 9*(2), 319–342. https://doi.org/10.1177/1461444807075015.

Fransen, M. L., Verlegh, P. W. J., Kirmani, A., & Smit, E. G. (2015). A typology of consumer strategies for resisting advertising, and a review of mechanisms for countering them. *International Journal of Advertising, 34*(1), 6–16.

Friestad, M., & Wright, P. (1994). The persuasion knowledge model: How people cope with persuasion attempts. *Journal of Consumer Research, 21*(1), 1–31.

Goldsmith, R. E., Lafferty, B. A., & Newell, S. J. (2000). The impact of corporate credibility and celebrity credibility on consumer reaction to advertisements and brands. *Journal of Advertising, 29*(3), 43–54.

Harms, B., Bijmolt, T. H. A., & Hoekstra, J. C. (2017). Digital native advertising: Practitioner perspectives and a research agenda. *Journal of Interactive Advertising, 17*, 1–12.

Hastak, M., & Jong-Won, P. (1990). Mediators of message sidedness effects on cognitive structure for involved and uninvolved audiences. *Advances in Consumer Research, 17*(1), 329–336.

Hayes, A. F., & Preacher, K. J. (2014). Statistical mediation analysis with a multicategorical independent variable. *British Journal of Mathematical and Statistical Psychology, 67*(3), 451–470.

Hovland, C. I., & Weiss, W. (1951). The influence of source credibility on communication effectiveness. *Public Opinion Quarterly, 15*(4), 635–650.

Igou, E. R., & Bless, H. (2003). Inferring the importance of arguments: Order effects and conversational rules. *Journal of Experimental Social Psychology, 39*(1), 91–99. https://doi.org/10.1016/S0022-1031(02)00509-7.

Jones, E. E., & Davis, K. E. (1965). From acts to dispositions the attribution process in person perception. *Advances in Experimental Social Psychology, 2*, 219–266. https://doi.org/10.1016/s0065-2601(08)60107-0

Kamins, M. A., & Assael, H. (1987). Two-sided versus one-sided appeals: A cognitive perspective on argumentation, source derogation, and the effect of disconfirming trial on belief change. *Journal of Marketing Research, 24*, 29–39.

Kiousis, S. (2001). Public trust or mistrust? Perceptions of media credibility in the information age. *Mass Communication and Society, 4*(4), 381–403. https://doi.org/10.1207/S15327825MCS0404_4.

Krouwer, S., Poels, K., & Paulussen, S. (2018). To disguise or to disclose? The influence of disclosure recognition and brand presence on readers' responses toward native advertisements in online news media. *Journal of Interactive Advertising, 17*(2), 124–137. https://doi.org/10.1080/15252019.2017.1381579.

Lafferty, B. A., & Goldsmith, R. E. (1999). Corporate credibility's role in consumers' attitudes and purchase intentions when a high versus a low credibility endorser is used in the ad. *Journal of Business Research, 44*(2), 109–116.

Lord, K. R., & Putrevu, S. (1993). Advertising and publicity: An information processing perspective. *Journal of Economic Psychology, 14*(1), 57–84.

Metzger, M. J., Flanagin, A. J., Eyal, K., Lemus, D. R., & McCann, R. M. (2003). Credibility for the 21st century: Integrating perspectives on source, message, and media credibility in the contemporary media environment. *Annals of the International Communication Association, 27*(1), 293–335.

Newman, N., Fletcher, R., Kalogeropoulos, A., & Nielsen, R. K. (2019). *Digital news report 2019*. Oxford: Reuters Institute for the Study of Journalism.

Petty, R. E., & Cacioppo, J. T. (1981). Issue involvement as a moderator of the effects on attitude of advertising content and context. *Advances in Consumer Research Volume 8*, 20–24.

Pornpitakpan, C. (2004). The persuasiveness of source credibility: A critical review of five decades' evidence. *Journal of Applied Social Psychology, 34*(2), 243–281.

Schauster, E. E., Ferrucci, P., & Neill, M. S. (2016). Native advertising is the new journalism: How deception affects social responsibility. *American Behavioral Scientist*. https://doi.org/10.1177/0002764216660135.

Settle, R. B., & Golden, L. L. (1974). Attribution theory and advertiser credibility. *Journal of Marketing Research, 11*(2), 181–185. https://doi.org/10.2307/3150556.

Sweetser, K. D., Ahn, S. J., Golan, G. J., & Hochman, A. (2016). Native advertising as a new public relations tactic. *American Behavioral Scientist*. https://doi.org/10.1177/0002764216660138.

Szykman, L. R., Bloom, P. N., & Blazing, J. (2004). Does corporate sponsorship of a socially-oriented message make a difference? An investigation of the effects of sponsorship identity on responses to an anti-drinking and driving message. *Journal of Consumer Psychology, 14*(1), 13–20. https://doi.org/10.1207/s15327663jcp1401and2_3.

Wojdynski, B. W. (2016). Native advertising: Engagement, deception, and implications for theory. In R. Borwn, V. Jones, & B. Ming Wang (Eds.), *The new advertising: Branding, content and consumer relationships in the data-driven social media era* (pp. 203–236). Santa Barbara: Praeger/ABC Clio.

Wojdynski, B. W., & Evans, N. J. (2015). Going native: Effects of disclosure position and language on the recognition and evaluation of online native advertising. *Journal of Advertising*, 157–168. https://doi.org/10.1080/00913367.2015.1115380.

A Thematic Exploration of Strong Emotional Appeals Based on Evolutionary Psychology

Serena D'Hooge and Patrick Vyncke

1 Introduction

Emotional appeals in advertising can attract attention and influence brand attitude, purchase intention and buying behavior (e.g. Alonso and Santos 2017; Faseur et al. 2015; Geuens et al. 2011; Panda et al. 2013; Taute et al. 2011; Williams 2012). There is, however, no research yet that presents a theoretically based and empirically tested overview of possible strong emotional appeals based on their content.

Previous studies on emotional appeals mostly used own pretested stimuli (e.g. Faseur et al. 2015; Geuens et al. 2011; Taute et al. 2011) or pictures from the International Affective Picture System (e.g. Alonso and Santos 2017; Morales et al. 2012). It is, however, unclear why these pictures evoke an emotional response. The current research aims to present an (not exhaustive) overview of strong emotional appeals based on their semantic content. This could be derived from evolutionary psychology that proposes general human goals, such as survival, care for kin or mating (e.g. Buss 2016; Kenrick et al. 2010). Sexual appeals, for instance, have been found to be strong emotional appeals in advertising (e.g. Reichert 2002). This can be linked to the evolutionarily determined mating goal. Other stimuli that are related to other evolutionary goals might work as strong emotional appeals just as well.

S. D'Hooge (✉) · P. Vyncke
University of Ghent, Ghent, Belgium

P. Vyncke
E-Mail: patrick.vyncke@ugent.be

After discussing the theoretical framework, we discuss the two performed studies. The first preliminary study is an exploration of the various evolutionary goals and the degree of importance that people attach to these goals. The second main study is an experimental study to test the affective reaction of people toward pictures that illustrate success in achieving or failure to achieve the various evolutionary goals. In addition, we discuss the differences according to life history variables: gender, life stages and parental status.

2 Theoretical Framework

2.1 Evolutionary Psychology

Evolutionary psychology is the amalgamation of evolutionary biology and psychology. It states that our human mind is in the same way evolved as a function of adaptive problems in the ancestral environment, as our bodily organs. Humans would have various 'mental organs' that are developed to each solve a particular adaptive problem. These adaptive problems are formed out of four basic selection mechanisms: natural, sexual, kin and social selection (Buss 2016; Saad 2013).

Natural selection is the mechanism in which nature selects those variants in inherited physical and mental characteristics and abilities that increase the carriers' chances of survival (Darwin 1859; Darwin and Wallace 1858). Survival not only contains basic physiological needs such as eating and drinking but also self-protection such as avoiding diseases, finding shelter, spotting and conquering predators (Buss 2016). While survival is a necessary precondition for reproduction, reproduction is the key to evolution. Consequently, sexual selection has been identified as a crucial mechanism next to natural selection. It is the process in which nature selects those physical and mental characteristics and abilities of an organism that increase its chances of reproductive success. Natural and sexual selection have been distinguished because some characteristics or abilities increase the organism's chances of reproduction but not of survival (e.g. a peacock's tale; Darwin 1871; Trivers 1972).

Fundamentally, organisms want to survive (natural selection) and reproduce themselves (sexual selection), but they also want to increase the chances of survival and reproduction of their offspring and other kin, because they have genes with them in common. Kin investment becomes investment in one's own success in terms of gene replication in the next generation (Hamilton 1964). Therefore, kin selection is introduced as the process in which nature selects the physical and mental characteristics and abilities that increase the chances of survival and reproduction of our kin. Finally, humans tend to also bond with others who are not kin—and therefore lack the typical kin-based genetic relatedness—because this may also result in benefits for themselves based on TIT-FOR-TAT interactions (Axelrod 1984). For instance, someone who is good at creating weapons could give a weapon to another unrelated human in return for some food. Therefore, a fourth selection mechanism—social selection—has been proposed. It is the process by which nature selects those physical and mental characteristics and abilities that increase people's chances to be socially successful (Roughgarden 2012). Out of these four evolutionarily determined selection mechanisms, universal human goals may be derived.

2.2 Human Goals

According to probably the best known inventory of human goals, that is the pyramid of needs developed by Maslow (1943), humans have five fundamental needs or motivations: immediate physiological needs (e.g. eating and drinking), safety needs (e.g. protection against physical danger), love/affection needs (e.g. finding a mate, belonging to a group), esteem needs (e.g. seeking status) and self-actualization needs (e.g. reaching one's full potential). However, this pyramid of needs has been debated by several researchers (for a discussion see Stoyanov 2017).

Kenrick and colleagues (2010) renovated the pyramid with a stronger theoretical base. They used evolutionary psychology as the basis of their model (see also Kenrick et al. 2017) and proposed seven, instead of five, fundamental motives with a distinctively evolutionary function: immediate physiological needs, self-protection, affiliation, status/esteem, mate acquisition, mate retention and parenting. Whereas Maslow (1943) included mate acquisition, mate retention and parenting into the affiliation need, Kenrick and colleagues (2010) argue that they have to be distinguished. Relationships between friends, family or lovers have functional (e.g. reproductive or not) and neurological differences (e.g. involving sexual arousal or sexual aversion) and are to be associated with different developmental periods (e.g. parenting can only occur when mating has been successful). Kenrick and colleagues removed self-actualization from their model because this cannot be seen as a distinct motive with a clear link to human evolutionary biology. Self-actualization can be integrated in both the status/esteem and the mating-related motives (e.g. striving to optimize a specific personal talent can be a means to (un)consciously achieve status/esteem or to attract a potential mate).

Neel and colleagues (2016) performed an empirical study and largely confirmed this motivational systems model. They distinguished self-protection and disease avoidance instead of immediate physiological needs and self-protection. Moreover, they discovered some subsets within affiliation (groups, exclusion concern and independence), mate retention (general and breakup concern) and kin care (family and children). To our knowledge, this is the only study that empirically tested these motives. Moreover, their survey focuses on people's current motivations and concerns, not on people's ultimate goals. For instance, if someone does not have children yet, bonding with his/her children might not be a current motive, but it still might be something he/she wants to achieve eventually. Although he/she does not have children yet, a picture of parent–child bonding might still work as a strong emotional appeal. Therefore, we first performed an exploratory study to investigate which ultimate human goals we can derive out of the four basic evolutionary selection mechanisms (natural, sexual, kin and social selection).

2.3 Evolutionary Goals and Emotional Appeals

Stimuli can be emotionally competent through their inherent nature (e.g. sweet food tastes good, a clear blue sky is stimulating, etc.), or become emotionally competent either just by previous exposure (cf. mere exposure theory (Zajonc 1968)) or because of the previous pairing with other affective stimuli (cf. evaluative conditioning theory (Martin and Levey 1978)). Most interesting for marketers are the stimuli that instinctively evoke an affective reaction by themselves because of the role they have played over the course of human evolution. These sorts of stimuli are interesting for marketers since they seem to 'naturally', spontaneously and – due to their evolutionary basis – probably universally evoke a positive/negative affective reaction, which may become the basis for emotionally charging the brand via processes of evaluative conditioning. Because evolutionary goals are deeply rooted into the human brain (Kenrick and Griskevicius 2013), we expect that emotionally competent stimuli provided by pictures that illustrate those goals, will instinctively evoke a strong affective reaction. Since we all (consciously or unconsciously) try to achieve these evolutionary goals, we expect pictures that illustrate success in achieving or failure to achieve these goals to evoke respectively a strong positive or strong negative affective reaction.

2.4 Differences According to Life History Variables

Likewise to the study of Neel and colleagues (2016) we wanted to investigate the differences according to various life history variables. Life history theory suggests that people's allocation of energy and resources differs according to various demographic variables, such as age and gender. As people have limited energy and resources to spend, they are facing several trade-offs, such as whether to spend their energy and resources on current or future reproduction. People can decide to focus on their own growth now in order to increase future reproductive success, or they could start reproducing themselves right now (Del Giudice et al. 2015). Although reproducing ourselves might be a key ultimate goal that we all (un)consciously try to achieve, the goal might become more prominent depending on our stage of life. Another example is that men are found to allocate more resources to mating, while women to parenting (mating-parenting trade-off), which might be reflected in a different degree of affective reactions toward pictures that illustrate mating or parenting (Beall and Schaller 2017).

Next to the basic demographic variables age and gender, we wanted to investigate the differences according to parental status, as reproduction is the key to evolution. Pictures of parenting might evoke a strong affective reaction in general, but this reaction might be stronger for people that have children compared to people that do not have children yet.

3 Preliminary Study

3.1 Method

We gathered 609 Flemish participants (52% women). Ages ranged from 19 to 87 ($M = 47$, $SE = 0.73$): 28% was aged 18 to 34, 24% 35 to 49, 28% 50 to 64 and 20% was 65 or older. 68% had children. An exploratory survey was performed in order to reveal different evolutionary goal dimensions. We gave the respondents a list of aspects belonging to the four evolutionary selection mechanisms and asked them in what degree these aspects will have had an influence to reach maximum happiness at the end of their lives. The aspects had to be rated from 'not at all influential' to 'very influential' on a 7 point Likert scale. The list of aspects was developed together with several academic researchers with and without knowledge of evolutionary theory (Table 1).

Table 1 The four selection mechanisms and the corresponding items

Natural selection	1. To have been able to provide for basic needs in terms of nutrition, housing, clothing and health 2. To have achieved a certain level of prosperity in order to have a comfortable life 3. Being saved from doom (accidents, disasters …) 4. To have had the feeling of having lived in a non-hostile environment (war, terror …) 5. To have had no enemies: not having been confronted with people who were hostile to you (stalkers, neighbor quarrels, bullying at work …) 6. To have had good health and have been spared from illnesses
Sexual selection	1. To have had a good sexual relationship with a partner that you found sexually attractive 2. To have been able to meet your sexual needs 3. To have had a romantic relationship with a partner who created a feeling of being loved 4. To have had a good and mature long-term relationship with a partner that shared love and suffering with you
Kin selection	1. To have had a good, close and warm relationship as a parent with your child(ren) 2. To have had a good, close and warm relationship as a grandparent with your grandchild(ren) 3. To have had a good, close and warm relationship as a child with your parent(s) 4. To have had a good, close and warm relationship with your brother(s) and/or sister(s) 5. To have had a good, close and warm relationship as a grandchild with your grandparents. 6. To have had a good, close and warm relationship with the rest of your family: uncles, aunts, cousins…
Social selection	1. To have had a good, close and warm friendship with one or a few dear friends 2. To have enjoyed a certain prestige and/or a high position in society or the groups you were a part of (colleagues, friends, acquaintances …) 3. To have had a wider circle of friends and acquaintances who gave you a sense of belonging

3.2 Results

Goal Dimensions

An alpha factor analysis with Promax rotation revealed five factors with eigenvalues greater than unity of which the total variance explained was high (65.48%). The first factor—**'survival'** ($\alpha = 0.83$)—consisted of the six items concerning the natural selection mechanism. The second factor consisted of the four items concerning sexual selection. However, like many other researchers (e.g. Kenrick et al. 2010; Li 2007), we propose to distinguish **'short term mating'** ($\alpha = 0.94$) from **'long term mating'** ($\alpha = 0.81$). Short term mating is the fundamental goal of humans to find someone to have sex with. Long term mating concerns the bonding of two partners because this benefits survival chances of their offspring. Sexual appeals, that are linked to short term mating, in advertising have been investigated a lot (Reichert 2002), while long term mating as an emotional appeal has not received much attention. The third factor—**'kin investment'** ($\alpha = 0.77$)—includes all items from the kin selection mechanism that represent bonding with people with whom we are genetically related: parents, grandparents, brother(s) and/or sister(s), and other family members. Bonding with children and grandchildren are distinguished from this. The reason for this could be that these items both relate to our own (direct gene) reproduction. Therefore, we will call this **'parental investment'**($\alpha = 0.79$). This is in line with the subfactors that were found in the study of Neel and colleagues (2016) for kin care: family and children. Finally, the three items concerning the social selection mechanism are found to strongly correlate. We will call this **'social investment'**($\alpha = 0.72$).

Goal Importance

All six goals were considered very important. A repeated measures ANOVA showed small significant differences between the perceived importance of the six goals ($F(4.03, 2447.01) = 156.33$, $p<0.001$, $\mu_p^2 = 0.21$). Parental investment was rated as the most important goal and short term mating as the least important goal (Table 2).

Differences in Goal Importance between Gender

The hierarchy differs between gender ($F(4.08, 2478.30) = 13.21$, $p<0.001$, $\mu_p^2 = 0.02$). A pairwise comparison test with Bonferroni adjustment revealed that men attach significant more importance to short term mating ($p<0.001$) and significant less importance to survival ($p = 0.001$), parental ($p = 0.009$), kin ($p = 0.016$) and

Table 2 The mean importance of each goal compared with the neutral value 3

EVOLUTIONARY GOAL	M (SE)	ONE SAMPLE T-TEST (Test Value = 3)
Survival	5.21 (0.03)	$t(608) = 78.17, p<0.001, d = 3.17$
Short term mating	4.39 (0.05)	$t(608) = 29.88, p<0.001, d = 1.21$
Long term mating	5.13 (0.04)	$t(608) = 54.11, p<0.001, d = 2.19$
Parental investment	5.28 (0.04)	$t(608) = 54.52, p<0.001, d = 2.21$
Kin investment	4.41 (0.04)	$t(608) = 33.17, p<0.001, d = 1.34$
Social investment	4.63 (0.04)	$t(608) = 45.14, p<0.001, d = 1.83$

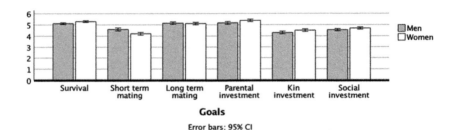

Fig. 1 Differences in mean importance of each goal compared between gender

social investment (p = 0.036) than women. No significant difference was found for long term mating (p = 0.660) (Fig. 1).

Differences in Goal Importance across Life Stages

Concerning life stages, we found significant differences for all goals (F(12.25, 2469.55) = 11.14, p<0.001, μ_p^2 = 0.05; short term mating: F(3,605) = 13.08, p<0.001, μ_p^2 = 0.06; long term mating: F(3,605) = 9.70, p<0.001, μ_p^2 = 0.05; parental investment: F(3,605) = 2.98, p = 0.031, μ_p^2 = 0.02; kin investment: F(3,605) = 10.60, p<0.001, μ_p^2 = 0.05 and social investment: F(3,605) = 12.39, p<0.001, μ_p^2 = 0.06), except for survival (F(3,605) = 2.25, p = 0.081, μ_p^2 = 0.01). The people in the oldest life stage attach significantly less importance to short (p ≤ 0.001) and long term mating (p ≤ 0.021) than the people in the younger life stages. The youngest life stage respondents attach significant less importance to parental investment than the oldest life stage respondents (p = 0.030) and more to kin (p ≤ 0.001) and social investment (p ≤ 0.005) than the older life stages (Fig. 2).

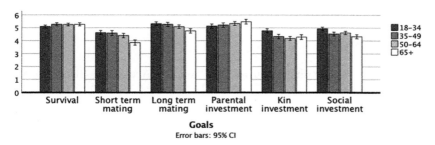

Fig. 2 Differences in mean importance of each goal compared across life stages

Differences in Goal Importance according to Parental Status

Finally, we did also find differences between respondents with and without children (F(4.05, 2460.44) = 23.86, p<0.001, μ_p^2 = 0.04). A pairwise comparison test with Bonferroni adjustment revealed that people with children find survival (p = 0.001) and parental investment (p<0.001) more important, and the other goals less important (short term mating: p = 0.007, long term mating: p = 0.025, kin investment: p<0.001, and social investment: p<0.001) than people without children (Fig. 3).

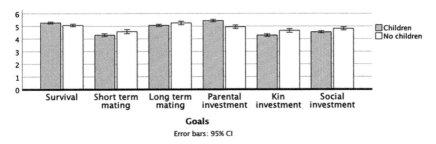

Fig. 3 Differences in mean importance of each goal according to parental status

4 Main Study

4.1 Method

We gathered 484 Flemish respondents (62% women). Ages (M = 40, SE = 0.82) ranged from 18 to 92 (43% aged 18 to 34; 24% aged 35 to 49; 22% aged 50 to 64 and 11% 65 or older) and 55% had children. An experimental study with a 6 (goals: survival, short term mating, long term mating, parental investment, kin investment and social investment) × 2 (success in achieving versus failure to achieve the goal) within subjects design was performed. Each respondent evaluated 72 pictures that belonged to the experimental design. The set included six subsets with one picture per condition. After the data collection, we calculated the mean affective reaction toward the six pictures for each condition.

The fit of the pictures with the various goals was pretested with 11 students with knowledge of evolutionary psychology. Each student received the same two large sets of pictures: one for success in achieving and one for failure to achieve the various goals. Per set, they had to assign each picture to one of the six goals. Only the pictures that every student assigned to the intended goal were selected.

The respondents of the main study had to evaluate every picture with a rating slider from 0 (gives me a very negative feeling) to 100 (gives me a very positive feeling). By providing it as a slider, respondents could move the slider quickly to the position that best fitted their primary feeling. This made it possible to evaluate a large number of pictures in a relatively short period. It also resulted in reactions that are based on gut feelings and it provided continuous data with a wide range. The slider format is found to be a valid and reliable method to measure affective reactions (Betella and Verschure 2016).

4.2 Results

General Results

Various one-sample t-tests confirmed that the pictures illustrating success in achieving or failure to achieve the goals significantly and largely scored respectively higher or lower than neutral (Table 3).

A repeated measures ANOVA with the six goals and success versus failure as within subjects factors, revealed a significant interaction effect (F(3.90, 1884.05) = 205.33, $p<0.001$, $\mu_p^2 = 0.30$). The difference between success and failure was significant for every goal (all $p<0.001$). A pairwise comparison with Bonferroni

Table 3 The mean affective reaction of every condition compared with the neutral value 50

EVOLUTIONARY GOAL	SUCCESS		FAILURE	
	Mean (SE)	One sample t-test (Test Value = 50)	Mean (SE)	One sample t-test (Test Value = 50)
Survival	76.01 (0.57)	t(483) = 45.72, p<0.001, d = 2.08	14.51 (0.48)	t(483) = −74.18, p<0.001, d = −3.37
Short term mating	76.49 (0.73)	t(483) = 36.09, p<0.001, d = 1.64	15.90 (0.47)	t(483) = −72.99, p<0.001, d = −3.32
Long term mating	83.91 (0.59)	t(483) = 57.19, p<0.001, d = 2.60	22.75 (0.54)	t(483) = −50.42, p<0.001, d = −2.29
Parental investment	84.14 (0.51)	t(483) = 67.14, p<0.001, d = 3.05	33.12 (0.56)	t(483) = −30.03, p<0.001, d = −1.36
Kin investment	84.80 (0.55)	t(483) = 62.95, p<0.001, d = 2.86	36.97 (0.72)	t(483) = −18.09, p<0.001, d = −0.82
Social investment	84.65 (0.47)	t(483) = 73.55, p<0.001, d = 3.34	16.92 (0.54)	t(483) = −61.41, p<0.001, d = −2.79

adjustment showed that the pictures of success in achieving survival and short term mating significantly scored lower than those of long term mating, parental, kin and social investment (p<0.001). For the pictures of failure to achieve the goals, we found significant differences between all goals (p ≤ 0.028), except between short term mating and social investment (p = 0.324). Survival evoked the most negative affective reaction, followed by short term mating and social investment, long term mating, parental investment and the least negative affective reaction toward failure to achieve kin investment.

Differences between Gender

A mixed ANOVA with the six goals and success versus failure as within subjects factors and gender as between subjects factor, resulted in no significant three-way interaction (F(3.91, 1884.66) = 1.98, p = 0.096, μ_p^2 = 0.004). Across all goals, women evaluated the images of success in achieving on average more positively (M = 82.60, SE = 0.69) than men (M = 80.17, SE = 0.98; p = 0.009), while they evaluated images of failure to achieve the goals more negatively (M = 21.44,

SE = 0.66) than men (M = 26.47, SE = 0.93; p<0.001) (F(1, 482) = 23.78, p<0.001, μ_p^2 = 0.05).

Differences across Life Stages

The same mixed ANOVA but with life stages as between subjects factor, did reveal a significant three-way interaction (F(11.81, 1882.28) = 3.97, p<0.001, μ_p^2 = 0.02). For the pictures of success in achieving the goals, we found a significant difference between the life stages for short term mating (F(3,478) = 4.78, p = 0.003, μ_p^2 = 0.03), parental (F(3,478) = 9.68, p<0.001, μ_p^2 = 0.06), kin (F(3,478) = 14.27, p<0.001, μ_p^2 = 0.08) and social investment (F(3,478) = 2.88, p = 0.035, μ_p^2 = 0.02). The people in the youngest life stage had a less positive affective reaction toward pictures of success in achieving parental (p ≤ 0.063) and kin investment (p ≤ 0.005) than the people in the older life stages, while the oldest life stage had a lower affective reaction toward pictures of success in achieving short term mating (p = 0.002) and social investment (p = 0.044) than the youngest life stage (Fig. 4).

For the pictures that illustrate failure to achieve the goals, we only found a significant difference for survival (F(3,478) = 3.31, p = 0.002, μ_p^2 = 0.02) and parental investment (F(3,478) = 8.25, p<0.001, μ_p^2 = 0.05), with a less negative affective reaction from the oldest life stages compared to the younger life stages for parental investment (p ≤ 0.035), and compared to the 50–64 year old respondents for survival (p = 0.015) (Fig. 5).

Differences according to Parental Status

A mixed ANOVA with the six goals and success versus failure as within subjects factors and parental status as between subjects factor, resulted in a significant

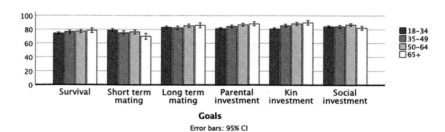

Fig. 4 Differences in mean affective reaction toward the pictures illustrating success in achieving the goals compared across life stages

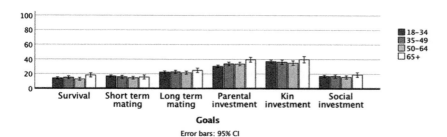

Fig. 5 Differences in mean affective reaction toward the pictures illustrating failure to achieve the goals compared across life stages

three-way interaction (F(3.93, 1.894.65) = 7.83, p<0.001, μ_p^2 = 0.02). For the pictures illustrating success in achieving the goals, a pairwise comparison with Bonferroni adjustment revealed a significant difference for survival (p = 0.016), parental investment (p<0.001) and kin investment (p<0.001). People with children reacted more positively to those pictures than people without children (Fig. 6).

For the pictures illustrating failure to achieve the goals, we only found a significant difference for parental investment (F(1, 482) = 11.19, p = 0.001, μ_p^2 = 0.02). Parents responded less negatively (M = 34.80, SE = 0.80) to those pictures than people without children (M = 31.06, SE = 0.76).

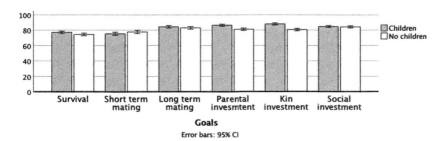

Fig. 6 Differences in mean affective reaction according to parental status toward the pictures illustrating success in achieving the goals

5   Conclusion and Discussion

Our preliminary study revealed six evolutionary goals (survival, short and long term mating, parental, kin and social investment) that are all found to be very important and that are broadly in line with the dimensions of previously proposed goal models. These findings could be useful for the development of an updated universal goal model. Our aim was not to update the model, but to investigate if these goals could work as dimensions for charting strong emotional appeals.

Our main study confirmed that pictures of success in achieving or failure to achieve the proposed goals evoke respectively strong positive or negative affective reactions. Not only sexual appeals, but also pictures of survival, couples, parents and their children, brother(s) and or sister(s) and groups of people would be strong emotional appeals in advertising. As we only measured affective reactions on the dimensional scale of pleasure, future research could measure arousal and dominance (Bradley and Lang 1994) or concrete emotions (love, hate, fear…).

In addition, men found short term mating more important than women did, but their affective reaction toward sexual images was not stronger. Women had stronger affective reactions across all pictures. This could just be a response bias as women are found to be more emotionally expressive than men (Parkins 2012).

Next, we only found small differences across life stages and parental status, meaning that the goals work as strong emotional appeals across all life stages and for people with and without offspring. Parents reacted slightly more positive to pictures of success in achieving survival. They also found this goal to be more important than people without children, but they did not react differently to pictures of failure to survive. People aged 65 or older reacted less negative to these pictures, while they found survival equally important as younger people. The reason could be that they already survived for a long time. Images of success in achieving short term mating evoked a less positive reaction for the oldest life stage respondents, who also found this goal less important than the people in the younger life stages. However, no difference was found for the pictures illustrating failure to achieve short term mating. Moreover, they did also find long term mating to be less important, while we found no differences in negative nor positive affective pictorial reactions. Likewise, people with children found short and long term mating less important, but their affective pictorial reactions did not differ. Images of success in achieving parental investment evoked less positive affective reactions for the youngest life stage than for older people. They also found the goal less important. Parents found this goal more important and rated pictures of success in achieving the goal more positively, but pictures of failure to achieve the goal less negatively than people without children. They might find the struggle in raising kids as normal and even necessary to improve their fitness. The affective reaction toward images of success in achieving kin investment were less positive for the youngest life stage respondents and more positive for parents, while they found this goal respectively more and less important. This could be due to the pictures showing very young brother(s) and/or sister(s), which could have activated the parental investment goal. No differences in the negative affective reaction toward pictures of failure to achieve kin investment were found.

As the differences in perceived importance and affective reactions are not entirely in line, this relation needs further research. The study should be replicated in other countries and the impact of other life history variables (e.g. slow vs fast strategies) should be investigated. Finally, we should note that the current paper does not present an exhaustive list of possible emotional appeals. It provides a framework for strong emotional appeals that would commonly evoke a strong innate affective reaction, based on evolutionary psychology. Humorous stimuli, for instance, can also be strong emotional appeals, but the direction and strength of the affective reaction depends on personal taste (Warren et al. 2019).

References

Alonso, M., & Santos, D. (2017). The influence of image valence on the attention paid to charity advertising. *Journal of Nonprofit & Public Sector Marketing, 29*(3), 346–363.

Axelrod, R. (1984). *The evolution of cooperation*. New York: Basic Books.

Beall, A. T., & Schaller, M. (2017). Evolution, motivation, and the mating/parenting trade – off. In: *Self and Identity*.

Betella, A., & Verschure, P. F. M. J. (2016). The affective slider: A digital self-assessment scale for the measurement of human emotions. *PLoS ONE, 11*(2), 1–11.

Bradley, M. M., & Lang, P. J. (1994). Measuring emotion: The self-assessment manikin and the semantic differential. *Journal of Behavior Therapy and Experimental Psychiatry, 25*(1), 49–59.

Buss, D. (2016). *Evolutionary psychology: The new science of the mind* (5th ed.). New York: Routledge.

Darwin, C. (1859). *On the origin of species by means of natural selection, or the preservation of favoured races in the struggle for life*. London: John Murray.

Darwin, C. (1871). *The descent of man and selection in relation to sex*. London: John Murray.

Darwin, C., & Wallace, A. (1858). On the tendency of species to form varieties; and on the perpetuation of varieties and species by natural means of selection. *Journal of the Proceedings of the Linnean Society of London (Zoology), 3*(9), 45–62.

Del Giudice, M., Gangestad, S. W., & Kaplan, H. S. (2015). Life History Theory and Evolutionary Psychology. In D. M. Buss (Ed.), *The Handbook of Evolutionary Psychology* (2nd ed., pp. 88–114). Hoboken, NJ: Wiley.

Faseur, T., Cauberghe, V., & Hudders, L. (2015). Social threat appeals in commercial advertising: The moderating impact of perceived level of self-efficacy and self-esteem on advertising effectiveness. *Communications, 40*(2), 171–183.

Geuens, M., Pelsmacker, P. D., & Faseur, T. (2011). Emotional advertising: Revisiting the role of product category. *Journal of Business Research, 64*(4), 418–426.

Hamilton, W. D. (1964). The genetical evolution of social behaviour II. *Journal of Theoretical Biology, 7*(1), 17–52.

Kenrick, D. T., & Griskevicius, V. (2013). *The rational animal: How evolution made us smarter than we think*. New York: Basic Books.

Kenrick, D. T., Griskevicius, V., Neuberg, S. L., & Schaller, M. (2010). Renovating the pyramid of needs: Contemporary extensions built upon ancient foundations. *Perspectives on Psychological Science, 5*(3), 292–314.

Li, N. P. (2007). Mate preference necessities in long- and short- term mating: People prioritize in themselves what their mates prioritize in them. *Acta Psychologica Sinica, 39*(3), 528–535.

Martin, I., & Levey, A. B. (1978). Evaluative conditioning. *Advances in Behaviour Research and Therapy, 1*(2), 57–102.

Maslow, A. H. (1943). A theory of human motivation. *Psychological Review, 50*(4), 370–396.

Morales, A. C., Wu, E. C., & Fitzsimons, G. J. (2012). How disgust enhances the effectiveness of fear appeals. *Journal of Marketing Research, 49*(3), 383–393.

Neel, R., Kenrick, D. T., White, A. E., & Neuberg, S. L. (2016). Individual differences in fundamental social motives. *Journal of Personality and Social Psychology, 110*(6), 887–907.

Panda, T. (2013). Does emotional appeal work in advertising ? The rationality behind using emotional appeal to create favorable brand attitude. *the IUP Journal of Brand Management, 10*(2), 7–23.

Panda, T., Panda, T.K., & Mishra, K.(2013). Does emotional appeal work in advertising? The rationality behind using emotional appeal tocreate favorable brand attitude. *The IUP Journal of Brand Management, 10*(2), 7–23.

Reichert, T. (2002). Sex in advertising research: A review of content, effects, and functions of sexual information in consumer advertising. *Annual Review of Sex Research, 13*(1), 241–273.

Roughgarden, J. (2012). The social selection alternative to sexual selection. *Philosophical Transactions of the Royal Society B, 367*, 2294–2303.

Saad, G. (2013). Evolutionary consumption. *Journal of Consumer Psychology, 23*(3), 351–371.

Schaller, M., Kenrick, D. T., Neel, R., & Neuberg, S. L. (2017). Evolution and human motivation: A fundamental motives framework. *Social and Personality Psychology Compass, 11*(6), 1–15.

Stoyanov, S. (2017). *A theory of human motivation*. London: Macat Library.

Taute, H. A., McQuitty, S., & Sautter, E. P. (2011). Emotional Information Management and Responses to Emotional Appeals. *Journal of Advertising, 40*(3), 31–44.

Trivers, R. L. (1972). Parental investment and sexual selection. In B. Campbell (Ed.), *Sexual selection and the descent of man, 1871–1971* (pp. 136–179). Chicago: Aldine.

Warren, C., Carter, E. P., Mcgraw, A. P., Warren, C., Carter, E. P., & Mcgraw, A. P. (2019). Being funny is not enough: The influence of perceived humor and negative emotional reactions on brand attitudes. *International Journal of Advertising, 38*(7), 1025–1045.

Williams, K. C. (2012). Fear appeal theory. *Research in Business and Economics Journal, 5*(1), 1–21.

Zajonc, R. B. (1968). Attitudinal effects of mere exposure. *Journal of Personality and Social Psychology, 9*(22), 1–27.

Half a Century of Super Bowl Commercials: A Content Analysis of Humorous Advertising Styles

Artemis Timamopoulou, Leonidas Hatzithomas, Christina Boutsouki, and Maria C. Voutsa

1   Introduction

Humor is an integral part of our everyday reality. It is a source of strength to compete with and face personal and social challenges as well as political disruptions (Berger 2008). Humor is imbedded in every culture (Berger 1987) and an individual's sense of humor reveals not only aspects of their personality but also their mode of social interaction (Lynch 2002).

As such, humor has been extensively researched and discussed in terms of its types, effectiveness, and outcomes (Weinberger and Gulas 1992, 2013; Eisend 2009). The present study discusses the evolution of humorous commercials and humor styles (types of humor) between 1969 and 2015 under the prism of the social change that shaped American society. Based on the logic and structure of Weinberger et al. (2015) study of humorous outdoor advertisements, a content analysis of actual Super Bowl advertisements and a review of both the social and micro-industry factors in the USA over a 45-year period provide the empirical

---

A. Timamopoulou (✉) · L. Hatzithomas
Department of Business Administration, University of Macedonia, Thessaloniki, Greece
E-Mail: art.timamopoulou@gmail.com

L. Hatzithomas
E-Mail: hatzithomas@uom.edu.gr

C. Boutsouki · M. C. Voutsa
Department of Economics, Aristotle University of Thessaloniki, Thessaloniki, Greece
E-Mail: chbouts@econ.auth.gr

M. C. Voutsa
E-Mail: mcvoutsa@econ.auh.gr

© The Author(s), under exclusive license to Springer Fachmedien Wiesbaden GmbH, part of Springer Nature 2021
M. Waiguny and S. Rosengren (eds.), *Advances in Advertising Research (Vol. XI)*, European Advertising Academy,
https://doi.org/10.1007/978-3-658-32201-4_10

underpinnings of the study. This is the first longitudinal, content analysis of TV commercials extending over half a century.

2 Background

Humor is one of the most effective communication tools that not only evokes pleasant feelings but is also associated with increased persuasion (Meyer 2000). Ever since the early'70 s humor was established as a popular advertising appeal accounting between 15% (Kelly and Solomon 1975) and 42% of all existing ads (Markiewicz 1974).

The first literature review on humor focused on its effectiveness on specific communication factors that it was found to influence (Sternthal and Craig 1973). Madden and Weinberger (1984) were the first to apply the findings of prior humorous research in the field of advertising to identify the level of agreement and congruence between advertising practitioners and the existing literature, thus setting the precedent for many humorous advertising studies to follow. Updating Sternthal and Craig's (1973) original literature review, Weinberger and Gulas (1992) examined some executional and/or situational factors that significantly influence the outcome of humorous messages. In the many studies to follow emphasis was given on the moderators of humorous ad appreciation (e.g. Swani et al. 2013) and the magnitude of the humorous advertising outcomes (Eisend 2009).

Advertising messages reflect the values, aesthetics and images of an existing culture (Pollay 1985), while at the same time they shape the prevailing culture through the images they portray (Pollay 1986). There seems to be a reciprocal relationship between advertising and culture expressed through the "mirror" vs. "mold" argument (Eisend 2009). The widespread belief that advertising is linked to societal changes (Phillips and McQuarrie 2002) has led historians to start reviewing and analyzing advertisements to comment on societal evolution (Pollay 1985).

Popular advertising appeals are further influenced by the prevailing advertising tactics and trends. A content analysis of over 2000 print ads illustrated in popular magazines between 1900 and 1980 (Pollay 1985) indicated an interaction between changing times and advertising strategies. This was further reinforced by Beard (2005) in a longitudinal analysis of humorous advertising based on past century marketing and advertising academic journals. Culture affects the use (Martin 2007) and appreciation (Speck 1991) of humor. Advertising humor in particular, is vastly influenced by societal changes both at a micro (advertising) and a macro (society) level (Weinberger et al. 2015). In the first ever content analysis of outdoor humorous advertisements extending over a period of 100 years, Weinberger et al. (2015) incorporated a historical and cultural analysis of the American society during the same period to investigate the acceptance of humor and the evolution of humor styles. They claim that the evolving social and cultural milieu, along with the cultural knowledge of audiences and the context in which executives create advertisements, are closely related to the level, styles, and elements of the humor employed. It is thus the objective of the present study to spread the theoretical and methodological foundations of Weinberger et al. (2015) study in TV commercials.

3   Super Bowl

Super Bowl is one of the most important American television shows (Schimmel 2011), in terms of anticipation and deliberation. Its fame and magnitude have surpassed the geographical boundaries of the American territory. By 1999, Super Bowl was broadcasted in 188 countries (Tomkovick et al. 2001). Due to the significance of Super Bowl, particular attention is given by the NFC to social responsibility issues (Babiak and Wolfe 2006). The commercial campaigns aired in Super Bowl have an impact both time and media wise (Kim et al. 2005). The commercial breaks during the game are a "must watch" (Kelley and Turley 2004) and often end up overshadowing the actual game (McAllister 1999). In 2003, 14% of the Super Bowl viewers claimed to have watched the game only for the commercials (Horovitz 2006), while in 2010, more than half the viewers (51%) stated to have enjoyed the commercials more than the actual game. With all this continuously rising attention, it becomes a priority for advertisers to invest in Super Bowl commercials (Siefert et al. 2009).

4   Sampling Frame and Method

Replicating the modus operandi of Weinberger et al. (2015) the present study employs secondary sources (see Batchelor and Scott 2007) to address the historical analysis of the American society over the 45-year period under study. Super Bowl's humorous advertisements were retrieved from Adland (Adland 2015) and grouped and content-analyzed in five distinct time periods; 1969–1979, 1980–1989, 1990–1999, 2000–2009 and 2010–2015. Out of the 2453 ads retrieved from Adland, 1675 ads that were broadcasted on a national level were content analyzed.

Table 1 Humor types and message element coding guidelines (adopted by Weinberger et al. 2015)

Humor type	Explanation	Message element	Explanation
Word play, puns, playful language	This form of humor uses wit and skillful use of language. It often includes double entendre. It is possible that the double word meaning is sexual and, if it is, the ad would be coded as a word play as well as sexual. Audience response to puns and word play is more often a groan than laughter Sometimes the double meaning of a word may be a spelling that implies a possible different meaning	*Vulgar*	Crude indecent, or obscene, particularly with regard to sex or bodily functions, showing a lack of taste or reasonable moderation
Warmth or sentiment	Gentle humor based in love, friendship and positive emotion. This type of humor often revolves around children, families, and/or pets. It may be the result of kids doing saying or doing something very adult which is unusual for kids to be doing	*Cartoon/comic*	A drawing, sketch, or computer animation with humorous intent

(continued)

Sixteen coders were trained on the task. They were all provided an explanatory table, along with sources and educational material on the different humor styles (Table 1). Written instructions for the classification of the ads into the humor-style categories were also provided. Each coder was coached on a sample of 200 non-Super Bowl commercials to ensure the reliability of the coding process.

Table 1 (continued)

Humor type	Explanation	Message element	Explanation
Sex, sexual innuendo, sexual allusion	This form of humor includes humor that is overtly sexual in nature, using nudity and/or direct sexual references. It also includes less overt suggestive sexual references. It often makes use of double entendre where one interpretation of the words or images in an ad is innocent and the other is sexual	*Children or animals*	A humorous ad where children or animals are a central focus of the ad. These ads generally capitalize on the 'cute' nature of kids and animals. E-Trade ads feature a talking baby

(continued)

In the main analysis, each of the coders analyzed approximately 210 commercials. All coders worked independently to determine the level of humorousness and classify the commercial in the predetermined (Weinberger et al. 2015) humor-style categories (Table 1). The coders watched every commercial twice. Inter-coder reliability coefficients ranged between 80 and 89%. Discrepancies amongst the coders were discussed and resolved.

Table 1 (continued)

Humor type	Explanation	Message element	Explanation
Nonsense	Silliness. This type of humor includes ridiculous pictures. Many of the children's books written by Dr. Seuss make use of nonsense humor as does Alice in Wonderland. Unusual, peculiar, absurd, silly, clownish, or odd situations, clumsiness, ignorance, grotesque, eccentric behavior, or characters, or exaggeration	*Stereotyping or racist*	Is this ad racist or stereotyped toward a group? Bald jokes, fat jokes, blond jokes, etc. are all forms of aggressive humor
Verbal or physical aggression	Physical, social psychological putdown of one's self, another person, or some other group of people or public figure, institutions using satire, sarcasm, ridicule, parody, or taking malicious pleasure in a person's situation or appearance. Slapstick humor in the style of the Three Stooges and pratfalls fit into the classification of aggressive humor. If the target is the joke teller, thenthis style of humor is self-deprecating		

5 Results

Tables 2 and 3 depict the percentage attributed to each category, while Fig. 1

Table 2 Humor and humor styles

Time-Period	Overall Humor N (%)	Word play N (%)	Warm N (%)	Nonsense N (%)	Sexual N (%)	Aggression N (%)
(I) 1969–1979	67 (37.6)	30 (44.8)	6 (9)	41 (61.2)	1 (1.5)	8 (11.9)
(II) 1980–1989	111 (48.9)	63 (56.8)	11 (9.9)	72 (64.9)	0 (0)	12 (10.8)
(III) 1990–1999	214 (53.1)	104 (48.6)	22 (10.3)	161 (75.2)	7 (3.3)	28 (13.1)
(IV) 2000–2009	280 (56.6)	93 (33.2)	18 (6.5)	232 (82.9)	18 (6.4)	54 (19.3)
(V) 2010–2015	210 (61)	62 (29.5)	18 (8.6)	170 (81)	15 (7.1)	38 (18.1)
Sheffe's Test	I < III, IV, V; II < V	II, III > IV, V		I, II < IV, V	II < V	

Table 3 Number and percentage of humor and humor elements

Time Period	Vulgarity N (%)	Stereotyping N (%)	Comic/Cartoon Characters N (%)	Children N (%)	Animals N (%)
(I) 1969–1979	0 (0)	4 (6)	5 (7.5)	5 (7.5)	3 (4.5)
(II) 1980–1989	6 (5.4)	2 (1.8)	7 (6.3)	9 (8.1)	9 (8.1)
(III) 1990–1999	8 (3.7)	1 (0.5)	39 (18.2)	30 (14)	34 (15.9)
(IV) 2000–2009	25 (8.9)	8 (2.9)	20 (7.1)	16 (5.7)	62 (22.1)
(V) 2010–2015	9 (4.3)	9 (4.3)	18 (8.6)	37 (17.6)	49 (23.3)
Sheffe's Test	I < IV		II < III; III > IV, V	IV < III, V	I, II < IV, V

illustrates the evolution of category use over time. Chi-square analysis revealed a statistically significant effect of the time period (decade) on all variables under

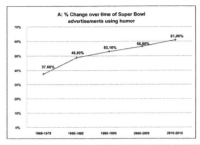
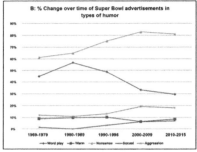
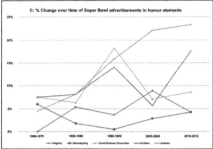

Fig. 1 Time-series graph of percentages

study; use of humor (χ^2 (4) = 29.702, p <0.001), word play (χ^2 (4) = 35.214, p <0.001), nonsense (χ^2 (4) = 25.991, p <0.001), sexual (χ^2 (4) = 12.782, p = 0.012), vulgarity (χ^2 (4) = 12.223, p = 0.016), comic/cartoon characters (χ^2(4) = 21.083, p <0.001), children (χ^2 (4) = 21.189, p <0.001), animals (χ^2 (4) = 23.791, p <0.001). In addition, the analysis of variance revealed a statistically insignificant effect of the time period on the use of warm/sentimental humor (χ^2 (4) = 2.676, p = 0.613) and aggression (χ^2 (4) = 7.371, p = 0.118), and a marginally statistically significant effect on the use of stereotypes (χ^2 (4) = 9.095, p = 0.059). Sheffe's test further revealed statistically significant variations in all categories over time.

6 Discussion

Based on Weinberger et al.'s (2015) study, the present paper addresses the issues associated with the evolution of humor and humor styles in advertising within the American societal context. The results indicate an increasing trend in the use of humor in Super Bowl advertising over the 45-year period examined, ranging from 38% during the'70 s to 61% by 2015 (see Table 2). The findings complement Weinberger et al. (2015) study that indicates an upward trend in the use of humor in billboard advertising over the past century.

The rising number of humorous advertisements could be mainly attributed to the wider acceptance of humor as an effective advertising strategy. Even though in the'70 s many advertising practitioners doubted the effectiveness of humorous advertising (Beard 2005), the'80 s saw a significant change in the adoption of emotional advertising (Batchelor and Stoddart 2007). The media spread further contributed to the rise of humor use (Beard 2005) resulting in the highest increase of humorous advertising in Super Bowl between the'70 s and'80 s, from 38 to 49% (Table 2). The increasing trend continued in the'90 s and the'00 s when the advertising sector widely accepted the use and recognized the significance of humor in advertising. During these decades both longitudinal Super Bowl advertising studies (e.g. Tomkovick et al. 2001) and advertising practitioners (Horovitz 2006) underline humor as the most successful advertising technique for Super Bowl commercials. This rising trend was further sustained in subsequent longitudinal studies (Kelley and Turley 2004).

Nonsense and word-play (puns) were the most frequently employed types of humor in Super Bowl humorous commercials throughout the entire 45-year period under study, compared to the other humor types (see Table 3). The frequent use of nonsense and puns was further addressed by other studies (e.g. McCullough and Taylor 1993; Weinberger et al. 2015), attributing the widespread use and appreciation to different cultures (McCullough and Taylor 1993).

Word-play is a low-risk type of humor (McCullough and Taylor 1993), hence a safe marketing choice. Word-play includes the resolution of a word-puzzle, thus originating from the incongruity (incongruity-resolution) theory (Shabbir and Thwaites 2007), the most common theory in humorous advertising (Speck 1991). Non-sense humor and word play were also the two most employed types of humor in billboard advertising over the same period (Weinberger et al. 2015). Throughout the whole period (1969 to 2015), non-sense humor was the prevailing type of humorous commercials in Super Bowl advertising (see Table 2), while word-play was found to be the prevailing type of humorous advertisements in outdoor advertising (Weinberger et al. 2015). This deviation in the use of humor types can be attributed to differences in media type advertising messages.

Warm/sentimental is a positive and mild type of humor, that involves arousal (Aaker et al. 1986) based either on arousal/safety (relief) or a combination of arousal-safety and incongruity theory (Speck 1991). According to the study's findings, warm/sentimental humor was, quiet, frequently employed during the'70 s and the'80 s, reaching its highest percentage (10%), during the nostalgic'80 s (see Table 3). However, during the twenties sexual humor emerged with aggressive humor significantly surpassing the use of warm/sentimental humor thus indicating important societal changes (see Table 3).

As warm/sentimental humor advertising illustrates images of pleasant and loving relationships (Aaker et al. 1986), it often involves elements significantly related to affection such as children and animals (Kelley and Turley 2004). Using children in Super Bowl advertising has been quite popular (Kelley and Turley 2004), while the use of animals was considered a very successful approach (Tomkovick et al. 2001; Kelley and Turley 2004). The present study highlights an increasing use of children and animals between the'70 s and'90 s, however, during the 2000s the use of children significantly dropped (6%) while the use of animals increased to an unprecedented level (22%) (see Table 3).

As both elements serve similar advertising strategies, it could be assumed that demographic changes and family structure transformations had a negative influence in the use of children in advertising. In fact, the percentage of unmarried adults increased by 21% between the'60 s and 2000s (Cohn et al. 2011), while the percentage of childless women doubled from the'70 s to the'00 s (Livingston and Cohn 2010). On the other hand, animals, as time passes, are not only companions and friends (Spears et al. 1996), but also, members of the family (Kennedy and McGarvey 2008), contributing to interpersonal affection. Animals in advertising have been found to transfer qualities to the products (Phillips 1996) and the brands (Lloyd and Woodside 2013). The comic/cartoon element has been highly used during the'90 s though with no particular pattern. Its use could be attributed to the emergence and wide viewership of adult animation series (see Table 3).

Aggressive and sexual humor falls under Freud's category of tendentious wit (McCullough and Taylor 1993). These types of humor have the ability to disguise the sensible moral subjects of violence (Speck 1991) and sex (Shabbir and Thwaites 2007), under the mantle of humor, while still addressing certain messages to society. Super Bowl advertising saw a slight increase in aggressive humor (almost 20% in'00 s), and a significant increase in sexual humor from 1990 to 2015 (see Table 2). In the last decade of the century sexual humor doubled, and aggressive humor more than doubled in Super Bowl ads (see Table 2) compared to the previous decade. These findings were similar to the ones recorded for outdoor advertising (Weinberger et al. 2015), suggesting a change in societies' ethics and moral values. The element of vulgarity, related to aggressive and sexual humor also more than doubled between the'90 s and'00 s (see Table 3).

Sexual humor, although found in a very small percentage of humorous Super Bowl advertisements during the'70 s, saw a significant increase in the'90 s and an even higher increase during the beginning of the new millennium (see Table 2). The low percentage of sexual humor in the'70 s was, possibly, the outcome of women's movements and the actions of organizations such as NOW, promoting women rights (Angley 2015). Nevertheless, during all previous decades, women being portrayed as sexual objects remained a core advertising technique (Zotos and Tsichla 2014). Its use is continuously increasing (see Table 2).

Stereotyping is yet, another concept of high societal significance. Stereotyping in Super Bowl humorous advertisements, followed a decreasing trend during the'80 s and the'90 s, but the millennium saw a significant increase reaching its prior percentage (6%) (see Table 3). Gender stereotyping was quite common during the'70 s, with advertisement portraying women in traditional roles; not, yet, reflecting the changes of women's roles in society (Plakoyiannaki and Zotos 2009). In the new millennium, though, traditional stereotyping was found to be decreasing both for males and females (Hatzithomas et al. 2016). The non-traditional stereotyping element that increased in the'00 s is, also, a more effective technique, especially when applied to humorous advertising (Eisend et al. 2014). The increase in stereotyping for Super Bowl humorous commercials, during the twenty-first century, reflects mainly the increase of a specific male non-traditional stereotype; that of men as losers (Hatzithomas et al. 2016). Such images are, also, related to humorous aggressive advertising targeting males (Gulas et al. 2010). Advertisers should be cautious, as stereotyping, concerning either males or females, ethnicities or minority groups, is a risky advertising technique.

7 Limitations and Future Research

The findings of this study are subject to specific limitations. Although the content-analysis was conducted and manipulated effectively in order to avoid issues concerning the objectivity and reliability of the analysis, known as the most vulnerable parts in the content-analysis methodology (Kolbe and Burnett 1991), the possibility of subjective judgments on behalf of the coders cannot be fully excluded.

Super Bowl advertising is, undoubtedly, a powerful sample for measuring the dominant advertising strategies, while gaining information about the prevailing culture of the American society. Nonetheless, in order to, further, confirm the results of the developments in humor and humor styles, longitudinal studies based on different samples should be conducted. For instance, a longitudinal analysis of print (magazine) advertisements for the same period or a similar analysis of the Clio award nominated and winning advertisements would be of interest.

The present study's results refer solemnly to the American society. Recognition of the method combining advertisements' content-analysis with historical and cultural analysis can lead to similar studies for other societies, worldwide.

References

Aaker, D. A., Stayman, D. M., & Hagerty, M. R. (1986). Warmth in advertising: Measurement, impact, and sequence effects. *Journal of Consumer Research, 12*(4), 365–381.

Adland (2015). Super Bowl: World's largest archive of Super Bowl commercials. https://adland.tv/SuperBowlCommercials. Accessed 15 Jan. 2015.

Angley, Natalie (2015): Sexist ads in the seventies. CNN online. https://edition.cnn.com/2015/07/22/living/seventies-sexist-ads/index.html. Accessed: 14. Nov. 2017.

Babiak, K., Wolfe, R. (2006). More than just a game? Corporate social responsibility and Super Bowl XL. *Sport Marketing Quarterly*, 15 (4).

Batchelor, B., & Stoddart, S. F. (2007). *The 1980s, american popular culture through history*. Westport: Greenwood press.

Beard, F. K. (2005). One hundred years of humor in American advertising. *Journal of Macromarketing, 25*(1), 54–65.

Berger, A. A. (1987). Humor: An introduction. *American Behavioral Scientist, 30*(3), 6–15.

Berger, A. A. (2008). On the gift of humor. *Europe's Journal of Psychology*, 4(2).

Cohn, D., Passel, J. S., Wang, W., Livingston, G. (2011). Barely half of US adults are married– A record low. Pew Research Center. https://www.pewsocialtrends.org/2011/12/14/barely-half-of-us-adults-are-married-a-record-low.

Eisend, M. (2009). A meta-analysis of humor in advertising. *Journal of the Academy of Marketing Science, 37*(2), 191–203.

Eisend, M., Plagemann, J., & Sollwedel, J. (2014). Gender roles and humor in advertising: The occurrence of stereotyping in humorous and nonhumorous advertising and its consequences for advertising effectiveness. *Journal of Advertising, 43*(3), 256–273.

Gulas, C. S., McKeage, K. K., & Weinberger, M. G. (2010). It's just a joke. *Journal of Advertising, 39*(4), 109–120.

Hatzithomas, L., Boutsouki, C., & Ziamou, P. (2016). A longitudinal analysis of the changing roles of gender in advertising: A content analysis of Super Bowl commercials. *International Journal of Advertising, 35*(5), 888–906.

Horovitz, B. (2006). Ten rules to make ads magical. USA Today online, [online] 2 March. https://usatoday30.usatoday.com/money/advertising/2006-02-03-super-ads-usat_x.htm.

Kelley, S. W., & Turley, L. W. (2004). The effect of content on perceived affect of Super Bowl commercials. *Journal of Sport Management, 18*(4), 398–420.

Kelly, J. P., & Solomon, P. J. (1975). Humor in television advertising. *Journal of Advertising*, 4(3), 31–35.

Kennedy, P. F., & McGarvey, M. G. (2008). Animal-companion depictions in women's magazine advertising. *Journal of Business Research, 61*(5), 424–430.

Kim, J., McMillan, S. J., & Hwang, J.-S. (2005). Strategies for the super bowl of advertising: An analysis of how the web is integrated into campaigns. *Journal of Interactive Advertising, 6*(1), 46–60.

Kolbe, R. H., & Burnett, M. S. (1991). Content-analysis research: An examination of applications with directives for improving research reliability and objectivity. *Journal of Consumer Research, 18*(2), 243–250.

Livingston, Gretchen; Cohn, D' Vera (2010): Childlessness up among all women; down among women with advanced degrees. Available from: https://www.pewsocialtrends.org/2010/06/25/childlessness-up-among-all-women-down-among-women-with-advanced-degrees/.

Lloyd, S., & Woodside, A. G. (2013). Animals, archetypes, and advertising (A3): The theory and the practice of customer brand symbolism. *Journal of Marketing Management, 29*(1–2), 5–25.

Lynch, O. H. (2002). Humorous communication: Finding a place for humor in communication research. *Communication Theory, 12*(4), 423–445.

Madden, T. J., & Weinberger, M. G. (1984). Humor in advertising: A practitioner view. *Journal of Advertising Research, 24*(4), 23–29.

Markiewicz, D. (1974). Effects of humor on persuasion. *Sociometry,* 407–422.

Martin, R. A., Ford, T. (2018). The psychology of humor: An integrative approach. Academic press.

McAllister, M. P. (1999). Super Bowl advertising as commercial celebration. *Communication Review (the), 3*(4), 403–428.

McCullough, L. S., & Taylor, R. K. (1993). Humor in American, British, and German Ads. *Industrial Marketing Management, 22*(1), 17–28.

Meyer, J. C. (2000). Humor as a double-edged sword: Four functions of humor in communication. *Communication Theory, 10*(3), 310–331.

Phillips, Barbara J. (1996): Advertising and the cultural meaning of animals. In: *ACR North American Advances.*

Phillips, B. J., & McQuarrie, E. F. (2002). The development, change, and transformation of rhetorical style in magazine advertisements 1954–1999. *Journal of Advertising, 31*(4), 1–13.

Plakoyiannaki, E., & Zotos, Y. (2009). Female role stereotypes in print advertising: Identifying associations with magazine and product categories. *European Journal of Marketing, 43*(11/12), 1411–1434.

Pollay, R. W. (1985). The subsiding sizzle: A descriptive history of print advertising, 1900–1980. *Journal of Marketing, 49*(3), 24–37.

Pollay, R. W. (1986). The distorted mirror: Reflections on the unintended consequences of advertising. *Journal of Marketing, 50*(2), 18–36.

Shabbir, H., & Thwaites, D. (2007). The use of humor to mask deceptive advertising: It's no laughing matter. *Journal of Advertising, 36*(2), 75–85.

Siefert, C. J., Kothuri, R., Jacobs, D. B., Levine, B., Plummer, J., & Marci, C. D. (2009). Winning the super "buzz" bowl: How biometrically-based emotional engagement correlates with online views and comments for super bowl advertisements. *Journal of Advertising Research, 49*(3), 293–303.

Spears, N. E., Mowen, J. C., & Chakraborty, G. (1996). Symbolic role of animals in print advertising: Content analysis and conceptual development. *Journal of Business Research, 37*(2), 87–95.

Speck, P. S. (1991). The humorous message taxonomy: A framework for the study of humorous ads. *Current Issues and Research in Advertising, 13*(1–2), 1–44.

Sternthal, B., & Craig, S. C. (1973). Humor in advertising. *Journal of Marketing, 37*(4), 12–18.

Swani, K., Weinberger, M. G., & Gulas, C. S. (2013). The impact of violent humor on advertising success: A gender perspective. *Journal of Advertising, 42*(4), 308–319.

Tomkovick, C., Yelkur, R., & Christians, L. (2001). The USA's biggest marketing event keeps getting bigger: An in-depth look at Super Bowl advertising in the 1990s. *Journal of Marketing Communications, 7*(2), 89–108.

Weinberger, M. G., & Gulas, C. S. (1992). The impact of humor in advertising: A review. *Journal of Advertising, 21*(4), 35–59.

Weinberger, M. G., Gulas, C. S., & Weinberger, M. F. (2015). Looking in through outdoor: A socio-cultural and historical perspective on the evolution of advertising humour. *International Journal of Advertising, 34*(3), 447–472.

Zotos, Y. C., & Tsichla, E. (2014). Female stereotypes in print advertising: A retrospective analysis. *Procedia-Social and Behavioral Sciences, 148,* 446–454.

Should Companies Use Tattooed Models in Their Advertisements?

Antonia Heberle and Heribert Gierl

1 Introduction

The probably oldest tattoos were recently found on two naturally mummified bodies from the Egypt's pre-dynastic period (4000-3100 BC). The male mummy denoted as Gebelein Man A has a tattoo depicting two horned animals on his upper right arm. The female mummy (Gebelein Woman) has even more tattoos—four small 's'-shaped motifs on her right shoulder, a tattoo on her upper right arm, and one on her lower abdomen. This discovery replaced the oldest finding of a tattoo on Ötzi the Iceman, a mummy found near the Ötz valley in the Alps, dating back to the late 4th millennium BC (Friedman et al. 2018). During history, tattoos were used all over the world for various reasons. They had a supernatural or magical meaning and were associated with protection against danger and diseases. In ancient Europe, tattoos were primarily used to mark slaves. The traditional motifs like an anchor, a swallow, a heart with a banner on it, or pin-up drawings became popular in Europe by the sailor James Cook in 1770 (Ruhnke 1974).

In the recent past, tattoos were rather assigned to men and especially used within male-dominated subcultures such as military groups, punk groups, motorcycle clubs, and street gangs. Because tattoos were associated with masculinity, tattooed men reached higher social acceptance than did tattooed women and women were motivated not to get a tattoo (Braunberger 2000; Atkinson 2002).

A. Heberle (✉) · H. Gierl
University of Augsburg, Augsburg, Germany
E-Mail: antonia.heberle@wiwi.uni-augsburg.de

H. Gierl
E-Mail: heribert.gierl@wiwi.uni-augsburg.de

© The Author(s), under exclusive license to Springer Fachmedien Wiesbaden GmbH, part of Springer Nature 2021
M. Waiguny and S. Rosengren (eds.), *Advances in Advertising Research (Vol. XI)*, European Advertising Academy,
https://doi.org/10.1007/978-3-658-32201-4_11

Thus, some years ago, the proportion of tattooed people was rather low. Researchers found that attitudes toward persons with tattoo were mostly negative (Forbes 2001; Degelman and Price 2002; Hawkes et al. 2004; Seiter and Hatch 2005; Swami and Furnham 2007). Tattooed people were evaluated as less physically attractive, less intelligent, less honest, more sexually promiscuous, and were perceived as heavy users of alcohol compared to untattooed people. Models depicted in advertisements or acting at fashion shows were not allowed to have a tattoo. If they had one, they had to cover it with make-up.

Today, tattoos are more prevalent in our daily life (https://tattoo-spirit.de). Hollywood movies, television programs including reality shows as well as soap operas, or sports events, especially soccer games—all show tattooed persons. Celebrities as well as unknown testimonials depicted in advertisements show their tattoos. There are even special model agencies for tattooed models and more and more brands decided to depict a tattooed model in their advertisements. Probably, the usage of tattoos in advertisements and in media is one of the reasons why tattoos gained higher social acceptance. Nowadays, tattoos are not necessarily associated with negative meanings (e.g., criminality, alcohol, or drug abuse) and not limited to persons of a certain age, gender, or a social group. For instance, Totten, Lipscomb, and Jones (2009) found that tattoos did not indicate any longer that this person is very sexually promiscuous, has a bad image, or abuses alcohol and drugs.

In the time span between 2016 and 2018, we conducted a pilot study (online-survey) among 3,363 persons in Germany (mean age = 23.76 years, 73.6% female, 80.1% students). 19.0% of the persons indicated to be tattooed. When looking separately at the male and female participants, we found that the portion of tattooed women (20.4%) is higher than the portion of tattooed men (15.3%). We surmise that these figures might even underestimate the true portion of tattooed young persons because some people might feel discomfort to admit in a survey to have a tattoo. Further, we asked the participants whether friends are tattooed or not. 72.8% indicated to have at least one tattooed person in their circle of friends. We also asked the persons to write down the major reason why they themselves (or if not, their friends) are tattooed. We classified the answers to this question and determined several types of reasons which are ex-post justification or explanations (Table 1). We found that 66.8% indicated reasons that are in favor of tattoos (e.g., tattoos as appropriate means to communicate to others, as means to please oneself, as a kind of memory, or as a signal of caesura in life) and that only 3.8% reported reasons that speak against tattoos (lost bet, drunkenness, or silliness). The remaining 29.4% did not report thoughts that are clearly either in

Table 1 Reasons why oneself or friends got a tattoo

	Subdimensions	Frequency
Tattoo as means to communicate to others	Tattoo as expression of rebellion to receive more attention (e.g., demonstrating the right to decide for oneself after the 18th birthday)	4.0%
	Tattoo as signal to belong to a particular group	5.6%
	Tattoo as expression of one's creativity and personality (e.g., intent to express one's individuality or uniqueness)	3.2%
	Tattoo as expression of "coolness"	1.4%
	Tattoo as expression of one's belongingness to a certain religion	1.6%
	Tattoo as proof of love (e.g., partner tattoo)	4.0%
	Tattoo as expression of one's willingness to follow fashion	6.0%
Tattoo as means to please oneself	Aesthetical and art-related benefits of a tattoo (e.g., body as a piece of art, body as a medium to implement artwork)	10.0%
	Tattoo as means of body embellishment (e.g., improving one's appearance, like jewelry, makes one's body look beautiful)	8.8%
	Covering unsightly scars (mostly due to self-injury)	2.4%
	Tattoo as a kind of pleasant self-injury	1.2%
Tattoo as an external memory	Tattoo as reminder and symbolic presence of deceased relatives, friends, and pets; aid to remember very special moments such as birthdays of one's children	13.2%

(continued)

Table 1 (continued)

	Subdimensions	Frequency
Tattoo as a caesura	Tattoo as signal indicating that a life section has past and a new section should begin (e.g., demonstrating one's strength that one was able to complete with a chapter in one's life and to be willing to start a "new beginning" in one's life)	5.4%
Tattoos to regret	Lost bet	1.0%
	Getting a tattoo while being drunken (e.g., "drunken in Prague")	2.2%
	Tattoo as a result of silliness	0.6%
Neutral	Diverse thoughts (e.g., about the person who painted the tattoo)	29.4%

favor or against tattoos. We conclude that the distribution of tattoos in Western societies is increasing and attitudes toward tattoos are predominantly positive.

Today, tattooed or body-painted models are frequently shown in print advertisements. There are manifold aspects, which might shape the effect of the presence of tattoos on models depicted in advertisements on brand evaluations. First, particular motifs, which are used as tattoos, could be liked or disliked (e.g., heart vs. dragon, small vs. large). Second, there might be a tattoo-motif/model interaction effect. A particular motif could be liked or disliked in combination with a particular model (e.g., a flower on a male vs. a female model). Third, in advertising practice, the image of the tattoo often is adopted as image on the product packaging; this practice might be liked or disliked. Fourth, consumers with own tattoos might react differently to tattooed models than untattooed consumers. Fifth, there might be gender effects: Male consumers might respond differently to tattooed male and female models than female consumers. In this paper, we focus on the latter aspect and examine whether there are gender effects. Investigations of the effectiveness of ads showing tattooed models depending on consumer and model gender could result in findings, which are beneficial for marketers.

2 Theoretical Considerations

Tattoos are attention-getting. Because we consider tattooed models, contact with tattoos likely increases the tendency in consumers to focus on their own gender role. In the tattoo condition, men become more aware of being male and women become more aware of being female. Transporting people into this mental state has consequences. Role theory (Rosenkrantz et al. 1968) predicts that persons have beliefs concerning the roles of each gender. Persons have expectations about the appearance and the behavior of women and men. Conforming to these expectations is rewarding for both persons—for the person who holds these expectations and for the person who conforms to these expectations (Workman and Johnson 1994). According to Atkinson (2002), there was a "long-standing association between tattooing and masculinity." Thus, we expect that female consumers respond favorably to tattooed male models (because the latter signal higher masculinity). However, if male consumers view a tattooed male model, they view a person who signals higher attractiveness for women. Due to rivalry among men as sexual partners of women, an aversion in male consumers toward tattooed male models is likely to exist. From our pilot study, we learned that many women get tattoos to improve the appearance of their body, e.g., want to look more beautiful due to likeable tattoo motifs. Because there is also rivalry among women with respect to their attractiveness for men, we expect that female consumers dislike tattooed female models. For men, there is no overt reason why a tattoo on a female model affects evaluations; exceptions might exist if the tattoo motif impairs perceptions of the female model's femininity.

3 Study 1: Exploratory Investigations of Gender Effects

We created two versions of advertisements for a large set of products. In one version, an untattooed model was shown, in the other version, the same model was tattooed. We examined the attitude toward the promoted products depending on the presence or absence of the tattoo on the model. The ads are shown in Fig. 1. In this experiment, we did not consider all model-gender/consumer-gender combinations for each of the brands.

In total, 1526 consumers participated in this experiment (mean age = 24.18 years, SD = 7.075, 63.2% female, 77.7% students). 15.6% indicated to be tattooed. Data were collected by the help of online surveys. After viewing one ad version, the test person indicated her/his attitude toward the promoted product.

Fig. 1 Test stimuli used in Study 1

S/he agreed or disagreed with: "The product is very appealing," "attractive," "likeable," and "interesting" ($\alpha = 0.869$). The results which are shown in Table 2 indicate that male consumers devaluate the product if a tattooed male compared to an untattooed male model is shown (F(1; 450) = 9.621, p = 0.002). Tattoos on female models do not affect product evaluations of male consumers (F(1; 109) =

Table 2 Results of Study 1

Brand	Sample size	Male consumer				Female consumer			
		Male model		Female model		Male model		Female model	
		Untattooed model	Tattooed model	Untattooed model	Tattooed model	Untattooed model	Tattooed model	Untattooed model	Tattooed model
Gerolsteiner mineral water	266	-	-	4.25 (1.33)	4.32 (1.61)	-	-	4.30 (1.30)	4.06 (1.38)
Maybelline mascara	99	-	-	-	-	-	-	3.43 (1.33)	3.16 (1.34)
Dove body lotion	186	-	-	-	-	-	-	3.41 (1.04)	2.84 (0.84)
Lancôme perfume	153	-	-	-	-	-	-	3.82 (1.46)	3.27 (1.12)
Nystalgia vodka (fictive brand)	237	-	-	-	-	-	-	3.25 (1.68)	2.86 (1.51)
Arizona soft drink	265	4.98 (1.37)	4.66 (1.65)	-	-	3.48 (1.19)	3.96 (1.38)	-	-
Axe shower gel	120	4.17 (1.53)	3.85 (1.47)	-	-	-	-	-	-
Boss perfume	200	4.05 (1.36)	3.43 (1.24)	-	-	-	-	-	-
Overall	1526	4.35 (1.46)	3.91 (1.52)	4.25 (1.33)	4.32 (1.61)	3.48 (1.19)	3.96 (1.38)	3.61 (1.47)	3.19 (1.31)

Note: Scale ranges from 1 = negative to 7 = positive attitude. Standard deviations in parentheses

0.054, NS). Female consumers indicate higher product evaluations if a male model is tattooed (F(1; 131) = 4.675, p = 0.032). On the contrary, if a female tattooed compared to a female untattooed model promotes a product, product evaluations of female consumers are deteriorated (F(1; 828) = 17.350, p < 0.001). Thus, the results conform to our expectations on gender effects when tattooed models are used.

4 Study 2: Effect of Using Tattooed Female Models on Responses of Young Female Consumers

The second study was based on a 2 (tattoo: absent, present) × 2 (images shown in the ad: product image, both product and model image) × 2 (promoted product: Coca Cola beverage, HTC smart phone) experimental between-subjects design. For each product, we created four versions of a print advertisement (Fig. 2).

In total, 385 female persons took part in the experiment (age between 18 and 32 years, mean age = 22.35 years, 97% students). Data were collected by conducting an online-survey in 2017 in Germany. 21% of the persons reported to have a tattoo. We checked whether the frequency of the usage of Cola beverages or smartphones, interest in the respective category, knowledge in the category,

TATTOO ABSENT		TATTOO PRESENT	
PRODUCT IMAGE	PRODUCT AND MODEL IMAGE	PRODUCT IMAGE	PRODUCT AND MODEL IMAGE

Fig. 2 Test stimuli used in Study 2

Table 3 Results of Study 2

Response variable	Tattoo absent		Tattoo present	
	Product image	Product and model image	Product image	Product and model image
Attitude toward the product	3.54 (1.32)	3.25 (1.31)	2.89 (1.36)	2.10 (1.07)
Attitude toward the model	-	4.38 (1.37)	-	3.74 (1.54)
Surprisingness of the ad	2.48 (1.05)	3.20 (1.29)	3.29 (1.55)	4.35 (1.47)

Note: Scales range from 1 = low (negative) to high (positive). Standard deviations in parentheses

and other control variables were constant across the conditions per product and did not find significant differences. To assess the attitude toward the promoted product, the test persons agreed or disagreed with "The product is very appealing," "attractive," "likeable," and "interesting" ($\alpha = 0.882$). The attitude toward the model (if depicted in the ad) was assessed by agreement with "The model is very attractive," "beautiful," "sexy," "pleasing," and "likeable" ($\alpha = 0.871$). To measure the surprisingness of the ad we asked the test persons to respond to "The ad is irritating," "surprises me," "astonishes me," and "makes me curious" ($\alpha = 0.773$). We aggregated data across the products because the effects of the other factors did not depend on the product. The findings (Table 3) show that the use of female models with tattoos resulted in less favorable product evaluations of female consumers than the use of female models without tattoos (untattooed model: M = 3.25, tattooed model: M = 2.10, $F(1;194) = 45.293$, $p<0.001$). The attitude toward tattooed models compared to untattooed models was less favorable whereas using tattoo-like images caused higher emotions of surprise ($ps<0.05$). There was also a negative effect of the usage of tattoo-like product images (tattoo absent: M = 3.54, tattoo present: M = 2.89). If the motif of the model's tattoo was adopted on the product, evaluations were even more negative.

5 Study 3: Replication Study

The replication study was based on a 2 (model image: tattooed, untattooed) × 2 (product image: tattoo-like, regular) × 2 (promoted product: Jean Paul Gaultier perfume, Nivea body milk) factorial between-subjects design. The versions of the ads are shown in Fig. 3.

In total, 696 female persons participated in the experiment (mean age = 25.13 years, 66% students, 18% indicated having a tattoo). The procedure and scales were adopted from Study 1. Cronbach's alphas were as follows: $\alpha = 0.744$ for the attitude toward the promoted product, $\alpha = 0.883$ for the attitude toward the model, and $\alpha = 0.769$ for the surprisingness of the ad. We aggregated data across the product factor. The mean values and standard deviations of the response variables are shown in Table 4. Again, we found that the depiction of a tattoo on a female model impairs product evaluations of female consumers (untattooed model: M = 4.09, tattooed model: M = 2.89, $F(1;365) = 87.128$, $p<0.001$). A rather similar effect was found when the motif of the model's tattoo was adopted as an image on the product packaging.

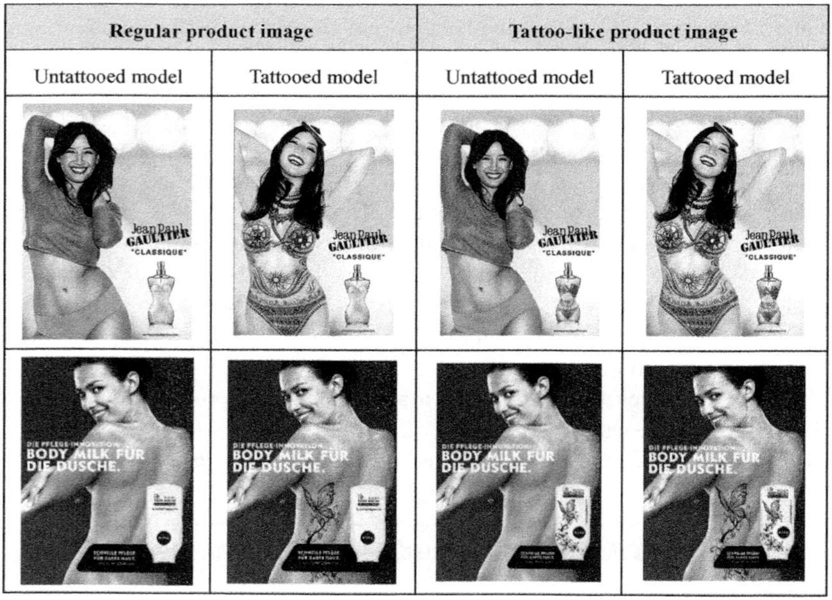

Fig. 3 Test stimuli used in Study 3

Table 4 Results of Study 3

Response variable	Regular product image		Tattoo-like product image	
	Untattooed model	Tattooed model	Untattooed model	Tattooed model
Attitude toward the product	4.09 (1.26)	2.89 (1.10)	4.10 (1.42)	2.88 (1.08)
Attitude toward the model	4.54 (1.21)	3.63 (1.37)	4.94 (1.11)	4.28 (1.41)
Surprisingness of the ad	2.65 (1.27)	3.59 (1.35)	3.01 (1.08)	3.89 (1.28)

Note: Scales range from 1 = low (negative) to high (positive). Standard deviations in parentheses

6 Study 4: Effect of Using Tattooed Male vs. Female Models on Responses of Young Male vs. Female Consumers

The fourth experiment was based on a 2 (model image: tattooed, untattooed) × 2 (model gender: male, female) × 2 (consumer gender: male, female) × 2 (promoted brand: Versicherungskammer Bayern, Check24) factorial between-subjects design. The Versicherungskammer Bayern is a well-known insurance company. Check24 is known as a provider of a wide variety of goods and services in the Internet (e.g., insurance, mobile phone contracts, energy, household appliances, and travel services). For each brand, we created four versions of an advertisement (Fig. 4). The versions differed with respect to showing a male or female model and regarding the fact whether the forearm of the model was tattooed or not.

In total, 535 persons took part in an online-survey. The test participants' age ranged from 16 to 46 years (mean age = 24.03 years, SD = 3.86). 46.5% were females, and 79.6% of the participants indicated to be student. Overall, 20.2% indicated to be tattooed (tattooed males: 15.7%, tattooed females: 25.3%). Data collection took place in 2018 in Germany. The link to the questionnaire has been distributed via social media; moreover, interviewers distributed a sheet of paper in pedestrian zones of two major German cities, which contained the link to the online questionnaire. The test participants could view one ad version as long as they wanted. Then, they had to complete the questionnaire. On each page of the questionnaire, the ad was depicted. Thus, while answering each question, the test participants were always exposed to the ad.

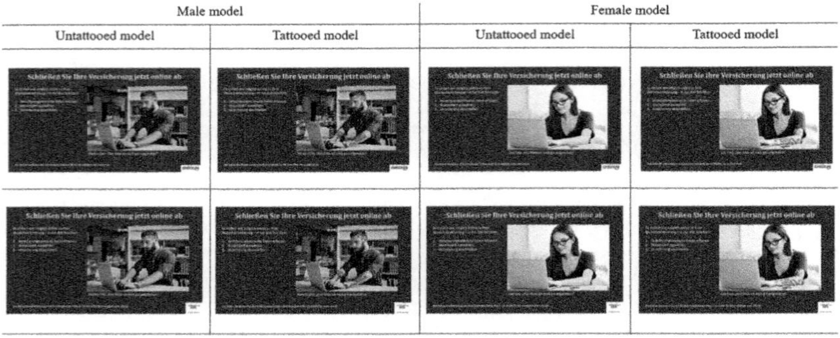

	Male model		Female model	
	Untattooed model	Tattooed model	Untattooed model	Tattooed model

Translation of the texts: "Take out your insurance online now. As easy as possible online to your desired insurance - in just three steps: 1. Enter insurance-relevant data. 2. Select desired tariff. 3. Take out insurance. Markus (26) [Lisa (26)]: 'Here I feel in good hands.' The online customer service of Versicherungskammer Bayern [Check24] is always available for you: www.vkw.de [www.check24.de]."

Fig. 4 Test stimuli used in Study 4

First, the test persons were requested to indicate all thoughts and feelings in response to the ad. Then, attitudes toward the promoted brand were assessed by agreement with: "The company is very appealing," "attractive," "good," "positive," and "likeable," "I would like to learn more about the company," "The ad made me very curious about the company," and "I easily could imagine to buy a service at this company" ($\alpha = 0.922$). Subsequently, the test persons evaluated the company. Company trustworthiness was assessed by agreement with: "The company is very trustworthy," "honest," "accommodating," "reliable," "does its best to solve customer problems," "supports the customers' interest," "is very concerned about its customers," and "is very credible" ($\alpha = 0.936$). To measure company innovativeness, we asked the persons to agree or disagree with: "The company is very innovative," "creative," and "modern" ($\alpha = 0.858$). Next, the depicted model was evaluated. Model competence was assessed by responding to: "The model is very intelligent," "competent," and "an expert" ($\alpha = 0.924$). Model trustworthiness was measured by: "The model is very honest," "credible," "trustworthy," and "reliable" ($\alpha = 0.933$). Moreover, the test participants were asked to judge the similarity of the model to their own person: "The model is very similar to me," "The model is like me," "The model behaves like me," "The model and me share many attitudes," "The model and me share many believes and values," and "The model likes the things I like" ($\alpha = 0.949$). The test persons also provided data about the model's extraordinariness: "The model evokes the feeling of curiosity," "The model makes me feel interested," "The model evokes feelings of surprise," and "The model evokes feelings of astonishment" ($\alpha = 0.808$). Finally, model identification was measured: "S/he is the sort of person I want to be myself," "S/he is someone I would like to emulate," "I think s/he could be a friend of mine," and "S/he would fit into my circle of friends" ($\alpha = 0.877$). All scales were seven-point scales. We averaged the items and analyzed the composite scores. We collapsed data across the brands because we did not find remarkable differences regarding the results. The mean values are reported in Table 5.

For the male-consumer/male-model condition, we found that consumers evaluated the promoted product more negatively, if a model with tattoo compared to a model without tattoo was shown ($F(1;140) = 71.999$, $p < 0.001$). In this condition, Hayes' (2013) mediation analysis with the model as independent variable (1 = tattoo vs. 0 = no tattoo) and brand evaluations as dependent variable showed that the company is evaluated as less trustworthy and less innovative and the model is perceived as lower in competence and lower in extraordinariness which spilled over onto brand evaluations. From the findings of the thought-listing task, we can add the finding that there were a rather large number of negative comments regarding tattooed models.

In the male-consumer/female-model condition, we observed a null effect of tattoos on brand evaluations ($F(1;142) = 0.026$, NS). The use of a tattoo had a positive mediating effect via company innovativeness. However, this effect seemed to be too weak to affect brand evaluations.

In the female-consumer/male-model condition, we found a positive tattoo effect on brand evaluations ($F(1;122) = 11.220$, $p < 0.001$). The mediation analysis showed that—in the tattooed-model condition—the company is more trustworthy and innovative and the model is more competent and extraordinary which spills over onto brand evaluations. The data from the thought-listing task showed that female persons reported only positive comments about tattoos on male models.

For the female consumer/female model condition, we expected a negative effect of a tattoo on brand evaluations (because Study 1, Study 2, and Study 3 had revealed a negative effect) but found a null effect ($F(1;123) = 1.419$, NS). The mediation analysis indicated a positive effect via company innovativeness; however, this effect is not strong enough to improve brand evaluations.

7 Implications for Practice

Our studies indicated that depicting tattooed female models in advertisements deteriorates attitudes of young female consumers toward the promoted product or showed that such depictions have a null effect. Male consumers respond negatively to tattooed male models, whereas female consumers respond positively

Table 5 Results of Study 4

Response variable	Male consumer						Female consumer					
	Male model		Female model				Male model		Female model			
	Untattooed model	Tattooed model	Untattooed model	Tattooed model			Untattooed model	Tattooed model	Untattooed model	Tattooed model		
Attitude toward the brand	4.17 (0.98)	2.66 (1.13)	3.76 (1.20)	3.79 (1.19)			3.08 (1.33)	3.87 (1.31)	3.85 (1.50)	4.14 (1.27)		
Company trustworthiness	4.19 (0.91)	3.16 (1.12)	3.89 (0.99)	4.02 (1.08)			3.46 (1.37)	3.91 (1.33)	3.92 (1.41)	4.23 (1.32)		
Company innovativeness	4.65 (1.12)	3.50 (1.54)	3.63 (1.58)	4.23 (1.33)			3.28 (1.54)	3.82 (1.42)	3.77 (1.61)	4.29 (1.44)		
Model competence	4.14 (1.02)	3.44 (1.12)	4.54 (1.13)	4.37 (1.21)			3.85 (1.52)	4.27 (1.27)	4.73 (1.20)	4.59 (1.18)		
Model trustworthiness	4.16 (1.05)	3.58 (1.15)	4.58 (1.19)	4.30 (1.23)			4.06 (1.41)	4.30 (1.18)	4.64 (1.22)	4.46 (1.17)		
Model-consumer similarity	3.54 (1.33)	2.50 (1.22)	2.74 (1.35)	2.95 (1.50)			2.82 (1.49)	3.32 (1.30)	3.46 (1.48)	3.46 (1.54)		
Model extraordinariness	3.00 (0.98)	2.33 (1.04)	2.62 (0.94)	2.99 (1.22)			2.89 (1.52)	3.44 (1.49)	3.11 (1.45)	3.43 (1.52)		
Identification with the model	3.80 (1.18)	2.73 (1.11)	3.05 (1.39)	3.06 (1.39)			2.84 (1.64)	3.70 (1.27)	3.47 (1.42)	3.55 (1.46)		

Note: Scales range from 1 = low (negative) to high (positive). Standard deviations in parentheses

to tattooed male models. Admittedly, our studies are only the starting point for examinations of effects of tattooed models in advertisements. Moreover, we did not manipulate the motif of the tattoo or its size. We did not consider responses of older consumers. When companies target young female consumers and show male models, we recommend considering tattooed male models. When companies target young male consumers, we recommend to refrain from showing tattooed male models.

References

Atkinson, M. (2002). Pretty in ink: Conformity, resistance, and negotiation in women's tattooing. *Sex Roles, 47*(5–6), 219–235.
Braunberger, C. (2000). Revolting bodies: The monster beauty of tattooed women. *NWSA Journal, 12*(2), 1–23.
Degelman, D., & Price, N. D. (2002). Tattoos and ratings of personal characteristics. *Psychological Reports, 90*(2), 507–514.
Forbes, G. B. (2001). College students with tattoos and piercings: Motives, family experiences, personality factors, and perception by others. *Psychological Reports, 89*(3), 774–786.
Friedman, R., Antoine, D., Talamo, S., Reimer, P. J., Taylor, J. H., Wills, B., & Mannino, M. A. (2018). Natural mummies from Predynastic Egypt reveal the world's earliest figural tattoos. *Journal of Archaeological Science, 92*, 116–125.
Hawkes, D., Senn, C. Y., & Thorn, C. (2004). Factors that influence attitudes toward women with tattoos. *Sex Roles, 50*(9–10), 593–604.
Hayes, A. F. (2013). *Introduction to mediation, moderation, and conditional process analysis: A regression-based approach*. New York: Guilford Press.
Rosenkrantz, P., Vogel, S., Bee, H., Broverman, I., & Broverman, D. M. (1968). Sex-role stereotypes and self-concepts in college students. *Journal of Consulting and Clinical Psychology, 32*(3), 287–295.
Ruhnke, Christa (1974): Die Tätowierung: eine sozio-kulturelle und medizinische Betrachtung. [The tattoo: A socio-cultural and medical consideration], PhD thesis, Marburg.
Seiter, J. S., & Hatch, S. (2005). Effect of tattoos on perceptions of credibility and attractiveness. *Psychological Reports, 96*(3), 1113–1120.
Swami, V., & Furnham, A. (2007). Unattractive, promiscuous and heavy drinkers: Perceptions of women with tattoos. *Body Image, 4*(4), 343–352.
Totten, J. W., Lipscomb, T. J., & Jones, M. A. (2009). Attitudes toward and stereotypes of persons with body art: Implications for marketing management. *Academy of Marketing Studies Journal, 13*(2), 77–96.
Workman, J. E., & Johnson, K. K. P. (1994). Effects of conformity and nonconformity to gender-role expectations for dress: Teachers versus students. *Adolescence, 29*(113), 207–223.

Creating Branded Entertainment that Resonates: Perspectives of Multinational Award Winners

Marthinus J. C. van Loggerenberg, Carla Enslin, and Marlize Terblanche-Smit

1 Introduction and Background

Branded entertainment is deemed to be an alternative or unconventional way to make brand contact (Duopoly 2014; Woodrooffe 2014; Graser 2015; Grinta 2016), as it steps out of the realm of traditional promotional initiatives (Thomas 2009). O'Guinn et al. (2009, pp. 612–613) defined branded entertainment as 'The development and support of any entertainment property (e.g. TV shows, theme park, short film, movie, or video game) where a primary objective is to feature one's brand or brands in an effort to impress and connect with consumers in a unique and compelling way'. Branded entertainment as a form of content creation has potential to break through commercial clutter and arrest target audience attention in a meaningful way (Bothun and Vollmer 2016; Ryan 2016).

Compelling content with ability to arrest attention is identified by the following characteristics: purpose-driven, relevant, exclusive, affirms the brand, and is stylistically appropriate (Figart 2011). Compelling branded entertainment that

M. J. C. van Loggerenberg (✉)
University of San Francisco, San Francisco, USA
E-Mail: mvanloggerenberg@usfca.edu

C. Enslin
IIE Vega School, Cape Town, South Africa
E-Mail: censlin@vegaschool.com

M. Terblanche-Smit
University of Stellenbosch Business School, Cape Town, South Africa
E-Mail: smitm@usb.ac.za

imbues an authentic narrative has considerable potential to establish a strong emotional connection with a target audience (Rose 2013; Valero 2014; Brenner 2015; Hudson and Tung 2016; Meyers 2018). Authentic narrative was introduced by the study to give form to narrative that is original, communicates the brand's identity and purpose and aligns with the target audience's value system in a meaningful way, with the potential to achieve brand resonance (Weiss 2014; Wiese 2015; Grinta 2016; Da Costa 2018; Jones 2018; Pereira 2018).

Kevin Lane Keller's brand resonance model indicates that various dimensions of brand resonance can be reached by impactful branded entertainment, such as enhanced brand attachment or emotional connection, establishing a sense of community and engagement, with the possibility of interactive effects between different brand resonance dimensions to exist such as higher levels of attachment leading to greater engagement (Keller 2009). Brand resonance is responsible for strategically growing brands (Keller 2001) and positively affecting brand experiences (Huang et al. 2015).

As advertisers are findings new ways to connect with especially a new generation of consumers, PJ Pereira, co-founder and chief creative officer of San Francisco-based Pereira & O'Dell and head juror at the 2017 Cannes Festival of Creativity, urged brand practitioners to familiarize themselves with the skill to create unique and memorable content, and brand experiences around entertainment that consumers will actively want to seek out (Pereira 2017). In the past Pereira, who also chaired the branded content and entertainment jury in 2016 for the Clio Awards, expressed concern that more quality content needs to be presented by the international advertising industry, stating 'We're still testing the waters and seeing what can be done, or can't'.

Pereira's sentiment is shared by various jurors of international award shows, industry influencers and academics over time, expressing concern over branded entertainment that is still trying to orientate itself in practice, its quality of expression and not achieving its strategic potential in terms of brand building (Weiss 2014; Morrison 2015; Wiese 2015; Emhoff 2016; MacCuish 2017; Keith in Dams 2019). Aidan McClure, Founding Partner and Chief Creative Officer at Wonderhood Studios, wrote a provocative article for Campaign UK (2020), stating that very few brands succeed at branded entertainment, calling it a 'scary landscape' to navigate. Those that do succeed are the 'brands with a very clear point of view on why they exist in this world, allowing them to rise above the weeds and tell a meaningful story that is authentic to them while being culturally relevant to people and, most importantly, entertaining', he said.

This research set out to suggest a practice-based perspective as result of a practice-based problem: many advertising practitioners and academics are still orientating themselves to identify the most pertinent challenges and understand the strategic significance of branded entertainment (Weiss 2014; Morrison 2015; Wiese 2015; Maconick 2016; Pereira 2017; Liffreing 2018). This occurs amidst a high demand for branded entertainment as a way to break through advertising clutter in a highly competitive, fast-evolving global mediascape (Ryan 2016).

2 Research Objectives

- To identify branded entertainment's value in brand communication practice. If the value and potential are understood, practitioners could plan and create branded entertainment that maximises such potential and contributes value in building brands by means of entertaining content.
- To identify challenges that branded entertainment is facing. If brand building practitioners can identify and overcome challenges in branded entertainment practice, a greater number of strategically significant branded entertainment campaigns may surface as result.
- To create a practice-based perspective to plan, create and execute impactful branded entertainment. Research findings may propose practice-based suggestions and principles in a more practice-focused way to address the research problem.

3 Research Design and Method

A qualitative methodology in the interpretivist paradigm approach (Guba and Lincoln 1981 cited by Plack 2005), was well suited to explore in-depth perspectives of primary research participants to address the research problem and inform the research objectives. In-depth interviews created an environment in which participants could express their thoughts on branded entertainment and the application thereof (Milena, Dainora and Alin 2008). This exploratory study thus relied on focused expert opinions in order to gain from participants' industry knowledge and experience.

Interviews were conducted across six continents between 2013–2015; Africa, North America, South America, Europe, Asia and Australasia, with a total of 15 advertising planners and creators who have received the highest international recognition of excellence in the form of multiple Grand Prix and Gold wins at the world's most respected advertising award shows in branded entertainment and content categories from 2012 to 2015 mainly at Cannes, the CLIO's, the One

Show awards, the WEBBY's, and in two isolated cases at Dubai Lynx and the Media Global Awards.

One participant was interviewed based on referral by participant James Mok, the Executive Creative Director for Asia–Pacific of Foote, Cone and Belding (FCB). This participant, Aste Gutiérrez, was based in China at the time of the interview and is one of the world's highest awarded creative directors and is regarded for consistent excellence in the field of branded content and entertainment (FWA 2017). Thus, 14 interviews were conducted using purposeful sampling and the additional interview was based on referral sampling. Refer to Table 1 for the sample selection.

4 Findings

The key findings on branded entertainment challenges and practical principles to create resonant branded entertainment follow.

4.1 Branded Entertainment's Value in Brand Communication

Overall participants agreed that the core value of branded entertainment as a means of alternative brand contact (North and Enslin 2007) is to break through commercial clutter and arrest the attention of a target audience in a meaningful way. Branded entertainment is becoming strategically more important in brand communication as the fundamental requirement to adhere to demand for entertainment in context of a fragmented and proliferated (mostly digital) mediascape. In addition, target audiences, in particular younger generations, choose to engage with brands that entertain them and branded entertainment has the ability to step up to the challenge. Another benefit that branded entertainment can deliver is that of a richer brand experience, allowing target audiences to either spend more time with the brand or have a higher level of engagement that may increase the possibility for making an emotional connection or active engagement which are both dimensions of brand resonance as stated by Keller (2009). These forms of resonance, identified as branded entertainment's strategic potential, along with the possibility of forming brand community or even possibly loyalty, also resonance dimensions (Keller 2001, 2009), may extrapolate to creating entertainment franchises based on consumer demand.

Table 1 Research sample

Awards (minimum to qualify for the sample selection criteria*)	Campaign	Agency	Participants (job titles as per time of interview)
	North America:		
Cannes Lions GRAND PRIX; CLIO GOLD	Intel & Toshiba's *The Beauty Inside*	Pereira & O'Dell *San Francisco*	Vice President & Executive Creative Director: **(1) Jaime Robinson**
Cannes Lions GOLD; CLIO GOLD	Mattel Inc's *Hot Wheels for Real*	Mistress *Los Angeles*	Founding Partner & Creative Director: **(2) Damien Eley**
Cannes Lions GOLD; CLIO GOLD	Village Voice Newspaper's *New York Writes Itself*	Leo Burnett *New York*	Managing Partner & Executive Creative Director: **(3) Kieran Antill**
	South America:		
Cannes Lions GOLD; The Wave (Latin America's largest advertising festival) GRAND PRIX	Coca Cola's *Coke Thirst Dolby Sound Experience*	J Walter Thompson *São Paulo*	Chief Creative Officer: **(4) Ricardo John**
	Europe:		
Cannes Lions GRAND PRIX; One Show BEST IN SHOW & GOLD in Branded Entertainment category	Volvo Truck's *Live Test Series*	Forsman & Bodenfors *Gothenburg*	Creative Director & Senior Partner: **(5) Björn Engström** Director Strategic Brand & Marketing Communications at Volvo Trucks: **(6) Annika Viberud**
Webby Awards GOLD; ADC Annual Awards (the oldest continuously running industry award show in the world; Part of the One Club for Creativity) GOLD	Deutsche Telekom's *Keep Moving*	DDB Tribal *Berlin*	Strategic Planning Director: **(7) Dr Gordon Euchler**
	Oceania:		
Cannes Lions GOLD; One Show GOLD	SPCA & MINI's *Driving Dogs*	FCB *Auckland*	Asia Pacific Executive Creative Director: **(8) James Mok**

(continued)

Table 1 (continued)

Awards (minimum to qualify for the sample selection criteria*)	Campaign	Agency	Participants (job titles as per time of interview)
	Africa:		
Dubai Lynx GRAND PRIX; Mena Cristals (reward the best advertising creations of the North African and Middle Eastern countries) GOLD	Mobinil's *Dayman Maabaad/ Always Together*	Leo Burnett *Cairo*	Managing Director: **(9) Amr Darwish**
Media Global Awards GOLD; IPRA (International Public Relations Association's communications awards) GOLD; Worth mentioning: GOLD at Africa's highly esteemed PRISM awards	KFC's *Journey of Hope*	Ogilvy *Johannesburg*	Group Account Director: **(10) Lauren McInnes** Senior Copy Writer: **(11) Irene Styger** KFC Senior Brand Manager for Sponsorships and CSI: **(12) Lauren Turnbull**
Cannes Lions GOLD; Loerie Awards GOLD (Largest gathering of brand communication industry in Africa and the Middle East)	Cape Town Tourism's *Send Your Facebook Profile to Cape Town*	Ogilvy *Cape Town*	Senior Art Director: **(13) Dean Paradise** & Senior Copywriter: **(14) Matthew Pullen**
Cannes, D&AD & Clio's, among others, in branded content and entertainment categories	Various	Fred & Farid *Shanghai*	Co-Head of Creative: **(15) Aste Gutiérrez**

*Sample selection criteria; at least a Grand Prix, meaning top honours, or Gold at one internationally acclaimed i.e. highest rated award show specifically in the branded entertainment category: (1) Cannes Lions International Festival of Creativity; (2) Design and Art Direction Awards (D&AD); (3) The One Show; (4) The CLIO Awards; (5) The London International Awards; (6) Dubai Lynx International Festival of Creativity; (7) The Webby Awards; (8) Festival of Media Global Awards; (9) The New York Festivals International Advertising Awards or (10) The ANDY Awards, as well as at least Gold at another award show that is preferably international but could be multi-continental with also an international judging panel (as requisite) that awarded the same piece of creative work

4.2 The Challenges Branded Entertainment is Facing

4.2.1 The Risk Factors

Client-side marketers in general do not necessarily want to dedicate too much resource to branded entertainment that could be seen as relatively high-risk investment with perceivably unreliable or unclear metrics. Branded entertainment could be regarded as high risk because of the unfamiliarity of the practice pertaining to the lack of cohesive understanding of the discipline which is supported by the literature (Wiese 2015; MacCuish 2017). Participant John, for instance, found that clients are more receptive to the idea of branded entertainment when presented with successful case studies. However, participant Gutiérrez warned that brands can fall into the trap of being 'me too' brands, mostly driven by clients' risk-adverse behaviour that fails in its sense of authenticity: 'The challenge is originality! So many clients just want to keep up with the Joneses and do not want to take the risk of creating something completely new and original'.

Findings furthermore suggest that the perception that branded entertainment takes abnormally long to conceptualise and produce, and that media costs are exuberantly more than for the average traditional advertising venture, is not necessarily true. As most branded entertainment is featured on digital media channels that on average costs less than traditional media channels to reach audiences, opportunity exists to invest in better quality content. Many brands also rely on the power of viral to leverage exposure in digital. However, this is dependent on the quality of the content and extent to which audiences resonate with the branded entertainment narrative. Braveness appears to play a pivotal role in deciding to undertake a branded entertainment project, especially in relation to the courage it takes to create original work that pushes boundaries.

4.2.2 Quality and Strategic Brand Building Significance of the Content

The most pertinent and elaborate finding relating to branded entertainment narrative exists in the identification of poor-quality (i.e. not compelling) or strategically insignificant content (i.e. content not conducive to resonance in building brand), as mentioned by most participants. It seems that a fair number of client-side marketers still approach branded entertainment with an overtly sales-orientated mindset (well-disguised advertising-driven attempt) that could taint any authentic narrative intent. This could be attributed to either reverting back to familiar commercial-centered practice or minimising risk of accountability. Paradise, for instance, remarked that 'too many clients in general are too serious about having to sell their product in a promotion piece' (referring to branded entertainment).

This however does not mean that one cannot express brand identity and product benefits in a creative way. Participant Mok argued that entertainment that should include or embody the brand message, and create a 'place for the commercial message' are not mutually exclusive; as long as the balance between the entertainment factor and the commercial message is treated with 'sensitivity' and caution'.

Poor quality content in context of establishing brand resonance could also be due to advertising agency-side strategists and creatives not yet mastering the skill of compelling narrative delivery in entertaining content. This is mainly because in most instances it seems challenging to unlearn advertising-driven thinking and application. Participant Eley said that he thinks industry has 'not looked at the difference between branded entertainment and traditional advertising for a long time'. Participants Eley and Antill caution that 'good' branded entertainment requires an extraordinary amount of effort and many creatives must learn how to approach and master the medium of entertainment and the sensitivity on how the content will be consumed by an intended target audience. Participant Mok hypothesised that agencies that 'miss the mark' are those that do not understand the relevance that the given brand should play in the target audience's lives, as that is the 'starting point' of 'good' branded entertainment. Many participants suggested that industry creatives should get better at telling stories but not at the cost of the brand message.

4.2.3 Nature of the Client-Agency Relationship

Client and agency need to be an aligned team in order to create strategically significant branded entertainment, according to participants Viberut, McInnes and Turnbull. Mutual trust is identified as a central denominator for agency-client relationships in creating branded entertainment for success. Clients interviewed also remarked on agencies having to display appreciation for brand- and marketing managers aligning their internal teams to buy into the idea of branded entertainment, usually with the principal criterium of branded entertainment being appropriate to solve the business challenge at hand, and not just to do it for the sake of doing branded entertainment. Participant Euchler remarked that branded entertainment is certainly not the norm and his advice is that agencies should not try to talk to clients about categories or definitions but rather talk about solutions to clients' problems. He emphasised that the discussion should rather be about solutions and not educating clients on promotional tools or 'categories.' Turnbull indicated very strong support of this notion. Participant Viberud remarked that there should be allowance for initial internal debate between client and agency to '… knock something into shape that is otherwise quite difficult to knock into shape'. She further reasoned that openness; collaboration and a sense of co-accountability make for a favourable and mature approach to branded entertainment from a client-agency relationship perspective.

4.3 Practice Principles for Resonant Branded Entertainment

General advice from participants was to create compelling narrative by means of a simple, unique and provocative idea that constitutes intrigue or drama ('compelling drama' as participant Mok put it), that most importantly speaks of the brand's identity and embodies emotional meaning. A concept with a universal or human truth, profound audience insight or even having the 'mass factor' or wider appeal could evoke engagement, and could even make branded entertainment 'go further' or 'travel' virally, according to participant Gutiérrez, contributing to its scalability and 'shareability'. Participant Mok said that industry has now realized that 'engagement and participation is fundamental to a rich connection' (with the target audience)'. Potential for brand communities and intended or behavioural brand loyalty as result of compelling authentic branded entertainment narrative does exist, however major value, according to some of the participants, are brands that invest in becoming entertainment franchises, like Red Bull and Nike, approaching entertainment strategically for long term brand success.

Participant Robinson also sees this as a strategic benefit of branded entertainment; where audiences want to open themselves up to engage with the brand because of its entertainment value. Audiences are more 'open to storytellers', according to Robinson, compared to advertisers or advertising in the classic sense of the word. She denoted that audiences generally want storytellers to succeed; to entertain them to constitute reaction or evoke emotion, even if the brand states that they are in position as author. Audiences seem to be more forgiving with the brand being placed in the story or the brand acting as catalyst for resolving the catharsis or tension point in the narrative, if they experience it to be compelling and delivered by a brand with genuine intent to entertain the audience. A critical finding of the research; compelling narrative by itself would not necessarily achieve resonance because it lacks the foundation of authentic narrative. It seems like an especially 'dangerous playground', according to participants Pullen and Paradise, as compelling narrative merely for entertainment's sake is highly likely to miss its strategic mark, i.e. to resonate. Findings do however suggest that authentic narrative is the backbone or central point of gravitas which without branded entertainment for resonance would not be able to exist. However, findings suggest that participants could draw comparisons between compelling authentic narrative and resonance. Seven key characteristics that should be evident in creating resonant branded entertainment follow with relation to its ability to evoke resonance.

4.3.1 Branded Entertainment Must Ideally be Generated by the Brand Itself

Most participants indicated that they think the narrative in branded entertainment should be generated by the brand, for it to be deemed authentic and should not be part of a third party's property, as in the case with product placement or sponsorships, for instance. Participant Robinson denoted that ownership gives a brand control over the branded entertainment narrative to such an extent that the brand can '… get an audience member to choose to spend time with your brand and to choose to engage with your brand in a way that they are letting your brand tell a story'. This means that narrative generated by the brand regarded as authentic can get a target audience to buy into the brand and the 'story' it consequently tells, with the probability that more time might be spent in heightened engagement, for instance, which in effect is a dimension of resonance (Keller 2001).

4.3.2 Branded Entertainment Narrative Must Align With the Brand's Identity

Almost all of the participants proactively reasoned that branded entertainment narrative must be brand-identity aligned in order for the branded entertainment to be considered authentic. Participant Engström stated that the brand's identity ought to be 'deeply integrated' into the narrative; to sit at the 'heart' of the narrative. In addition, the brand identity communicated in the narrative must also align with the overarching brand narrative to evoke a sense of trust and credibility that is important to achieve resonance. It also seems that the trust and credibility that a clear brand identity in the narrative offers may evoke engagement and even provide a better possibility for emotional attachment with the brand. Engagement and emotional attachment are two dimensions of resonance (Keller 2001).

4.3.3 Branded Entertainment Narrative Must be Original

The majority of participants indicated that branded entertainment narrative ought to be original as it is deemed as the 'genesis' (Paradise) of a branded entertainment initiative. It should never imitate another idea, especially the mimicking of another successful branded entertainment campaign as a way to minimise client risk as it could permanently harm a brand's credibility. Darwish in particular warned against this, attributing '… why a lot of the branded entertainment isn't particularly that good; because it is a copy of a copy of a copy of a copy'. Findings show that authentic narrative should be original because in addition to brand credibility it can drive brand attachment and engagement. Attachment and engagement are dimensions of brand resonance (Keller 2001). A copy of someone else's idea would be regarded as inauthentic and deplete the potential for brand resonance.

4.3.4 Branded Entertainment Narrative Must Embody Emotional Meaning

Almost all of the participants proactively identified branded entertainment narrative to carry emotional meaning in order for that branded entertainment to be regarded as authentic based on target audience relevance; their attitudes, motivations, behaviours, culture, sub-culture, belief systems, localisms, vernacular and shared experiences are among some of the indicators. This delivered a highly satisfactory return, meaning that this narrative characteristic can be reckoned as one of the more important narrative characteristics for authenticity. The narrative in branded entertainment allows for establishing 'an emotional connection between the product and the content in the way that the audience likes to see it', according to participant John. The findings, among many other as it delivered a very rich dataset, suggest that branded entertainment narrative that can show a values-alignment between the brand and the target-audience is likely to create an attitudinal attachment to the brand (and resonance for that matter) because the narrative is regarded as authentic. It seems that the possibility also may exist to establish or sway a sense of loyalty from consumers, according to participant Darwish. Emotional attachment, engagement and loyalty are dimensions of brand resonance (Keller 2001). This is supported further by the literature (Hudson and Tung 2016; Meyers 2018).

4.3.5 Branded Entertainment Narrative Must Have a Genuine Intent to Entertain

Almost all of the participants proactively identified branded entertainment narrative to have a genuine intent to entertain in order for the branded entertainment to be regarded as authentic. This delivered a highly satisfactory return and can be reckoned as one of the more important narrative characteristics for authenticity. According to participant Eley '… being true to the customer is the guiding light'; meaning that you have their best interest at heart by offering utility in the form of entertainment, never intrusive. Findings suggest that branded entertainment narrative needs to be sincere towards a target audience and must come across as being genuine/ 'for real' due to its honesty, simplicity and humanness. An emotional connection or attitudinal attachment to the brand is identified as dimensions of brand resonance by Keller (2001). It comes across in the findings that a brand should align naturally versus exist in a forced and artificial relationship with the narrative.

4.3.6 Branded Entertainment Narrative Must be Believable

Plausibility or for the branded entertainment narrative to come across as 'genuine', seems to have played a significant role in the various branded entertainment initiatives as indicated by most of the participants. In addition to the literature finding that authentic narrative ought to be believable from a coherence and plausibility point of view (Yale 2012; Patel 2017), participants suggested that the narrative ought to come across as being 'real' (participant Styger) with respect to narrative methods like suspended disbelief, for instance. The narrative should be something that is of 'truth' (participant Euchler) and not something that is engineered to impress without substance. Additionally, the central character in the narrative ought to align with the motivation or intent of the brand for the branded entertainment. Only then would it be found to have integrity, credibility and trustworthiness, and will it propel a target audience engagement, a dimension of resonance as indicated by Keller (2001).

4.3.7 Branded Entertainment Narrative Must Imbue a Sense of Considered Craft

The research findings suggest that craft or a sense of considered craft is a contributing factor to maximise potential for brand resonance that is deeply grounded in authenticity. The branded entertainment narrative must come across as highly considered and 'crafted in a way that speaks of authenticity', participant Antill expressed. He continues to state that authentic narrative in the context of craft is not necessarily budget-dependent. It seems that consideration and craft of branded entertainment narrative speak to 'type' of authenticity (Carroll and Wheaton 2009), love of production, and pride in the brand's original work as author of the entertainment. This means that the brand not only satisfies expectation but it also provides the opportunity to show integrity and to contribute to a positive perception of a brand that may lead to a sense of affinity. Affinity, one can reason, is integral to an emotional connection or attitudinal attachment that is a dimension of brand resonance as indicated by Keller (2001).

5 Conclusions

Branded entertainment's value still evidently lies in its alternative brand contact format and ability to offer rich brand experiences, now becoming more expected by younger generation consumers. Its main challenge still seems to be poor quality content because creating compelling, authentic entertainment narratives are yet to be mastered by advertisers. From the seven branded entertainment principles explored, three seemed to surface significantly more than others: brand identity alignment for strategic significance, emotional meaning embodiment for purposeful entertainment, and a genuine intent to entertain to counter any perception of being an intrusive, well-disguised 'advertising'-driven initiative. The objective of branded entertainment is ultimately to provide utility to target audiences by means of entertainment.

Considering that principle drives practice it can be concluded that authentic branded entertainment narrative that is compelling to a target audience seems to be key to this type of communication effort to achieve brand resonance.

6 Value of the Study

The findings of this research add to the body of knowledge on branded entertainment principles. It can specifically assist brand communication decision makers to strategically plan and creatively produce successful branded entertainment campaigns towards resonance; campaigns that can establish authentic depth in their relationships with consumers, built on trust and integrity.

References

Bothun, D., Vollmer, C. (2016). Entertainment & Media Industry Trends. In: *Strategy &: A PWC report.* https://www.strategyand.pwc.com/perspectives/2016-entertainment-media-industry-trends. Accessed 20 Nov 2016.

Brenner, M. (2015). Millennials Don't Want Ads. They Want Stories. In: *Entrepreneur,* October 22. https://www.entrepreneur.com/article/250243. Accessed 12 Dec 2017.

Carroll, G. R., Wheaton, D. R. (2009). The Organizational Construction of Authenticity: An Examination of Contemporary Food and Dining in the U.S. In: *A Collaboration Between Stanford University and Chicago Magazine.* https://www.faculty-gsb.stanford.edu/carroll/pages/documents/Auth_paper_V94.pdf. Accessed 15 Apr 2015.

Da Costa, C. (2018). How to Create a Brand Story That Connect with Audiences and Drive Sales. In: *Forbes,* January 31. https://www.forbes.com/sites/celinnedacosta/2018/01/

31/how-to-create-a-brand-story-that-connects-with-audiences-and-drives-sales/#5f28a9 873d34. Accessed 15 Sept 2019.

Dams, T. (2019). Branded Content Campaigns Help Ads Cut Through Clutter. In: *Variety*, June 17. https://variety.com/2019/biz/festivals/branded-content-help-commercials-producers-cut-through-ad-clutter-1203238594/. Accessed 23 Jan 2020.

Duopoly (2014). Branded Entertainment: A New Production Financing Paradigm - White Paper 3: The Future of Branded Entertainment. By: *Canadian Media Production Association*, April. https://www.omdc.on.ca/Assets/Research/Research+Reports/The-future-of-branded-entertainment/The-future-of-branded-entertainment_en.pdf. Accessed 15 June 2015.

Emhoff, K. (2016). What Makes Great Branded Entertainment and Content? In: *D&AD*, N.D. https://www.dandad.org/en/d-ad-branded-content-features-opinion/. Accessed 22 Nov 2016.

Figart, Mark (2011): The Five Characteristics of Compelling Content. By: *Digett*, July 21. https://www.digett.com/insights/five-characteristics-compelling-content. Accessed 13 Jan 2020.

FWA (2017). Aste Gutiérrez; Creative Director at BBH Asia Pacific, Handling Regional Nike. In: *The FWA*, April. https://thefwa.com/interviews/aste-gutierrez. Accessed 28 Mar 2018.

Graser, M. (2014). The Best Branded Entertainment of 2014. In: *Variety*, December 22. https://variety.com/2014/biz/news/the-best-branded-entertainment-of-2014-1201373904/. Accessed 7 Sept 2016.

Grinta, E. (2016). The art and science of branded entertainment strategy. In: *Best of Branded Content Marketing*, March 4. https://bobcm.net/2016/03/04/the-art-and-science-of-branded-entertainment-strategy/. Accessed 14 Sept 2016.

Guba, E. G., & Lincoln, Y. S. (1994). Competing paradigms in qualitative research. In N. Denzin & Y. Lincoln (Eds.), *Handbook of Qualitative Research*. Thousand Oaks: Sage.

Huang, R., Lee, S. H., Kim, HaeJung, & Evans, L. (2015). The impact of brand experiences on brand resonance in multi-channel fashion retailing. *Journal of Research in Interactive Marketing, 9*(2), 129–147.

Hudson, S., & Tung, V. (2016). Appealing to tourists via branded entertainment: From theory to practice. *Journal of Travel & Tourism Marketing, 33*(1), 123–137.

Liffreing, I. (2018). The Merging of Advertsing and Entertainment Had Led to Talent Shortfall. In: *Digiday*, February 12. https://digiday.com/marketing/merging-advertising-entertainment-led-talent-shortfall/. Accessed 14 Oct 2019.

Jones, K. (2018). Why Authentic Content Marketing Matters Now More Than Ever. In: *Search Engine Journal*, April 9. https://www.searchenginejournal.com/authentic-content-marketing/239597/. Accessed 16 Sept 2019.

Keller, K. L. (2001). Building Customer-based Brand Equity: A Blueprint for Creating Strong Brands. In: *Marketing Science Institute*, Cambridge, USA: Report no. 01–107. https://anandahussein.lecture.ub.ac.id/files/2015/09/article-4.pdf. Accessed 10 July 2013.

Keller, K. L. (2009). Hitting the Branding Sweet Spot: How to Best Manage Marketing's Trade-offs. In: *Marketing Science Institute: Conference Presentation*. https://www.msi.org/conferences/presentations/hitting-the-branding-sweetspot-how-to-best-manage-marketings-trade-offs/. Accessed 26 Nov 2014.

MacCuish, A. (2017). Branded Entertainment Is Entering a Brave New World. In: *Campaign,* April 21. https://www.campaignlive.co.uk/article/brand-entertainment-entering-brave-new-world/1430950. Accessed 28 Apr 2017.

Maconick, R. (2016). Why Marketers Must Move Beyond 'Branded Content' and Create Entertainment. In: Adweek, October 28, available at https://www.adweek.com/brand-marketing/why-next-step-brands-become-creators-entertainment-174330/. Accessed 14 Jan 2017.

McClure, A. (2020). Meet the Scary New Landscape of Branded Entertainment. In: *Campaign,* January 6. https://www.campaignlive.co.uk/article/meet-scary-new-landscape-brand-funded-entertainment/1668915. Accessed 23 Jan 2020.

Meyers, C. B. (2018). Branded Entertainment Reshapes Media Ecosystem. By: *Carsey-Wolf Center.* https://carseywolf.ucsb.edu/wp-content/uploads/2018/02/Meyers_BrandedEntertainment.pdf. Accessed 20 Apr 2018.

Milena, Z. R., Dainora, G., & Alin, S. (2008). Qualitative research methods: A comparison between focus group and in-depth interview. *Annals of the University of Oradea, Economics Science Series, 17*(4), 1279–1283.

Morrison, M. (2015). No Grand Prix for Branded Content Lions – Again for Second Year Jury Awarded No Top Prize, Citing Lack of Standout Content, Category Definition Issues. In: *Advertising Age,* June 27. https://adage.com/article/special-report-cannes-lions/grand-prix-branded-content-lions/299256/. Accessed 20 Apr 2016.

North, E. J., Enslin, C. (2007). Development of a Conceptual Model to Alternative Brand Contact Planning in the South African Marketing and Communications Industry. *International Retail and Marketing Review, 3*(1), 28–41.

O'Guinn, T., Allen, C., Semenik, R. J. (2009). *Advertising and Integrated Brand Promotion.* USA: South-Western Cengage Learning. 5th Ed.

Patel, S. (2017). How to Use Content to Get Your Audience to Trust You. By: *Content Marketing Institute,* Febraury 12. https://contentmarketinginstitute.com/2017/02/content-audience-trust/. Accessed 12 Dec 2019.

Pereira, P. J. (2017). Branded Entertainment Is Worthy of Your Money and Time. In: *Forbes,* August 24. https://www.forbes.com/sites/forbesagencycouncil/2017/08/24/branded-entertainment-is-worthy-of-your-money-and-time/#187bf8975722. Accessed 14 Jan 2019.

Pereira, P. J. (2018). *The art of branded entertainment.* London: Peter Owen.

Rose, J. (2013). Let Me Entertain You: The Rise of Branded Entertainment. *The Guardian,* September 26. https://www.theguardian.com/media-network/2013/sep/26/branded-entertainment-content-marketing. Accessed 31 Oct 2013.

Ryan, T. (2016). 5 Realities About Branded Entertainment That Every Creator Must Know - The New Form of Advertising: Branded Entertainment. By: *Tar Productions.* https://tarproductions.com/2016/04/26/5-realities-about-branded-entertainment-every-creator-should-know/. Accessed 20 Sept 2016.

Thomas, H. (2009). How to Target an Audience – Version 5: Advertising Funded Programming. By: *Busvannah Communications.* https://www.busvannah.co.za/wp-content/Book_AFP%20-%20Web%20version.pdf. Accessed 7 Oct 2016.

Valero, D. (2014). *Branded entertainment: Deal making strategies & techniques for industry professionals.* Florida: J. Ross Publishing.

Weiss, P. (2014). Branded Content, the Cannes Lions Festival, and the Search for Human Connection. In: *The Content Strategist,* July 15. https://contently.com/strategist/2014/07/

15/%E2%80%8Bbranded-content-the-cannes-lions-festival-and-the-search-for-human-connection/. Accessed 12 Nov 2016.

Wiese, M. (2015). Q&A with Mike Wiese, Chair of Branded Content & Entertainment at Dubai Lynx. By: *J Walter Thompson*, 28 January. https://www.jwt.com/blog/people/qa-with-mike-wiese-chair-of-branded-content-entertainment-at-dubai-lynx/. Accessed 23 Sept 2016.

Woodrooffe, S. (2014). Reimagining Branded Entertainment: Q&A with CAA Marketing's Jesse Coulter. In: *Sparksheet*, May 28. https://sparksheet.com/reimagining-branded-entertainment-qa-caa-marketings-jesse-coulter/. Accessed 6 Sept 2016.

Yale, R. (2012). Narrative Believability Scale. https://www.robertyale.com/nbs-22/. Accessed 27 Mar 2013.

Advertising Music and the Effects of Incongruity Resolution on Consumer Response

Morteza Abolhasani, Steve Oakes, and Zahra Golrokhi

1 Introduction

Music is considered as one of the most important executional cues in advertisements. It is a ubiquitous phenomenon in the context of television and radio advertising, with more than 94% of advertisements incorporating a certain type of music (Allan 2008). Music accounts for a significant commercial advantage in the context of advertising by producing favorable associations with the product/brand (Gorn 1982), contributing to the message (Hung 2000), and by attracting consumers' attention and enhancing message recall (Yalch 1991).

Previous research highlights the effects of various objective characteristics of music such as key and tempo (Kellaris and Kent 1993), complexity (North and Hargreaves 1998), frequency (Sunaga 2018) and volume (Kellaris and Rice 1993), as well as subjective characteristics of music such as liking (Dube et al. 1995),

---

Morteza Abolhasaai I The Open University I Morteza.abolhasani@open.ac.uk
Steve Oakes I University of Liverpool I Sekaos60@liverpool.ac.uk
Zahra Golrokhi I The Open University I Zahra.golrokhi@open.ac.uk

---

M. Abolhasani (✉)
The Open University/Business School, Milton Keynes, UK
E-Mail: Morteza.abolhasani@open.ac.uk

S. Oakes
University of Liverpool/Management School, Liverpool, UK
E-Mail: Sekaos60@liverpool.ac.uk

Z. Golrokhi
School of Engineering & Innovation, The Open University, Milton Keynes, UK
E-Mail: Zahra.golrokhi@open.ac.uk

© The Author(s), under exclusive license to Springer Fachmedien Wiesbaden GmbH, part of Springer Nature 2021
M. Waiguny and S. Rosengren (eds.), *Advances in Advertising Research (Vol. XI)*, European Advertising Academy,
https://doi.org/10.1007/978-3-658-32201-4_13

familiarity (Bailey and Areni 2006), arousal (Mattila and Wirtz 2001), and mood induction (Alpert and Alpert 1990). The existing empirical research (Abolhasani and Oakes 2017; Alpert et al. 2005; North MacKenzie et al. 2004; Oakes and North 2006) mainly addressed the influence of music/advertising congruity and how it enhances communications effectiveness, recall of advertising information, brand attitude, affective response, as well as purchase intent.

To date, little research has focused on the effects of deliberate musical incongruity in advertising on communications effectiveness and reinforcing the advertising proposition. The present research investigates the effects of mildly incongruent music on consumer responses to advertising. Advertising effectiveness depends on the extent to which consumers process the information that is being communicated in a message (Jurca and Madlberger 2015). Advertisers may be able to use the novelty, surprise, or unexpectedness of incongruent music in order to enhance consumers' affective, cognitive, and behavioral responses to advertising. Findings from existing studies using non-musical stimuli provide a theoretical counterargument underpinning the benefits of using incongruity in advertising (e.g., Heckler and Childers 1992). Studies drawing on incongruity, either in non-traditional advertising campaigns such as in-game advertising (Lewis and porter 2010) or in the context of inconsistent brand communication (Halkias and Kokkinaki 2011) suggest that a moderate degree of incongruity positively influences advertising effectiveness. These studies reveal how using information that is incongruent with prior expectations may lead to more effortful and complicated processing, enhancing associative memory pathways. In this context, using a mildly incongruent stimulus may be more effective in penetrating the perceptual screen of an audience to attract attention to the advertisement and enhance the identification of the primary theme and message of the advertisement. To this end, the present research aims to demonstrate the effects of artful musical incongruity (mild incongruity) on consumers' cognitive and behavioral responses to advertising.

2 Twin Components Congruity Framework

Heckler and Childers (1992) propose a general framework for congruity that postulates two components; *relevancy* and *expectancy*. While Heckler and Childers' (1992) study investigates the effects of congruity in the context of print advertising, the present study attempts to redefine and refine the twin component distinction as the framework for congruity to examine the impact of in/congruity between the advertising message and music. A key objective of this research is to integrate *country of origin musical congruity* and *genre congruity* in a single congruity framework through focusing more closely upon the twin components of congruity (relevancy and expectancy). A further objective is to examine how various quadrants of musical congruity (discussed in the context of print advertising by Heckler and Childers 1992) including relevant/unexpected, relevant/unexpected, irrelevant/expected, and irrelevant/unexpected influence consumers' cognitive and behavioral responses in the context of music and advertising.

Hypotheses

Although existing research studies examine the effects of background music on recall (e.g., Oakes and North 2006; Fraser and Bradford 2013; Guido et al. 2016; North et al. 2016), they have not addressed the question using unexpected/relevant music. Unexpected information presents a diversion from the norm and attracts viewers' attention more than expected information (Haberland and Dacin 1992).

Consumers' attitudes towards the advertisement represent individuals' internal evaluations of the overall advertising stimulus. Resource matching notions (Meyers-Levy and Peracchio 1995) seem to provide a valuable perspective regarding the complex relationship between music-message congruity, cognitive processing, and attitudes. This framework suggests that music incongruent with an advertising message may consume cognitive resources, thus inhibiting processing which may lead to adversely affecting consumer attitudes towards the advertisement. However, regarding moderate incongruity when using an unexpected but relevant piece of music, the underlying meaning of purposeful musical incongruity may be resolved through allocation of cognitive resources, thus enhancing attitude through a pleasurable resolution of the detected musical incongruity in the advertisement.

Various pieces of music may portray different meaning and images. For example, classical music is considered to be sophisticated, upscale, prestigious, and high quality, whereas dance music may be considered to be hedonic, exciting and trendy (North and Hargreaves 1998). Various genres of music associate different genre-related qualities or attributes to the brand image. For example, attributes of various pieces of music used in a restaurant advertisement may be transferred to the restaurant brand, forming a distinctive image for the advertised restaurant.

It is proposed that musical expectancy influences attention, depth of processing, and image (Craton et al. 2017). However, extreme violation of musical expectations may demand a high level of attention that could make the music the center of attention, and compete for cognitive resources that would otherwise be used for processing the advertising information. The mildly incongruent treatment (unexpected/relevant) may enhance brand image as a result of the successful incongruity resolution that takes place in the minds of consumers.

The existing literature has investigated the influence of background music on a range of restaurant patrons' behavior such as flavor pleasantness and overall impression of food (Fiegel et al. 2014) and consumer spending (North et al. 2003), but there is a lack of research investigating the effects of background music in advertisements on expectations of food and service quality. While the Mehrabian-Russel model (Mehrabian and Russel 1974) proposes that individuals respond emotionally to environmental stimuli such as background music, leading to an approach-avoidance behavior, background music in advertisements may also affect consumers' responses to advertisements.

Research (e.g., Abolhasani et al. 2017) demonstrates how selecting a congruously perceived genre of music enhances consumers' purchase intent. However, the mild incongruity as a result of selecting an unexpected/relevant musical genre may be resolved by the consumers in an equally successful manner. This fruitful incongruity resolution may be a reinforcing element in enhancing purchase intent. Therefore, from the discussions above, it can be proposed that:

H1. Unexpected/relevant music in advertising enhances consumers' recall of information.

H2. Unexpected/relevant music in advertising produces the most favorable attitudes towards the advertisement.

H3. Unexpected/relevant music in advertising enhances consumers' perceived image of the advertised restaurant.

H4. Unexpected/relevant music enhances consumers' expectation of food and service quality.

H5. Unexpected/relevant music enhances consumers' purchase intent.

3 Design and Participants

An advertisement copy was recorded to promote a fictitious, authentically Italian restaurant. Brief excerpts of vocal pieces of music were used in advertisement copies to be prepared for the manipulation checks. Stimulus congruity was manipulated in a pre-test involving eight treatments through within-subjects design in which all the participants in the manipulation checks were exposed to every treatment. This would establish the efficacy of the musical manipulations representing the different treatment conditions of *relevancy* and *expectancy*. An objective of conducting the manipulation test was to inform choice of musical treatments for relevancy/expectancy quadrants.

Having established the final four musical treatments (Fig. 1), a between-subjects design was initiated through which each group of participants were exposed to only one advertisement treatment and asked to answer a set of questions. A total of 141 first year undergraduate students participated in the experiment; 33 in the "Expected/Irrelevant", 35 in the "Expected/Relevant", 37 in the "Unexpected/Irrelevant", and 36 in the "Unexpected/Relevant" treatments. The mean age of participants was 18.6, and the genr distribution was 62% male and 38% female.

		RELEVANCY	
		RELEVANT	*IRRELEVANT*
EXPECTANCY	*EXPECTED*	Expected/Relevant (congruent) Italian Opera, Pavarotti "La Dona e Mobile"	Expected/Irrelevant (Incongruent) Italian Reggae, Roberto Ferri "Italian Brothers Reggae"
	UNEXPECTED	Unexpected/Relevant (Mildly Incongruent) Opera Reggae Mashup, Puccini Verdi feat Donizetti Rossini "Pasta Grooves"	Unexpected/Irrelevant (Severely Incongruent) Caribbean Reggae, El Chacal "Pa' la Camara"

Fig. 1 Musical in/congruity quadrants

4 Findings

The findings presented in this section illustrate how purposeful use of unexpected/relevant music representing an artful musical incongruity may positively affect consumers' responses to advertising through examining the impacts on a range of dependent variables including recall of information, attitude towards the advertisement, perceived image of the brand, perceived quality, as well as purchase intent.

4.1 Mild (moderate) Musical Incongruity and its Effects on Recall of Advertising Information

H1 of the present study tests whether *unexpected/relevant music in advertising will enhance consumers' recall of information*. The recall of advertising information in various in/congruity quadrants was examined through three different measures.

The first measure to examine recall was the extent to which participants exposed to various quadrants were able to recall the restaurant *brand name*. For this purpose, a frequency test was conducted which revealed that a higher percentage of participants listening to the unexpected/relevant treatment (91.7%) recalled the brand name correctly, while this figure was 85.7% for expected/relevant, 78.8% for expected/irrelevant, and 73% for unexpected/irrelevant treatments.

The second measure to examine recall of information was the extent to which participants were able to recall the *advertising slogan*. A frequency test showed that the unexpected/relevant quadrant produced the highest level for recall of advertising slogan (86.1%), while this figure was 77.1% for expected/relevant, 75.8% for expected/irrelevant, and 75.7% for unexpected/irrelevant quadrants.

Furthermore, an ANOVA test revealed a statistically significant difference between in/congruity quadrants in recalling the *advertising claims*, thus supporting *H1*:

- Recall of advertising claims ($F(3, 137) = 5.08; p < 0.01$)

A Tukey test revealed that the unexpected/relevant ($M = 3.92, SD = 0.97$) quadrant produced a significantly higher level of recall of advertising claims compared to expected/irrelevant ($M = 3.21, SD = 1.05$) and unexpected/irrelevant ($M = 3.14, SD = 1.00$) quadrants. There was no significant difference in recalling advertising claims between unexpected/relevant ($M = 3.92, SD = 0.97$) and expected/relevant ($M = 3.66$, $SD = 0.91$) or between any other combination of quadrants.

4.2 Effects of Unexpected/Relevant Music on Ad Attitude

ANOVA test results revealed a statistically significant difference between treatments in terms of the influence of various in/congruity quadrants on the attitude towards the advertisement, partially supporting *H2* revealing that *unexpected/relevant music in advertising will produce the most favourable attitudes towards the advertisement:*

- Enjoyable/Not enjoyable ($F(3, 137) = 8.06$; $p < 0.001$)
- Not entertaining/Entertaining ($F(3, 137) = 5.25$; $p < 0.01$)

4.3 Mild Musical Incongruity and its Impact on Perceived Image of The Brand

One-way ANOVA results demonstrated a statistically significant difference between in/congruity quadrants in terms of the influence on the perceived restaurant image for all of the items, thus supporting *H3* revealing that *unexpected/relevant music in advertising will enhance consumers' perceived image of the restaurant:*

- Dull/Exciting ($F(3, 137) = 26.79$; $p < 0.001$)
- Pleasant/Unpleasant ($F(3, 137) = 31.35$; $p < 0.001$)
- Tense/Relaxing ($F(3, 137) = 44.65$; $p < 0.001$)
- Uncool/Cool ($F(3, 137) = 32.45$; $p < 0.001$)
- Appealing/Unappealing ($F(3, 137) = 25.12$; $p < 0.001$)

4.4 Impact of Mild Incongruity on Expectation of Quality

ANOVA tests revealed a statistically significant difference between in/congruity quadrants in perception of food and service quality, partially supporting *H4* indicating that *unexpected/relevant music will enhance consumers' expectation of food quality:*

- Food quality ($F(3, 137) = 12.77$, $p < 0.001$)
- Service quality ($F(3, 137) = 5.95$, $p < 0.01$)

4.5 Mild Incongruity in Advertisements and Consumers' Purchase Intent

An ANOVA test revealed a statistically significant difference between different in/congruity quadrants in terms of consumers' purchase intention, thus supporting *H5* revealing that *unexpected/relevant music will enhance consumers' purchase intent:*

- Purchase intention ($F(3, 137) = 19.88$), $p < 0.01$)

A Tukey test revealed that the unexpected/relevant ($M = 3.39$, $SD = 0.96$) quadrant produced a significantly higher intention to visit the restaurant amongst participants compared to expected/irrelevant ($M = 2.70$, $SD = 0.98$) and unexpected/irrelevant ($M = 2.51$, $SD = 1.02$) quadrants. There was no significant difference in purchase intent between unexpected/relevant ($M = 3.39$, $SD = 0.96$) and expected/relevant ($M = 3.17$, $SD = 0.92$) quadrants or between any other in/congruity quadrants.

5 Discussion

The current study developed, refined, and redefined the concept of musical congruity in advertising through adapting Heckler and Childers' (1992) congruity model. Findings indicate how the deliberate crafting of musical incongruity can be used to engage and amuse consumers, and advocate a hypothetical continuum of artful, deliberate deviation of musical incongruity proposing that resolving such musical incongruity may enhance consumers' responses such as recall, ad attitude, perception of brand image and quality, as well as their purchase intent. The findings suggest that the unexpected/relevant incongruity quadrant represented by Italian opera/reggae mashup produced the highest level of recall for all three recall components. Findings emphasize the importance of contextual incongruity to the aesthetic and indicate how the unexpected combining of two songs from contrasting genres (opera and reggae) may often create humorous effects capable of generating more cognitive resources to resolve the incongruity.

Drawing on Mandler's schema incongruity theory (1982), the current study depicts resolution strategies for incongruity related to different changes in schema structure. The findings reveal that the internal processing activities consumers embrace in an attempt to resolve varying levels of incongruity may have evident consequences for their cognitive and affective (reflected in perceptions, recall, attitude formation, and persuasion) responses to advertising. This confirms the argument made by schema incongruity theory that moderate schema-stimulus discrepancies can be successfully resolved, resulting in more positive subsequent responses through a psychological reward mechanism (Mandler 1982; Meyers-Levy and Tybout 1989). Such positive affect is believed to result from increased feelings of control and self-efficacy accompanying the "I get it" response (Bandura 1977). Positive feelings and emotions combined with a continued cognitive appreciation of resolution are then likely to enhance attitudes, perceptions, and evaluations of the advertisement and the brand.

6 Conclusion

It has been observed that the existing research around the use of incongruity in advertisements does not produce conclusive findings (Halkias and Kokkinaki 2014; Segev et al. 2014). For instance, Torn and Dahlen (2007) reveal how the discrepancy between the advertisement and brand schema may result in increasing attention, better recall, and a more positive ad attitude, compared to congruent advertisements. On the other hand, Dahlen et al. (2008) demonstrate that the incongruity between advertisement and the brand may reduce the credibility of the ad and lead to lower ad attitude, compared to congruity. The review of literature, however, shows that the existing studies implement a dichotomous operationalization of incongruity that solely discerns what is congruent and what is not, neglecting the differences in the level of incongruity (Jhang et al. 2012; Han et al. 2013). The current research addressed this flaw in the context of musical incongruity in advertising, demonstrating how mild musical incongruity in advertising enables consumers to focus their attention and allows them to muster accessible cognitive resources for an intentional exploration of the incongruent event, resulting in enhancing consumers' affective, cognitive, and behavioral responses to advertising through resolving the incongruity.

References

Abolhasani, M., Oakes, S., & Oakes, H. (2017). Music in advertising and consumer identity: The search for Heideggerian authenticity. *Marketing Theory, 17*(4), 473–490.

Alpert, M. I., Alpert, J. I., & Maltz, E. N. (2005). Purchase occasion influence on the role of music in advertising. *Journal of Business Research, 58*(3), 369–376.

Alpert, J. I., & Alpert, M. I. (1990). Music influences on mood and purchase intentions. *Psychology & Marketing, 7*(2), 109–133.

Allan, D. (2008). A content analysis of music placement in prime-time television advertising. *Journal of Advertising Research, 48*(3), 404–417.

Bailey, N., & Areni, C. S. (2006). When a few minutes sound like a lifetime: Does atmospheric music expand or contract perceived time? *Journal of Retailing, 82*(3), 189–202.

Bandura, A. (1977). *Social learning theory*. Englewood Cliffs: Prentice Hall.

Craton, L. G., Lantos, G. P., & Leventhal, R. C. (2017). Results may vary: Overcoming variability in consumer response to advertising music. *Psychology & Marketing, 34*(1), 19–39.

Dahlen, M., Rosengren, S., Törn, F., & Öhman, N. (2008). Could placing ads wrong be right? Advertising effects of thematic incongruence. *Journal of Advertising, 37*(3), 57–67.

Dube, L., Chebat, J. C., & Morin, S. (1995). The effects of background music on consumers' desire to affiliate in buyer-seller interactions. *Psychology & Marketing, 12*(4), 305–319.

Fiegel, A., Meullenet, J. F., Harrington, R. J., Humble, R., & Seo, H. S. (2014). Background music genre can modulate flavor pleasantness and overall impression of food stimuli. *Appetite, 76,* 144–152.

Fraser, C., & Bradford, J. A. (2013). Music to your brain: Background music changes are processed first, reducing ad message recall. *Psychology & Marketing, 30*(1), 62–75.

Gorn, G. J. (1982). The effects of music in advertising on choice behavior: A classical conditioning approach. *the Journal of Marketing, 46*(1), 94–101.

Guido, G., Peluso, A. M., Mileti, A., Capestro, M., Cambo, L., & Pisanello, P. (2016). Effects of background music endings on consumer memory in advertising. *International Journal of Advertising, 35*(3), 504–518.

Haberland, G. S., & Dacin, P. A. (1992). The development of a measure to assess viewers' judgments of the creativity of an advertisement: A preliminary study. *NA-Advances in Consumer Research, 19*(1), 818–825.

Halkias, G., & Kokkinaki, F. (2011). Increasing advertising effectiveness through incongruity-based tactics: The moderating role of consumer involvement. *Journal of Marketing Communications, 19*(3), 1–16.

Halkias, G., & Kokkinaki, F. (2014). The degree of ad-brand incongruity and the distinction between schema-driven and stimulus-driven attitudes. *Journal of Advertising, 43*(4), 397–409.

Han, S., Choi, J., Kim, H., Davis, J. A., & Lee, K. Y. (2013). The effectiveness of image congruence and the moderating effects of sponsor motive and cheering event fit in sponsorship. *International Journal of Advertising, 32*(2), 301–317.

Heckler, S. E., & Childers, T. L. (1992). The Role of expectancy and relevancy in memory for verbal and visual information: What Is incongruency? *Journal of Consumer Research, 18*(4), 475–492.

Hung, K. (2000). Narrative music in congruent and incongruent tv advertising. *Journal of Advertising, 29*(1), 25–34.
Jhang, J. H., Grant, S. J., & Campbell, M. C. (2012). Get it? Got it. Good! Enhancing new product acceptance by facilitating resolution of extreme incongruity. *Journal of Marketing Research, 49*(2), 247–259.
Jurca, M. A., & Madlberger, M. (2015). Ambient advertising characteristics and schema incongruity as drivers of advertising effectiveness. *Journal of Marketing Communications, 21*(1), 48–64.
Kellaris, J. J., Cox, A. D. & Cox, D. (1993). The effect of background music on ad processing: A contingency explanation. *Journal of Marketing, 57*(4), 114–125.
Lewis, B., & Porter, L. (2010). In-game advertising effects: Examining player perceptions of advertising schema congruity in a massively multiplayer online role-playing game. *Journal of Interactive Advertising, 10*(2), 46–60.
Mandler, G. (1982). The structure of value: Accounting for taste. In S.C. H. Margaret & S.T. Fiske (eds.), *Affect and cognition* (pp. 3–36). Hillsday: Lawrence Erlbaum.
Mattila, A. S., & Wirtz, J. (2001). Congruency of scent and music as a driver of in-store evaluations and behavior. *Journal of Retailing, 77*(2), 273–289.
Mehrabian, A., & Russell, J. A. (1974). *An approach to environmental psychology*. Boston: MIT Press.
Meyers-Levy, J., & Peracchio, L. A. (1995). Understanding the effects of color: How the correspondence between available and required resources affects attitudes. *Journal of Consumer Research, 22*(2), 121–138.
Meyers-Levy, J., & Tybout, A. M. (1989). Schema congruity as a basis for product evaluation. *Journal of Consumer Research, 16*(1), 39–54.
North, A. C., & Hargreaves, D. J. (1998). The effect of music on atmosphere and purchase intentions in a Cafeterial. *Journal of Applied Social Psychology, 28*(24), 2254–2273.
North, A. C., Mackenzie, L. C., Law, R. M., & Hargreaves, D. J. (2004). The effects of musical and voice "Fit" on responses to advertisements. *Journal of Applied Social Psychology, 34*(8), 1675–1708.
North, A. C., Sheridan, L. P., & Areni, C. S. (2016). Music congruity effects on product memory, perception, and choice. *Journal of Retailing, 92*(1), 83–95.
North, A. C., Shilcock, A., & Hargreaves, D. J. (2003). The effect of musical style on restaurant customers' spending. *Environment and Behavior, 35*(5), 712–718.
Oakes, S., & North, A. (2006). The impact of background musical tempo and timbre congruity upon ad content recall and affective response. *Applied Cognitive Psychology, 20*(4), 505–520.
Segev, S., Ruvio, A., Shoham, A., & Velan, D. (2014). Acculturation and consumer loyalty among immigrants: A cross-national study. *European Journal of Marketing, 48*(9/10), 1579–1599.
Sunaga, T. (2018). How the sound frequency of background music influences consumers' perceptions and decision making. *Psychology & Marketing, 35*(4), 253–267.
Torn, F., & Dahlen, M. (2007). Effects of brand incongruent advertising in competitive settings. *ACR European Advances*.
Yalch, R. F. (1991). Memory in jingle jungle: Music as a mnemonic device in communicating advertising slogans. *Journal of Applied Psychology, 76*(2), 268–275.

The Sound Factor in Autoplay Mobile Video Ads

Eunah Kim and Jisu Huh

1   Introduction

Autoplay video ads, defined as "a video ad or an ad linked with video content that initiates "play" without user interaction or without an explicit action to start the video (essentially automatically starting without a "play" button being clicked by the user)" (IAB 2018), are widely adopted across different digital media platforms. While autoplay video ads can be displayed with either 'sound-on' or 'sound-off,' many ads default to the sound-on option to draw more attention from viewers. While sound-on autoplay video ads can be effective in capturing viewer attention, concerns have been raised over their potentially negative impacts on consumer reactions, because such ads could disturb consumers by the sudden burst of sound and the forced attention caused by the sound could be highly annoying (Spartz 2017).

The potentially negative effects of autoplay sound-on video ads on viewers' responses could be even more problematic when these ads are shown on mobile devices. As most people carry their smartphones with them everywhere, including public places, there is a good chance that sound-on video ads would automatically start to play, making an unexpected noise at ill-timed moments. If your phone makes sudden noise because of a video ad automatically playing in public spaces, such as on a bus or in a classroom, you would be surprised and might be

E. Kim (✉) · J. Huh
University of Minnesota, Minneapolis, USA
E-Mail: kimx5125@umn.edu

J. Huh
E-Mail: jhuh@umn.edu

embarrassed by the sudden sound, which would likely cause negative reaction to the ad. While most other types of advertising designed to draw higher attention only impact the viewers, autoplay sound-on video ads playing on mobile devices can impact not only the viewers but also others nearby.

Despite the growing attention to autoplay mobile video ads and the controversies surrounding the sound-on play option, previous studies on digital video advertising have primarily focused on video ads in non-mobile media contexts (e.g. Lee and Lee 2011; Li and Lo 2015). In addition, to our best knowledge, no prior research has investigated the effects of autoplay video ads by comparing the sound-on and sound-off conditions in the mobile media context.

To fill the research gap and to advance the emerging research on digital video advertising, this study investigates the effects of autoplay video ads in mobile apps, with a specific focus on how the presence of sound at the start of the autoplay video ad affects consumers' brand-related memory and attitudes in both short-term and longer-term. As a theoretical framework, the limited capacity model of mediated message processing (LCMP) is applied to predict potentially different effects of sound-on and sound-off autoplay video ads on consumers' memory. Expectancy violation theory (EVT) is also applied to examine effects of sound-on vs. sound-off autoplay video ads on consumers' attitudinal reactions at the time of ad exposure. Additionally, changes in consumer attitudes toward the ad and the brand over time are predicted based on the mere exposure effect. The following section will review these theories and related research, which will lead to the development of hypotheses for this study.

2 Literature Review

2.1 LCMP and Sound-On vs. Sound-Off Mobile Video Ad Effects On Memory

Attention to media messages and subsequent memory outcomes have been examined through various theoretical frameworks. Among the different theories, LCMP provides an excellent theoretical guidance for investigating whether sound-on vs. sound-off autoplay mobile video ads would lead to different consumer responses in terms of attention and memory.

LCMP, which was originally developed to investigate television message processing, theorizes that information processing occurs through three sub-processes: information encoding, storage, and retrieval (Lang 2000). In an encoding process, where individuals are exposed to a mediated message, it is determined which information will be transformed into mental representation for further processing. This process can occur with or without the message recipient's intention. When information is intentionally selected, individuals pay conscious attention to the particular information based on their selection goals or needs, whereas automatic selection happens without the message recipient's intention and it is driven by particular message elements or characteristics that elicit orienting responses. Second, storage is the process where the selected information is stored in memory. In this process, the association between the previously encoded information and new information facilitates the information storage. Last, retrieval is the subprocess of reactivating a specific piece of stored information in working memory, which is considered the outcome of learning (Lang 2000).

Research has demonstrated that message stimuli including unexpected occurrences, changes, or novelty can facilitate automatic selection of information for encoding (Graham 1997), which affects the outcome of information processing. Because humans have limited cognitive resources, such stimuli that stand out from their environment are more likely to get attention for further information processing, and in turn, receive cognitive resources for the process (Lang 2006). That is, cognitive allocation in the encoding process may lead to higher levels of attention and facilitate further steps of information processing.

Applying LCMP to the current study, if you hear a sudden sound from an autoplay video ad while using a mobile app, more cognitive resources would be allocated to the ad regardless of your intention. The allocated cognitive resources will be used to transform ad-related information into mental representation. In contrast, when exposed to a sound-off video ad, fewer cognitive resources would be allocated to the ad while primary cognitive resources will be used for processing the mobile app content that is being used. Therefore, a sound-on autoplay ad would consume more cognitive resources for information encoding and, in turn, generate stronger memory of the ad. Thus, it is predicted:

H1: A sound-on autoplay mobile video ad will generate stronger memory of a) the ad and b) the advertised brand than a sound-off ad.

2.2 EVT and Sound-On vs. Sound-Off Mobile Video Ad Effects On Attitude

While sound-on autoplay video ads are predicted to receive more attention and generate stronger memory than sound-off ads, questions remain as to whether sound-on autoplay ads would cause a positive or negative impact on consumer attitudes. Guided by Expectancy Violations Theory (EVT), this study predicts that consumer expectancy about mobile ads in general can affect their attitudes toward the ad and the brand. EVT, proposed by Burgoon (1978), posits that individuals hold certain expectations of what will happen in social situations, such as communication events. According to this theory, individuals anticipate others' behavior in social situations and evaluate the actions in terms of the congruence with their expectations of acceptable actions within each situation (Burgoon and Hale 1988). Then, whether the expectancy is met or violated, and if the expectancy violation is regarded as positive or negative, will impact communication outcomes (Burgoon et al. 2016). A negative violation occurs when the actual behavior is less favorable than the expectancy, and this would elicit more negative outcomes than when the expectancy is met.

While EVT was originally developed to explain individuals' expectancy and expectancy violation in interpersonal communication, this theory has been applied to the mediated communication context as well. Previous studies have demonstrated that humans also consider non-human objects, such as communication media, as social actors and hold expectations about them (e.g. Leshner et al. 1998), which extends the possible application of EVT to other types of communication than interpersonal communication. In addition, Siegel and Burgoon (2002) suggest that individuals have expectations about communication messages, and the violation of the established expectations about the messages can affect message effectiveness.

According to EVT, consumers would have certain expectancy about mobile communication and mobile ads based on their knowledge and experience. The violation or confirmation of such expectancy can influence consumer reactions to sound-on vs. sound-off autoplay mobile video ads. Particularly, mobile media users would likely hold expectancy about the extent to which they can control their mobile media use experience. Because digital media provides greater user control than traditional media (McMillan and Hwang 2002), when consumers feel that certain mobile ads cause loss of control, they would likely perceive the ads as more intrusive than those in the traditional media environment. As a result, the perceived annoyance or intrusiveness of the ads could lead to negative attitudes toward the ad and a negative impact on brand attitudes (MacKenzie and Lutz 1989).

Applying this reasoning to the current study, when consumers are exposed to a sound-on autoplay video ad while using their mobile devices, they would likely perceive the ad as intrusive, and feel their control over their media experience is reduced, leading to negative attitude toward the ad and the brand. In addition, as research has suggested, consumer attitudes toward ads tend to differ across different media (Logan 2013), and consumers' perceptions about their mobile devices can influence their attitudinal responses to sound-on vs. sound-off mobile autoplay video ads. As a majority of today's smartphone users keep their phones on themselves or nearby almost all the time during their waking hours (Pew Research Center 2015), people use mobile phones not only when they are alone in private but also when they are out in public spaces. When individuals experience a sound-on autoplay video ad while using mobile phones in places where sounded media use is not expected, such as in public transportation or in a work meeting, the sound coming from their devices can irritate and embarrass the mobile phone users, which may generate negative attitudes toward the ad and brand. Thus, the following hypotheses are posed:

> H2: A sound-on autoplay mobile video ad will generate more negative attitudes toward a) the ad and b) the brand than a sound-off ad.
>
> H3: Expectancy about mobile video ads will moderate the effect of the sound-on vs. sound-off variable on consumer attitudes. Specifically, the negative effect of a sound-on mobile video ad will be lower among those with higher expectancy of sound-on mobile video ads.

2.3 Mere Exposure and Delayed Effects of Sound on Attitudes

Although sound-on autoplay video ads may elicit more negative attitudes than sound-off ads at the time of ad exposure, one might question whether consumers' attitudes might change over time, especially due to the superior memory effect of sound-on video ads. The research on delayed effects of ads, which primarily focuses on the impact of ad repetition, suggests that attitudinal responses are more likely to decay over time while memory effects remains relatively stable. For example, Kronrod and Huber (2018) found that a more frequently advertised brand led to higher annoyance at the time of advertising but, several weeks later, consumers developed greater preference for the brand. Possible explanation for this finding is that, while brand memory tends to remain relatively stable, initial annoyance caused by ad repetition seem to fade. In addition, research has shown that higher brand memory enhances consumers' familiarity with the ad and the advertised brand, which, in turn, exerts a positive impact on brand attitude (Fang et al. 2007).

Delayed ad effects enhancing attitudes based on familiarity can be explained by mere exposure effect theory. Mere exposure effect posits that people tend to develop preference for a stimulus they have been previously exposed to because the mere exposure makes the stimulus more accessible to their perception than others (Zajonc 2001). Although there have been arguments over whether the mere exposure effect is a product of implicit processing or not (Stafford and Grimes 2012), researchers suggest that exposure to an object elicits a sense of familiarity that makes the object less threatening, leading to more favorable attitudes toward it (Janiszewski 1993; Zajonc 2001). Indeed, empirical research has established that mere exposure to ads can influence attitude toward the ad and the advertised brand (Janiszewski 1993). According to the perspective of familiarity-based mere exposure effect, consumer memory would likely enhance familiarity, which can elicit a positive impact on attitudinal reactions (Campbell and Keller 2003; Janiszewski and Meyvis 2001). Applying this logic, if sound-on autoplay video ads catch more attention from consumers and are better remembered than sound-off ads, as expected in Hypothesis 1, consumers' initial negative reaction to sound-on video ads could turn into more positive attitudes over time due to enhanced familiarity. Thus, we predict:

> H4: A sound-on autoplay mobile video ad will generate a positive attitude change over time (i.e., relatively more positive attitude at a later time than attitude immediately after ad exposure), while such attitude change will not likely occur with a sound-off ad.

3   Method

3.1   Study Design and Stimuli

An experiment was conducted with a between-subjects design with two experimental conditions: autoplay mobile app video ads with either 1) sound-on or 2) sound-off. To investigate both immediate and delayed ad effects, the data collection was performed in two stages: post-exposure measurement (Time 1) and week-after measurement (Time 2). For experimental stimuli, a mock mobile app was built for Android mobile devices by using Android Studio, and autoplay video ads for fictitious brands were created and inserted into the mock mobile app (Fig. 1). The mobile app was created as a home decoration advice app, because home design apps typically consist of silent content, such as text or images rather than videos, which can make sound-on autoplay video ads stand out more prominently. The main page of the app presented pictures of three different concepts for home design: contemporary, traditional, and farmhouse. When participants

Fig. 1 Mock mobile app including an autoplay video ad stimulus

tapped on one of these pictures, they were directed to a linked page presenting more pictures and related information under the selected design concept.

The experimental treatment video ad was placed on one of the linked pages. To enhance external validity, ads for two different product categories (an app-based food delivery service and a travel information website) were initially used, resulting in a total of four video ads. The video ads were created by editing existing ads for each product category. One ad for each product was set for autoplay with sound on by default, and the other for autoplay with sound off. Each video ad had a run time of 15 seconds. Fictitious brand names were used for all video ads to ensure no bias caused by any pre-existing brand familiarity or attitudes. Brand names were presented throughout the duration of the ads on the lower left corner of the screen and also shown on the center of the screen at the end.

The experimental stimuli and questionnaires were pre-tested in a pilot study ($N = 19$). The results showed that five out of seven participants who viewed the ad for the travel information website did not remember the ad at all regardless of the experimental conditions; whereas all but one participant who viewed the app-based delivery service ad remembered the ad. The possible explanation for this result might be that the ad for the app-based delivery service included many eye-catching elements, such as vivid colors and anthropomorphized objects, while the travel website ad did not have such attention-grabbing elements. Since the purpose of the main study was to examine whether sound-on and sound-off ads draw different levels of attention from consumers, we decided to use only the app-based delivery ads for the main study.

3.2 Participants and Procedure

A total of 105 undergraduate students were recruited in exchange for extra course credit. To disguise the original purpose of the study, participants were told that this study was conducted to test a new mobile app that would be launched soon. To approximate a naturalistic setting where participants would typically use their phones out in public, the data collection was carried out at a student lounge on a university campus, instead of a controlled research lab environment. The student lounge was furnished with sofas and tables and also had several TV screens on the wall, and oftentimes crowded.

Upon arrival at the study location, participants were randomly assigned to one of the experimental conditions (sound-on vs. -off) and were provided with a smartphone with the mock mobile app pre-installed. When participants tapped on one of the three home design themes on the main page, they were directed to pages presenting text and images related to the corresponding design theme. On one of the pages of the mobile app, a video ad automatically played with sound on or off, depending on the assigned condition. Participants were asked to browse all pages in the mobile app to make sure that they were exposed to the video ad inserted on one of the pages. After browsing the app as long as they wanted, participants were asked to fill out a printed questionnaire on their app use experiences, including their memory and attitude toward the video ad they saw.

A week later, participants received an email asking to participate in the follow-up study, which was executed online through Qualtrics. The length of time delay was determined based on the previous studies that examined delayed effects (e.g. Burke and Edell 1986). Only participants who had reported that they had noticed the video ad at Time 1 were invited to the online follow-up (Time 2). Each participant's responses collected at the two different stages were matched for statistical analysis using the email addresses that participants provided.

3.3 Measures

In both stages of data collection, a screening question was asked about whether participants noticed and remembered the video ad placed inside the mobile app, those who did not remember the ad were excluded from the analysis. Regarding ad recall, unaided ad recall and ad content recall were measured. First, unaided ad recall was measured in the post-exposure questionnaire by asking participants to write down everything they remembered about the mobile app they used. The presence of ad-related mentions in participants' responses was coded dichotomously ($1 = yes$, $0 = no$). For ad content recall, participants were asked to write down any of the ad content they could recall, which the number of elements correctly mentioned was counted. While unaided recall of the ad was measured only in the post-exposure questionnaire, ad content recall was measured in both of the data collection stages. Brand recall was measured by asking participants to write down the brand name shown in the ad. The responses were coded into three categories ($2 = correct$, $1 = partially correct$, $0 = incorrect/I don't know$). For brand recognition, participants were instructed to choose one out of the four possible answer choices. Brand recall and recognition were assessed at both Time 1 and Time 2.

Attitude toward the ad was measured using nine 7-point semantic differential scales (Laczniak and Muehling 1993), anchored by *not attractive-attractive, bad-good, unpleasant-pleasant, unappealing-appealing, dull-dynamic, depressing-refreshing, not enjoyable-enjoyable, uninteresting-interesting, not likable-likable* (Cronbach's $\alpha = 0.93$). Brand attitude was measured by five 7-point semantic differential scales, anchored by *unappealing-appealing, bad-good, unpleasant-pleasant, unfavorable-favorable, unlikable-likable* (Cronbach's $\alpha = 0.96$). Attitudes toward the ad and the brand were measured at both Time 1 and Time 2.

Participants' expectancy about mobile video ads was measured with two 7-point Likert scales, adapted from Afifi and Metts (1998). The items began with *"When I use apps on my smartphone, I usually expect to see..."* and ended in *1) "video advertisements which are silent"*, and *2) "video advertisements which play with sound on"*. The first item was reverse-coded and averaged with the second item to create a summated score indicating the level of expectancy of sound-on mobile video ads.

Product involvement was measured as a potential confounding factor (Laczniak and Muehling 1990), using Zaichkowsky's (1987) five 7-point semantic differential scales (*unimportant-important, irrelevant-relevant, mundane-fascinating, unappealing-appealing, and uninvolving-involving*) (Cronbach's $\alpha = 0.91$). Demographic information was also obtained at the end of the post-exposure questionnaire.

4 Results

4.1 Sample Characteristics and Randomization Check

Among the 105 participants who signed up for this study, 87 ($N_{sound\text{-}on} = 44$, $N_{sound\text{-}off} = 43$) completed the post-exposure questionnaire, resulting in a response rate of 82.8%. Among the 87 participants, 79 ($N_{sound\text{-}on} = 43$, $N_{sound\text{-}off} = 36$) were qualified for the week-after measurement, of which 58 of the invited participants completed the survey ($N_{sound\text{-}on} = 30$, $N_{sound\text{-}off} = 28$) (see Table 1 for complete information on response rates). A majority (64.4%) of the 87 participants identified themselves as White/Caucasian, and 63.2% of the participants were female. The average age was 21 years old ($SD = 3.22$).

Chi-square tests and *t*-tests were conducted for the randomization check, and the results showed no significant differences between the experimental conditions for gender ($\chi^2 = 0.01$, $df = 1$, $p = 0.95$), race ($\chi^2 = 2.71$, $df = 1$, $p = 0.10$), age ($M_{sound\text{-}on} = 21.55$, $M_{sound\text{-}off} = 20.79$; $t(85) = 1.12$, $p = 0.27$), and product involvement ($M_{sound\text{-}on} = 4.67$, $M_{sound\text{-}off} = 5.02$; $t(75) = -1.14$, $p = 0.67$). Thus, the randomization was deemed successful.

Table 1 Sample and completion rates (The base of the percentages is Time 1 sample size)

	Time 1 (Participated)		Time 2 (Qualified)		Time 2 (Completed)	
	N	%	N	%	N	%
Sound-on	44	100%	43	97.7	30	68.2
Sound-off	43	100%	36	83.7	28	65.1
Total	87	100%	79	90.8	58	66.7

4.2 Hypothesis Testing

H1: Effects of sound-on vs. -off on memory

Hypothesis 1 predicted that a sound-on autoplay video ad would generate a stronger memory of a) the ad and b) the brand than a sound-off ad. Multiple measures were utilized to test this. First, a chi-square test was conducted to examine the effect of the sound-on vs. -off variable on unaided recall of the ad, which the result showed that unaided ad recall was not significantly different between the two conditions ($\chi^2 = .10$, $df = 1$, $p = .76$). Second, recall of ad content elements was analyzed using a t-test, and the result indicated a significant difference ($t(77) = 3.15$, $p < .01$); such that the mean recall score in the sound-on condition ($M = 2.26$, $SD = 1.31$) was higher than that of the sound-off condition ($M = 1.53$, $SD = 1.13$). Third, brand recall and recognition were analyzed by conducting chi-square tests. Both of the analysis results showed that the differences were statistically non-significant: (1) chi-square test with the brand recall variable – sound-on brand recall = 18.6%, sound-off brand recall = 19.4%, $\chi^2 = .01$, $df = 1$, $p = .92$; (2) chi-square test with the brand recognition variable – sound-on brand recognition = 36.4%, sound-off brand recognition = 32.6%, $\chi^2 = .14$, $df = 1$, $p = .71$. Thus, H1a was partially supported for ad content memory, but H1b was not supported.

H2: Effects of sound-on vs. -off on attitudes

Hypothesis 2 predicted that a sound-on ad would generate more negative attitudes toward a) the ad and b) the brand than would a sound-off ad. The descriptive statistics seemed to indicate that the sound-on ad generated lower attitude toward the ad ($M_{sound-on} = 3.67$, $SD = 1.28$; $M_{sound-off} = 4.03$, $SD = 1.05$) and attitude toward the brand ($M_{sound-on} = 4.45$, $SD = 1.33$; $M_{sound-off} = 4.83$, $SD = 1.01$), compared to the sound-off condition. However, t-tests showed that the differences were not significant (ad attitude: $t(77) = -1.35$, $p = 1.81$; brand attitude: $t(76) = -1.41$, $p = 1.65$). Thus, H2 was not supported.

H3: Moderating effects of sound-on mobile video ad expectancy

Hypothesis 3 predicted that expectancy of mobile video ads would moderate the effects of the sound-on vs. -off variable on consumers' attitudes toward a) the ad and b) the brand. A general linear model analysis was performed to test the hypothesis and the results showed no significant moderating effect of expectancy of mobile video ads (sound factor – $F = 0.04$, $p = 0.85$; expectancy – $F = 0.77$, $p = 0.39$; interaction term – $F = 0.52$, $p = 0.47$). Thus, H3 was not supported.

H4: Delayed effects on attitudes.

Hypothesis 4 predicted that a sound-on ad would generate a positive attitude change over time, while such attitude change would not occur in the sound-off ad condition. Results of a paired sample *t*-test comparing attitude scores between Time 1 and Time 2 showed that in the sound-on condition, attitude toward the ad increased after time delay ($M_{Time2-Time1} = 0.33$, $SD = 0.80$), and the difference was statistically significant ($t(29) = 2.26$, $p = 0.03$) (see Table 2). In the sound-off condition, however, ad attitude scores at Time 1 and Time 2 were not significantly different ($M_{Time2-Time1} = 0.28$, $SD = 0.82$, $t(25) = 1.73$, $p = 0.10$).

Regarding brand attitude, the same paired sample *t*-tests were conducted. In the sound-on condition, the difference in brand attitude between Time 1 and Time 2 was only slight ($M_{Time2-Time1} = 0.06$, $SD = 0.77$) and statistically non-significant ($t(29) = 0.43$, $p = 0.67$). Similarly, in the sound-off condition as well, the difference in brand attitude between Time 1 and Time 2 ($M_{Time2-Time1} = 0.25$, $SD = 0.99$) was non-significant ($t(25) = 1.26$, $p = 0.22$). Therefore, H4 was partially supported for the change in attitude toward the ad, but not for brand attitude.

5 Discussion

5.1 Summary of Findings and Contributions

This study examined the effects of the sound-on vs. -off factor in mobile autoplay video ads on consumer memory and attitude as well as investigated potential moderating effect of consumers' expectancy about mobile video ads. Additionally, we tested the possibility of time-delayed effects of the sound factor on attitudes. The results demonstrated that a sound-on autoplay video ad generated stronger recall of the ad content than did a sound-off ad, which is consistent with LCMP (Lang 2000). However, no significant differences were found in brand memory.

Of particular interest and significance is that, in terms of the attitudinal outcomes, although the sound factor did not cause significant effect on attitudes toward the ad and the brand, the sound-on ad condition generated significant changes of ad attitude in a positive direction over time, while the sound-off condition did not. This finding is consistent with our hypothesis based on the mere exposure effect

Table 2 Paired sample *t*-test for changes in ad attitude

	Time1		Time2		Paired Differences (Time2 - Time1)						
	M	SD	M	SD	M	SD	95% CI		t	df	p
Sound-on	4.01	1.17	4.34	0.89	0.33	0.80	0.03	0.63	2.26	29	0.03
Sound-off	4.41	0.83	4.68	1.06	0.28	0.82	-0.05	0.61	1.73	25	0.10

theory and related prior research that suggested delayed attitudinal effects based on familiarity (Fang et al. 2007).

This study makes important theoretical contributions advancing the emerging research on digital video advertising, and offers meaningful practical implications. First, as the first research on the effects of the sound factor in mobile video advertising, this study adds unique new insight into digital video advertising effects. Our findings provide important empirical evidence supporting the commonly-held belief about a superior memory effect of sound-on ads, at least for memory of ad content, but refuting the presumed negative effects on attitudinal outcomes. While digital video advertising shares many similarities with traditional TV advertising, there are some unique characteristics distinguishing the two. Moreover, video advertising on personal mobile devices has some unique characteristics compared to video advertising on other digital media (Kim et al. 2019). The sound factor is unique and particularly important for video ads placed in mobile apps. Future researchers are encouraged to further examine this variable and other message and media factors that are unique to mobile devices.

Second, the finding that negative attitudes may decay, but familiarity caused by higher memory effects of sound-on ads can positively impact consumer attitudes over time, is particularly noteworthy. While a majority of the prior research in digital video advertising tends to focus on and present rather negative responses, such as ad irritation, ad intrusiveness, negative attitude, and ad avoidance (Kim et al. 2019), research findings could be different if such outcome variables are measured in a longer term with some time delay.

Third, the methodological approach of this study contributes to advancing digital video advertising and mobile advertising research. Unlike lab experiments or scenario-based approaches widely used in these research fields, the current study approximates the situation where consumers typically use their mobile devices in public. To enhance the ecological validity of the knowledge generated by research on mobile advertising, researchers are strongly encouraged to develop study design and data collection methods that resemble the distinctive nature of mobile device use and mobile ad exposure.

For practitioners, this study's findings suggest that reluctance or total avoidance of sound-on mobile video ads out of fear of irritating consumers might not be warranted. When used appropriately, sound-on ads could generate a better ad memory outcome, which, in turn, could lead to improved attitudinal outcomes with time delay, although the unexpected sound might generate negative attitude at the moment of ad exposure. Given that most purchase decisions are made after some time delay since ad exposure, using attention-grabbing features producing automatic orienting responses could improve ad outcomes.

5.2 Limitations and Suggestions for Future Research

While this study offers some interesting findings, some of the hypotheses were not supported partly due to a small sample size and low statistical power. In addition, this study allowed participants to freely use the mock mobile app, without mentioning or drawing their attention to the embedded ad. While this approach contributed to enhanced ecological validity, it also increased dropout rates because many of the initial participants did not notice nor recall the stimulus ad. Also, this study's use of a student sample reduces generalizability of the findings.

Limitations of this study suggest opportunities for future research. Building on this study, future research is encouraged to further examine the sound factor and other important strategic factors in mobile video advertising, using larger and more generalizable samples. Also, to overcome the limitation of a single ad exposure in an artificial experimental design, future research should consider examining cumulative effects of ad exposure by placing an autoplay video ad in multiple places in a real mobile app, or allowing participants to use multiple mobile apps that include real autoplay video ads.

As consumers steadily shift their media viewing more toward mobile devices, video ads in the mobile environment rapidly expand, and digital advertising on mobile devices increases much faster than on desktops, more research on mobile video advertising is warranted. Especially considering the distinctive characteristics of video ads in the mobile environment, future research should pay special attention to the mobile-specific advertising factors and unique challenges facing advertisers.

References

Afifi, W. A., & Metts, S. (1998). Characteristics and consequences of expectation violations in close relationships. *Journal of Social and Personal Relationships, 15*(3), 365–392.

Burgoon, J. K. (1978). A communication model of personal space violations: Explication and an initial test. *Human Communication Research, 4*(2), 129–142.

Burgoon, J. K., & Hale, J. L. (1988). Nonverbal expectancy violations: Model elaboration and application to immediacy behaviors. *Communications Monographs, 55*(1), 58–79.

Burke, M. C., & Edell, J. A. (1986). Ad reactions over time: Capturing changes in the real world. *Journal of Consumer Research, 13*(1), 114–118.

Campbell, M. C., & Keller, K. L. (2003). Brand familiarity and advertising repetition effects. *Journal of Consumer Research, 30*(2), 292–304.

Fang, X., Singh, S., & Ahluwalia, R. (2007). An examination of different explanations for the mere exposure effect. *Journal of Consumer Research, 34*(1), 97–103.

Graham, F. K. (1997). Afterward: Pre-attentive processing and passive and active attention. In P. J. Lang, R. F. Simons, M. Balaban, & R. Simons (Eds.), *Attention and orienting: Sensory and motivational processes* (pp. 417–452). Hillsdale: Erlbaum.

IAB. (2018). IAB Digital video glossary. https://www.iab.com/wp-content/uploads/2019/07/IAB_Digital-Video-Glossary-2018.pdf.

Janiszewski, C. (1993). Preattentive mere exposure effects. *Journal of Consumer Research, 20*(3), 376–392.

Janiszewski, C., & Meyvis, T. (2001). Effects of brand logo complexity, repetition, and spacing on processing fluency and judgment. *Journal of Consumer Research, 28*(1), 18–32.

Kim, S., Lee, J., & Huh, J. (2019). Digital video advertising. In S. Rodgers & E. Thorson (Eds.), *Advertising theory* (2nd ed., pp. 382–403). New York: Routledge.

Kronrod, A., & Huber, J. (2018). Ad wearout wearout: How time can reverse the negative effect of frequent advertising repetition on brand preference. *International Journal of Research in Marketing, 36*(2), 306–324.

Laczniak, R. N., & Muehling, D. D. (1990). Delayed effects of advertising moderated by involvement. *Journal of Business Research, 20*(3), 263–277.

Laczniak, R. N., & Muehling, D. D. (1993). Toward a better understanding of the role of advertising message involvement in ad processing. *Psychology & Marketing, 10*(4), 301–319.

Lang, A. (2000). The limited capacity model of mediated message processing. *Journal of Communication, 50*(1), 46–70.

Lang, A. (2006). Using the limited capacity model of motivated mediated message processing to design effective cancer communication messages. *Journal of Communication, 56*(suppl_1), 57–80.

Lee, J., & Lee, M. (2011). Factors influencing the intention to watch online video advertising. *Cyberpsychology, Behavior, and Social Networking, 14*(10), 619–624.

Leshner, G., Reeves, B., & Nass, C. (1998). Switching channels: The effects of television channels on the mental representations of television news. *Journal of Broadcasting & Electronic Media, 42*(1), 21–33.

Li, H., & Lo, H.-Y. (2015). Do you recognize its brand? The effectiveness of online in-stream video advertisements. *Journal of Advertising, 44*(3), 208–218.

Logan, K. (2013). And now a word from our sponsor: Do consumers perceive advertising on traditional television and online streaming video differently? *Journal of Marketing Communications, 19*(4), 258–276.

MacKenzie, S., & Lutz, R. (1989). An empirical examination of the structural antecedents of attitude toward the ad in an advertising pretesting context. *Journal of Marketing, 53*(2), 48–65.

McMillan, S. J., & Hwang, J.-S. (2002). Measures of perceived interactivity: An exploration of the role of direction of communication, user control, and time in shaping perceptions of interactivity. *Journal of Advertising, 31*(3), 29–42.

Pew Research Center. (2015). Americans' views on mobile etiquette. https://www.pewresearch.org/internet/2015/08/26/americans-views-on-mobile-etiquette/.

Siegel, J. T., Burgoon, J. K. (2002). Expectancy theory approaches to prevention: Violating adolescent expectations to increase the effectiveness of public service announcements. *Mass Media and Drug Prevention: Classic and Contemporary Theories and Research*, 163–186.

Spartz, E. (2017). Are Facebook's recent changes to videos affecting its user experience? *AdWeek*. https://www.adweek.com/digital/emerson-spartz-dose-guest-post-facebook-changes-videos-user-experience.

Stafford, T., & Grimes, A. (2012). Memory enhances the mere exposure effect. *Psychology & Marketing, 29*(12), 995–1003.

Zaichkowsky, J. L. (1987). The emotional affect of product involvement. In M. Wallendorf & P. Anderson (Eds.), *Advances in Consumer Research* (Vol. 14, pp. 32–35). Provo: Association for Consumer Research.

Zajonc, R. B. (2001). Mere exposure: A gateway to the subliminal. *Current Directions in Psychological Science, 10*(6), 224–228.

Battle-Weary Women: The Female Creatives Fighting for Leadership in Advertising Management

Helen Thompson-Whiteside

1 The Gender Problem

Advertising still has a gender problem. Practitioners such as Kevin Roberts, the executive chairman of Saatchi and Saatchi, might argue that the debate about gender is "over" and chief creative officer of MandC, and Justin Tindall may well claim to be "bored of diversity", but despite on-going discussions, women are still under-represented at the top of creative departments in all countries (Grow et al. 2012), accounting for less than 15% of all creative directors worldwide (Grow and Deng 2014; Wohl and Stein 2016). So, who is bored now?

Women continue to fight for equality but the problem remains. Many women feel defeated by the challenges they face as they seek advancement, with some feeling that it is easier to leave the industry than to change it (Bronwin 2018). Women face on-going sexual harassment, now considered one of the biggest problems facing the industry (Kemp 2018). They appear to be losing the battle for equal representation in creative leadership (Mallia and Windels 2018) which severely limits the influence they can have on the adverts that are made. Unsurprisingly perhaps, advertising is criticised for its representation of women (JWT Intelligence 2017), in particular for its use of harmful gender stereotypes (Advertising Standards Authority 2018), and the ways in which it objectifies women (Stein 2017). Advertising is credited with the power and responsibility to reflect society (Shabbir et al. 2019; Windels 2016), yet the industry appears to be out of touch with the changing role of the female consumer and the aspirations of

H. Thompson-Whiteside (✉)
Portsmouth Business School, University of Portsmouth, Portsmouth, UK
E-Mail: helen.thompson-whiteside@port.ac.uk

its female creatives. Women may now exert unprecedented levels of influence on the market place (3% conference), but they still make up only 23.5 per cent of creative teams globally (Deng and Grow 2018) and account for an even smaller minority of creative directors worldwide, leaving advertising's claims to reflect the increasingly powerful female consumer seriously undermined.

1.1   Why Does The Gender Problem Persist?

The problem of female representation and gender inequality in creative advertising has been widely discussed by academics and practitioners alike. The progression of women to creative leadership is not due to insufficient numbers in the pipeline. Women make up around half of the advertising workforce in the US, UK and Spain (Windels and Mallia 2015), but few make it to leadership positions (Grow et al. 2012; Grow and Deng 2014). Speaking in 2016, Kevin Roberts implied that women lack the ambition for leadership, while advertising scholars have put forward a number of structural and cultural reasons for this stubborn problem. One of the much-cited barriers is the culture of advertising's creative departments, which have been built on a male paradigm and shaped by male norms (Nixon and Crewe 2004; Stuhlfaut 2011). In these departments, personality factors more often associated with men such as competitiveness, perseverance, toughness, and a thick skin are seen as important factors for success (Grow and Broyles 2011; Mallia 2009; Windels and Lee 2012). Even the language used to describe the creative process appears to be gendered, with reference to "war rooms" and "territories" (Turnbull and Wheeler 2017, pp.185–186). The existing culture demands long working hours (Mallia 2009; Mallia and Windels 2011) and has traditionally been poor at providing flexible work arrangements (Mallia 2009; Mallia and Windels 2011) for employees, presenting particular difficulties for mothers (Grow and Broyles 2011; Mallia 2009) when they return to the workplace. The identity of creative director is perceived to be male with many male creative directors hiring in their own image, often leaving women struggling for recognition, or even access to certain accounts (Broyles and Grow 2008; Singh and Lepitak 2018). The net result is that women can often feel like outsiders in advertising's creative departments, feeling that they must emulate male behaviours in order to succeed, which can feel inauthentic or inappropriate for them, (Thompson-Whiteside et al. 2020).

There have been concerted efforts made by campaigning groups, such as 3% Conference in the US, Creative Equals in the UK and See it Be it from Cannes Lions, but change has been slow. No one issue or barrier has been isolated as the main problem. Instead, women are seen to be operating under a "cloud of masculinity" (Grow and Deng 2015, p. 10) with a number of factors conspiring to impede their progress. To date, a number of theories have been brought to bear on the gender issue including; situated learning theory (Windels and Mallia 2015), creativity (Grow and Broyles 2011) and impression management (Thompson-Whiteside et al. 2020). While this has drawn a number of valuable insights, this type of theory-led research might be precluding other insights (Belk and Sobh 2019). It is acknowledged that there are still gaps in our understanding of this persistent issue (Windels and Mallia 2015). Therefore, this study sought to explore the experiences of female creatives by taking an open approach, capturing both "retrospective and real-time accounts" (Gioia et al. 2013, p. 19) of female creatives' experiences, guided by just one broad question:

> *RQ: What has been your experience of seeking career progression in a creative advertising department?*

2 Methods

An abductive approach to data collection (Gioia et al. 2013) was adopted, allowing the researcher to follow wherever participants took the conversation as they responded to this guiding question. This approach allows the researcher to uncover experiences and interpretations of this gendered-environment as put forward by female participants, rather than the researcher imposing a priori constructs at the data collection stage. The researcher can therefore be open to much-needed fresh insights and interpretations of the persistent problem of gender inequality in creative advertising. Given the exploratory nature of the study, a qualitative methodology was employed to learn more about women's own constructions of their experiences through in-depth interviews. Interviews lasted up to 60 min and were undertaken face-to-face and via telephone with 25 female creatives from a range of agencies in the USA, UK and mainland Europe.

Data analysis
Table 1 provides a graphic representation of how the data was structured by the researcher progressing from raw data to themes. These were identified through close analysis of how participants described their experience, staying true to the wording they used. This process also facilitates the researcher in starting to move from thinking of the data in terms of simply methodology, to developing a theoretical viewpoint (Gioia et al. 2013).

Tab. 1 Data structure

First order themes	Second Order themes	Aggregate dimensions
Creative God Army general Clique of men Being like one of the lads Socialising out of work Being included Humour Banter	Leadership identity Uncomfortable Workplace culture Fitting in	Rules of engagement
Willing to run the gauntlet Pitching ideas Under fire Too many opinions Putting your head above the parapet Back lash Need for self-promotion Getting soul crushed Door is closed	Risk Criticism Standing out Exposure Double standards	At the front line

(continued)

3 Findings

Interviewees discussed their experience making extended use of military allusions to convey the struggle they, and other women, experience in being accepted, and granted authority by the community of practice in which they operate. One overarching warfare metaphor with four related sub-themes were identified in the data: *Rules of engagement*; *At the front line*, *Battle-weary women*; and; *New model army*. Verbatim quotes are included to illustrate the themes and the dimensions that result from the aggregation of these.

Tab. 1 (continued)

First order themes	Second Order themes	Aggregate dimensions
Tired of fighting Not the army Problems with system Working hours Nothing new Lack of equality Fight for recognition Return from maternity leave	Exploitative system Tired Motherhood No change	Battle-weary
Need for something new Army of change makers Fight for a new system Cooperation not competition New ways of working Banging the drum for equality Social media for recognition Breaking away	Desire for new system Equality Personal branding Opportunity Freedom	New-model army

4 Rules Of Engagement

Respondents described creative departments bound by codes or rules which dictate what is acceptable in creative departments. They describe the space as shaped by, *"a clique of men"*, and led by men who they liken to *"creative gods"* or *"army generals"*. Male behaviours are privileged in this space. As the minority coming into this space, women feel that they must conform to be granted access, or accorded the right to participate in the community. To comply with the established *rules of engagement,* women emulate male behaviours *"to be one of the lads"* and participate in humour and social activities which can often feel inappropriate and uncomfortable. Some participants describe making a conscious decision to abide by these rules or codes of conduct, while they noted that other female colleagues struggled, or had left agencies after finding they could not conform in the ways that the male culture demands.

5 At The Front Line

Participants describe the process of pitching and defending their creative ideas as akin to being *"at the front line"*. They recognise the need to put themselves forward, and engage in self-promotion but use the language of warfare to describe their experience. They speak of *"running the gauntlet"* or putting their *"head above the parapet"* when they share their ideas and opinions. They often feel attacked and describe the experience as coming *"under fire"*. One woman describes the behaviour of men saying, *"creative male directors in advertising are allowed to be so difficult and violent, I've been in meetings where [men] have thrown chairs, thrown phones, screamed, sworn at people, got people fired"*. Current practice requires creatives to not only advance, but also defend their ideas. However, women describe receiving harsh criticism from men, with defensive action considered to be equally unwelcome. Assertive women appear to experience a backlash, being seen as *"disruptive...difficult and aggressive"*. Many participants spoke of a on-going fight for inclusion and recognition.

6 Battle-Weary Women

For some women, front-line experience has honed their skills, brought affirmation and led to career progress. While for others constant criticism and resistance injects self-doubt and brings fatigue. Women report being tired of the struggle, *"I don't want to go to work and fight, I'm not at war here, like I didn't join the army"*. Others question the wisdom of the current fight, *"why are we looking for equality in an exploitive system, we need to be saying something totally different"*. This leads many to not only question but reject the culture of traditional ad agencies. Some keep fighting, and in their words, *"banging the drum"*, while others shift to less front-line roles in planning and account management. Some female creatives simply leave, choosing to move to smaller independent agencies or to work for themselves.

7   New Model Army

There were signs however of a new tribe of women emerging, a *new model army*, who are creating new cultures outside of traditional agencies or moving for change within them. There is *"a massive army of women right now who want things to change"*, *"who want to be a part a system where [we] are equal in telling those stories about women"*. Rather than continuing to struggle for verification within an existing system, women with a sense of agency are taking opportunities to shape new cultures and experiment with new styles of creative production, *"things are starting to loosen up a bit on the edges"*. They are rejecting the existing practices, and replacing these with the co-creation of ideas and business solutions. This *new- model army* of women recognise the need for female creatives to engage in personal narrative building, leveraged through self-promotion, social media and networks.

8   Discussion

Consistent with previous research, the women in this study describe a number of cultural and structural barriers they have encountered as they work and seek career progression within advertising's strongly gendered creative departments. However, this study additionally finds that female creatives consistently use metaphor to describe their experience of advertising's strongly-gendered workplaces, likening their struggle for recognition and career progression to war.

Metaphors allow two unrelated concepts to be connected to produce a new understanding of reality (Morgan 1980). Using war metaphors appears to allow women to more effectively convey their experiences by drawing on a more familiar image, such as war. Perhaps their choice of metaphor is not surprising, given that since the 1980's comparisons between marketing and warfare have been made by both academics and practitioners alike (Cornelissen 2003; Delbaere and Slobodzian 2018; Kotler and Singh 1981; Ries and Trout 1986; Rindfleisch 1996). The widespread use of military-style language within the marketing sphere is both commonplace, and a widely accepted metaphor. References are often made to the planning, launching, implementation and control of offensive and defensive strategies, tactics and campaigns, positioning, targets, the entering and penetrating of territories and markets, all with the ultimate aim of winning customers, beating, and even destroying competitors (Rindfleisch 1996; Saren 2007). In this way, metaphor has been used to map a familiar domain, such as warfare on to another, perhaps less-familiar domain (Morgan 1980) such as marketing, making concepts easier to understand, communicate and recall (Delbaere and Slobodzian 2014, 2018). Indeed, the conception of marketing as war has proved to be an enduring metaphor, which has successfully popularised marketing and advertising concepts, and even been used to describe elements of the creative process (Turnbull and Wheeler 2017), but the findings of this study suggest it might also describe the workplace itself.

Conceiving of marketing as warfare has been successful in conveying urgency and action (Delbaere and Slobodzian 2018). However, metaphor can also be limited or even problematic. Limited in that any metaphor can only ever provide partial understanding, as they can explain and highlight some aspects of a phenomenon, but obscure or downplay others (Brown 2008; Rindfleisch 1996). Problematic in that their application may go beyond initial intentions. For example, conceiving of marketing as war has been useful in communicating a range of marketing activities. Military language helps describe the launch of a campaign, the need to defend territory, win customers and beat the competition, but this language is seen as "highly gendered" (Saren 2007 p. 12) and its prevalence is problematic when it goes further to suggest, and even sanction combative behaviours and attitudes (Lakoff and Johnson 1980) in the workplace.

Prior research has highlighted the use of metaphor as a form of identity work (Carollo and Guerci 2018; Nyberg and Svenningsson 2014) and as a cognitive coping strategy (Carollo and Guerci 2018) but to the best of the researcher's knowledge, the role of metaphor in shaping the workplace has not previously been identified. Therefore this study contributes to our understanding of a lack of female creative leaders by suggesting that the prevalence of war-like metaphors to describe both marketing activity and elements of advertising's creative process, has had unintended consequences for female creatives by suggesting and legitimising combative behaviours and attitudes in the workplace.

9 Conclusion

This study has found that the current norms within the creative departments require female creatives to convince others of the value of their work and their leadership abilities, within a community of practice which they find aggressive and even hostile. Women are fighting to participate in their community, but the acceptance and affirmation of these behaviours is limited, or at best inconsistent. Negative feedback and criticism, undermine women's confidence and even their future motivation to progress, which leads many female creatives to withdraw, or even exit the field. The net result is that few women reach positions of creative leadership with female creative directors still a small minority of all creative directors worldwide. The challenges of women in advertising have been well documented in the literature but this study also suggests that employees may be further impacted by marketing's most dominant metaphor. This paper therefore contributes to our understanding of the barriers women face within advertising's creative departments. It would appear that marketing-as-warfare is no longer simply a description. Instead it may have become a prescription by suggesting combative work-place behaviours and attitudes which negatively shape the experiences of women. If as Brown (2008) argues, it is only those metaphors which continue to fit the managerial environment which survive, then we should be deeply concerned that the metaphor of marketing appears to be intact, and still proving useful in describing the experience of women within the field. As Delbaere and Slobodzian (2018, p. 391) argue, marketing has a metaphor problem, but understanding it may just help us better understand advertising's gender problem.

References

Advertising Standards Authority. (2018). New rule to ban harmful gender stereotypes next year. https://www.asa.org.uk/news/new-rule-to-ban-harmful-gender-stereotypes-next-year.html.
Belk, R., & Sobh, R. (2019). No assemblage required: On pursuing original consumer culture theory. *Marketing Theory, 19*(4), 489–507.
Bronwin, F. (2018). Why leaving adland is the easy option. https://www.campaignlive.co.uk/article/why-leaving-adland-easy-option/1456315.
Brown, S. (2008). Are marketing's metaphors good for it? *the Marketing Review, 8*(3), 209–221.
Broyles, S. J., & Grow, J. M. (2008). Creative women in advertising agencies: why so few "babes in boyland"? *Journal of Consumer Marketing, 25*, 4.
Carollo, L., & Guerci, M. (2018). 'Activists in a suit': Paradoxes and metaphors in sustainability managers' identity work. *Journal of Business Ethics, 148*(2), 249–268.
Cornelissen, J. P. (2003). Metaphor as a method in the domain of marketing. *Psychology & Marketing, 20*(3), 209–225.
Delbaere, M., & Slobodzian, A. D. (2019). Marketing's metaphors have expired: An argument for a new dominant metaphor. *Marketing Theory, 19*(3), 391–401.
Deng, T., and Grow, J.M. (2018). Gender segregation revealed: Five years of red books data tell a global story. *Advertising & Society Quarterly, 19*, 3.
Gioia, D. A., Corley, K. G., & Hamilton, A. L. (2013). Seeking qualitative rigor in inductive research: Notes on the Gioia methodology. *Organizational Research Methods, 16*(1), 15–31.

Grow, J., and Broyles, S. J. (2011). Unspoken rules of the creative game: Insights to shape the next generation from top advertising creative women. *Advertising & Society Review, 12*, 1.

Grow, J. M., and Deng,T. (2014). Sex segregation in advertising creative departments across the globe. *Advertising and Society Review, 14*, 4.

Grow, J. M., and Deng, T., (2015). Tokens in a man's world: Women in creative advertising departments. *Media Report to Women*.

Grow, J., Roca, D., & Broyles, S. J. (2012). Vanishing acts: Creative women in Spain and the United States. *International Journal of Advertising, 31*(3), 657–679.

JWT Intelligence. (2017). Gender bias in advertising. https://seejane.org/research-informs-empowers/gender-bias-advertising/.

Kemp, N. (2018). Time to campaign exposes reality of sexual harassment in advertising. https://www.campaignlive.co.uk/article/timeto-campaign-exposes-reality-sexual-harassment-advertising/1497555.

Kotler, P., & Singh, R. (1981). Marketing warfare in the 1980s. *the Journal of Business Strategy, 1*(3), 30.

Lakoff, G., & Johnson, M. (1980). The metaphorical structure of the human conceptual system. *Cognitive Science, 4*(2), 195–208.

Mallia, K. L. (2009). Rare birds: Why so few women become ad agency creative directors. *Advertising and Society Review, 10*, 3.

Mallia, K. L., & Windels, K. (2011). Will changing media change the world? An exploratory investigation of the impact of digital advertising on opportunities for creative women. *Journal of interactive advertising, 11*(2), 30–44.

Mallia, K. L., and Windels,K. (2018). Female representation among advertising's creative elite: A content analysis of the communication arts advertising annual. *Advertising and Society Quarterly, 18*, 4.

Morgan, G. (1980). Paradigms, metaphors, and puzzle solving in organization theory. *Administrative Science Quarterly, 25*, 605–622.

Nixon, S., & Crewe, B. (2004). Pleasure at work? Gender, consumption and work-based identities in the creative industries. *Consumption Markets and Culture, 7*(2), 129–147.

Nyberg, D., & Sveningsson, S. (2014). Paradoxes of authentic leadership: Leader identity struggles. *Leadership, 10*(4), 437–455.

Ries, A., and Trout, J. (1986). Marketing warfare. *Journal of Consumer Marketing*, 77–82.

Rindfleisch, A. (1996). Marketing as warfare: Reassessing a dominant metaphor. *Business Horizons, 39*(5), 3–10.

Saren, M. (2007). Marketing is everything: the view from the street. *Marketing Intelligence & Planning*, 11–16.

Shabbir, H. A., Maalouf, H., Griessmair, M., Colmekcioglu, N., & Akhtar, P. (2019). Exploring perceptions of advertising ethics: An informant-derived approach. *Journal of Business Ethics, 159*(3), 727–744.

Singh, S., and Lepitak, S. (2018). Less than a fifth of top industry creative awards won by women. https://www.thedrum.com/news/2018/02/06/less-fifth-top-industry-creative-awards-won-by-women.

Delbaere, M., & Slobodzian, A. D. (2019). Marketing's metaphors have expired: An argument for a new dominant metaphor. *Marketing Theory, 19*(3), 391–401.

Stein. L., (2017). Cannes Bans Gender Bias. https://adage.com/article/agency-news/cannes-bannes-gender-bias-womennotobjects/307847/.

Stuhlfaut, M. W. (2011). The creative code: An organisational influence on the creative process in advertising. *International Journal of Advertising, 30*(2), 283–304.

Thompson-Whiteside, H., Turnbull, S., & Howe-Walsh, L. (2018). *Developing an authentic personal brand using impression management behaviours.* In Qualitative Market Research: An International Journal, 166–181.

Thompson-Whiteside, H., Turnbull, S., & Howe-Walsh, L. (2020). Advertising: Should creative women be expected to 'fake it?'. *Journal of Marketing Management,* 1–26. DOI: 10.1080/0267257X.2019.1707704

Turnbull, S., & Wheeler, C. (2017). The advertising creative process: A study of UK agencies. *Journal of Marketing Communications, 23*(2), 176–194.

Windels, K. (2016). Stereotypical or just typical: How do US practitioners view the role and function of gender stereotypes in advertisements? *International Journal of Advertising, 35*(5), 864–887.

Windels, K., & Lee, W. N. (2012). The construction of gender and creativity in advertising creative departments. *Gender in Management: An International Journal, 27*(8), 502–519.

Windels, K., & Mallia, K. L. (2015). How being female impacts learning and career growth in advertising creative departments. *Employee Relations, 37*(1), 122–140.

Wohl, J. and Stein, L. (2016). Ad industry hits 'inflection point' on women. Now what? https://adage.com/article/special-report-women-to-watch/ad-industry-hits-inflection-point-women/304210/.

Can Market Mavens Be Negative Word of Mouth Senders? the Moderating Role of Assumed-Competence and Gender

Keigo Taketani and Kei Mineo

1   Introduction

Today's consumers often make their purchase decisions by relying on word-of-mouth (WOM) and electronic word-of-mouth (eWOM) information, as prior research suggests that WOM/eWOM influences brand attitude (Herr, Kardes, and Kim 1991), product evaluation (Bone 1995), switching behavior (Wangenheim and Bayón 2004), and sales (Chevalier and Mayzlin 2006; Duan et al. 2008; You et al. 2015). Many marketers thus focus on influencer marketing when promoting their products and services (Keller and Fay 2012).

Still, firms are concerned about negative WOM. Today consumer negative WOM can spread instantly worldwide via the Internet (Ward and Ostrom 2006). Since negative WOM can seriously damage sales and company reputation, marketers are interested in how to suppress negative WOM rather than simply promoting positive WOM (Williams and Buttle 2014). As identifying consumers who may disseminate influential negative WOM has become an important research topic both academically and managerially, this paper focuses on "market maven" concept (Feick and Price 1987).

This work was supported by JSPS KAKENHI Grant Numbers JP17K13811.

K. Taketani (✉)
Komazawa University, Tokyo, Japan
E-Mail: taketani@komazawa-u.ac.jp

K. Mineo
Kindai University, Osaka, Japan
E-Mail: mineok@bus.kindai.ac.jp

Market mavens are consumers with general marketplace expertise who can provide useful information to other consumers (Feick and Price 1987). Because "the differentiation between market mavens and nonmavens is gradual rather than dichotomous" (Wangenheim 2005, p. 70), we use the term "market mavenism" rather than market maven. Specifically, consumers with high market mavenism denotes market maven in this paper. Although multiple research efforts have examined market mavenism (Abratt et al. 1995; Barnes and Pressey 2012; Flynn and Goldsmith 2017; Goodey and East 2008; Gauri et al. 2016; Price et al. 1995; Ruvio and Shoham 2007), little is known about the precise relationship between market mavenism and negative WOM (Wangenheim (2005) is one the few studies investigating this relationship). That is surprising, given the strong influence of consumers who have high market mavenism.

This study thus has two purposes: (1) Determine whether market mavenism positively affects negative WOM/eWOM intention and (2) better understand this relationship by testing the moderating role of assumed-competence based on undervaluing others (Hayamizu et al. 2004). This personal trait "is a form of illusory competence which one gains by demeaning others" (Hayamizu et al. 2004, p. 128), as developed and applied in the field of educational psychology. The current study assumes that this trait amplifies the positive effects of market mavenism on negative WOM/eWOM intention, as explained below.

2 Literature Review and Research Hypotheses

2.1 Negative WOM as Complaint Behaviour

If consumers experience dissatisfaction with provided goods and services, they react in various ways (e.g., seeking redress, revenge, product switching, no action), all of which are referred to as consumer complaint behavior (Grégoire et al. 2018; Hirschman 1970; Istanbulluoglu et al. 2017; Singh 1988). Singh (1988) classified such complaint behavior into three categories: voice responses (e.g., seeking redress), third-party responses (e.g., taking legal action), and private responses (e.g., negative WOM).

Richins (1983) conducted foundational research on negative WOM and reported that the more consumers negatively perceive a company's responsiveness to a complaint, the more they engage in negative WOM activity. Sundaram, Mitra, and Webster (1998) focused on consumer motives for engaging in negative WOM. Applying the critical incident technique, they identified four motives: altruistic, anxiety reduction, vengeance, and advice seeking. Hennig-Thurau, Gwinner,

Walsh, and Gremler (2004) also reported on the motives for eWOM engagement by identifying motives similar to those reported by Sundaram and Webster (1998) (e.g., concern for other consumers, venting negative feelings). In addition, they discovered motives unique to the online context (e.g., platform assistance) and reported that the number of comments on online platforms can vary widely from consumer to consumer (value ranging from 1 to 1800, $SD = 107$). Their findings suggested two types of information diffusion consumers: influencers and non-influencers.

2.2 Market Mavenism as Predictor of Negative WOM

For information diffusion, market mavens (i.e., consumers with high market mavenism) are important (Abratt et al. 1995; Slama and Williams 1990). Market mavens are defined as those "individuals who have information about many kinds of products, places to shop, and other facets of markets, and initiate discussions with consumers and respond to requests from consumers for market information" (Feick and Price 1987, p. 85). Consumers with high market mavenism in real life (i.e., offline) are also more likely to have high market mavenism in different channels (e.g., web, virtual world) unlike consumers with low market mavenism (Barnes and Pressey 2012).

A market maven is often seen as similar to an "opinion leader (OL)" and "early adopter (EA)" as an influencer. However, there are two differences (Feick and Price 1987). First, the knowledge of the OL and EA is category specific, as a market maven has general marketplace expertise (e.g., knowledge of changes in pricing, new stores). Second, unlike the OL and EA, a market maven does not need to be a purchaser. In this study, market maven is distinguished from the other concepts.

Since consumers with high market mavenism are important as targeted influencers, numerous studies have worked to identify their profiles. Using that research, market mavenism positively correlates with innovativeness (Feick and Price 1987; Ruvio and Shoham 2007), self-esteem (Clark and Goldsmith 2005), Big Five personality traits (Flynn and Goldsmith 2017; Goodey and East 2008), altruism and market helping behavior (Price et al. 1995; Walsh et al. 2004), attitude toward ads (Sudbury-Riley 2016), and heavy coupon usage (Price et al. 1988).

However, despite its importance, little is known about the relationship between market mavenism and negative WOM beyond Wangenheim's efforts (2005). Using cognitive dissonance theory, Wangenheim (2005) found that consumers with high market mavenism are more likely to engage in post-switching negative WOM to reduce post-decision dissonance. The current study does not necessarily limit its efforts to "post-switching" negative WOM, but rather assumes that market mavenism positively correlates with negative WOM in general, similar to Wangenheim (2005), for two reasons. First, the self-image of "smart shopper" which market mavens emphasize (Feick and Price 1987; Wangenheim 2005) can be maintained and improved by properly criticizing goods and services. This contention is supported by previous research arguing that "in an effort to preserve their self-esteem and their esteem in the eyes of observers, they may become negatively critical of the intelligence or the intellectual work of others" (Amabile 1983, p. 147). Through experiments using book reviews, Amabile (1983) revealed that negative reviewers are seen as less likable, but more intelligent than positive reviewers. Second, consumers with high market mavenism may engage in negative WOM partially for altruistic reasons (Hennig-Thurau et al. 2004; Sundaram et al. 1998). Because market mavenism positively correlates with altruism and market-helping behavior (Price et al. 1995), the implication is that consumers with high market mavenism may engage in negative WOM to prevent other consumers from experiencing service failure. Given this previous research, the following hypothesis is proposed:

H1: Market mavenism positively influences a consumer's (a) negative WOM intention and (b) negative eWOM intention.

2.3 The Moderating Role of Assumed-Competence

To understand the relationship between market mavenism and negative WOM and eWOM intention, this paper adopted the concept of assumed-competence based on undervaluing others (Hayamizu et al. 2004). Assumed-competence "is a form of illusory competence which one gains by demeaning others" (Hayamizu et al. 2004, p. 128). It can be measured by views like "There are a lot of insensitive people around me." The concept was developed to explain the tendency of today's Japanese adolescents to become angry easily and to feel less sadness (Hayamizu et al. 2004). The relationship between assumed-competence and age as having a U-shaped curve (Hayamizu et al. 2007) was then confirmed as a value that is higher in younger individuals and older persons than those who are middle-aged.

More importantly, assumed-competence was distinguished from self-esteem (Hayamizu et al. 2004). While self-esteem relates to positive experiences (e.g., success in sports, achieving good grades), assumed-competence did not display a strong relationship. Using meta-analysis (n = 6367), Okada and Oshio (2012) confirmed that the correlation was quite low and suggested that the concepts were nearly unrelated.

According to an earlier study involving American university students (n = 168), people with high assumed-competence are less inclined to communicate with family and friends than those with low assumed-competence (Hayamizu et al. 2010). That study also revealed that American students score slightly higher for assumed-competence than Japanese students.

Furthermore, people with high assumed-competence are inclined to attack others to confirm their own competence based on both definition and empirical evidence (e.g., Hayamizu (ed.) 2012; Matsumoto et al. 2009). For example, Matsumoto et al. (2009) conducted a survey of Japanese high school students (n = 1062) to examine the relationship between assumed-competence and bullying (physical, verbal, and indirect bullying). They found that students with high assumed-competence had a tendency to engage in bullying more than those with low assumed-competence. Thus, we can hypothesize that assumed-competence amplifies the effect of market mavenism on negative WOM and eWOM. Consumers with high market mavenism may engage in negative WOM, criticizing products/services to maintain and/or improve their "smart shopper" self-image. This tendency is more pronounced in consumers with high assumed-competence. Therefore, the following hypothesis is offered:

H2: When consumer assumed-competence is high, the effect of market mavenism on (a) negative WOM intention and (b) negative eWOM intention is stronger than when consumer assumed-competence is low.

2.4 The Potential Moderating Role of Gender

Interestingly, gender differences exist in motivations among consumers with high market mavenism. Goodey and East (2008) pointed out that the "sexes differed so much on certain personality variables that any overall profile of a market maven could be misleading" (p. 272). For instance, they reported that agreeableness has positive effects on mavenism in females but negative effects in males. Also, there are positive correlations between mavenism and some personalities for males only (openness; self-esteem; materialism). Furthermore, their study revealed moderate negative correlations between market mavenism and demographic factors in females only: age and education.

With insufficient empirical evidence and a lack of theoretical frameworks, the above findings imply that it is reasonable to assume some gender differences in the effects of market mavenism and the interactions of market mavenism and assumed-competence on negative WOM/eWOM intention. For instance, it is likely that the effects of market mavenism and its interactions are more salient in males than in females because market mavens may criticize products or services to enhance their self-esteem (i.e., construction of self-image as smart shopper). As mentioned earlier, self-image has a positive correlation with market mavenism only in males (Goodey and East 2008). Therefore, male market mavens may be inclined to engage more in negative WOM/eWOM than female market mavens.

Based on the above discussions, it is necessary to analyze the effects of market mavenism and its interaction separately by gender. Thus, the following research question (RQ) is offered:

RQ: With respect to the effect of market mavenism and the interaction effect of market mavenism × assumed-competence, are there any differences between females and males?

Figure 1 illustrates the conceptual model proposed in this study.

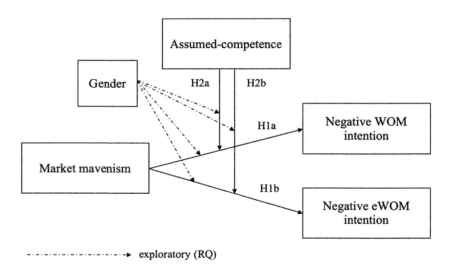

Fig. 1 The Conceptual Model

3 Methods and Results

3.1 Participants and Procedure

The hypotheses were tested using an online survey via a professional research firm that recruits respondents from its own consumer panel. The data were collected in January 2017. The participants were 1,500 Japanese adults who had experienced dissatisfaction with products/services within the past year; 57.1% were females and 42.9% were males. The average age of the sample was 44.76.

The survey measured market mavenism (6 items adapted from Feick and Price 1987, $\alpha = 0.94$, CR $= 0.94$, AVE $= 0.73$), assumed-competence (11 items, Hayamizu et al. 2004, $\alpha = 0.91$, CR $= 0.91$, AVE $= 0.47$), negative offline WOM intention (1 item stating "In case you feel dissatisfied with products or services, you talk about the information face-to-face"), and negative eWOM intention (1 item stating "In case you feel dissatisfied with products or services, you send the information over the Internet such as through an SNS") (see Appendix). The scales in English were translated into Japanese.[1] All items were measured using a 7-point Likert scale (1 = strongly disagree; 7 = strongly agree). All scale reliabilities and convergent validities were also deemed statistically acceptable. The correlation between market mavenism and assumed-competence ($r = 0.06$, $p < 0.05$) was quite low and well below the average variance extracted (AVE), indicating good discriminant validity (Voorhees, Brady, Calantone, and Ramirez 2016).

3.2 Hypotheses Testing

To test H1a and H2a, the negative WOM intention on market mavenism, assumed-competence, and market mavenism × assumed-competence interaction were tested using an SPSS macro PROCESS (Hayes 2018, Model 1) and an HAD Ver.16.056 statistical application (Shimizu 2016). All variables were mean-centered to minimize multicollinearity. The variance inflation factors (VIFs) were well below 10 (highest VIF $= 1.03$). Analysis revealed that the positive effect of market mavenism on negative WOM intention was statistically significant ($\beta = 0.17$, $p < 0.01$), thus supporting H1a (see Table 1. However, market mavenism × assumed-

---

[1] Assumed-competence was measured using the Japanese version of the market mavenism scale (Hayamizu 2006). We referred to the Japanese version of the market mavenism scale (Sakai 2016) as well. This study confirmed the reliability of the scale (N = 1687, $\alpha = .92$).

Table 1 Results of Regression Analysis

	Negative WOM intention			Negative eWOM intention		
Predictor	All (N = 1500)	Female (n = 857)	Male (n = 643)	All (N = 1500)	Female (n = 857)	Male (n = 643)
Market mavenism (MM)	.172***	.151***	.177***	.206***	.190***	.219***
Assumed-competence (AC)	.113***	.154***	.078**	.107***	.142***	.059
MM × AC	.008	-.046	.065*	.077***	.034	.128***
R^2	.044***	.052***	.043**	.060***	.060***	.067***

Note: *$p < .10$; **$p < .05$; ***$p < .01$, Table reports standardized betas

competence interaction was not significant ($\beta = 0.01$, n. s.). Thus, H2a was not supported.

To test H1b and H2b, negativeeWOM intention on mavenism, assumed-competence, and market mavenism × assumed-competence interaction were regressed.[2] This analysis revealed that the positive effect of market mavenism on negative eWoM intention was statistically significant ($\beta = 0.21$, $p < 0.01$), thereby supporting H1b. More importantly, market mavenism × assumed-competence interaction was significant ($\beta = 0.08$, $p < 0.01$) (Table 2).

The two-way interaction effect on negative eWOM intention was explored using a simple slope analysis (Spiller et al. 2013). The result indicated that at low levels of assumed-competence ($-1SD$), market mavenism had a significant positive effect on negative eWOM intention ($\beta = 0.14$, $p < 0.01$), while at high levels of assumed-competence ($+1SD$), market mavenism had a stronger positive effect on negative eWOM intention ($\beta = 0.27$, $p < 0.01$). These results supported H1b (see Fig. 2). We discuss the possible reason why the interaction effect was significant for negative eWOM intention only and not for negative WOM intention.

---

[2] Because the floor effect was confirmed for negative eWOM intention ($M = 2.22$, $SD = 1.62$), a Tobit model analysis was also conducted. No substantial differences between the estimation model (i.e., ordinary least squares (OLS) and Tobit) for the H1b and H2b tests emerged. We report the results of OLS in Table 1.

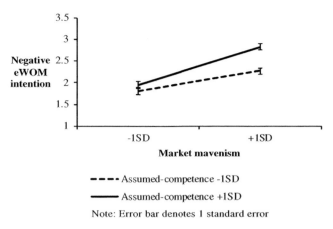

Fig. 2 Results of a Simple Slope Anaysis (Negative eWOM intention)

3.3 Exploratory Analysis of Gender Effect

Gender is the basic for and vital standard of segmentation. Gender segmentation is utilized for many products and services. Thus, it is essential for marketers engaging in customer services to understand any differences stemming from gender. To deepen the understanding of the relationships among market mavenism, assumed-competence, and WOM/eWOM intention, the same analyses for male and female respondents were conducted separately (see Table 1) since previous research has reported gender differences for market mavens' WOM motivation (Goodey and East 2008), as discussed earlier. Here we focus on the particularly interesting results about the interaction effect.

These results indicated that for males the interaction effect on negative WOM intention is marginally significant ($\beta = 0.07$, $p < 0.10$), and the positive effect of market mavenism is stronger at high assumed-competence levels ($\beta = 0.23$, $p < 0.01$) than at low assumed-competence levels ($\beta = 0.14$, $p < 0.05$). For females, no significant interaction effect ($\beta = -0.05$, $n.s.$) was observed. Furthermore, while the interaction effect on negative eWOM was significant for males ($\beta = 0.13$, $p < 0.01$), it was not significant for females ($\beta = 0.03$, $n.s.$). For males, the positive effect of market mavenism was stronger at high assumed-competence levels ($\beta = 0.32$, $p < 0.01$) than at low assumed-competence levels ($\beta = 0.11$, p

<0.05). In other words, neither H2a nor H2b was supported for females, but both were supported for males.

4 Discussion

4.1 Summary

Recently consumers have come to rely on WOM information when they make a purchase (Keller and Fay 2012; You et al. 2015). To obtain quality goods or services, on one hand, consumers check SNSs or brand websites and also get a lot of information from friends and colleagues. On the other hand, consumers who experience dissatisfaction are likely to talk with their family, friends, and colleagues (Singh 1988). With the prevalence of mobile technology and SNSs, they can easily share their dissatisfaction with millions of people. Thus, marketers pay heightened attention to negative WOM and its suppression (Williams and Buttle 2014). This paper provides a new perspective to resolve the issue effectively by revealing the effects of consumer traits for promoting negative WOM.

This paper focused on the potential effects of market mavenism and assumed-competence on negative WOM and eWOM intention. The analyses that were conducted revealed that as H1a and H1b did hypothesize, market mavenism positively influences negative WOM and eWOM intention. Further, the positive influence of market mavenism on negative eWOM intention is stronger in consumers with high assumed-competence than for those with low assumed-competence (H2b). However, it was determined that the moderating effect of assumed-competence was not supported in the case of negative WOM intention (H2a). Further, an exploratory analysis showed there were gender differences in the interaction effect of market maven and assumed-competence.

These findings do make important theoretical contributions to the negative WOM, market mavenism, and assumed-competence literature. First, it was determined that market mavenism is an important predictor of negative WOM/eWOM intention. Although prior studies have revealed that market mavenism does have a positively correlated positive WOM intention (e.g., Feick and Price 1987), little has been known about the effect of market mavenism on negative WOM intention. Wangenheim (2005) did demonstrate that market mavenism increases postswitching negative word of mouth using cognitive dissonance theory. The current study extended those findings by revealing that market mavenism enhances not only postswitching negative WOM, but also negative WOM in general. It also confirmed the impact on negative eWOM intention that was not ever examined explicitly.

Second, these findings show the usefulness of the concept of assumed-competence in the marketing context. It is the first research that has applied this educational psychology concept specifically to marketing research. By introducing the concept, this study elaborates on the effects of market mavenism and found that assumed-competence amplifies the positive effect of market mavenism on negative eWOM intention. This result suggests that not all market mavens will engage in eWOM.

Third, we offer a new perspective on the relationship between market mavenism and gender. Flynn and Goldsmith (2017) suggested that "gender might play an important role in the psychology of mavenism that cannot be ignored" (p. 123). The results from the current study further support this suggestion. Specifically, market mavenism × assumed-competence on negative WOM intention is marginally supported for males, although in the combined data, the effect was cancelled out (H2a was not supported, see Table 1). This result implies that if a researcher is interested in the interaction effect of market mavenism and a psychographic variable, then the gender effect must also be considered.

The current findings also have valuable implications for actual practice. First, marketers should be cautious about consumers with high market mavenism and assumed-competence in service recovery situations. As indicated in the literature review, many researchers have investigated this profile. Marketers will benefit from these findings whenever they engage in complaint handling. In particular, male market mavens with high assumed-competence are more likely to engage in negative WOM behavior. According to prior research (Hayamizu et al. 2007), the relationship between assumed-competence and age follows a U-shaped curve, which means that the score is higher in younger and older individuals than in the middle-aged. Thus, marketers should pay special attention to younger and older market mavens.

Second, if firms consider the current findings, they will be able to implement more effective customer relationship management (cf. Wangenheim 2005). Firms should especially manage market mavens with high assumed-competence so as not to lose them. Thus, marketers engaging in customer relationship management should utilize profiles of market mavens revealed in prior research as their target.

Third, marketers who set a target customer based on gender have to take its effect into account. As the exploratory analysis demonstrated, the interaction of market mavenism and assumed-competence did not influence negative WOM/eWOM intentions for females. This implies that female market mavens have different negative WOM motivations than male market mavens. Still, the study is in an early stage of research, and future research should elaborate the results in this regard.

Certain limitations of this study should be addressed in future research. First, the mediator variables between market mavenism and negative WOM/eWOM intentions should be examined. This paper assumed the mechanism to be altruism and improving self-image based on theoretical backgrounds. However, the mechanism has not been empirically examined. Future research should elaborate this relationship. Then, the effects of gender should be examined further. The current analysis produced a theoretically interesting result; however, it was just exploratory research. Further research is needed to confirm the findings. Finally, future research should be conducted in a different context so as to confirm external validity.

Appendix Scale Items

Market mavenism (Feick and Price 1987)		Mean (SD)	factor loadings
1	I like introducing new brands and products to my friends	4.23 (1.74)	0.83
2	I like helping people by providing them with information about many kind of products	4.66 (1.63)	0.83
3	People ask me for information about products, places to shop, or sales	4.04 (1.68)	0.89
4	If someone asked where to get the best buy on several types of products, I could tell him or her where to shop	4.51 (1.58)	0.87
5	My friends think of me as a good source of information when it comes to new products or sales	3.82 (1.66)	0.86
6	Think about a person who has information about a variety of products and likes to share this information with others. This person knows about new products, sales, stores, and so on, but does not necessarily feel he or she is an expert on one particular product. How well would you say that this description fits you?	4.06 (1.62)	0.84
Assumed-competence (Hayamizu et al. 2004)			
1	There are a lot of insensitive people around me	3.02 (1.43)	0.62

	Market mavenism (Feick and Price 1987)	Mean (SD)	factor loadings
2	Looking at the way others work, I feel that they are inefficient	3.75 (1.55)	0.73
3	I think that there are many people who talk nonsense at a meeting	3.51 (1.52)	0.74
4	I think that there are lot of people who look great but in fact they are unsophisticated and unknowledgeable	3.71 (1.56)	0.74
5	I wonder why others could not understand such a simple task	3.57 (1.55)	0.82
6	It seems to me that there are few efficient people around me whom I can trust with important task	2.85 (1.48)	0.70
7	Looking at others, it seems to me that they are failures	3.15 (1.53)	0.82
8	When my opinion is not supported, I think the other party is not intelligent enough to understand me	3.00 (1.44)	0.62
9	I think that most people who are managing Japan are not so great	3.04 (1.52)	0.59
10	I think that there quite a number of people in the world who achieve high status without much effort	3.94 (1.66)	0.52
11	I think that there are too many people who have no common sense	4.11 (1.51)	0.60
	Negative WOM intention (Original)		
1	In case you feel dissatisfied with products or services, you talk the information face-to-face	2.88 (1.81)	–
	Negative eWOM intention (Original)		
1	In case you feel dissatisfied with products or services, you send the information over the Internet such as SNS	2.22 (1.62)	–

References

Abratt, R., Nel, D., & Nezer, C. (1995). Role of the market maven in retailing: A general marketplace influencer. *Journal of Business and Psychology, 10*(1), 31–55.

Amabile, T. M. (1983). Brilliant but cruel: Perception of negative evaluators. *Journal of Experimental Social Psychology, 19*(2), 146–156.

Barnes, S. J., & Pressey, A. D. (2012). In search of the "Meta-Maven": An examination of market maven behavior across real-life, web, and virtual world marketing channels. *Psychology & Marketing, 29*(3), 167–185.

Bone, P. F. (1995). Word-of-mouth effects on short-term and long-term product judgments. *Journal of Business Research, 32*(3), 213–223.

Chevalier, J. A., & Mayzlin, D. (2006). The effect of word of mouth on sales: Online book reviews. *Journal of Marketing Research, 43*(3), 345–354.

Clark, R. A., & Goldsmith, R. E. (2005). Market mavens: Psychological influences. *Psychology & Marketing, 22*(4), 289–312.

Duan, W., Gu, B., & Whinston, A. B. (2008). The dynamics of online word-of-mouth and product sales: An empirical investigation of the movie industry. *Journal of Retailing, 84*(2), 233–242.

Feick, L. F., & Price, L. L. (1987). The market maven: A diffuser of marketplace information. *Journal of Marketing, 51*(1), 83–97.

Flynn, L. R., & Goldsmith, R. E. (2017). Filling some gaps in market mavenism research. *Journal of Consumer Behaviour, 16*(2), 121–129.

Gauri, D. K., Harmon-Kizer, T. R., & Talukdar, D. (2016). Antecedents and outcomes of market mavenism: Insight based on survey and purchase data. *Journal of Business Research, 69*(3), 1053–1060.

Goodey, C., & East, R. (2008). Testing the market maven concept. *Journal of Marketing Management, 24*(3–4), 265–282.

Grégoire, Y., Ghadami, F., Laporte, S., Sénécal, S., & Larocque, D. (2018). How can firms stop customer revenge? the effects of direct and indirect revenge on post-complaint responses . *Journal of the Academy of Marketing Science, 46*(6), 1052–1071.

Hayamizu, T. (2006). *Tanin wo mikudasu wakamono tachi*. Tokyo: Kodansha (published in Japanese).

Hayamizu, T. (ed.). (2012). Kasouteki yuunoukan no sinrigaku [Psychology of assumed-competence based on undervaluing others], Kyoto: Kitaoji Shobou (published in Japanese).

Hayamizu, T., Kino, K., & Takagi, K. (2007). Effects of age and competence type on the emotiotns: Focusing on sadness and anger. *Japanese Psychological Research, 49*(3), 211–221.

Hayamizu, T., Kino, K., Takagi, K., & Tan, E.-H. (2004). Assumed-competence based on undervaluing others as a determinant of emotions: Focusing on anger and sadness. *Asia Pacific Education Review, 5*(2), 127–135.

Hayamizu, T., Y. Nozaki, and T. Umemoto. (2010). Assumed-competence based on undervaluing others among American college students. *Bulletin of the Graduate School of Education and Human Development (Nagoya University) 57*, 47–59 (published in Japanese).

Hayes, A. F. (2018). *Introduction to Mediation, Moderation, and Conditional Process Analysis* (2nd ed.). New York: Guilford.
Hennig-Thurau, T., Gwinner, K. P., Walsh, G., & Gremler, D. D. (2004). Electronic word-of-mouth via consumer-opinion platforms: What motivates consumers to articulate themselves on the internet? *Journal of Interactive Marketing, 18*(1), 38–52.
Herr, P. M., Kardes, F. R., & Kim, J. (1991). Effects of word-of-mouth and product-attribute information on persuasion: An accessibility-diagnosticity perspective. *Journal of Consumer Research, 17*(4), 454–462.
Hirschman, A. O. (1970). *Exit, Voice, and Loyalty: Responses to decline in firms, organizations, and states.* Cambridge M. A.: Harvard University Press.
Istanbulluoglu, D., Leek, S., & Szmigin, I. T. (2017). Beyond exit and voice: Developing an integrated taxonomy of consumer complaining behavior. *European Journal of Marketing, 51*(5/6), 1109–1128.
Keller, E., & Fay, B. (2012). *The face-to-face book: Why real relationship rule in a digital marketplace.* New York: FreePress.
Matsumoto, M., M. Yamamoto, & Hayamizu, T. (2009). Relation between assumed-competence and bullying in high school students. *Japanese Journal of Educational Psychology 57,* 432–441 (published in Japanese).
Okada, R., & Oshio, S. (2012). *1–3: Rinsetsugainen (jikoai, jisonkanjyou) tono ruijiten to souiten, in Kasouteki yuunoukan no sinrigaku [Psychology of assumed-competence based on undervaluing others],* T. Hayamizu (ed.), 15–34, Kyoto: Kitaoji Shobou (published in Japanese).
Price, L. L., Feick, L. F., & Guskey-Federouch, A. (1988). Couponing behaviors of the market maven: Profile of a super couponer. *Advances in Consumer Research, 15,* 354–359.
Price, L. L., Feick, L. F., & Guskey, A. (1995). Everyday market helping behavior. *Journal of Public Policy & Marketing, 14*(2), 255–266.
Richins, M. L. (1983). Negative word-of-mouth by dissatisfied consumers: A pilot study. *Journal of Marketing, 47*(1), 68–78.
Ruvio, A., & Shoham, A. (2007). Innovativeness, exploratory behavior, market mavenship, and opinion leadership: An empirical examination in the Asian context. *Psychology & Marketing, 24*(8), 703–722.
Sudbury-Riley, L. (2016). The baby boomer market maven in the United Kingdom: An experienced diffuser of marketplace information. *Journal of Marketing Management, 32*(7–8), 716–749.
Sakai, N. (2016). Typology of media followers: Offering potential for new models of advertising that will connect. *Bulletin of Nikkei Advertising Research Institute, 50* (4), 3–12 (published in Japanese).
Shimizu, H. (2016). An introduction to the statistical free software HAD: Suggestions to improve teaching, learning and practice data analysis. *Journal of Media, Information and Communication, 1,* 59–73 (published in Japanese).
Singh, J. (1988). Consumer complaint intentions and behavior: Definitional and taxonomical issues. *Journal of Marketing, 52*(1), 93–107.
Slama, M. E., & Williams, T. G. (1990). Generalization of the market maven's information provision tendency. *Advances in Consumer Research, 17,* 48–52.

Spiller, S. A., Fitzsimons, G. J., & Lynch, J. G., Jr., and McClelland. (2013). Spotlights, floodlights, and the magic number zero: Simple effects tests in moderated regression. *Journal of Marketing Research, 50*(2), 277–288.

Sundaram, D. S., Mitra, K., & Webster, C. (1998). Word-of-mouth communications: A motivational analysis. *Advances in Consumer Research, 25,* 527–531.

Voorhees, C. M., Brady, M. K., Calantone, R., & Ramirez, E. (2016). Discriminant validity testing in marketing: An analysis, causes for concern, and proposed remedies. *Journal of the Academy of Marketing Science, 44*(1), 119–134.

Walsh, G., Gwinner, K. P., & Swanson, S. R. (2004). What makes mavens tick? Exploring the Motives of Market Mavens' Initiation of Information Diffusion. *Journal of Consumer Marketing, 21*(2), 109–122.

Wangenheim, F. v. (2005). Postswitching Negative Word of Mouth. *Journal of Service Research, 8*(1), 67–78.

Wangenheim, Fv., & Bayón, T. (2004). The effect of word of mouth on services switching. *European Journal of Marketing, 38*(9/10), 1173–1185.

Ward, J. C., & Ostrom, A. L. (2006). Complaining to the masses: The role of protest framing in customer-created complaint web sites. *Journal of Consumer Research, 33*(2), 220–230.

William, M., & Buttle, F. (2014). Managing negative word-of-mouth: An exploratory study. *Journal of Marketing Management, 30*(13–14), 1423–1447.

You, Y., Vadakkepatt, G. G., & Joshi, A. M. (2015). A meta-analysis of electronic word-of-mouth elasticity. *Journal of Marketing, 79*(2), 19–39.

Gender Responses to Emotional Appeals in Advertising: Comparing Self-Reports and Facial Expressions

Eirini Tsichla, Maria C. Voutsa, Kostoula Margariti, and Leonidas Hatzithomas

1 Introduction

Emotional appeals in advertising represent one of the most frequently used creative strategies. Considering that their effectiveness lies on consumers' subjective reactions to emotions, understanding gender differences in affective responses can form the basis for the development of successful advertising messages (Schwarz et al. 2015). Prior research has highlighted various gender reactions across different emotional appeals in advertising. For instance, women appear to be more receptive towards subtle advertisements that appeal to warmth and affection (Schwarz et al. 2015), while men are more positive towards aggressive, violent and provocative advertisements (Swani et al. 2013).

These differences have been attributed to biological and most importantly social factors (Putrevu 2001; Weinberger et al. 2016). The paternalistic social standards have "constructed" a fragile, susceptible identity for women and a dominant, dynamic role for men (Meyers-Levy and Sternthal 1991). In this light, women learn to effortlessly express their emotions (Simon and Nath 2004), while men are told to oppress their emotions towards third parties, in order to maintain a strong social image (Gallois and Callan 1986). Research findings corroborate to

E. Tsichla (✉) · M. C. Voutsa · K. Margariti · L. Hatzithomas
Department of Business Administration, University of Macedonia, Thessaloniki, Greece
E-Mail: etsichla@uowm.gr

M. C. Voutsa
E-Mail: mcvoutsa@econ.auth.gr

L. Hatzithomas
E-Mail: hatzithomas@uom.edu.gr

the above pattern, as men avoid revealing that they are enjoying an advertisement that depicts warm emotions when they are watching it in the presence of others (Fisher and Dubé 2005). Nonetheless, there is no evidence on how women experience advertising appeals that are incompatible with the traditional female stereotype. The proposed study aims to navigate these waters and elucidate the nature of women's emotional experience when exposed to advertisements that display scenes of aggressiveness.

In a comprehensive review of emotion measurement in advertising, Poels and Dewitte (2006) distinguished between two types of measures of emotions in advertising: a) self-reports and b) autonomic, encompassing heart rate, skin conductance and facial expressions. The majority of the relevant literature has extensively used self-assessment questionnaires in order to capture the emotional experience of subjects during their exposure to advertising messages. Nonetheless, the limitations of these measures have been widely acknowledged, urging the need to focus on applied research in order to directly observe human behavior (Baumeister et al. 2007). Considering that the validity of self-reports for measuring emotions can be biased by cognitive or social desirability constraints, the measurement of autonomic reactions may cater for the weaknesses of self-evaluation measures as they capture emotional responses beyond the subjects' control (Poels and Dewitte 2006) that can hardly be manipulated by research subjects (Cacioppo and Petty 1985; Wang and Minor 2008). Autonomic measures may record respondents' brain activity, heart rate fluctuation, skin conductance variation, eye movement and facial expressions (Lewinski et al. 2014). However, with the exception of facial recognition software, the majority of the aforementioned measurement tools are invasive (Hamelin et al. 2017), posing ecological validity concerns. Thus, they are seldom used in advertising research. The proposed study aims to contribute to the literature on emotion measurement in advertising research through the combined use of a self-evaluation questionnaire and facial expression analysis. In particular, the study aims to trace whether the expressed emotions portrayed in the participants' faces, detected by a facial recognition software during their exposure to emotional advertising stimuli, coincide with their self-reports.

Therefore, the objective of this study is to address the following research questions:

(a) What are the emotional reactions reported by men and women when they are exposed to warm, aggressive and emotionally neutral advertising stimuli?

(b) What are the expressed emotions (as detected by the analysis of facial expressions) shown by both genders, upon their exposure to warm, aggressive and emotionally neutral advertising stimuli?

2 Literature Review

2.1 Gender Differences in the Expression of Emotion

The perception of gender differences in their emotional responses is one of the most dominant and commonplace stereotypes. *"Everyone knows the prevailing emotion stereotype: She is emotional, he is not"* (Shields 2002, p. 3). Numerous studies support that gender differences in terms of the expression of emotional experience are arising from the roles undertaken by men and women in the society (Eagly 1987; Wood and Rhodes 1992). According to the normative theory of Hochschild (1975), the differences between men and women in emotional reactions and expressiveness converge with gender specific beliefs of the underlying culture. Hence, gender stereotypes signify the way in which people should (or shouldn't) feel and express under different circumstances. Thus, when emotional experience deviates from pre-specified rules, people are more inclined to manage and ultimately repress their feelings, in order to demonstrate a more appropriate emotional behavior.

Differences in social roles form the foundation of stereotypical beliefs about the expected emotional behaviors of men and women. Women are described as emotionally expressive and unstable, preoccupied not only with their own emotional world but with that of others as well (Bakan 1966; Grossman and Wood 1993). On the other hand, contemporary male stereotypes are either linked with the desire for dominance and superiority or with the stoicism associated with the strict avoidance of behaviors that reflect sensitivity (Eagly et al. 2000; Fisher and Dubé 2005).

3 Hypotheses Development

Emotional appeals in advertising can be categorized in terms of valence as positive (e.g. warmth, love) and negative (e.g. guilt, aggression, shame, fear). Aggression covers a wide range of behaviors, situations and events that may cause harm and injury of varying sorts and differing magnitudes (Berkowitz 1993). On the other hand, warmth is defined as a positive, gentle and volatile emotion and as part of empathetic emotional response (Coke et al. 1978). Aaker and Bruzzone (1981) argue that warmth is associated to advertisements that are using sentimental, "family and friends" creative approaches, which attempt to make viewers feel good about themselves.

The relationship between emotional reactions and advertising evaluation is likely to be colored by gender. Men have been found to prefer advertising scenarios that promote competitiveness and demonstrate authority (Prakash 1992) as well as more violent advertising scenarios than women (Swani et al. 2013). On the contrary, research evidence demonstrates that warm appeals are more effective in raising brand awareness and loyalty for women compared to men (Aaker and Stayman 1989; Geuens and de Pelsmacker 1998).

In addition, relevant studies reveal the existence of differences in the emotional expressivity of men and women that can be traced in the greater desire of men to adapt their emotional profile in what they consider to be appropriate or socially acceptable (Fischer and Manstead 2000; Fisher and Dubé 2005). In particular, men often experience emotions incongruent to the male stereotype in private conditions, but they avoid the expression of these very emotions when they are in the public sphere (Fisher and Dubé 2005). As far as women are concerned, research conducted by Hoffman et al. (2005) showed that women perceive the expressiveness and orientation towards others as a fundamental characteristic of their femininity, highlighting the potential influence of gender clichés on their responses.

Following the preceding analysis, gender reactions in emotional advertising appeals are expected to vary in terms of the type of appeal (aggression, warmth and non-emotional) and the congruence of the particular emotional appeal to the gender stereotype. Specifically, the incongruence between the appeal and the gender's emotional stereotype would lead to lower levels of positive and higher levels of negative emotions.

H1: Males who are exposed to an aggressive advertising appeal will report more positive and less negative emotions compared to females

H2: Females who are exposed to a warm advertising appeal will report more positive and less negative emotions compared to males

H3: No significant differences are expected between males' and females' emotional responses for the non-emotional advertising appeal

Although numerous studies have examined emotions using self-report questionnaires, it should be emphasized that these measures are subject to the influence of gender stereotypes and social desirability bias (Grossman and Wood 1993; Hess et al. 2000). In that sense, the strong tendency of people in presenting themselves favorably is likely to distort the information retrieved from such measures. Thus, participants may be unwilling to give an honest answer, providing information that reflects reality with less accuracy, due to self-defense or impression management concerns (Maccoby and Maccoby 1954). This phenomenon is known as social desirability bias and can be a critical issue in several research designs, as the presence of the researcher may invoke a desire to save face (Stodel 2015).

According to LaFrance and Banaji (1992), gender differences tend to occur in terms of emotional expressiveness rather than emotional experience. Thus, there is a possibility that the reported differences in emotional reactions between males and females is an illusion created by stereotypes so deeply engraved in popular culture, that can predispose participants' answers (McRae et al. 2008). However, autonomic measures such as the analysis of facial expressions are outside of the respondent's conscious appraisal and hence provide a more accurate assessment of the respondent's emotional reactions (Poels and Dewitte 2006), less affected by social desirability. Facial expressions can be measured through electromyography (EMG), using coding systems like the Facial Action Coding System (FACS) (Ekman and Friesen 1978) and more recently, automated facial expression recognition systems. Studies using such measures suggest the absence of differences between the two genders in terms of emotional responses (e.g. Danner et al. 2014; Hamelin et al. 2017). Therefore, it would be reasonable to assume that facial expression analysis would suggest the absence of differences between the two genders such as:

H4: The effect of gender on positive and negative emotions will not be significant when participants' emotions are captured through the analysis of facial expressions

4 Methodology

4.1 Participants and Experimental Design

In order to test the research hypotheses a 2 (sex: male or female) × 3 (emotional appeal: warmth, aggression, non-emotional appeal) between-subjects experiment was conducted. The study recruited students from a large university in Northern Greece. The experimental procedure in all three scenarios was identical. Two researchers (a male and a female) were present during the procedure. Participants were distributed in three experimental groups: the first group was exposed to a warm advertisement, the second group watched the aggressive advertisement, while the third experienced the non-emotional one. The total sample of the experiment comprised of 54 respondents (28 males). All subjects were instructed to watch the advertisement on a computer screen and then complete a questionnaire that measured their emotional reactions.

4.2 Stimulus Materials

For the purpose of the experimental procedure one TV commercial for a filter coffee brand was created by a professional advertising agency. The use of TV commercials has been qualified for the experiment, since they are able to express precisely the different emotional appeals, namely, warmth and aggression. In contrast, when static print advertisements are used in experimental procedures for the study of advertising effectiveness, emotional variations tend to be very small (Weinberger and Gulas 1992).

The choice of the product was based on a pretest with 48 participants that were instructed to report their feelings regarding 14 different types of products. Coffee is a low involvement product that appeals to both sexes and was associated with both warmth and aggressiveness. In order to increase the ecological validity of the study, the coffee brand shown in the advertisement is an actual brand that is not available in Greece. Items measuring familiarity with the brand were included in the questionnaire in order to rule out potential bias due to existing attitudes and beliefs about the brand. Each advertisement was developed in three different versions (a warm, an aggressive, and a non-emotional version). The manipulation of the emotional appeals was based on the character that performed the main role in the scenario. The ad depicted a man, making coffee and sipping from his mug with delight, when a female character approached and gently tried to take his mug. In the aggressive scenario the man threatens the woman with a knife and takes the mug back. In the warm version, the man offers affectionately to the woman a strawberry cake which she savours with enjoyment, while he is gently taking the mug from her hand. In the non-emotional version, the man simply denies to give his mug to the woman.

4.3 Measures

The emotional reactions triggered by the advertisements were measured by the 22-item scale developed by Holbrook and Batra (1987). The questions focused on emotions of happiness (positive emotion), sadness, anger and fear (negative emotions). These emotions can also be detected by the FaceReader 8.0 software. Manipulation checks of the emotional appeals of warmth and aggression were conducted using the items developed by Swani et al. (2013). All variables were measured using five-point Likert scales ranging from (1) "strongly disagree" to (5) "strongly agree." During participants' exposure to the advertisements, their facial expressions were recorded with the use of a computer camera and analyzed through FaceReader 8.0 (Noldus Information Technology) software in order to be compared with their responses provided in the self-reported questionnaires.

4.4 Results

Perceived warmth was higher for the warm ad ($M = 3.72$) compared to the non-emotional ($M = 2.85$, $p = 0.038$) and the aggressive ($M = 2.86$, $p = 0.028$) ad ($F(2, 51) = 4.586$, $p = 0.015$). Perceived aggressiveness was also higher for the aggressive ad ($M = 3.1$) than the non-emotional ($M = 1.56$, $p < 0.001$) and the warm ad ($M = 1.13$, $p < 0.001$) ($F(2, 51) = 21.255$, $p < 0.001$) which indicates a successful manipulation.

A 2 (sex: male or female) × 3 (emotional appeal: warmth, aggression, non-emotional) between-subjects multivariate analysis of variance (MANOVA) was conducted. Happiness, sadness, fear and anger were treated as dependent variables in order to test hypotheses H1-3 (Table 1).

The MANOVA analysis indicates that the main effect of emotional appeal ($F(8, 86) = 10.526$, $p < 0.001$; Wilk's $\Lambda = 0.255$; partial $\eta^2 = 0.495$) and gender ($F(4, 43) = 6.92$, $p < 0.001$; Wilk's $\Lambda = 0.608$; partial $\eta^2 = 0.392$) was statistically significant.

The interaction effect of the type of emotional appeal and gender was also significant ($F(8, 86) = 13.323$, $p < 0.001$; Wilk's $\Lambda = 0.199$; partial $\eta^2 = 0.553$). As initially assumed, this interaction also exerted a statistically significant effect on all emotions. In order to test the moderating effect of gender on emotional responses, planned contrasts were performed (Fig. 1).

The findings reveal that in the case of the aggressive ad females express more sadness ($p < 0.001$; Fig. 1b), anger ($p < 0.001$; Fig. 1c), and fear ($p < 0.001$; Fig. 1d) than males, while males express more happiness than females ($p < 0.001$; Fig. 1a). Hence, hypothesis H1 is supported. When exposed to the warm ad, females express higher levels of happiness than males ($p < 0.001$; Fig. 1a), while no statistically significant differences were reported between genders on negative

Table 1 Descriptive statistics, mean (Standard Error) scores of manipulation measurements and dependent variables

Dependent variables		Emotional Appeal	M	F	p-value	F—statistic
Happy	SR	Aggressive	2.79 (0.2)	1.17 (0.2)	<0.001	$F(2, 46) =$ 44.734, $p < 0.001$
		Warm	1.54 (0.22)	3.87 (0.23)	<0.001	
		Non-emotional	1.42 (0.21)	1.13 (0.23)	0.362	
Sad	SR	Aggressive	0.94 (0.11)	1.79 (0.11)	<0.001	$F(2, 46) =$ 10.833, $p < 0.001$
		Warm	0.98 (0.12)	1.11 (0.13)	0.489	
		Non-emotional	1.07 (0.11)	0.91 (0.12)	0.357	
Angry	SR	Aggressive	0.95 (0.11)	2.31 (0.11)	<0.001	$F(2, 46) =$ 26.060, $p < 0.001$
		Warm	0.94 (0.12)	1.13 (0.13)	0.289	
		Non-emotional	1.06 (0.11)	0.89 (0.12)	0.333	
Fear	SR	Aggressive	0.98 (0.12)	1.72 (0.12)	<0.001	$F(2, 46) =$ 6.509, $p = 0.003$
		Warm	0.95 (0.13)	1.07 (0.13)	0.528	
		Non-emotional	1.02 (0.12)	0.95 (0.13)	0.687	
Happy	FE	Aggressive	0.094 (0.03)	0.118 (0.03)	0.584	$F(2, 46) =$ 10.793, $p < 0.001$
		Warm	−0.013 (0.04)	0.299 (0.04)	<0.001	
		Non-emotional	0.012 (0.03)	0.044 (0.04)	0.522	
Sad	FE	Aggressive	0.012 (0.01)	0.058 (0.01)	0.008	$F(2, 46) =$ 2.981, $p = 0.061$
		Warm	0.028 (0.01)	0.014 (0.01)	0.472	

(continued)

Table 1 (continued)

Dependent variables		Emotional Appeal	M	F	p-value	F—statistic
		Non-emotional	0.008 (0.01)	0.02 (0.01)	0.529	
Angry	FE	Aggressive	0.174 (0.03)	0.111 (0.03)	0.176	$F(2, 46) =$ 2.319, $p = 0.11$
		Warm	0.046 (0.04)	−0.024 (0.04)	0.202	
		Non-emotional	−0.031 (0.03)	0.047 (0.04)	0.151	
Fear	FE	Aggressive	0.001 (0.0)	0.003 (0.0)	0.220	$F(2, 46) =$ 0.341, $p = 0.713$
		Warm	0.002 (0.0)	0.006 (0.0)	0.095	
		Non-emotional	0.001 (0.0)	0.002 (0.0)	0.609	

Note. All scale-items were on a 5-point Likert scale; SR—Self-report; FE—Facial Expressions, M—Males, F—Females

emotions ($ps > 0.29$). Therefore, H2 is partially supported. No statistically significant differences were reported between males' and females' emotional reactions for the non-emotional ad ($ps > 0.33$). Hence, hypothesis H3 is supported.

As far as the analysis of facial expressions is concerned, the interaction effect of the type of emotional appeals and gender also exerted a statistically significant effect on happiness ($F(2, 46) = 10.793, p < 0.001$) and sadness ($F(2, 46) = 2.981, p = 0.061$; Table 1). Specifically, when exposed to the warm ad, females show higher levels of happiness ($p < 0.001$; Fig. 2a), whereas when exposed to the aggressive ad they demonstrate higher levels of sadness compared to males ($p = 0.008$; Fig. 2b). As a result, H4 is partially supported.

5 Discussion

In line with prior findings (Geuens and de Pelsmacker 1998; Swani et al. 2013), this study suggests that the main effects and the interaction effect of the type of emotional appeals and gender are statistically significant. Particularly, the research shows that an aggressive advertising appeal evokes higher levels of happiness

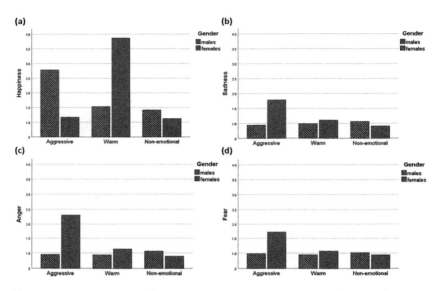

Fig. 1 Two-way interaction effects of self-report measurements (Hypotheses H1-3)

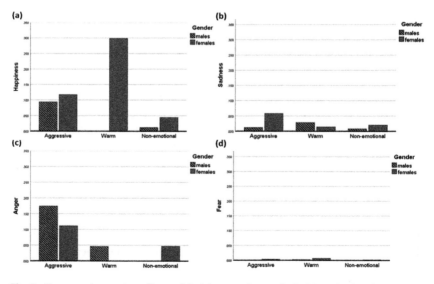

Fig. 2 Two-way interaction effects of facial expression analysis (Hypothesis H4)

and lower levels of sadness, fear and anger for males whereas a warm advertising appeal evokes higher levels of happiness for females. Similar to expectations, no significant differences were reported after participants' exposure to the nonemotional advertising appeal. Finally, the facial expression analysis revealed that males and females portray similar responses towards the advertisements except for women, who generated higher levels of happiness for the warm ad and higher levels of sadness for the aggressive ad. It is interesting that although several women reported negative emotions such as anger and fear for the aggressive advertisement, such emotions were not evident in their facial expression analysis. This difference could be interpreted from a social desirability viewpoint, that dictates gender appropriate responses that coincide with their sensitive, fragile nature and an aversion for violence and aggression.

The findings draw important managerial implications that could benefit the marketers' and advertisers' efforts to communicate with their target groups by highlighting the effectiveness of warmth and aggressiveness to evoke emotional reactions and by specifying these very emotions for men and women. In addition, the results indicate that aggressive appeals should be treated with caution if they are addressed to a female audience, as they instill negative affective responses and ultimately, may create a backlash against the sponsor of the message.

Further research could broaden the subject area and face some limitations of the present study. Considering that culture plays an important role affecting emotional expressivity, future research could recruit participants from different cultural backgrounds, enhancing the generalizability of the findings. Moreover, this study employed a small sample of participants and thus constitutes a modest beginning for the thorough understanding of the subject area that needs to be corroborated by studies with larger sample sizes.

References

Aaker, D. A., & Bruzzone, D. E. (1981). Viewer perceptions of prime-time television advertising. *Journal of Advertising Research, 21*(5), 15–23.
Aaker, D. A., & Stayman, D. M. (1989). What mediates the emotional response to advertising? The case of warmth. In P. Cafferata & A. M. Tybout (Eds.), *Cognitive and affective responses to advertising* (pp. 287–304). Lexinton: Lexington.
Bakan, D. (1966). *The duality of human existence.* Chicago: Rand McNally.
Baumeister, R. F., Vohs, K. D., & Funder, D. C. (2007). Psychology as the science of self-reports and finger movements: Whatever happened to actual behavior? *Perspectives on Psychological Science, 2*(4), 396–403.

Berkowitz, L. (1993). *Aggression: Its causes, consequences, and control.* New York: McGraw-Hill.

Cacioppo, J. T., & Petty, R. E. (1985). Physiological responses and advertising effects: Is the cup half full or half empty? *Psychology & Marketing, 2*(2), 115–126.

Coke, J. S., Batson, D. C., & McDavis, K. (1978). Empathic mediation of helping: A two-stage model. *Journal of Personality and Social Psychology, 36*(7), 752–766.

Danner, L., Sidorkina, L., Joechl, M., & Duerrschmid, K. (2014). Make a face! Implicit and explicit measurement of facial expressions elicited by orange juices using face reading technology. *Food Quality and Preference, 32*(Part B), 167–172.

Eagly, A. H. (1987). *Sex differences in social behavior: A social-role interpretation.* Hillsdale: Erlbaum.

Eagly, A. H., Wood, W., & Diekman, A. B. (2000). Social role theory of sex differences and similarities: A current appraisal. In T. Eckes & H. M. Trautner (Eds.), *The developmental social psychology of gender* (pp. 123–174). New York: Psychology Press.

Ekman, P., & Friesen, W. V. (1978). *The facial action coding system.* Palo Alto: Consulting Psychologists Press.

Fischer, A. H., & Manstead, A. S. R. (2000). The relation between gender and emotions in different cultures. In A. H. Fischer (Ed.), *Gender and emotion: Social psychological perspectives* (pp. 71–94). Cambridge: Cambridge University Press.

Fisher, R. J., & Dube, L. (2005). Gender differences in responses to emotional advertising: A social desirability perspective. *Journal of Consumer Research, 31*(4), 850–858.

Gallois, C., & Callan, V. J. (1986). Decoding emotional messages: Influence of ethnicity, sex, message type, and channel. *Journal of Personality and Social Psychology, 51*(4), 755–762.

Geuens, M., & De Pelsmacker, P. (1998). Need for Cognition and the Moderating Role of the Intensity of Warm and Humorous Advertising Appeals. *Asia Pacific Advances in Consumer Research, 3,* 74–80.

Grossman, M., & Wood, W. (1993). Sex differences in intensity of emotional experience: A social role interpretation. *Journal of Personality and Social Psychology, 65*(5), 1010–1022.

Hamelin, N., El Moujahid, O., & Thaichon, P. (2017). Emotion and advertising effectiveness: A novel facial expression analysis approach. *Journal of Retailing and Consumer Services, 36*(C), 103–111.

Hess, U., Senécal, S., Kirouac, G., Herrera, P., Philippot, P., & Kleck, R. E. (2000). Emotional expressivity in men and women: Stereotypes and self-perceptions. *Cognition & Emotion, 14*(5), 609–642.

Hochschild, A. R. (1975). The sociology of feeling and emotion: Selected possibilities. In M. Millman & R. M. Kantor (Eds.), *Another voice: Feminist perspectives on social life and social science* (pp. 208–307). New York: Anchor Books.

Hoffman, R. M., Hattie, J. A., & Borders, D. L. (2005). Personal Definitions of Masculinity and Femininity as an Aspect of Gender Self-Concept. *Journal of Humanistic Counseling, Education, and Development, 44*(1), 66–83.

Holbrook, M. B., & Rajeev, B. (1987). Assessing the role of emotions as mediators of consumer responses to advertising. *Journal of Consumer Research, 14*(3), 404–420.

LaFrance, M., & Banaji, M. (1992). Toward a reconsideration of the gender-emotion relationship. In M. S. Clark (Ed.), *Emotion and social behavior* (pp. 178–201). Thousand Oaks: Sage.

Lewinski, P., Fransen, M. L., & Tan, Ed. S. H. (2014). Predicting advertising effectiveness by facial expressions in response to amusing persuasive stimuli. *Journal of Neuroscience, Psychology and Economics, 7*(1), 1–14.

Maccoby, E. E., & Maccoby, N. (1954). The interview: A tool of social science. In L. Gardner (Ed.), *Handbook of social psychology* (Vol. I, pp. 449–487). Cambridge: Addison-Wesley.

McRae, K., Ochsner, K. N., Mauss, I. B., Gabrieli, J. J. D., & Gross, J. J. (2008). Gender differences in emotion regulation: An fMRI study of cognitive reappraisal. *Group Processes & Intergroup Relations, 11*(2), 143–162.

Meyers-Levy, J., & Sternthal, B. (1991). Gender differences in the use of message cues and judgments. *Journal of Marketing Research, 28*(1), 84–96.

Poels, K., & Dewitte, S. (2006). How to capture the heart? Reviewing 20 years of emotion measurement in advertising. *Journal of Advertising Research, 46*(1), 18–37.

Prakash, V. (1992). Sex roles and advertising preferences. *Journal of Advertising Research, 32*(3), 43–52.

Putrevu, S. (2001). Exploring the origins and information processing differences between men and women: Implications for advertisers. *Academy of Marketing Science Review, 10*(1), 1–13.

Schwarz, U., Hoffmann, S., & Katharina, H. (2015). Do men and women laugh about different types of humor? A comparison of satire, sentimental comedy, and comic wit in print ads. *Journal of Current Issues & Research in Advertising, 36*(1), 70–87.

Shields, S. A. (2002). *Speaking from the heart: Gender and the social meaning of emotion.* UK: Cambridge University Press.

Simon, R. W., & Nath, L. E. (2004). Gender and emotion in the United States: Do men and women differ in self-reports of feelings and expressive behavior? *American Journal of Sociology, 109*(5), 1137–1176.

Stodel, M. (2015). But what will people think? Getting beyond social desirability bias by increasing cognitive load. *International Journal of Market Research, 57*(2), 313–322.

Swani, K., Weinberger, M. G., & Gulas, C. S. (2013). The impact of violent humor on advertising success: A gender perspective. *Journal of Advertising, 42*(4), 308–319.

Wang, Y. J., & Minor, M. S. (2008). Validity, reliability, and applicability of psychophysiological techniques in marketing research. *Psychology and Marketing, 25*(2), 197–232.

Weinberger, M. G., & Gulas, C. S. (1992). The impact of humor in advertising: A review. *Journal of Advertising, 21*(4), 35–59.

Weinberger, M. G., Swani, K., Yoon, H. J., & Gulas, C. S. (2016). Understanding responses to comedic advertising aggression: The role of vividness and gender identity. *International Journal of Advertising, 36*(4), 562–587.

Wood, W., & Rhodes, N. (1992). Sex differences in interaction style in task groups. In C. L. Ridgeway (Ed.), *Gender, interaction, and inequality* (pp. 97–121). New York: Springer.

Sustainability and Diversity Labels in Job Ads and Their Effect on Employer Brands

Denise F. Kleiss and Martin K. J. Waiguny

1 Introduction

Nowadays talent management and competition are considered a global phenomenon. Competition does not only happen at a local level, but has moved internationally and people are willing to change jobs and locations more often (Macey and Schneider 2008). Employment markets are characterized by high competition, and obtaining suitable human resources in a competitive market becomes more difficult. A survey by Manpower (2015) including 750 employers in 42 countries indicated that 38% struggle to fill positions, 45% face a shortage of candidates and these percentages continue to increase in recent years (Manpower 2015).

Human Resource Managers and executives who want their company to be regarded as having one of the most attractive workplaces can play a key role in ensuring that what a company is showing publicly outside aligns with how their employees are treated inside (Strandberg 2009; Wilden et al. 2010). In order to win this war for talents, business have to focus on marketing themselves rather than just their products or services (Ritz and Sinelli 2018). In response companies are trying to adopt ways to attract suitable candidates in order to fill key positions. The challenge for HR is to make employer branding so attractive that it withstands the value-fit of the attracted generation (Salmen 2012).

D. F. Kleiss (✉) · M. K. J. Waiguny
IMC University of Applied Sciences Krems, Krems, Austria
E-Mail: denise.kleiss@fh-krems.ac.at

M. K. J. Waiguny
E-Mail: martin.waiguny@fh-krems.ac.at

When referring to the image, especially Corporate Social Responsibility (CSR) plays a crucial role. Employers are adopting various CSR activities that reflect their overall commitments, ecological footprint, caring for the communities and diversity, which reflect the image that the company wishes to portray (Grosser and Moon 2005). The employer brand is used to issue unique benefits to current and potential employees and highlight distinctive strengths of the organization (Viot and Benraiss-Noailles 2014).

Enhancing the employer brand through CSR activities is a complex matter, especially when communicating them in job advertisements. Studies in the domain of investigating the relationship between CSR and recruiting mostly used complex descriptions of the organizations' behaviors (Bauer and Aiman-Smith 1996; Duarte et al. 2014; Turban and Greening 1997), which does not reflect reality of job-advertisements where potential recruits only have some limited information and the potential employer is limited by the space of the job ad.

In consumer research, certification standards are often signaled by visible labels or seals attached (Jahn et al. 2005). In recent times certification seals and labels for CSR like sustainability or diversity issues show increased popularity, examples include "baby friendly company", "rainbow tick", or "equal salary" as well as all kinds of organic labels such as fairtrade labels, or the PRME Sustainable Development Goals wheel. Also, accreditations such as "Top Employer", "Great Place to Work" signal that the working conditions for employees are appealing. When a company earns such a label, it can promote its qualification by displaying it on the website, and use the label as an employer branding tool, to attract job candidates. An "employer of choice" label functions as a distinctive quality signal that attracts better candidates and reduces turnover (Dineen and Allen 2016).

Therefore the aim of this study is to explore the relationship, if there is any between CSR activities provided through different labels in job advertisements, and if there is a desire to pursue a job in an ecological and diversity friendly company. While there is considerable research on fairtrade, organic and eco labels in the product domain, their effect in employer branding show less research.

2 The Role of CSR (in Particular Diversity and Sustainability) in Recruitment

Prior literature indicates that communicating CSR activities increases organizational attractiveness to potential employees by reinforcing perceptions of person-organization fit (Gully et al. 2013; Jones et al. 2014). The message content of a job advertisement serves as an important tool, which a potential applicant can use to become better acquainted with an organization before deciding on whether or not to apply for a job (Barber and Roehling 1993; Perkins et al. 2000; Ganesan et al. 2018). Analyzing the nature of a job advertisement and the effect on the perception of applicants about a job has gained importance in recent years (Breaugh 2013). Previous studies indicate the link between environmental management and recruitment (Jackson et al. 2011) and companies try to gain a reputation of being a green employer, as this reputation leads to increased ability to attract new talents (Phillips 2007).

2.1 CSR in Employer Branding

Corporate Social Responsibility refers to the integration of enterprises social, environmental, ethical and philanthropic responsibilities towards society into its operations, processes and core business strategy in cooperation with relevant stakeholders (Bowen 1953). CSR is about "creating economic value in a way that also creates value for society by addressing its needs and challenges" (Porter and Kramer 2006, p. 74). The motivation of CSR is based on an ethical obligation, driven by the leaders' personal values and integrity to serve society. Nearly two-thirds of members of the millennial generation consider a company's social reputation when deciding where to shop, and nine out of ten would switch brands based on their perception of a firm's commitment to social responsibility (Bohlander et al. 2013). The limited research on CSR practices and their influence on recruiting generally show a positive effect (Grolleau et al. 2012; Bauer and Aiman-Smith 1996; Duarte et al. 2014; Jones et al. 2010) of CSR on company attractiveness for prospective employees, yet until now different CSR activities have not been the aim of the research as fairly all research was considering ecological responsibility only.

Besides the ecological footprint, equality and diversity are major issues in CSR and workplaces. All employees have a right to not be discriminated against unfairly and blocked in their careers for reasons that have nothing to do with their abilities in relation to their work. Diversity Management includes factors such as age, gender, ethnicity, political and religious beliefs, disability and sexual orientation. Being considered an employer that believes in and promotes equality is likely to contribute to the organizations image, thus bringing benefits that relate to CSR and being recognized as an employer of choice.

Although a lot of CSR can be communicated and experienced by actual employees, for recruiting only limited information about the CSR activities can be conveyed. Thus the next chapter investigates the role of job ads as a major communication tool in recruiting.

2.2 Job Advertisements and Communicating the Employer Brand

Research has shown that potential employees compare the image of organizations with their own values, needs and personalities. If there is a match with ones' own values, then the organization becomes attractive, therefor it is important to create a positive image to increase employer attractiveness (Sivertzen et al. 2013). Potential job seekers consider job advertisements that contain larger amounts of information more credible (Allen et al. 2004) and attractive (Allen et al. 2007). Enhancing interest in a position is achievable through the inclusion of position specific information, which can assist applicants in determining whether there exists a person-organization fit (Roberson et al. 2005). Therefore in a first step potential applicants are screening job advertisements for information to establish this person-organization fit.

One challenge in recruiting is creating a superior value proposition to convince people to work for and stay with the organization. Employers have to find ways of making jobs appealing, challenging and worthwhile in order to encourage highly qualified individuals to apply (Wilden et al. 2010; Suff 2006). So far a small amount of research investigated elements of job ads to communicate certain attributes of a company.

Dowling (1988) studied the impact of recruitment advertisements on the recruiting process and job content and stated that recruiting advertisements are the first engagement that potential job seekers have with organizations. Rafaeli and Oliver (1998) examined the intention of people behind reading employment advertisements. The authors suggested a process of sense making of employment and identified employment ads to be a useful source, where job seekers read job ads, not only to search for the particular job, but also to get information about the job environment. Robertson et al. (2005) studied the effects of recruitment messages on applicant attraction using experimental design with data obtained from 171 college-level job seekers. According to the authors, detailed recruitment messages lead to enhanced perceptions or organizational attributes, which influence the applicants' intention to apply for a job. A study by Blackman (2006) examined three variables (the use of the word "Graduate", the use of pictures, and mentioning career paths or opportunities for development and promotion) that influence attention to advertisements and the intention to apply for advertised positions among 97 final year commerce students. The results highlighted the importance of the word "Graduate" and supports a three-step model, that an advertisement should attract a reader's attention, should create interest to motivate further reading by a potential applicant, and also needs to create a positive desire or attitude toward applying for a position. (Blackman 2006; Chandor 1976; Dwyer 1999) Ganesan et al. (2018) clarify the role of instrumental and symbolic attributes and dimensions of job ad design and message content play a vital role in fostering organizational attractiveness that cultivate application intention in potential job seekers. In the initial stages of recruitment, job ads are a major vehicle for communicating information about an organization and the job. This should help attract, hire, and retain individuals who share the values that are shared by the organizations that reinforce them.

Yet in particular CSR is complicated to communicate in a short and rather specific information format like a job-description.

Drawing on findings from consumer behaviour research, demonstration of the importance of certificates and labels based on standards is noticeable (Jahn et al. 2005; Carrero and Valor 2012).

Standards can be defined as "rules for common and voluntary use, decided by one or several people or organizations" (Brunsson et al. 2012) CSR standards are considered an umbrella term to describe certain pre-defined rules or procedures to guide, assess, measure, verify and / or communicate the social and environmental performance of firms (Gilbert and Rasche 2011).

"Certification is the voluntary assessment and approval by an (accredited) party on an (accredited) standard" (Meuwissen et al. 2003). Certification standards are more focused on compliance with a set of expected practices, behaviours and principles. Companies that pass an audit are awarded with a seal of approval for a specific period (e.g. fairtrade, organic certifications, etc.). Labels can support information asymmetries in markets. These asymmetries exist because consumers cannot directly observe the social or environmental characteristics of company processes. Labels transform the unobservable attributes to observable search attributes. Labels communicate to consumers that a product conforms to the codified requirements of a specific standard (Rasche et. al. 2017). If certifiers succeed in revealing critical aspects and opportunity behaviour, then quality assurance concepts will support in building a positive reputation, which is necessary to serve as a reliable quality signal (Jahn et al. 2005). Despite the widespread use of labels in product marketing, they are seldom found in recruitment and job advertisements.

2.3 Signals in Job Ads Using Labels

Signaling theory (Spence 1973) is commonly used to explain how applicant attraction to a recruiting organization may or can be influenced by information or signals about organizational characteristics revealed during recruitment activities (Connelly et al. 2011; Celani and Singh 2011). Applicants understand many recruitment-related activities as signals of unknown organizational characteristics (Turban and Cable 2003), and recruiter characteristics and/or behavior (Ganesan et al. 2018, Rynes 1991).

Signaling theory (Spence 1973) suggest that when decision-makers are faced with uncertainty and incomplete information, they use the information they have as the basis for inferences about missing information. Signaling is the idea that one party conveys some information about itself to another party. It is useful for describing behaviour when two parties (individuals or organizations) have access to different information (information asymmetry). The two parties could get around the problem of asymmetric information by having one party send a signal that would reveal some piece of relevant information to the other party. That party would then interpret the signal and adjust their purchasing behaviour accordingly. A job applicant might engage in behaviours to reduce information asymmetry that hampers the selection ability of prospective employers. A perceivable action that is intended evolves to indicate an otherwise not perceivable quality about the signallers' environment (Spence 1973; Connelly et al. 2011). Ultimately the purpose of the signal is to indicate a certain quality or characteristic (Celani and Singh 2011).

A study by Guillot-Soulez et al. (2019) analyzed the distinct and combined influence of two employer certification labels "Great Place to Work" reflecting social commitment and "Ecological" reflecting ecological commitments, in recruitment advertising with the organization's attractiveness to potential candidates. The study consisted of 320 higher education management students. According to their study a "Great place to work" label appears more attractive than an "Ecological" label for signaling the attractiveness of a potential employer. Also adding multiple labels does not appear to improve organizational attractiveness. (Guillot-Soulet et al. 2019).

Signals gained through the inclusion of CSR information in recruitment advertisements taken from CSR labels can contribute to an applicants' ability to assess the match between the organization and the individual. Therefor in this study a variety of labels were used, to send signals to prospective job seekers, to determine whether CSR label(s) will lead to an increased attractiveness of an organization compared to a company with no label. Rynes (1991) suggested that recruitment activities serve as signals to applicants about unknown organizational attributes, and applicants may interpret a signal positively or negatively and generalize the assessment or other aspects of the organization. Also the research by Allen et al. (2004) and Allen et al. (2007) demonstrates the richer job ads the more credible they are. Similar are the prepositions of Ganesan et al. (2018) which suggest the richer an job ad with several dimension the more signals it will send to prospective workforce.Thus adding CSR related signaling labels will also enhance the information richness.

> *H1: Displaying CSR related certification label(s) would lead to an increased rating of attractiveness and reputational measure of the company compared to a control group with no label.*

Besides the pure existence of labels, also the associations connected to labels are an area of interest. Common labels in the product domain like "organic" or "Fairtrade" immediately remind the viewer and furthermore provide valuable information in the attitude formation of the company (Rousseau 2015). Yet effects have proven different from rather marginal (Lacreneux et al. 2012, Bauer et al. 2013) to influential (Rousseau 2015); in consumer choices and even in consumers taste perceptions (Lee et al. 2013). Drawing on classic association theory (Albarracín and Vargas 2010) the labels serve as a prime to activate certain associations, thus we assume that even if they are only shallowly processed, different labels will lead to different attitudinal effects, as the labels will activate different sets of associations.

> *H2: There is a difference in the rating of the attractiveness and reputational measures between the different types of CSR related labels.*
>
> *H3: Different CSR related labels will change the influence of reputational measures on the perceived attractiveness of the employer brand.*

An interesting factor in researching these labels is the number of labels shown. Particularly with certificates, companies tend to show their competence and activities by complying with several certifications. Considering processing likelihood dual processing models would suggest that based on motivations, we process information differently (Chen and Chaiken 1999; Petty and Cacioppo 1986; Petty et al. 1994; Petty and Wegner 1999). Considering job-advertisements, the actual content of the job advertisement is the content the applicant is motivated to read. However, labels are likely to be peripherally or heuristically processed as they are usually placed below or above descriptive information. Shallow processing implies that we relate and evaluate based on simple heuristics (Chen and Chaiken 1999) – like the more the better – thus a company with many labels should be rated better compared to single label ones. On the other hand Guillot-Soulez et al. (2019) findings suggest that more labels of the same signal does not increase the attractiveness of the employer brand. Yet we assume that using mixed signals however will show a positive effect. Association activation would suggest that the more different concepts are presented the more associations should be activated (Gawronski and Bodenhausen 2006). Yet with this activation, it is to investigate if the number of labels and in particular mixed forms of signals interact.

H4: Multiple different labels will lead to a more positive evaluation of the employer.

3 Studies

Two experimental online studies investigate the proposed effects of CSR related labels on the attractiveness of the employer brand. Study 1 establishes the main effect for the different signals while study 2 aims to investigate the role of multiple labels.

3.1 Study 1

Study 1 is a single factorial online experimental study investigating the main effect of the presence of different labels with different signals (ecological, mixed, LGBTQI-pride) in comparison to a job ad with no label.

3.1.1 Design

We created a fictitious company named "Malamart" which is a pet-products retail chain that is hiring a marketing assistant. The English job-ads featured the company which had branches in France, Austria and the Czech Republic. The CSR label(s) were displayed at the bottom of the job offer. We created four groups, one with no label, a group with a sustainability, one with a mixed diversity-sustainability accredited label and one with a pride-standards label. The labels were designed based on thorough research of different accreditation labels and we followed similar standards with a simplistic design to reflect reality.

3.1.2 Measures

Three items (bad-good, unappealing-appealing, unattractive-attractive) on a 7-point semantic differential assessed the attitude towards the employer brand (AEB = 4.45, sd = 1.072, alpha = 0.834). Furthermore we asked a set of questions about the reputation of Malamart: whether participants rate the brand "as an attractive employer" (AEM = 4.61, sd = 1.032), "employs high ethical standards" (EST = 4.42, sd = 0.913), "follows a sustainable strategy" (SST = 4.40, sd = 1.077), "is a company of high moral standards" (MST = 4.49, sd = 0.926), "cares for its staff" (CST = 4.56, sd = 0.953), and "celebrates different backgrounds (age, gender, sexual orientation, etc.) of their staff" (CDB = 4.71, sd = 1.026). To test that there are no differences in the general attitudes towards diversity between the groups we employed the diversity acceptance scale as suggested by Beck et al. (2018).

3.1.3 Procedure

To introduce participants to the topic of recruitment questions about their current employment status were asked. Then they were randomly assigned into one of the four experimental groups and displayed one of the job advertisements. Directly after the job-ad, the attitude towards the company, the reputational measures and the acceptance of diversity were assessed. The survey form closes with demographical data and a debriefing of the participants about the purpose of the study.

3.1.4 Sample

We utilized a micro working platform (Clickworker.de) to invite potential participants who were offered 30cts for completion. Due to the use of click-worker for data collection, a rigorous screening process of the data was employed. First, the data was checked for extreme outliers, second a line-by-line check identified participants who did not sufficiently fill in the questionnaire, and finally we employed a time check (Leiner 2013). In total 134 participants completed the study. After carrying out all the checks 24 participants (17.9%) were discarded and 110 participants provided useable data. Checks in regards to age, gender and the diversity acceptance revealed no differences between the groups.

3.1.5 Results

A one-way Anova was employed to test Hypotheses 1 and 2. Table 1 summarizes the mean scores of the groups. Contrast analysis checked whether the control group was significantly different to the combined groups with labels. In particular the reputation variables moral standards (MST: $T(106) = 2.239, p = 0.027$),

Table 1 Effects of different Label Signals on Attitude and Reputation of the Employer Brand

DV	No label (a)	Sustainability (b)	Sustainability & Diversity (c)	Diversity (d)	$F(3,107)$	p
AEB	4.26[b]	4.89[a,d]	4.56	4.12[b]	2.967	0.035
AEM	4.54	4.89[d]	4.89[d]	4.17[b,c]	3.411	0.020
EST	4.38	4.56	4.56	4.20	0.991	0.400
SST	4.35	4.63	4.52	4.13	1.158	0.329
MST	4.15[b]	4.93[a,d]	4.52	4.37[b]	3.555	0.017
CST	4.23[b,c]	4.96[a,d]	4.78[a]	4.30[b]	4.194	0.008
CDB	4.42[c]	4.56[c]	5.11[a,b]	4.73	2.347	0.077

caring for staff (CST: $T(106) = 2.191, p = 0.031$) and celebrating diverse backgrounds (CDB: $T(106) = 1.667, p = 0.098$) showed significances. Thus, H1 is partly confirmed adding labels to the job ads lead to more positive attitudes and reputation.

To test H2 comparisons were calculated in groups, the letters in Table 1 indicate if a value is significantly different to another one. It shows that the effect of the sustainable claim is sending stronger signals than the diversity (LGBTQI-pride) signal. Interestingly the diversity label did not influence the dependent variables in comparison to the control group, and though not significant for most dependent variables the "pride standards" label performed lowest. This already indicates that these labels, even if only quickly processed, can activate a set of associations and influence positively as negatively the employer brands reputation. One limitation of study 1 is the different design of the labels. Therefore in study 2 a set of similar labels and a mix with a non-CSR label in form of a quality label was used to further test whether different associations are present.

H3 assumes that the attitude is influenced by different reputational measures as a result of the exposure to the label. Therefore we calculated a set of regression models which are reported in Table 2. The overall model suggests that only attractiveness of the employer significantly influences the attitude towards the employer brand. However looking into the regression models for the separate groups, except for the pride label, attractive employer had a significant positive influence. Yet not surprisingly for the no label condition several factors influence the attitude towards the employer brand and interestingly having high moral standards had a negative influence. For the sustainability logo the most surprising effect is the negative influence of sustainable strategy on attitude towards the employer brand.

Table 2 Influence of the Reputational Measures on the Attitude towards the Employer Brand

Source	Overall	No label	Sustainability	Sustainability & Diversity	Diversity
AEM	0.427**	0.361*	0.417**	0.517**	0.380
EST	0.105	−0.131	0.340	0.124	−0.054
SST	0.076	0.493**	−0.486*	0.170	0.112
MST	0.061	−0.447**	0.437	−0.103	0.235
CST	0.151	0.458*	−0.013	−0.003	0.158
CDB	0.070	−0.040	0.065	0.251	0.188

*coefficient is significant on p<.05; **coefficent is significant on p<.01

Interestingly in the moment using the pride information (the mixed label and the pride label) there is no clear influence of the reputational measures on AEB.

3.2 Study 2

Study 2 investigates in particular the role of multiple labels and also we extended the diversity message by a more general diversity claim (equal employer) and a more LGTBQI related claim (pride similar as in study 1) to see whether the LGBTI signal might have led to neutral or negative associations.

3.2.1 Design

Study 2 employs two numbers of labels (1 vs. 3) by three signal of labels (eco vs. mixed vs. diversity) design. An additional control group with a single quality label served to see if there is a difference, or if any label irrespective of the signal has fairly the same effect. We used the same job announcement as in study 1 however this time it was translated to German as the participants were from Germany and Austria. A set of similar looking labels for the single label conditions were created. All created labels are shown in Fig. 1. We created two eco labels and two diversity labels.

In the multiple label condition, we showed three labels whereas the label in the middle was kept constant by utilizing the quality label. For the mixed (eco-signal and diversity signal), we counterbalanced the order and the mix (two random out of the 4 labels, above).

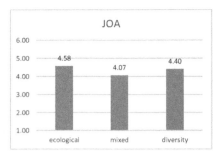 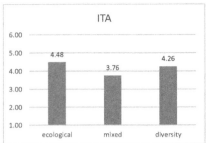

Fig. 1 Types of signals

3.3 Measures

In study 2 we added how attractive the job offer is (JOA = 4.33, sd = 1.498), and if participants consider applying (ITA = 4.15, sd = 1.735) both measured on a 7point scale. The other measures remained the same as in study 1: AEB = 4.60, sd = 1.311; AEM = 4.69, sd = 1.298; EST = 4.41, sd = 1.130; SST = 4.51, sd = 1.140; MST = 4.66, sd = 1.131; CST = 4.88, sd = 1.125; CDB = 4.71, sd = 1.310.

3.3.1 Procedure
Study 2 followed the same procedure as study 1, the new measures were integrated in existing pages. The measures regarding the job offer were directly assessed after showing the job offer the order of all other questions were not altered, however for the reputational measures we randomized them within the question set to avoid order effects.

3.3.2 Sample
322 participants completed the survey, again the sample through the micro working service Clickworker. Again here a time check was employed as a check for outliers with no variance behaviour in answering. The final sample after data clearing consists of 274 participants (discarding 48 participants, 14.9%); again the large majority failed the time checks as suggested by (Leiner 2013). As the job ad targeted junior level applicants we targeted 18 to 35 year old click workers, the average age is 27.75 years. 50.7% were female, 48.9% male and 0.4% provided no information on gender.

Table 3 Results of the ANOVA for the single label comparison

DV	Eco (a)	Sustainability & Diversity (b)	Diversity (c)	Quality (d)	$F(3,151)$	p
AEB	4.89	4.68	4.35	4.42	1.318	0.271
JOA	4.76	4.17	4.45	4.17	1.693	0.171
ITA	4.91^{b,d}	3.90^a	4.35	3.94^a	3.675	0.014
AEM	5.00	4.62^d	4.26^d	4.83^{b,c}	2.462	0.065
EST	4.61	4.36	4.61	4.25	1.212	0.307
SST	4.63	4.40	4.52	4.22	1.137	0.336
MST	4.89	4.45	4.65	4.78	1.335	0.265
CST	5.04	4.93	4.87	4.92	0.174	0.914
CDB	4.87	4.62	4.74	4.78	0.286	0.836

letters show significant differences between the groups

3.3.3 Results

To test H2 again, whether the seals can send different signals we compared the 3 single CSR label groups with the control group with the quality label in a one way ANOVA. Table 3 reports the mean scores, significance levels and the results of the pairwise comparisons.

While we could observe slight differences for the intentions to apply and employer attractiveness, it seems that just having any certification label already improves the ratings. Compared to study 1 where the main differences were with the control group, in study 2 the quality label group underperformed in regards to AEM compared to eco-signal label. Besides the dual comparisons, we ran a contrast test combining all CSR labels in comparison to the quality label, with the same result that there was no significant difference. Thus our data suggest that irrespective from the signal adding labels can create benefits.

To investigate the effects if multiple labels generate a difference (H4) we performed a two way ANOVAs for the variables. For the attractiveness of the job-offer (JOA: $F(2,232) = 2.304$, $p = 0.100$) and for the intentions to apply (ITA: $F(2,232) = 3.836$, $p = 0.023$) the analyses showed a (marginal) significant main effect of the signals of the CSR-labels. For both variables the mixed signals of diversity and ecologically underperformed compared to the single signals (Fig. 1).

The main effect for the single vs. multiple labels also showed significant results for the intentions to apply ($F(1,232) = 3.954$, $p = 0.048$). The single labels showed a higher likelihood rating compared to the multiple labels (ITA$_{single}$ =

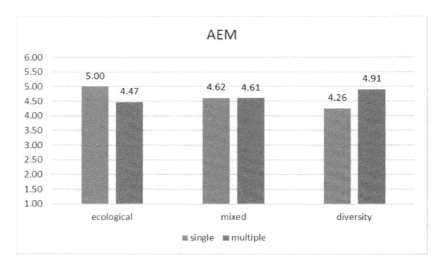

Fig. 2 Interaction effect of label count and label signal

4.39, $ITA_{multiple} = 3.94$). For attitudinal measures brand attitude ($F(2,232) = 2.851$, $p = 0.060$) and that the company is an attractive employer ($F(2,232) = 3.829$, $p = 0.023$) showed significant interaction effects. Contrast analyses show that the difference for the brand attitude is only in reference to the eco labels. The single label generated a more favourable brand attitude rating compared to the multiple eco labels ($AEB_{single} = 4.89$ vs. $AEB_{multiple} = 4.35$; $F(1,232) = 3.524$, $p = 0.062$). There were no significant other effects. The result for the rating that the company is an attractive employer is similar. Also here for the eco label the single condition leads to a more positive rating compared to the multiple label condition ($AEM_{single} = 5.00$ vs. $AEM_{multiple} = 4.47$; $F(2,232) = 3.294$, $p = 0.071$). The effect is reversed for the diversity labels ($AEM_{single} = 4.26$ vs. $AEM_{multiple} = 4.91$, $F(2,232) = 4.368$, $p = 0.038$) as Fig. 2 demonstrates.

4 Implications and Discussion

Our results suggest that CSR related labels can positively influence the perceptions of prospective employers. Yet it seems that the signal the company cares about, the environment is regarded more positively by the participants compared to the diversity related labels. The questions whether a mixed or focused signal label should be used for conveying the CSR activities of a company our results would suggest that the mixed approach does not perform any worse compared to the single ones. Except for one measure, the mixed signals always either created similar ratings like the focused signals or created higher values. Thus, we would recommend a mixed certificate labels approach.

According to the study by Guillot-Soulez et al. (2019) organizations should only communicate a "Great place to work" label rather than an ecological label, as adding multiple labels didn't appear to be more attractive. Yet our results show when having other CSR related signals like diversity and ecological mixed approaches to the labels do not underperform. Future studies however might look into more detail into more variants of signals of the CSR domain.

The matter is still under research and further studies will be implemented. Limitations include that artificial brands were used and that participants might reflect on the chosen industry. In future experiments, the industry and the setup of the company will change. Additionally, we selected a job offer at junior level; other levels might alter the results as well as the position offered. Future experiments therefor will change the elements to garner a more holistic view. Finally, we used the diversity with a rather strong LGTBQI signal, future studies should also include other forms of diversity like gender equality, disabilities, etc. as well as not only looking into the ecological certification but also other social CSR activities.

References

Albarracín, D., & Vargas, P. (2010). Attitudes and persuasion. In S. T. Fiske, B. D. Gilbert, & L. Gardner (Eds.), Handbook of consumer psychology (pp. 394–427). Hoboken: Wiley.

Allen, D. G., Mahto, R. V., & Otondo, R. F. (2007). Web-based recruitment: Effects of information, organizational brand, and attitudes toward a Web site on applicant attraction. *Journal of Applied Psychology, 92*(6), 1696.

Allen, D. G., Scotter, J., & Otondo, R. F. (2004). Recruitment communication media: Impact on prehire outcomes. *Personnel Psychology, 57*(1), 143–171.

Barber, A. E., & Roehling, M. V. (1993). Job postings and the decision to interview: A verbal protocol analysis. *Journal of Applied Psychology, 78*(5), 845–856.

Bauer, H. H., Heinrich, D., & Schäfer, D. B. (2013). The effects of organic labels on global, local, and private brands: More hype than substance? *Journal of Business Research, 66*(8), 1035–1043.

Bauer, T. N., & Aiman-Smith, L. (1996). Green career choices: The influence of ecological stance on recruiting. *Journal of Business Psychology, 10*(4), 445–458.

Beck, K. L., Acevedo-Polakovich, I. D., Lyons, E., Estevez, J., Sevecke, J. R., Rossman, D. L., et al. (2018). The youth diversity acceptance scale: Development and validity. *Measurement and Evaluation in Counseling and Development, 51*(2), 71–83.

Blackman, A. (2006). Graduate students responses to recruitment advertisements. *Journal of Business Communication, 43*(4), 367–388.

Bowen, D. (1953). *Corporate Social Responsibility: Verantwortungsvolle Unternehmensführung in Theorie und Praxis* (2nd ed.). Berlin: Springer.

Bohlander, G. W., & Snell, S. A. (2013). Principles of human resource management (16th ed.). South-Western: Cengage Learning.

Brunsson, N., Rasche, A., & Seidl, D. (2012). The dynamics of standardization: Three perspectives on standards in organization studies. *Organization Studies, 33*(5–6), 613–632.

Carrero, I., & Valor, C. (2012). CSR-labelled products in retailers' assortment: A comparative study of British and Spanish retailers. *International Journal of Retail & Distribution Management, 40*(8), 629–652.

Celani, A., & Singh, P. (2011). Signaling theory and applicant attraction outcomes. *Personnel Review, 40*(2), 222–238.

Chen, S., Chaiken, S. (1999). The Heuristic-Systematic Model in Its Broader Context. In S. Chaiken & Y. Trope (Eds.), Dual-process theories in social psychology (pp. 73–96). The Guilford Press, New York.

Connelly, B. L., Certo, S. T., Ireland, R. D., & Reutzel, C. R. (2011). Signaling theory: A review and assessment. *Journal of Management, 37*(1), 39–67.

Dineen, B., & Allen, D. (2016). Third party employment branding: Human capital inflows and outflows following "best places to work" certifications. *Academy of Management Journal, 59*(1), 90–112.

Duarte, A., Gomes, D., & Das Neves, J. (2014). Tell me your socially responsible practices, I will tell you how attractive for recruitment you are! The impact of perceived CSR on organizational attractiveness. *Tékhne, 12*, 22–29.

Gawronski, B., & Bodenhausen, G. V. (2006). Associative and propositional processes in evaluation: An integrative review of implicit and explicit attitude change. *Psychological Bulletin, 132*(5), 692.

Ganesan, M., Antony, S., & George, E. (2018). Dimensions of job advertisement as signals for achieving job seeker's application intention. Journal of Management Development, 37(5), 425–434.

Gilbert, D. U., & Rasche, A. (2011). Accountability in a global economy: The emergence of international accountability standards. Business Ethics Quarterly, 21(1), 23–44.

Grolleau, G., Mzoughi, N., & Pekovic, S. (2012). Green not (only) for profit: An empirical examination of the effect of environmental-related standards on employees' recruitment. *Resource and Energy Economics, 34*(1), 74–92.

Grosser and Moon, (2005). *Corporate Responsibility* (2nd ed.). Oxford University Press: Oxford.

Guillot-Soulet, C., Saint-Onge, S., & Soulez, S. (2019). Linking employer labels in recruitment advertising, governance mode and organizational attractiveness. *Recherche et Applications en Marketing, 34*(3), 5–26.

Jahn, G., Schramm, M., & Spiller, A. (2005). The reliability of certification: Quality labels as a consumer policy tool. *Journal of Consumer Policy, 28*(1), 53–73.

Jones, D. A., Willness, C. R., & Madey, S. (2010). *Why are job seekers attracted to socially responsible companies? Testing uunderlying mechanisms.* Paper presented at the Academy of Management Proceedings.

Larceneux, F., Benoit-Moreau, F., & Renaudin, V. (2012). Why might organic labels fail to influence consumer choices? Marginal labelling and brand equity effects. Journal of Consumer Policy, 35(1), 85–104.

Lee, W. C. J., Shimizu, M., Kniffin, K. M., & Wansink, B. (2013). You taste what you see: Do organic labels bias taste perceptions? *Food Quality and Preference, 29*(1), 33–39.

Leiner, D. J. (2013). *Too fast, too straight, too weird: Post hoc identification of meaningless data in internet surveys.* Working Paper. LMU Munich.

Macey, W. H., & Schneider, B. (2008). The meaning of employee engagement. *Industrial and Organizational Psychology: Perspectives on Science and Practice, 1*(1), 3–30.

Manpower. (2015). Talent shortage survey. Manpower Groups. https://www.manpowergroup.com/wps/wcm/connect/right-br-pt/microsites/talentshortagesurvey-2015

Meuwissen, M. P., Velthuis, A. G. J., Hogeveen, H., & Huirne, R. B. (2003). Technical and economic considerations about traceability and certification in livestock production chains. in Velthuis, A.G.J., Unnevehr, L.J., Hogeveen, H. & Huirne, R.B.M eds.: New approaches to food safety economics, 41-54, Kluwer Academic Publishers, Dordrecht.

Petty, R. E., & Cacioppo, C. (1986). The elaboration likelihood model of persuasion. *Advances in Experimental Social Psychology, 19,* 123–195.

Petty, R. E., Cacioppo, J. T., Strathman, A. J., & Priester, J. R. (1994). To think or not to think, exploring two routes to persuasion. In S. Shavitt & T. Brock (Eds.), *Persuasion: psychological insights and perspectives* (pp. 113–147). Thousand Oaks: Sage.

Petty, R. E., & Wegner, D. T. (1999). The elaboration likelihood model: current status and controversies. In S. Chaiken & Y. Trope (Eds.), *Dual-process theories in social psychology* (pp. 41–72). The Guilford Press: New York.

Porter, M. E., & Kramer, M. R. (2006). Strategy and society: The link between competitive advantage and corporate social responsibility. *Harvard Business Review, 84*(12), 78–92.

Rasche, A., Moon, J., & Morsing, M. (2017). *Corporate social responsibility. Strategy, communication, Governance.* Cambridge University Press: Cambridge.

Rafaeli, A., & Oliver, A. L. (1998). Employment ads: A configuration research agenda. Journal of Management Inquiry, 7(4), 342–358.

Ritz, A., & Sinelli, P. (2018). Talents Management – Überblick und konzeptionelle Grundlagen. In A. Ritz & N. Thom, *Talent Management: Talents identifizieren, Kompetenzen entwickeln, Leistungsträger erhalten.* Wiesbaden: Springer Fachmedien.

Roberson, Q. M., Collins, C. J., & Oreg, S. (2005). The effects of recruitment message specificity on applicant attraction to organizations. *Journal of Business Psychology, 19*(3), 319–339.

Rousseau, S. (2015). The role of organic and fair trade labels when choosing chocolate. *Food Quality and Preference, 44,* 92–100.

Rynes, S. L. (1991). Recruitment, job choice, and post-hire consequences: A call for new research directions. In M. D. Dunnette & L. M. Hough (Eds.), *Handbook of industrial and organizational psychology* (2nd ed., Vol. 2, pp. 299–444). Consulting Psychology Press: Palo Alto.

Salmen, S. (2012). Die Suche von Top-Mitarbeitern im War for Talent! In B. Rath & S. Salmen (Eds.), *Recruiting im Social Weg: Talentmanagement 2.0* (2nd ed., pp. 21–53). Göttinger: Business Village GmbH.

Sivertzen, A., Ragnhild, E., & Olafsen, A. (2013). Employer branding employer attractiveness and the use of social media. *Journal of Product and brand Management, 22*, 473–483

Spence, M. (1973). Job market signaling. *Quarterly Journal of Economics, 87*, 355–374.

Strandberg, C. (2009). *The role of human resource management in corporate social responsibility.* Burnay. Strandberg Consulting: Report for Canada.

Suff, R. (2006). *Human resource management (2ed).The right person for the right role: using competency in recruitment and selection.* Oxford University Press: Oxford.

Turban, D. B., & Cable, D. M. (2003). Firm reputation and applicant pool characteristics. *Journal of Organizational Behaviour, 24*, 733–751.

Turban, D. B., & Greening, D. W. (1997). Corporate social performance and organizational attractiveness to prospective employees. *Academy of Management Journal, 40*(3), 658–672.

Viot, C., & Benraiss-Noailles, L. (2014). Employeurs demarquez-vous! La marque employeur, un gisement de valeur inexploite? *Management International, 18*(3), 60–81.

Wilden, R., Gudergan, S., & Lings, I. (2010). Employer branding: Strategic implications for staff recruitment. *Journal of Marketing Management, 26*(1–2), 56–73.

Children's Perceptions of Sponsorship Disclosures in Online Influencer Videos

Esther Rozendaal, Eva A. van Reijmersdal, and Margot J. van der Goot

1 Introduction

As sponsoring in online influencer videos is gaining popularity, advertising- and media regulators are tightening the guidelines for commercial content in YouTube videos (e.g., the European Union's Audiovisual Media Services Directive [AVMSD], and the United States' Federal Trade Commission). An important part of these stricter guidelines is the obligatory inclusion of disclosures, in order to increase the transparency and fairness of sponsored online influencer videos (European Commission, 2018; Einstein, 2015; Federal Trade Commission 2010). In these videos, persuasive messages are embedded into the entertaining content of influencers which makes it hard for audiences to recognize its persuasive nature. Disclosures can help audiences to better recognize the commercial nature of sponsored online influencer videos and potentially facilitate more critical processing of these videos. Minors in particular are in need of sponsorship disclosures as they have greater difficulty than adults to recognize the persuasive nature of

E. Rozendaal (✉)
Erasmus School of Social and Behavioural Sciences, Erasmus University Rotterdam, Rotterdam, Netherlands
E-Mail: rozendaal@essb.eur.nl

E. A. van Reijmersdal · M. J. van der Goot
Amsterdam School of Communication Research, University of Amsterdam, Amsterdam, Netherlands
E-Mail: e.a.vanreijmersdal@uva.nl

M. J. van der Goot
E-Mail: m.j.vandergoot@uva.nl

embedded advertising formats (De Veirman et al. 2019; Hudders et al. 2017; De Pauw et al. 2017). Therefore, the tightened regulations stress the importance of including disclosures in online influencer videos with an underage audience, in a way that is adequate in light of minors' capacity to understand them (CAP, 2017; Stichting Reclame Code, 2014).

Several studies have experimentally investigated the effect of disclosures in sponsored content on minors (e.g., An & Stern, 2011; De Jans 2019; De Pauw et al. 2017; Panic et al. 2012; Van Reijmersdal et al. 2017). However, only a few of these studies specifically focused on disclosures in online influencer videos (De Jans et al. 2019; Van Reijmersdal et al. 2020). Moreover, these studies showed mixed effects of disclosures regarding enhancing minors' recognition and understanding of sponsored content, including influencer videos. In order to interpret and theoretically explain these mixed findings, more insight into minors' perceptions of sponsorship disclosures is needed. Based on the Motivation-Opportunity-Ability model (MacInnes et al. 1991) it is expected that minors' perceptions and understanding of sponsorship disclosures drive their motivation, opportunity, and/or ability (MOA) to process the disclosure and the sponsored content and, as such, may help or hinder the effectiveness of disclosures. For example, the extent to which children perceive disclosures to be helpful in recognizing sponsored influencer videos likely determines their motivation to pay attention to the disclosure. And, the extent to which children understand the purpose of sponsorship disclosures, likely determines their ability to critically process sponsoring in influencer videos.

Unfortunately, existing research fails to provide a deep understanding of how minors perceive sponsorship disclosures, mainly due to the experimental nature of the studies. Qualitative research is more suitable to expose minors' perceptions. Therefore, using a qualitative research approach (i.e., interviews), the main aim of the present study is to provide in-depth insights into 10- to 16-year-olds' perceptions of various types of sponsorship disclosures in sponsored online influencer videos.

One earlier study explored adolescents' perceptions of disclosures for sponsored influencer videos, showing that disclosures are appreciated as long as they do not disturb the entertaining value of the sponsored video (Van Dam & Van Reijmersdal, 2019). The current study extends this existing research by focusing not only on children's perceptions of the relevance and usefulness of sponsorship disclosures, but also on their awareness and understanding of such disclosures. Moreover, the current study extends the study by Van Dam and Van Reijmersdal by focusing on children's perceptions of a wider variety of disclosures that are currently part of disclosure guidelines, namely a disclosure presented in text before the start or at the start of the video, a disclosure in the description below the sponsored video, and a spoken disclosure by the influencer. These insights are not only valuable for our theoretical understanding of disclosure effects among minors, but are also necessary to guide the development of regulatory guidelines on age-appropriate disclosures with the ultimate aim of making the commercial nature of online influencer videos transparent to minors.

The present study focuses on children aged 10 to 16, an age group in which major changes are taking place in the development of advertising literacy, especially in the context of digital advertising and online influencer marketing (Hudders et al. 2017; Van Dam & Van Reijmersdal, 2019). This is on the one hand because children in this age group gain increasingly more experience with digital advertising, and on the other hand because their perspective taking skills are vastly developing. This allows them to better understand the intentions of others, including online advertisers and social media influencers (Moses and Baldwin 2005). However, insights from developmental and media psychology indicate that, even if children do have a well-developed level of advertising literacy, they still experience difficulty activating and applying this literacy when confronted with advertising. Because 10- to 16 year olds' executive functions (e.g., working memory, inhibitory control, attentional flexibility) are still emerging, they experience more difficulties with monitoring and controlling their thoughts, feelings, and actions than adults (Best & Miller, 2010). As a result, their ability to activate their advertising literacy and to elaborate critically on the commercial intent of digital advertising may be lower, especially when the advertising is integrated in attractive and engaging social media posts (e.g., sponsored YouTube videos; Rozendaal et al. 2011). Thus, 10 to 16 year olds are rapidly developing their digital advertising literacy, but still encounter difficulties to activate and use this literacy as a critical coping mechanism. This may influence the perceptions 10- to 16-year olds have of sponsorship disclosures in online influencer videos, making them an interesting group to study.

2 Theoretical Background

2.1 Disclosure Awareness

Experimental studies have shown that awareness and memory of disclosures tend to be low (for an overview see Boerman & Van Reijmersdal, 2016). Even in experimental settings with forced exposure, many participants do not notice or remember sponsorship disclosures. This is problematic since studies have shown that awareness of disclosures is crucial for disclosures to have the intended effect on enhancing transparency (e.g., Van Reijmersdal et al. 2020; Wojdynski & Evans, 2016). If disclosures go unnoticed, the opportunity for audiences to process the disclosure is low. As a consequence, viewers are less likely to critically process the sponsored content in light of the knowledge they have about the commercial nature of sponsored content (Van Reijmersdal et al. 2020). Experimental studies using eye tracking have indeed shown that visual attention to disclosures among children and adults is an important mechanism that underlies disclosure effects (Boerman et al. 2015; Guo et al. 2018; Van Reijmersdal et al. 2020; Wojdynski & Evans, 2016).

Research among adults has shown that the format of the disclosure impacts awareness (Boerman et al. 2015; Wojdynski & Evans, 2016). For example, an experiment showed that text accompanied by a logo gained more visual attention than only a logo (Boerman et al. 2015), and other studies showed that the position and prominence of the disclosure determined disclosure awareness (Wojdynski & Evans, 2016). In the present study, we focus on three types of disclosures that are currently part of disclosure guidelines: a disclosure presented in text before the video starts, a disclosure in the description below the sponsored video, and a spoken disclosure by the influencer. We explore children's awareness of these disclosures, and investigate whether awareness differs for the three different disclosure types. We pose the following research question:

RQ1: How aware are 10- to 16-year-olds of various disclosure types in sponsored online influencer videos?

2.2 Disclosure Understanding

The general purpose of sponsorship disclosures in online influencer videos is to help audiences recognize sponsoring. Experimental studies showed that sponsorship disclosures are sometimes successful and sometimes unsuccessful in helping minors to recognize and understand the commercial nature of sponsoring in influencer videos (De Jans et al. 2019; Van Reijmersdal et al. 2020). However, these studies did not take minors' understanding of the purpose of the investigated disclosures into account. This may explain the lack of clear evidence for the effectiveness of sponsorship disclosures among minors: Minors who do not understand the purpose of disclosures, are probably less able to process the sponsored influencer video in light of their general knowledge about the commercial nature of sponsored content, which makes disclosures less effective for these minors.

Besides minors' understanding of the *purpose* of sponsorship disclosures, minors' understanding of the *meaning* of the disclosures may also drive their ability to critically process sponsoring in influencer videos, and thus play a role in disclosure effectiveness. Influencers use a wide variety of disclosure messages in their sponsored videos. They, for example, disclose a commercial partnership by stating 'I created this video in collaboration with [brand x]' or 'I would like to thank [brand name] for this cool collaboration, thank you [brand name]'. The term 'collaboration' in these disclosures refers to the influencer marketing business model, which is based on a mutual agreement between a brand and an influencer (Federal Trade Commission, 2009, 2010). Agreements can range from the influencers receiving money (i.e., paid sponsorship) or free products (i.e., unpaid sponsorship). The term 'collaboration' in disclosures must be understood in the context of this business model, but the question is whether children possess the relevant background knowledge to interpret disclosures in this intended way.

In the present study, we explore children's understanding of the purpose and meaning of disclosure messages that refer to a collaboration between the influencer and a brand, since this type of disclosure message is most common. We pose the following research question:

RQ2: What do 10- to 16-year-olds understand about the purpose and meaning of disclosures?

2.3 Disclosure Evaluations

Advertising- and media regulators have decided that disclosures are useful and beneficial for young viewers of influencer videos. But what do minors themselves think about this? Do they find sponsorship disclosures necessary and helpful? Insights into minors' opinions of and preferences for certain types of disclosures can help to gain a better understanding of the effectiveness of such disclosures. Although some research focused on adults' opinions about whether sponsored content in television programs and movies should be disclosed (Gupta et al. 2000; Hudson et al. 2008; Van Reijmersdal et al. 2013), no such research exists among minor audiences. The studies among adults show that disclosing sponsored content may be perceived as informative and helpful as audiences may become aware of something that used to be hidden in entertainment (Gupta et al. 2000; Hudson et al. 2008). However, disclosures can also be perceived as intrusive and patronizing as viewers may feel that their judgments are underestimated and that they are not taken seriously as authorities think they need to be warned and protected

(Reijmersdal et al. 2013). This may lead to resistance and negative evaluations of the disclosures (Brehm and Brehm 1981).

Another question is how disclosures should be formulated and formatted. To date, no research has shown what minors consider as the most appropriate and informative formulation, format, and place of disclosures in online influencer videos. Therefore, the present study investigates minors' attitudes toward and preferences for influencer video disclosure formulation (i.e., 'paid collaboration' or 'collaboration'), format (i.e., in text or spoken) and location (i.e., before the video, in the video, or in the description). This leads to the following research question:

> *RQ3: How do 10- to 16-year-olds evaluate various disclosure types in sponsored online influencer videos?*

3 Method

3.1 Sampling and Procedure

A total of 38 children aged 10 to 16 with various backgrounds (level of education, gender, place of residence, ethnicity) were interviewed in friend duos. The children were recruited by a professional research company. All children were interviewed by the same professional female interviewer. The interviews lasted around 75 min. During the interview, children watched two videos, each with a different disclosure: one video with a textual disclosure ('this video contains a collaboration with [brand name]') and one with a spoken disclosure (e.g., 'I created this video in collaboration with [brand x]' or 'I would like to thank [brand name] for this cool collaboration, thank you [brand name])'). The order in which they watched the video with either the textual or the spoken disclosure was randomized. After each video, the interviewer asked the children about their perceptions of the video, the sponsoring and the disclosure. After talking about the second video, children were asked about the description below the video and the disclosure in this description.

Each friend duo watched two out of nine videos based on the videos' suitability for the friend duo's age and gender. We used nine existing sponsored videos of popular male and female YouTubers. The videos included a variety of genres: beauty videos, sketches, vlogs, and gaming. The sponsoring products were shampoo, make up, toys, games, household appliances, baking products, apps, and travels.

3.2 Analysis

We used procedures that are described in the grounded theory approach (Charmaz, 2014; Strauss & Corbin, 1998). The interviews were transcribed verbatim and subjected to open coding.. We read the interviews in light of our research questions, and particularly looked for variation in children's perceptions. To enhance the credibility and transparency of our findings, we extensively discussed the coding with all three researchers (researcher triangulation), and we included the perceptions of a broad sample of children with various ages and backgrounds (data triangulation). We believe that new interviews would not result in substantially new insights regarding our research questions (saturation).

4 Results

4.1 Disclosure Awareness

Awareness was not the same for the three disclosure types. First, disclosures in the video description were noticed the least. Some children said that they usually do not read the descriptions and thus are not exposed to the disclosures in the descriptions.

> *'There is a lot of information (in the description), but we never read it'*
>
> (boy and girl, 10- and 12-years-old).
>
> *'Only in the description is bad because then they make it too easy for themselves: Like "I do it, but nobody sees it"'*
>
> (boys, 13-years old)

Second, textual disclosures before the start of the video are also barely noticed. Children feel like a screen with text before the video is not a part of the video itself. They only start paying attention once the video has started.

> *'Oh you mean that text at the beginning. I didn't read it'*
>
> (girls, 16-years old)

Third, awareness was highest for spoken disclosures. They said that a spoken disclosure somewhere at the beginning of the video has the best chance of being noticed (compared to a spoken disclosure near the end of the video) because they rarely watch a video until the end.

> *'Usually everyone just watches the beginning [of the video] and if they don't like it then they go to something else. And sometimes people go away, halfway through the video, to watch another video'*
>
> (boys, 13-years old).

Interestingly, most children did not notice the disclosure spontaneously, which means that they did not talk about it unless the interviewer directly asked questions about it. Typically it was only then that children realized that they had come across the disclosure somewhere. When asked if they ever notice these kinds of disclosures in YouTube videos, the children said they rarely see them. An explanation for this may be that many children say they usually also do other things (put on makeup, do homework, eat, send WhatsApp messages) when they watch YouTube videos. Because of this multitasking they do not process the content of the YouTube video for the full 100%. In addition, they watch YouTube videos mainly because of entertainment and relaxation and therefore do not seem to have a critical attitude while watching.

4.2 Disclosure Understanding

The interviews reveal a divide in children's level of understanding of the disclosures. On one end of the spectrum there are children who show a good understanding of the purpose and meaning of disclosures. When confronted with disclosures that refer to collaborations between influencers and brands, these children show a well-developed understanding of the business model of influencer marketing. The analyses indicate that these children are typically older or higher educated. Some children are confused about the meaning of "collaboration" and "paid collaboration". Others seem to understand well that with a paid partnership the YouTuber is paid by a brand or has received products.

> *'Collaboration" is enough ("paid" does not need to added). Then I understand that it is advertising. It is clear to me that it is paid'*
>
> (boys, 12- and 14-years-old)
>
> *'Paid collaboration can be two different things. It is also possible that he has received products [in addition to having received money]'*

(boys, 13-years-old)

Interviewer: 'But how did you know it was advertising?' *'It was stated in the beginning: "In cooperation with XXX"'*

(boys, 12- and 13-years-old)

Interviewer: 'And what does it mean, that he said that it is a collaboration?' *'That he got big money for this. "I will use all this stuff, so that I get even more money"; that's it basically'*

(boys, 15- and 16 years-old)

On the other end of the spectrum there are children who have difficulty understanding the purpose of disclosures, and who do not understand that brands are featured in influencer videos for commercial reasons and that often (financial) compensation is part of the deal. For these children, the term "collaboration" means that the YouTuber and the brand help each other and support each other (just like at school); they do not think it has anything to do with money. Even when the disclosure states that there is a financial collaboration, these children are confused about the process behind the video or show no understanding of the business model of influencers. Some children even think that paid collaboration means that the YouTuber had to pay the brand for showing it in the video.

'I think collaboration is a good name. Because that is what it is, they help each other. Advertising is different.'

(boys, 10- and 12-years-old).

'Paid collaboration means that he [the YouTuber] had to pay for it...".

(boy and girl, 10-years-old)

An interesting finding is that some children see the textual disclosure as a form of advertising for the brand rather than a "warning" for the fact that the video is sponsored. Especially for the textual disclosure, they think it is a promotional message from the brand. As a result, they find it annoying to see the disclosure.

'I think such a text in advance in a black screen is a bit too much .. then I think it is really too much advertising.'

(boy and girl, 10-years-old)

4.3 Disclosure Evaluations

On the one end, there are children who do not care whether disclosures are present or not. They feel they do not need that information, and they do not really care whether a video is sponsored or not.

> *'I totally don't care (whether there is a disclosure or not)'*
>
> (girls, 15- and 16-years-old)
>
> *Interviewer: 'What do you think about such a text [disclosure] at the start of the video?'*
> *'Fine, I did not see it anyway'.*
>
> (girls, 15- and 16-years-old)
>
> *'I don't think it's* [the fact that the video is sponsored] *important to know myself. If other people want to know, I think that's fine, but I don't know why they would want to'*
>
> (boy and girl, 11- and 10-years-old)

On the other end, there are children who do acknowledge the need for disclosures.

> *'If they do not disclose it, I think it is annoying, because then I start thinking: is this commercial or not?'*
>
> (girls, 15-years-old).
>
> *'I think you should always say it. Otherwise it feels like you are secretly being persuaded'*
>
> (boys, 12- and 14-years old)
>
> *'I think it's good, because it's also better for viewers because they don't have to think [about whether a video is sponsored or not]'*
>
> (boys, 10- and 12-years old)

These children want to know whether a video is sponsored or not, not only for themselves but they think it is important for others too.

> *'It is especially important for younger children, because they are more vulnerable'*
>
> (girls, 16-year-olds)

With respect to disclosure types, there are children who prefer a textual disclosure before the start of the video over a spoken disclosure, because this stands out the most and because then they know what they are watching from the beginning

> 'I prefer the first option [text before start of the video]. Because it is faster (...) If it is in the end, often I am not watching videos till the end'
>
> (girls, 11- and 14 years-old)

There are also children who prefer spoken disclosures over textual disclosures and disclosures in descriptions. They feel that a spoken disclosure is more sincere than a textual disclosure.

> 'I think spoken is better than just text. With a spoken disclosure you can check whether he is sincere'
>
> (boys, 13-years-old).
>
> 'The text before the video appears to be a less sincere, more like: this has to be done'
>
> (boys, 12- and 14-years old)

Other children prefer a spoken disclosure, because in a text it is too obvious that a brand is being promoted in the video. These children see the disclosure itself as a form of advertising, rather than as a warning that a video is sponsored.

The children think disclosures in the video description are less sincere.

> '(A disclosure) only in the description is bad, because then you take the easy way out: like "I do it (use the disclosure), but no one will notice"'
>
> (boys, 13-years-old).

5 Conclusion and Discussion

This study aimed to give insight into children's perceptions of disclosures in sponsored influencer videos. It shows that there are differences between children in their awareness, understanding, and evaluations of disclosures. Better awareness and understanding of disclosures seem to be associated with better developed advertising literacy, in particular a better understanding of the business model behind influencer marketing.

In addition, children's perceptions differ between disclosure types. Children express relatively more awareness, better understanding and more positive attitudes toward spoken disclosures than toward textual disclosures before the video or in the description below the video.

5.1 Theoretical and Practical Implications

The present study has several theoretical implications. First, it provides explanations for the mixed findings found in experiments investigating the effect of disclosures among minors (e.g., An & Stern, 2011; De Jans 2019; De Pauw et al. 2017; Panic et al. 2012; Van Reijmersdal et al. 2017). In the interviews, children indicated that they hardly pay attention to textual disclosures, which is likely to explain the lack of effects of disclosures on advertising recognition found in previous studies (An & Stern, 2011; Panic et al. 2012). Our study also shows the confusions regarding the formulations 'collaboration' and 'paid collaboration,' which may explain why some studies found effects whereas others did not (e.g., De Jans et al. 2019; De Pauw et al. 2017; Van Reijmersdal et al. 2017). If children do not notice or do not understand the meaning of a sponsorship disclosure (due to vague or complex formulations), their *opportunity* to process and make sense of the disclosure is low. As a result, the disclosure will be less effective in triggering children's advertising literacy and critical coping strategies (Van Reijmersdal et al. 2020).

The second theoretical implication is that our study reveals important differences between children in their perceptions of disclosures. For example, children differ greatly in the extent to which they consider sponsorship disclosures necessary and relevant. Our findings show that there are children who do see the need for disclosures. However, in line with earlier research by Van Dam and Van Reijmersdal (2019), our findings also show that there are also children who seem to prefer to be left in the dark with regard to the content's sponsorship rather than to be informed about it. Children who find disclosures less important are probably also less motivated to pay attention to disclosures and think about its meaning and purpose. They also processed the sponsored influencer video less critically. Our study also showed that children differ in their level of advertising literacy with regard to sponsored influencer videos. Children who are less aware of the business model of influencer marketing are also less able to understand the purpose and meaning of sponsorship disclosures in online influencer videos. These individual differences in children's *motivation* and *ability* to process and understand sponsorship disclosure need to be taken into account in future theory building and empirical research, to refine our understanding of how disclosures affect children.

For legislators and in particular for the implementation of the European AVMSD, our study implies that spoken disclosures somewhere at the beginning of the video have the highest chance of being noticed and appreciated. In addition, explicit terms such as 'paid' are helpful for children to understand the persuasive intent of sponsored influencer videos.

5.2 Limitations and Suggestions for Future Research

Our study has several limitations worth noting. First, children talked about a variety of sponsored online influencer videos in this study. However, the study is limited to the specific genre of influencer videos. Future research is needed to illuminate minors' perceptions of disclosures for other types of sponsored videos (e.g., music videos) and other types of influencer content that are not audio-visual (e.g., Instagram posts).

Second, the findings of our study offer some insights into the characteristics that make disclosures more or less noticeable and understandable (e.g., formulation, location, modality). However, more systematic research is needed to explore how sponsorship disclosures should be formulated and implemented in order to be noticeable and well understood by children.

Finally, this study provides rich qualitative insights into children's perceptions of disclosures and their role in the transparency of sponsored influencer videos. A next step would be to conduct a quantitative study (for example a survey) in which these perceptions can be examined on a larger scale. Similarly, some of the preferences for specific types of disclosures may be tested in experimental studies for actual effectiveness in enhancing children's understanding of the persuasive nature of sponsored influencer videos.

Acknowledgements
This study was funded by the *Dutch Media Authority* and field work was done by *Youngworks*. The authors thank Eline Metske for her help with the study design and the data collection.

References

An, S., & Stern, S. (2011). Mitigating the effects of advergames on children. *Journal of Advertising, 40*(1), 43–56.

Best, J. R., & Miller, P. H. (2010). A developmental perspective on executive function. *Child Development, 81*(6), 1641–1660.

Boerman, S. C., Van Reijmersdal, E. A., & Neijens, P. C. (2015). Using eye tracking to understand the effects of brand placement disclosure types in television programs. *Journal of Advertising, 44*(3), 196–207.

CAP. (2017). *Advertising Codes*. Retrieved from https://www.asa.org.uk/advice-online/affiliate-marketing.html

Charmaz, K. (2014). *Constructing grounded theory*. Thousand Oaks: Sage.

De Jans, S., Cauberghe, V., & Hudders, L. (2019). How an advertising disclosure alerts young adolescents to sponsored vlogs: The moderating role of a peer-based advertising literacy intervention through an informational vlog. *Journal of Advertising*, 1–17.

De Jans, S., Vanwesenbeeck, I., Cauberghe, V., Hudders, L., Rozendaal, E., & Van Reijmersdal, E. A. (2018). The development and testing of a child-inspired advertising disclosure to alert children to digital and embedded advertising. *Journal of Advertising, 47*(3), 255–269.

De Pauw, P., De Wolf, R., Hudders, L., & Cauberghe, V. (2017). From persuasive messages to tactics: Exploring children's knowledge and judgement of new advertising formats. *New Media and Society, 20*(7), 2604–2628.

Einstein, B. R. (2015): Reading between the lines: The rise of native advertising and the FTC's inability to regulate it. In: *Brook. J. Corp. Fin. and Com. L., 10*, 225.

European Commission. (2018): Revision of the audiovisual media services directive (AVMSD). Retrieved from https://ec.europa.eu/digital-single-market/en/revision-audiovisual-media-services-directive-avmsd

Federal Trade Commission. (2009). 16 CFR part 255: Guides concerning the use of endorsements and testimonials in advertising. Retrieved from https://www.ftc.gov/sites/default/files/attachments/press-releases/ftc-publishes-final-guides-governing-endorsements-testimonials/091005revisedendorsementguides.pdf

Federal Trade Commission. (2010). 15 U.S.C. §§ 41–58; section 5: Unfair or deceptive acts or practices. Retrieved from https://www.federalreserve.gov/boarddocs/supmanual/cch/ftca.pdf

Guo, F., Ye, G., Duffy, V. G., Li, M., & Ding, Y. (2018). Applying eye tracking and electroencephalography to evaluate the effects of placement disclosures on brand responses. *Journal of Consumer Behaviour, 17*(6), 519–531.

Gupta, P. B., Balasubramanian, S. K., & Klassen, M. L. (2000). Viewers' evaluations of product placements in movies: Public policy issues and managerial implications. *Journal of Current Issues & Research in Advertising, 22*(2), 41–52.

Hudders, L., De Pauw, P., Cauberghe, V., Panic, K., Zarouali, B., & Rozendaal, E. (2017). Shedding new light on how advertising literacy can affect children's processing of embedded advertising formats: A future research agenda. *Journal of Advertising, 46*(2), 333–349.

Hudson, S., Hudson, D., & Peloza, J. (2008). Meet the parents: A parents' perspective on product placement in children's films. *Journal of Business Ethics, 80*(2), 289–304.

MacInnis, D. J., Moorman, C., & Jaworski, B. J. (1991). Enhancing consumers' motivation, ability, and opportunity to process brand information from ads: Conceptual framework and managerial implications. *Journal of Marketing, 55*(1), 32–53.

Panic, K., Hudders, L., Destoop, K., Cauberghe, V., & De Pelsmacker, P. (2012). Children and a changing media environment: Investigating Persuasion Knowledge for integrated advertising formats. In: *11th International conference on Research in Advertising (ICORIA 2012): The changing roles of advertising*.

Stichting Reclame Code. (2014). Reclamecode social media (RSM). Retrieved from https://www.reclamecode.nl/nrc/pagina.asp?paginaID=289%20anddeel=2

Strauss, A., & Corbin, J. (1998). *Basics of qualitative research techniques*. Thousand Oaks: Sage.

Van Dam, S., & Van Reijmersdal, E. (2019). Insights in adolescents' advertising literacy, perceptions and responses regarding sponsored influencer videos and disclosures. *Cyberpsychology: Journal of Psychosocial Research on Cyberspace, 13*(2), 1–19.

Van Reijmersdal, E. A., Boerman, S. C., Buijzen, M., & Rozendaal, E. (2017). This is advertising! Effects of disclosing television brand placement on adolescents. *Journal of Youth and Adolescence, 46*(2), 328–342.

Van Reijmersdal, E. A., Rozendaal, E., Hudders, L., Van Wesenbeeck, I., & Cauberghe, V. (2020). Effects of Disclosing Influencer Marketing in Videos: An Eye Tracking Study among Children in Early Adolescence. *Journal of Interactive Marketing, 49*(February), 94–106.

Van Reijmersdal, E. A., Tutaj, K., & Boerman, S. C. (2013). The effects of brand placement disclosures on skepticism and brand memory. *Communication: The European Journal of Communication Research, 38*(2), 127–146.

Wojdynski, B. W., & Evans, N. J. (2016). Going native: Effects of disclosure position and language on the recognition and evaluation of online native advertising. *Journal of Advertising, 45*(2), 157–168.

Family Decision Making and Vacation Functions in Summer Tourism – The Case of Austrian Families

Stephanie Tischler

1 Introduction

Family-decision making has changed considerably in recent years (Bronner and de Hoog 2008, p. 165). Additionally, new family structures and the complexity of modified family relationships affect the decision making process greatly (Tinson et al. 2008). According to Schänzel and Yeoman (2015) the tourism industry requires a better understanding of these changes in family purchasing decision processes.

Family vacation functions have been particularly under-researched and longitudinal studies have been requested by several authors (Lehto et al. 2009; Fu et al. 2014; Shaw et al. 2008). Furthermore, a better understanding of the benefits of travelling in relation to family cohesion is needed (Durko and Petrick 2013). As differences in general behaviours of various family types have been identified, it is therefore important to gain a deeper understanding of family vacation behaviour regarding family types (Tinson et al. 2008). Furthermore, practitioners in the tourism industry need a better understanding of these complex purchasing decisions, as destination choice and holiday activities are normally discussed among all family members, including children (Schänzel and Yeoman 2015).

This study aims to 1) investigate the vacation functions perceived by Austrian families, 2) examine possible developments in these functions between 2016 and 2018 in order to bring in a longitudinal perspective and 3) study the decision-making style of Austrian families when planning a summer vacation.

S. Tischler (✉)
IMC University of Applied Sciences Krems, Krems, Austria
E-Mail: stephanie.tischler@fh-krems.ac.at

2   Theoretical Background

Schänzel et al. (2005) define family holidays as "[...] leisure travel away from home for more than one day undertaken by a family group, itself defined as at least one child and one adult." Families can therefore be described as decision-making units which are looking to collect joint experiences while being on vacation (Bronner and de Hoog 2008, p. 967; Lehto et al. 2012, p. 835; Gram 2005, p. 6).

However, it has to be considered that there is a great diversity of family forms (Schänzel et al. 2005). Regardless of the family form, research shows that vacation activities provide opportunities for interactions among all family members (Lehto et al. 2009). Attention should be paid to families as decision-making units not only because of their significant market share and size but also because of the effects family holidays have on family relationships (Lehto et al. 2012, p. 835).

The reasons why families go on holiday differ significantly from the reasons why individuals do so (Backer and Schänzel 2013). Family holidays are usually less about escape and stress reduction, than about spending time together as a family (Schänzel 2012).

Lehto et al. (2009) showed that family vacations contribute positively to family bonding, communication and solidarity. Fu et al. (2014) identified five different functions of family vacations: "Bonding and Sharing", "Communication", "Escape and Relaxation", "Children's Learning" and "Novelty Seeking". Vacation bonds families together, as sharing experiences and taking a family vacation foster positive bonds among family members (Fu et al. 2014). Similarly, the importance of family togetherness for families was highlighted by Shaw et al. (2008). In their opinion, the creation of positive memories and experiences is a key motivation to travel together. Similarly, Durko and Petrick (2013) state that family travelling creates strong family bonds and life-time memories. However, the aim of being together might also cause a dilemma, as parents' and children's preferred holiday activities might diverge. While children mainly prefer play and activities, parents also seek room for rest (Gram 2005).

Spending time together has to be seen as an important motive, as holidays provide families with the opportunity of compensating for their working life and daily routine. During their vacation the family has the opportunity to solve tasks and problems together and new activities and stimuli enable families to gain new experiences. Family vacations can thus combine greater individual freedom and a more in-depth family connection (Busse and Ströhlein 1991, p. 230–231).

Nevertheless, the reasons for family vacation and holiday choice have evolved over recent years. Bronner and de Hoog (2008) claim that family holidays are now

"[…] a joint decision, in which family members discuss, seek out information to use in the discussion, employ disagreement-resolution strategies and come finally to a joint choice". Additionally, they emphasize that holiday choices are more of a joint affair compared to other choices.

Children's opinions are usually highly significant for parents as they hope their children will be pleased with the vacation. This can be achieved early by involving them in deciding on the destination. Depending on the children's age, this can be done by simply notifying them about the intention or actively involving them in selecting a travel destination (Gram 2005, p. 20–21). Children are not only co-decision makers when deciding on the destination. Family vacation requires detailed planning beforehand, not only about activities on-site but also about financial resources and necessary provisions (Srnec et al. 2016, p. 432).

During this decision-making process, the amount of influence over the family may differ between its members and subdecisions. For vacation satisfaction, it is nevertheless crucial that parents consider the needs of their children during planning and decision-making (Tinson et al. 2008). Family purchasing decisions have become more democratic and are discussed among all family members. Children are and want to be involved in the decision-making process (Carr 2011). However, children cannot be considered as a homogeneous group. Age has to be considered an important differentiator, as various age groups have different requirements (Schänzel and Yeoman 2015). Older children are supposed to have more influence than younger children due to their perception and understanding of different products and services. Furthermore, they may have already developed argumentation and negotiation techniques for persuading their parents to purchase a certain service (Martensen and Grønholdt 2008, p. 14). Decrop (2006, pp. 145–147) for example, stated that decisions about on-site activities such as tours, activities, attractions are most often made by the children, which is the result of parents sacrificing their own desires in order to please their children.

However, it has to be considered, that booking behaviour in family tourism is not only influenced by the family members and their roles but also by other people's recommendations and opinions (Fletcher et al. 2013, p. 51). Furthermore, travel information is obtained through intermediaries and online. Therefore, tour operators, travel agencies and online forums and platforms are forced to adjust to the demand of families requiring detailed information about a destination or service before booking especially with regards to the infrastructure and the activities offered (Schänzel and Yeoman 2015, p. 143) in order to meet the families' holiday motives and needs.

3 Methodology

The aim of the research was to shed light on vacation functions, as perceived by Austrian families as well as the decision-making style of Austrian families. This required quantification of data as well as application of measurement techniques and statistical analysis, leading to the decision to use a quantitative method using a multiple cross-sectional design. The first survey was conducted face-to-face among Austrian families in April and May 2016. The same method was used for the second survey, which was carried out in March and April 2018. The target population consisted of Austrian parents having at least one child under 18 years of age. The applied quota sampling strategy determined a proportion of 30% families with one child, 50% families with two children, 20% families with three or more children, where at least one child had to be under the age of 18. These quota represent the approximate structure of Austrian families. This sampling approach resulted in a sample size of n = 229 usable interviews in 2016 and n = 260 in 2018.

The questionnaire that was used for this study was pre-tested in order to minimise errors and biases. The original language of the questionnaire was German as this was the mother tongue of all respondents. The questions covered the range of vacation functions based on Fu et al. (2014): bonding and sharing, communication, escape/relaxation, children's learning as well as novelty seeking. Following the approach of these authors, family vacation functions were measured by perceived levels of importance, ranging from "never important to me (1)" to "always important to me (5)" on a 5-point Likert scale. The items covering the family decision making process were based on the factor "domestic familial decisions" described in the analysis of Ozdipciner et al. (2010) regarding purchase decision attributes.

Demographic and statistical questions such as age and gender of the respondents, number of children, age of children and residential area were placed at the beginning of the questionnaire to ensure fulfilment of pre-determined quota. Families who were not eligible to take part in the survey excluded immediately after they answered these initial questions.

Ethical behaviour was kept in mind at all stages of the research as families including children have to be treated as a sensitive target group. Participation in the survey was voluntary and respondents had the right to refuse to answer any question. Participants were given the information that any personal information or data would be treated as confidential and anonymous and that they had the right to access research findings at any time. All aspects of the research were designed with the intention not to mislead the participants regarding any aspect of the research (Jennings 2010, p. 99).

All questionnaires were checked, coded and entered into the computer. Consistency checks were done in order to ensure that data were logically consistent (Malhotra et al. 2012, p. 597). Participants' verbatim responses were coded. Mutually exclusive and collectively exhaustive category codes were developed (Malhotra et al. 2012, p. 595). Data analysis was done with SPSS, version 23. The internal consistency of the scale used to measure perceived vacation functions was tested and classified as reliable (Cronbach's $\alpha = 0.76$) (Fantapié Altobelli 2011, p. 165).

Similar to Fu et al. (2014), an exploratory factor analysis was performed on the vacation functions. Additionally, Kruskal–Wallis tests as well as Mann–Whitney-U tests were carried out to investigate group differences.

4 Findings

As suggested by the literature (e.g. Bronner and de Hoog 2008) children are usually involved in the decision-making process. Results of the 2018 study show that in general 64.1% of all respondents reported involving their children in all or most vacation decisions, 21.4% claimed to do so at least sometimes. 14.5% include them only rarely or not at all.

Findings therefore indicate that making the decision to book a vacation is typically a family decision. 42.9% of all respondents strongly agree with the statement that they make this decision as a family. The same holds true for the duration and how much to pay. The destination tends not to be seen as a family decision. Here, only 10.9% see this as a clear-cut family decision-making process (scaling point 1 "strongly agree"; see Table 1).

Based on the performed Kruskal–Wallis tests, none of these decisions differ with regard to family size (according to the number of children) or gender of parent. However, one difference regarding the age of the parents appears: Parents aged between 30 and 40 are less likely to make their decision on a family basis. Here, parents under the age of 30 and above 40 are more likely to decide this jointly ($\chi 2(2) = 8.468, p = 0.014$).

Additionally, differences related to the family structure can be observed: when investigating single parents (S) and mothers/fathers living with another partner than the biological mother/father of their child(ren) (blended families) (B) compared to those in a traditional family structure (T), several differences appear (see Table 2). Single parents are less likely to make the decision of buying a vacation

Table 1 Domestic family decisions

	strongly agree (1)	agree (2)	neutral (3)	rather disagree (4)	strongly disagree (5)	Mean	SD
we make the decision of buying a vacation as a family	42.9%	30.7%	18.5%	3.8%	4.2%	1.96	1.07
we decide as a family how long we should stay on vacation	33.6%	31.1%	16.8%	10.9%	7.6%	2.28	1.25
we decide how much to pay as a family	30.4%	15.6%	20.7%	18.6%	14.8%	2.72	1.44
we decide where to go on vacation on familial grounds	10.9%	22.3%	25.6%	14.7%	26.5%	3.24	1.35

Table 2 Decision making according to family structure

	Family structure	N	Mean	SD	Sig. (P<0.05)	Group differences (P<0.05)
we make the decision of buying a vacation as a family	single parent (S)	24	3.33	1.341	0.000	T = B < S
	traditional family (T)	189	2.13	1.180		
	blended family (B)	24	2.38	1.209		
we decide as a family how long we should stay on vacation	single parent (S)	24	2.54	1.285	0.006	S = B > T
	traditional family (T)	189	1.83	0.964		
	blended family (B)	24	2.38	1.377		
we decide how much to pay as a family	single parent (S)	24	3.67	1.465	0.002	T = B < S
	traditional family (T)	189	2.56	1.396		
	blended family (B)	24	2.96	1.429		
we decide where to go on vacation on familial grounds	single parent (S)	24	3.33	1.341	0.748	S = T = B
	traditional family (T)	189	3.26	1.321		
	blended family (B)	24	3.04	1.546		

on a family basis ($\chi2(2) = 10.212$, $p = 0.006$). Similarly, they are less likely to decide jointly on how much to pay ($\chi2(2) = 12.847$, $p = 0.002$). The decision on the length of a vacation is usually more of a joint affair in traditional families, compared to single parents and blended families ($\chi2(2) = 17.224$, $p = 0.000$).

In order to further investigate the various vacation functions, an exploratory factor analysis was conducted using the results of the 2018 study regarding the 20 statements based on the concept of (Fu et al. 2014). For this, the Varimax procedure using Kaiser Normalization was employed. Regarding the extraction method, principal component analysis was used to extract factors with eigenvalues greater than 1. The Kaiser–Meyer–Olkin measure of sampling adequacy was .84, and therefore above the commonly recommended value of .6. Bartlett's test of sphericity was significant ($\chi 2(190) = 2177.34$, $p < .001$). The diagonals of the anti-image correlation matrix were also all over 0.7. Given these overall indicators, factor analysis was deemed to be suitable with all 20 items.

The performed factor analysis resulted in a 5-factor solution similar to Fu et al. (2014). Together, the 5 dimensions accounted for 66.28% of the variance in data set, which is slightly below the total amount of variance explained in the sample of Fu et al. (2014) (73.95%) (see Table 3).

Table 3 Factor solution based on exploratory factor analysis

	Novelty Seeking and Knowledge	Bonding and Sharing	Communi-cation	Escape/ Relaxation	Children's Learning
tasting authentic local food	0.866				
experiencing a different culture	0.802				
children can learn culture, history and people (or, I can learn culture, history and people)	0.830				
extending children's knowledge (or, extending my knowledge)	0.629				
doing things together		0.633			
making memories together		0.743			
having fun with family members		0.828			
sharing quality time together		0.761			

(continued)

Table 3 (continued)

	Novelty Seeking and Knowledge	Bonding and Sharing	Communi-cation	Escape/ Relaxation	Children's Learning
being together as a family		0.605			
respecting family members decisions			0.650		
sharing different opinions			0.566		
increasing communication			0.775		
finding more things in common			0.591		
bonding more strongly			0.732		
escaping from the routine life				0.870	
getting away from the demands at home				0.831	
getting a change from a busy job/ school				0.800	
relaxing				0.406	
broadening children's view (or, broadening my view)					0.734
experiencing new things together					0.756
% of variance explained	15.74	15.25	14.67	12.60	8.04
Eigenvalues	6.079	3.115	1.895	1.136	1.030
Cronbach's Alpha	0.855	0.794	0.817	0.751	0.674
N of items	4	5	5	4	2

The factors explaining most of the variance are "Novelty Seeking and Knowledge" (15.74%) as well as "Bonding and Sharing" (15.25%), followed by "Communication" (14.67%). This is notably different to the results of the study of Fu et al. (2014), where "Bonding and Sharing" was by far the most important factor with regard to the variance explained (46.04%) and all other factors explained less than 10% of the variance. This great importance of togetherness and family bonding is not only documented in previous studies but also stressed by the tourism industry (Carr 2011). The learning aspect explains least of the variance in this study (8.04%) and also little in Fu's (2014) study (5.95%). However, the learning that can occur in the holiday environment should not be devalued (Carr 2011), as holidays provide an excellent opportunity for learning social and practical skills as well as transmitting family-specific skills and establishing family values (Schänzel 2013).

When investigating the tested vacation functions individually, findings show that the most important functions are "doing things together", "making memories together", "having fun with family members", "sharing quality time together" as well as "being together as a family". The least important functions are those related to culinary and cultural aspects: "tasting authentic local food" and "experiencing a different culture" tend not to be perceived as important family vacation functions. When investigating the longitudinal perspective, a few changes between 2016 and 2018 appear. "Doing things together", "increasing communication", "bonding more strongly" and "experiencing a different culture" seem to have become less important, while "respecting family members decisions", "escaping from routine life" and "getting away from the demands at home" seem to have become more important in 2018. All in all, findings suggest that the escape/relaxation factor has become more important (see Table 4).

The results of performing Kruskal–Wallis tests revealed that (at the 5% significance level) none of the vacation functions differed significantly among family structures (single parent family vs. blended vs. traditional family). Similarly, no differences in family vacations functions with regard to family size (number of children) can be observed.

In contrast to this, significant differences appeared when investigating the gender aspect by performing Mann–Whitney-U tests: the importance of nine tested family vacations functions varied between males and females. "Sharing quality time together" ($U = 4,548.5$, $p = 0.011$), "respecting family members decisions" ($U = 4,724.5$, $p = 0.043$), "sharing different opinions" ($U = 4,548.5$, $p = 0.011$), "increasing communication" ($U = 4,609.5$, $p = 0.013$), "bonding more strongly" ($U = 4,801.0$, $p = 0.018$), "children or I can learn about culture, history and people" ($U = 4,681.0$, $p = 0.020$), "extending children's or my own knowledge" ($U = 4,817.0$, $p = 0.034$), "broadening children's or my own view" ($U = 4,605.0$, $p = 0.009$) and "experiencing a different culture" ($U = 4,598.5$, $p = 0.011$) are more important to mothers. This suggests that the communication as well as the children's learning factors are valued higher by mothers, which confirms the findings of (Fu et al. 2014).

Table 4 Vacation functions per year

Vacation functions	N	Year	Very important (1)	Important (2)	Neu-tral (3)	Rather not impor-tant (4)	Not important at all (5)	Mean	SD	Sig (P<0.05)	Group differences (P<0.05)
Doing things together	229	2016	83.0%	14.4%	1.3%	0.4%	0.9%	1.22	0.574	0.002	2018>2016
	239	2018	71.1%	21.8%	6.3%	0.4%	0.4%	1.37	0.661		
Making memories together	229	2016	83.4%	13.5%	1.7%	0.9%	0.4%	1.21	0.556	0.642	2018 = 2016
	238	2018	84.9%	13.0%	1.3%	0.0%	0.8%	1.19	0.530		
Having fun with family members	229	2016	83.8%	13.1%	1.7%	0.4%	0.9%	1.21	0.579	0.963	2018 = 2016
	239	2018	83.7%	13.0%	3.3%	0.0%	0.0%	1.20	0.475		
Sharing quality time together	229	2016	86.5%	9.6%	2.6%	0.9%	0.4%	1.19	0.560	0.406	2018 = 2016
	239	2018	83.7%	11.7%	3.3%	0.8%	0.4%	1.23	0.586		
Being together as a family	229	2016	83.0%	14.0%	2.6%	0.0%	0.4%	1.21	0.521	0.106	2018 = 2016
	239	2018	88.3%	9.2%	2.1%	0.0%	0.4%	1.15	0.439		
Respecting family members decisions	229	2016	31.0%	34.1%	23.1%	9.2%	2.6%	2.18	1.056	0.000	2018<2016
	235	2018	48.1%	35.7%	11.5%	2.6%	2.1%	1.75	0.911		
Sharing different opinions	229	2016	28.8%	31.4%	28.4%	10.0%	1.3%	2.24	1.020	0.147	2018 = 2016
	237	2018	23.2%	32.5%	40.8%	7.6%	5.9%	2.41	1.103		
Increasing communication	229	2016	35.4%	38.0%	18.8%	6.6%	1.3%	2.00	0.962	0.029	2018>2016
	238	2018	28.2%	37.8%	21.9%	8.0%	5.0%	2.24	1.103		

(continued)

Table 4 (continued)

Vacation functions	N	Year	Very important (1)	Impor-tant (2)	Neu-tral (3)	Rather not impor-tant (4)	Not important at all (5)	Mean	SD	Sig (P<0.05)	Group differences (P<0.05)
Finding more things in common	228	2016	35.5%	35.5%	22.8%	5.3%	0.9%	2.00	0.936	0.504	2018 = 2016
	239	2018	42.3%	28.9%	18.4%	5.9%	4.6%	2.02	1.123		
Bonding more strongly	229	2016	74.7%	14.8%	9.6%	0.0%	0.9%	1.37	0.692	0.006	2018 > 2016
	239	2018	63.2%	21.4%	9.6%	2.1%	3.8%	1.62	1.005		
Children or I can learn about culture, history and people	229	2016	34.1%	39.7%	16.2%	8.3%	1.7%	2.04	0.997	0.077	2018 = 2016
	238	2018	31.5%	30.7%	26.5%	6.3%	5.0%	2.23	1.113		
Extending children's or my own knowledge	229	2016	41.0%	38.0%	13.5%	6.6%	0.9%	1.88	0.936	0.340	2018 = 2016
	239	2018	39.7%	33.5%	16.7%	5.9%	4.2%	2.01	1.087		
Broadening children's or my own view	229	2016	40.6%	35.8%	18.8%	4.4%	0.4%	1.88	0.893	0.082	2018 = 2016
	238	2018	48.3%	33.6%	12.6%	2.9%	2.5%	1.78	0.953		
Experiencing new things together	229	2016	65.1%	28.5%	5.7%	0.0%	0.9%	1.42	0.642	0.321	2018 = 2016
	239	2018	61.1%	30.1%	7.5%	0.4%	0.8%	1.50	0.727		
Escaping from the routine life	229	2016	45.9%	25.3%	15.7%	7.9%	5.2%	2.01	1.186	0.006	2018 < 2016
	239	2018	57.7%	21.3%	13.8%	5.0%	2.1%	1.72	1.016		

(continued)

Table 4 (continued)

Vacation functions	N	Year	Very important (1)	Important (2)	Neu-tral (3)	Rather not impor-tant (4)	Not important at all (5)	Mean	SD	Sig (P<0.05)	Group differences (P<0.05)
Getting away from the demands at home	229	2016	36.2%	22.7%	19.7%	14.0%	7.4%	2.34	1.296	0.003	2018<2016
	239	2018	48.1%	23.0%	15.5%	7.1%	6.3%	2.00	1.221		
Getting a change from busy job, school, work	228	2016	51.8%	28.5%	12.7%	5.3%	1.8%	1.77	0.982	0.051	2018 = 2016
	238	2018	61.3%	21.8%	12.2%	3.4%	1.3%	1.61	0.915		
Relaxing	229	2016	69.0%	20.1%	9.6%	1.3%	0.0%	1.43	0.720	0.911	2018 = 2016
	238	2018	69.3%	20.6%	8.4%	0.4%	1.3%	1.44	0.770		
Tasting authentic local food	229	2016	27.9%	37.6%	22.7%	8.7%	3.1%	2.21	1.044	0.525	2018 = 2016
	239	2018	28.5%	33.1%	23.8%	9.2%	5.4%	2.30	1.138		
Experiencing a different culture	228	2016	29.8%	32.0%	23.7%	11.8%	2.6%	2.25	1.089	0.003	2018>2016
	239	2018	21.3%	28.9%	26.8%	14.2%	8.8%	2.60	1.218		

5   Conclusion

This study investigated the vacation functions perceived by Austrian families and studied the decision-making style of Austrian families in planning a vacation. Results confirm that making the decision to book a vacation is typically a family decision.

Furthermore, as requested by Tinson et al. (2008), this study tried to shed light on the differences regarding various family structures. Findings show that single parents are less likely to make the buying and budget decision on a family basis. Besides, single parents and blended families are less likely to decide on the length of a vacation jointly. Additionally, this research aimed at investigating differences in the decision-making style regarding family size and gender. However, no differences regarding family size (based on the number of children) and gender of parent can be seen.

Based on family vacation functions defined in earlier research, this study empirically assessed family vacation functions with regard to family structure. Whereas differences in the decision-making style can be seen with regard to family structure as described above, none of the tested family vacations functions were found to be related to family structure and size.

This research further aimed at investigating family vacation functions. The most important factors are "novelty seeking and knowledge" as well as "bonding and sharing", which are not only significant motives documented in the literature, but also heavily used in marketing and advertising efforts of the tourism industry. Findings at hand therefore confirm the importance of family bonding as a main motivator for family holidays. Nevertheless, relaxation and learning should not be underestimated in family tourism.

Communicating the relaxation aspect is especially important, as mothers are more likely to perceive family vacation as an opportunity to get escape home and/or work-based stress and enjoy a temporary break (Fu et al. 2014), but report a less positive and less relaxing vacation experience compared to fathers because of ongoing caregiving duties (Schänzel et al. 2005) and genderdized roles are most often maintained (Mottiar and Quinn 2012). This fact is especially important, when considering mothers living in blended households and single-parent households as they report even greater child involvement and duties (Tinson et al. 2008).

As the findings at hand furthermore suggest that children's learning is a factor that is highly valued by mothers and women appear to be particularly influential in the vacation decision-making process (Koc 2004; Mottiar and Quinn 2004), the learning aspect is recommended to appear in marketing and advertising of tourism companies. Learning social and practical skills, transmitting family-specific skills and establishing family values and traditions shapes the family's social identity and contributes to generativity (Schänzel 2013).

For marketers, it is important to have information on the holiday decision-making process, as they need to know who makes the decision and on what basis (Schänzel 2012, p. 57). Findings confirm that children are to be seen as influencers and co-decision makers as suggested by Gram (2005, p. 20).

With this study, a first step was made towards analysing longitudinal developments in family vacation functions. Although the investigation of short, two-year differences is clearly limited, this first comparison shall lay the basis for upcoming studies in terms of two-year cycles. These first comparisons suggest that the escape/relaxation factor has become more important since the first study in 2016.

For practitioners it is important to understand that based on their structure, Austrian families do not differ greatly regarding their decision-making style and their pursued vacation functions. However, it is important to monitor these aspects regularly, as family vacation functions seem to evolve over time.

This research is limited with regard to sample sizes for both studies, as well as the above-mentioned restricted time frame under consideration, for evaluating changes in the long-run. It is therefore recommended to repeat these analyses at regular intervals.

Additionally, as children cannot be considered as a homogeneous group, their age should be considered as a further differentiator in further studies, as various age groups might have different holiday motives and requirements. Finally, the perspective of the children themselves should be taken into consideration, as the two mentioned studies solely examined the perspective of parents. Investigating these"[…] childhood experiences based on children's voices, rather than adults' or experts' assumptions, is essential in advancing tourism scholarship and industry knowledge, and will contribute to developing a more inclusive view of tourism and its impacts." (Poria and Timothy 2014, p. 95).

References

Backer, E., & Schänzel, H. (2013). Family holidays—Vacation or obli-cation? *Tourism Recreation Research, 38*(2), 159–173.

Bronner, F., & de Hoog, R. (2008). Agreement and disagreement in family vacation decision-making. *Tourism Management, 29*(5), 967–979.

Busse, G., & Ströhlein, G. (1991). Familienurlaub: Anspruch und Realisierung. *Freizeitpädagogik, 13*(3), 230–242.

Carr, N. (2011). *Children's and families' holiday experiences*. Milton Park: Routledge.

Decrop, A. (2006). *Vacation decision making.* Wallingford: CABI Publishing.
Durko, A. M., & Petrick, J. F. (2013). Family and relationship benefits of travel experiences. A literature review. *Journal of Travel Research, 52*(6), 720–730.
Fantapié Altobelli, C. 2011. *Marktforschung. Methoden, Anwendungen, Praxisbeispiele.* Konstanz: UVK.
Fletcher, J., Fyall, A., Gilbert, D., & Wanhill, S. (2013). *Tourism: Principles and practice* (5th ed.). Harlow: Pearson Education Limited.
Fu, X., Lehto, X., & Park, O. (2014). What does vacation do to our family? Contrasting the perspectives of parents and children. *Journal of Travel & Tourism Marketing, 31*(4), 461–475.
Gram, M. (2005). Family holidays. A qualitative analysis of family holiday experiences. *Scandinavian Journal of Hospitality and Tourism, 5*(1), 2–22.
Jennings, G. (2010). *Tourism research.* Milton: Wiley.
Koc, E. (2004). The role of family members in the family holiday purchase decision-making process. *International Journal of Hospitality & Tourism Administration, 5*(2), 85–102.
Lehto, X., Choi, S., Lin, Y.-C., & MacDermid, S. M. (2009). Vacation and family functioning. *Annals of Tourism Research, 36*(3), 459–479.
Lehto, X., Lin, Y.-C., Chen, Y., & Choi, S. (2012). Family vacation activities and family cohesion. *Journal of Travel & Tourism Marketing, 29*(8), 835–850
Malhotra, N. K., Birks, D. F., & Wills, P. (2012). *Marketing research: An applied approach.* Harlow: Pearson.
Martensen, A., & Grønholdt, L. (2008). Children's influence on family decision making. *Innovative Marketing, 4*(4), 14–22.
Mottiar, Z., & Quinn, D. (2004). Couple dynamics in household tourism decision making: Women as the gatekeepers? *Journal of Vacation Marketing, 10*(2), 149–160.
Mottiar, Z., & Quinn, D. (2012). Is a self-catering holiday with the family really a holiday for mothers? Examining the balance of household responsibilities while on holiday from a female perspective. *Hospitality & Society, 2*(2), 197–214.
Ozdipciner, N. S., Li, X., & Uysal, M. (2010). An examination of purchase decision-making criteria: A case of Turkey as a destination. *Journal of Hospitality Marketing & Management, 19*(5), 514–527.
Poria, Y., & Timothy, D. J. (2014). Where are the children in tourism research? *Annals of Tourism Research, 47,* 93–95.
Schänzel, H. (2012). The context of family tourism. In H. Schänzel, I. Yeoman, & E. Baker (Eds.), *Family tourism. Multidiscipinary perspectives* (pp. 17–29). Bristol: Channel View Publications.
Schänzel, H. (2013). The importance of 'Social' in family tourism. *Asia-Pacific Journal of Innovation in Hospitality and Tourism* 2 (1).
Schänzel, H., Smith, K. A., & Weaver, A. (2005). Family holidays: A research review and application to New Zealand. *Annals of Leisure Research, 8*(2–3), 105–123.
Schänzel, H., & Yeoman, I. (2015). Trends in family tourism. *Journal of Tourism Futures, 1*(2), 141–147.
Shaw, S. M., Havitz, M. E., & Delamere, F. (2008). "I decided to invest in my kids" memories": Family vacations, memories, and the social construction of the family." *Tourism, Culture & Communication, 8*(1), 13–26.

Srnec, T., Lončarić, D., & Prodan, M. P. (2016). Family vacation decision making process: Evidence from croatia. *Tourism & Hospitality Industry 2016, Conference Proceedings,* 432–445.

Tinson, J., Nancarrow, C., & Brace, I. (2008). Purchase decision making and the increasing significance of family types. *Journal of Consumer Marketing, 25*(1), 45–56.

Replicating the CSR-Advertising-Effectiveness Model: Do Consumers' Attitudes Towards Corporate Socially Responsible Behavior in the Pharmaceutical Industry Change Over Time?

Isabell Koinig, Sandra Diehl, and Barbara Mueller

1 Introduction

In recent years, the concept of Corporate Social Responsibility (CSR) has begun to resonate with consumers throughout the world. Stemming from growing consumer pressure, both corporations and policy makers are increasingly concerned with CSR, which has been defined as "the continuing commitment by business to contribute to economic development while improving the quality of life of the workforce and their families as well as of the community and society at large" (World Business Council for Sustainable Development, 2000). Consumers are playing a leading role in encouraging corporations to expand upon, as well as publicly disclose their CSR efforts (Nielsen 2012).

An industry survey revealed that consumers expressed concerns over how business operate, and demanded that companies not only support social issues, but

I. Koinig (✉) · S. Diehl
University of Klagenfurt, Klagenfurt, Austria
E-Mail: Isabelle.Koinig@aau.at

S. Diehl
E-Mail: Sandra.Diehl@aau.at

B. Mueller
San Diego State University, San Diego, USA
E-Mail: muelle1@sdsu.edu

also advocate change by creating awareness of these problems (Cone Communications 2013). Earlier surveys found consumers were most concerned about environmental causes, such as water accessibility, as well as social issues, such as fighting poverty and disease (Cone Communications 2013; Nielsen, 2014a). In more recent surveys, the top issues consumers wanted companies to address were social development (Deloitte 2018) and fighting hunger (Nielsen 2018). In 2012, nearly half of all consumers (46 %) were willing to reward firms that went beyond legal obligations by purchasing their products (Nielsen 2012). Just two years later, the number had increased to 55 % (Nielsen 2014b). By 2017, this number reached 87 % among the general population (Cone Communications 2017). Nielsen's 2015 survey also confirmed that companies can benefit from publicizing their CSR engagements, with the sales of such firms outperforming companies that failed to do so (Nielsen 2015). Yet, CSR messages were often perceived as confusing (70 %; Cone Communications 2013). Consequently, consumers expected companies to provide evidence of the good that they do (59 %; Cone Communications 2015). Since companies have begun to take these statistics to heart, consumers' confusion regarding CSR message content has decreased, and integrated CSR initiatives were found to be most effective (Nielsen 2018). CSR has gained momentum in nearly every industry, and the pharmaceutical industry is no exception (McPeak and Guo 2014).

2 CSR in the Pharmaceutical Industry

The benchmark for pharma companies to behave ethically is high. Consumers expect pharmaceutical firms to act both in an ethically and socially responsible fashion, and to provide affordable drugs to the public (Nussbaum 2009). Further, they should not disguise their drugs' potential side effects in their advertising disclosures, but instead provide balanced information (Roblek and Bertoncelj 2014). Connecting the core concerns of profit and ethics is particularly crucial in the health sector (Mueller 2011; Smith 2008). Qualifying as a "controversial sector" (Sroka and Szanto 2018) the industry's reputation unfortunately "keeps getting worse" (Silverman 2016). Support for social causes in the health-care field might allow drug manufacturers to redeem themselves from accusations of engaging in unsound business practices (Koinig 2016; Koinig et al. 2017a). The integration of social and sustainable message elements, therefore, presents a potential strategy to counteract declining public trust (Fontanarosa et al. 2004), however, this may involve shifting funds from R&D and promotional activities towards CSR projects (Yang et al. 2019; Wang and Xu 2011).

2.1 Study Purpose

Academic studies addressing CSR activities in the pharmaceutical industry have dealt with a variety of CSR-related topics (e.g., see Droppert and Bennett 2015; Salton and Jones 2015; Smith 2008) and have received an increasing amount of attention in recent years (Cook et al. 2018; Yang et al. 2019; Filho et al. 2019; Lee et al. 2019). The rationale for this study is three-fold: first, few studies have addressed responses to CSR advertising appeals in one or more pharma markets (Koinig et al. 2017c; Lee et al. 2019); second, limited research has been conducted in the area of non-prescription or over-the-counter drug advertising (Koinig 2016; Koinig et al. 2017a 2017b 2017c, 2017d; Koinig et al. 2018a, 2018b); and third, replication studies addressing the reception of CSR message over time are missing from the debate. In general, a replication study describes "a duplication of a previously published empirical study, and is concerned with assessing whether similar findings can be obtained upon repeating the study" (Hubbard and Armstrong 1994, p. 236). Calls for replication studies have increased (Eisend et al. 2016; Royne 2018). Despite the fact that replications studies are sometimes criticized for not making a "new" contribution (Kerr et al. 2016; Royne 2018), they are useful in ensuring the robustness of results and conceptual models (Faber 2002; Eisend et al. 2016) as well as upholding existing knowledge (Nosek et al. 2012). Additionally, problems associated with single investigations can be overcome (Eisend et al. 2016; Kerr et al. 2016). The present study qualifies as an inter-study replication, meaning that a subsequent study was conducted at a later point in time, by the same authors, using identical stimuli (Easley et al. 2000). This approach is especially useful in testing for the reproducibility of results, making it the strongest form of replication (Sternthal et al. 1987). Industry studies have provided evidence that consumers' concerns regarding corporate social engagements are on the rise. Hence, studies investigating consumer responses to CSR in advertising are called for (Mohr et al. 2001). Given the findings from Nielsen and Cone Communications, it is of value to investigate whether an upswing in interest in CSR would also be reflected in consumer attitudes toward pharma advertisements employing CSR appeals, attitudes toward the product, and purchase intent.

2.2 Rationale for Country Selection

The countries examined are Germany and Austria. The largest share of OTC drug revenues in Europe was generated by Germany, which represented 18.2 % of the continent's total market value (MarketLine 2016), and a market value of € 3.7 billion in 2019. By 2023, the market is expected to be worth € 3.8 billion (Statista 2019b). In Austria, the OTC market volume is estimated at € 600 million for 2019 and is expected to reach € 643 by 2023 (Statista 2019b). Overall, the global OTC market is currently estimated at € 92.2 billion and is forecast to reach a market volume of more than 96 billion by 2023 (Statista 2019c).

2.3 Study Population

122 subjects were surveyed in 2013, and 81 subjects in 2018. They were recruited in mid-sized cities. In terms of age, respondents were between 18 and 82 years old, with an average age of 35 years in 2013, and 33 years in 2018. Female/male participation was almost equally distributed in both datasets (f = 54 %; m = 46 %).

2.4 Stimulus Ad Design

An ad was designed to promote a fictitious pain reliever with the brand name Senza, produced by the fictitious pharmaceutical manufacturer ProSante. The CSR ad employed a mix of two established appeal types, combining elements of both informative and emotional messages, which is on the rise in the pharmaceutical industry (Koinig et al. 2017c). A fictitious CSR message was included in the ad, which was based on the successful CSR initiative by Procter and Gamble linking Pampers and UNICEF. Its inclusion in the ad was intended to raise awareness of Tetanus. For every package of Senza sold, one crucial vaccination to reduce maternal and infant morbidity would be donated. This health cause, a humane-oriented CSR appeal (Diehl et al. 2015), was seen as a good fit for a pharmaceutical marketer. Ads and questionnaires were translated from English into German via the translation/back-translation method. The OTC drug ad is depicted in Fig. 1.

3 Conceptual Model and Hypotheses

Research has begun to address how consumers respond to CSR appeals. While Tiang et al. (2011) and Diehl et al. (2015) developed and tested models analyzing consumers' processing of CSR information, the CSR-Advertising Effectiveness model (Koinig et al. 2017c) expanded existing research by placing a special focus

Getting the best out of life despite pain – with Senza!

Generally, pain surfaces when prostaglandins are created – those are substances that increase the likelihood of pain and are at times accompanied by fever.

What now? The solution is Senza!
Senza is an effective, non-sterioidal, well-tolerated anti-inflammatory drug (NSAID) which inhibits enzymes triggering swelling and pain (cyclooxygenase) and, thus, prevents the creation of prostaglandins.

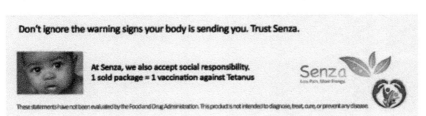

Fig. 1 OTC drug advert incl. a corporate social appeal (Koinig 2016)

on the pharmaceutical industry. The theory-based model proposes that consumers' general attitudes towards CSR will impact their evaluations of an OTC drug ad using a CSR appeal (H1). Consumers' perceived social responsibility on the part of the firm as garnered from the ad is expected to affect their product evaluations (H2a) and purchase intentions (H2b). Moreover, company-cause-fit is presumed to influence both consumers' ad evaluations (H3a) and product evaluations (H3b), while consumers' ad evaluations are expected to influence their product evaluations (H4), which are in turn expected to exercise an impact on consumers' purchase intentions (H5). Finally, consumers' willingness to increase their purchases of products manufactured by socially responsible corporations is assumed to elevate their purchasing likelihood (H6). As numerous industry studies have found consumers' concerns regarding CSR to be on the rise globally (Cone Communications 2017; Nielsen 2018), this is also predicted to hold true for Austria and Germany. Consequently, we expect all CSR-related paths (H1-H3 and H6) to be more pronounced for the 2018 sample as compared to the 2013 sample. The conceptual model is depicted in Fig. 2.

All variables were derived from established scales (see Koinig et al. 2017c). As factor analyses revealed the items of the all multi-item variables in 2013 and 2018 to load on one single factor and to have acceptable Cronbach α values, they were combined for analysis. Answers to each question were reported on a 7-point

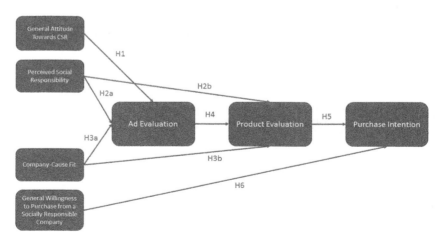

Fig. 2 Conceptual Model including Hypotheses (Koinig et al. 2017c)

Likert scale ranging from (1) 'I do not agree at all' to (7) 'I fully agree' (see Tabs. 1 and 2).

4 Results

Measurement Model
We first conducted a confirmatory factor analysis (CFA) to assess the measurement model, which showed good model fit.

Structural Equation Model
Table 2 presents the results of the structural equation model for the complete dataset. The model shows acceptable global fit measures (CFI = .942; IFI = .943; CMIN/DF = 1.973; RMSEA = .070). The factors within the SEM are latent constructs measured by observable variables (items).

Hypothesis H1 proposed that more positive attitudes towards corporate social engagement would also lead to more favorable evaluations of an ad with a CSR appeal. While consumers' attitudes towards CSR were above average (M_{2013} = 5.2008; M_{2018} = 5.2963; t = .447, p = n..s.), path oefficients were neither significant for the 2013 nor for the 2018 sample (-.89 vs. -.88; CR = -.017, p = n.s.). Hence, hypothesis H1 is rejected in both data sets.

Hypothesis H2a predicted that respondents' perceived CSR engagement positively influenced how they evaluated an advertising message with a CSR appeal. In general, consumers' perceived CSR engagement on the part of the company was slightly below or at average (M_{2013} = 3.7377; M_{2018} = 4.0494; t = -1.332, p = n.s.), as were consumers' ad evaluations (M_{2013} = 3.7582; M_{2018} = 3.8364; t = $-.360$, p = n.s.). Results showed that a higher perceived CSR engagement on the part of the company indeed led to more favorable ad evaluations, with positive and highly significant path coefficients (r_{2013} = .334, p = .000 vs. r_{2018} = .347, p = .006; CR = .281, p = n.s.). Hypothesis H2a is confirmed by both datasets.

Hypothesis H2b predicted that if respondents perceived a high level of CSR engagement on the part of a company, they would also evaluate the advertised product more positively. Consumers' product evaluations were below average (M_{2013} = 3.4016; M_{2018} = 3.3889; t = .059, p = n.s.) and the assumption that respondents' perceived CSR engagement would influence their product evaluations was not confirmed in 2013 (r = .107, p = n.s.), but was in 2018 (r = .241, p = .008). The critical ratio comparison uncovers highly significant differences between the two path coefficients (CR = 4.411, p = .000). Consequently, hypothesis H2b was rejected for the 2013 dataset, yet accepted for the 2018 dataset.

Table 1 Items with means and standard deviations, per year

Variables and Items	2013		2018	
	M	SD	M	SD
General Attitude Towards CSR (a: .883)	5.2003	1.49884	5.2963	1.47644
I think positively about enterprises winch act socially responsible.				
It is important to me that enterprises increasingly consider social issues.				
Ad Evaluation (a: .914) Overall, I find the ad	3.7582	1.53504	3.3364	1.48543
favorable				
interesting				
positive				
pleasant				
Product Evaluation (a: .938)	3.4016	1.47023	3.3339	1.53603
The advertised product (Senza) makes a good impression.				
Senza is of high quality.				
Senza is attractive,				
Senza is appealing.				
Purchase Intention (a: .952)	2.6749	1.74576	2.8436	1.71843
I could imagine trying SENZA.				
I could imagine buying SENZA.				
I could imagine SENZA being one of my most likely choices for my next purchases.				
Company-Cause-Fit:	3.7213	1.96777	3.8025	1.81259
I think that fooSante donating vaccines to reduce infant death caused by Tetanus presents a good match between the company and the cause.				
Increased Purchasing Intention from A Socially Responsible Company	4.7049	1.81667	4.6543	1.8108
I would increasingly purchase products from enterprises winch act socially responsible.				
Perceived Social Responsibility	3.7377	1.70949	4.0494	1.50749
I have the impression jfrgSflBfg (producer of Senza) is a socially responsible company.				

Table 2 Measures of global fit for the measurement model

	x^2	df	X^2/df	RMSEA	IFI	CFI
Sample n = 242						
SEM	363,108	184	1.973	0.07	0.943	0.942
CFA	383,168	174	2.203	0.077	0.934	0.932

Notes: RMSEA = root mean squared error of approximation; IFI: incremental fit index; CFI: comparative fit index

Hypothesis H3a postulated that if the perceived company-cause-fit was high, respondents' evaluations would be more favorable. Consumers perceived a moderate fit between the advertised CSR initiative and the company profile (M_{2013} = 3.7213; M_{2018} = 3.8025; t = -.297, p = n.s.). Path coefficients were highly significant in both 2013 (r = .415, p = .000) and 2018 (r = .366, p = .002; CR: -.201, p = n.s.). Hypothesis H3a is thus supported by all datasets.

H3b proposed that if respondents perceived a high level of perceived fit between the company and the supported cause, they would also evaluate the product more favourably. This relationship could neither be confirmed for the 2013 dataset (r = -.047, p = n.s.), nor for the 2018 dataset (r = -.031, p = n.s.; CR = .069, p = n.s.). Consequently, hypothesis H3b has so be rejected.

Hypothesis H4 suggested that if respondents evaluated the CSR ad appeal positively, their product evaluations would be more favorable. For both datasets, paths were highly significant (2013: r = .809, p = .000; 2018: r = .643, p = .000; CR: -.405, p = n.s.). Hypothesis H4 is thus supported for both data sets.

Hypothesis H5 attempted to determine whether more positive product evaluations would be positively linked to respondents' purchase intentions. Although consumers' purchase intentions were not highly pronounced in either dataset (M_{2013} = 2.6749; M_{2018} = 2.8436; t = .498, p = n.s.), regression weights of path coefficients were highly significant (r_{2013} = .733, p = .000; r_{2018} = .783, p = .000). Besides, the critical ratio was significant (CR = -1.965, p = .000), supporting hypothesis H5.

Hypothesis H6 assumed that an increased general willingness on behalf of consumers to purchase from socially responsible firms would lead to a greater likelihood of purchasing the advertised product. Overall, consumers appeared to increasingly consider purchasing from socially engaged companies (M_{2013} = 4.7049; M_{2018} = 4.6543; t = .195, p = n.s.). For the 2013 dataset, path coefficients were not significant (r = .070, p = n.s.), while they were in the 2018 dataset (r = .185, p = .007). The values however, did not significantly differ in

Table 3 Results of the structural equation model for the two independent data sets

Path	Hypothesis			2013	2018
General Attitude towards CSR		Ad Evaluation	H 1	-.089 n.s	-.088 n.s
Perceived Corporate Social Responsibility		Ad Evaluation	H 2a	.334 ***	347 ***
Perceived Corporate Social Responsibility	—	Product Evaluation	H 2b	.107 n.s	241 ***
Company-Cause Fit	—	Ad Evaluation	H 3a	415 ***	.366 ***
Company-Cause Fit	—	Product Evaluation	H 3b	-.047 n.s	-.031 n.s
Ad Evaluation	—	Product Evaluation	H 4	809 ***	.643 ***
Product Evaluation	—	Purchase Intention	H 5	.733 ***	.783 ***
Increased Purchase Intention from A Socially Responsible Company	—	Purchase Intention	H 6	.070 n.s	185 ***

*** p<0.01 ** p<0.05 * p<0.10

terms of strength (CR = 1.743, p = n.s.). Thus, hypothesis H6 is rejected for the 2013 dataset, but supported for the 2018 dataset.

Table 3 in the Appendix provides an overview of the coefficients and significance levels for the hypotheses proposed in this study for both groups. Fig. 3 depicts the conceptual model, including the confirmed hypotheses for both data sets.

5 Discussion of Results and Implications

The purpose of the present study was to replicate a previous investigation and explore whether consumers' attitudes towards CSR shifted when comparing data

2013

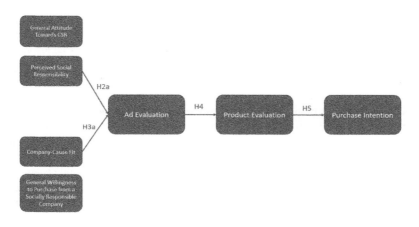

2018

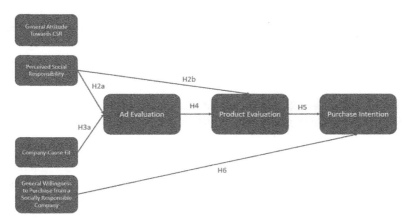

Fig. 3 Conceptual Model including confirmed Hypotheses for 2013 and 2018

from two points in time. As such, it qualifies as an inter-study replication (Easley et al. 2000). Much like the trend revealed by industry surveys, the expectation was that there would be an upswing in interest in CSR even in just half a decade, and this would be reflected in consumer attitudes toward ads employing CSR appeals, attitudes toward the product, and ultimately purchase intention. Via analysis of the model, we explored the relationships between the different variables for 2013 and 2018.

Results indicate that even though consumers generally attributed importance to socially responsible behavior, it did not influence their perceptions of a specific CSR advertising message. Findings however confirmed that if consumers perceived an advertiser to be socially responsible, this positively influenced their ad evaluations. Corporate social engagement was also expected to influence respondents' product evaluations; while results did not confirm any direct link for the 2013 dataset, they did for the 2018 dataset. This finding is of interest in that it might indicate that consumers are paying greater attention and are more receptive to CSR messages communicated by advertisers. Company-cause fit was found to exercise a positive influence on respondents' ad evaluations of the CSR message but failed to impact their product evaluations in both datasets. Nonetheless, an indirect effect of company-cause-fit (via ad evaluation) was supported. If ad evaluations were positive, they significantly influenced respondents' product evaluations; these, in turn, had an impact on their purchase intentions. While respondents claimed to prefer to purchase from socially responsible manufacturers, this general willingness was not found to influence their purchase intentions in 2013. For the 2018 dataset, however, a positive influence was noted, again indicating that CSR has gained in importance for consumers and exerted an increasing influence on their behavior.

In total, the study shows that the model tested in 2013 could be largely replicated by the data of 2018. The present study confirmed the benefits of utilizing a CSR appeal as part of a non-prescription drug advertisement for the German-speaking market, highlighting that – as consumers' preferences shift – some relationships are likely to increase over time. The question of whether consumers' attitudes towards CSR, as well their evaluations of a CSR advert promoting an OTC drug, change over time can be answered as follows: No significant differences in mean comparisons could be confirmed through t-tests, and only two significant changes in path coefficients surfaced when conducting critical-ratio comparisons, which both indicate an increased relevance of CSR. Perceived CSR engagement of the company was found to more strongly affect consumers' product evaluations, suggesting that companies can indeed benefit from stressing their environmental or social engagements in their promotional messages, which is likely to "spill over" to their product evaluations. The relationship between consumers' product evaluations and their purchase intentions was more pronounced in 2018. One additional path turned out to be significant in 2018, which was not significant in the 2013 dataset: consumers' general willingness to increasingly purchase from companies whose engagement goes beyond what is required by law on purchase intention. This suggests, in line with findings by Cook et al. (2018), that public disclosure of CSR initiatives indeed has positive effects for corporations.

6 Limitations and Directions for Future Research

Several limitations are related to this investigation. First, this study only offers insight to pharmaceutical manufacturers use of CSR appeals. Second, it is advisable to replicate the study with an existing pharma product and also with a product that addresses different health issues. It might also be fruitful to test consumer responses to different social and even environmental engagements. The proposed model was largely replicated from a previous study and tested for changes in consumers' attitudes towards CSR engagements; hence, additional replication studies might be needed to test for differences over a longer period of time and with larger samples. In addition, findings may well vary based on consumer demographics, including sex and age, as well as educational background.

References

Cone Communications. (2013). Global CSR Study. Available from: https://www.energystar.gov/sites/default/files/asset/document/2013_cone_communicationsecho_global_csr_study.pdf. Accessed: 2. Dec. 2016.
Cone Communications. (2015). Global CSR Study. Available from: https://www.conecomm.com/2015-cone-communications-ebiquity-global-csr-study-pdf/. Accessed: 29. Nov. 2016.
Cone Communications. (2017). 2017 Cone Communications CSR Study. Available from: https://www.conecomm.com/2017-cone-communications-csr-study-pdf. Accessed: 20. Mar. 2019.
Cook, L., Lavin, H., & Zilic, I. (2018). An exploratory analysis of corporate social responsibility reporting in US pharmaceutical companies. *Journal of Communication Management, 22*(2), 197–211.
Deloitte. (2018). 2018 Deloitte millennial survey. Available from: https://www2.deloitte.com/de/de/pages/innovation/contents/Millennial-Survey-2018.html. Accessed: 20. Mar. 2019.

Diehl, S., Terlutter, R., & Mueller, B. (2015). Doing good matters to consumers: the effectiveness of humane-oriented appeals in cross-cultural standardized advertising campaigns. *International Journal of Advertising 35(4)*. doi:https://doi.org/10.1080/02650487.2015.1077606.

Droppert, H., & Bennett, S. (2015). Corporate social responsibility in global health: An exploratory study of multinational pharmaceutical firms. *Globalization and Health, 11*, 15.

Easley, R. W., Madden, C., & Dunn, M. (2000). Conducting marketing science: The role of replication in the research process. *Journal of Business Research, 48*, 83–92.

Eisend, M., Franke, G. R., & Leigh, J. H. (2016). Reinquiries in advertising research. *Journal of Advertising, 45(1)*, 1–3.

Faber, R. (2002). From the editor: A glance backward and the view ahead. *Journal of Advertising, 31(4)*, 5–7.

Filho, C. F. S., De Benedicto, S. C., Sagahara, C. R., & Georges, M. R. R. (2019). Corporate Social Responsibility of Pharmaceutical Industry in Brazil. *International Journal of Humanities and Social Sciences 9(1)*. doi:https://doi.org/10.30845/ijhss.v9n1p4

Fontanarosa, P. B., Rennie, D., & DeAngelis, C. D. (2004). Postmarketing surveillance-lack of vigilance: Lack of trust. *Journal of the American Marketing Association, 292*, 2647–2650.

Hubbard, R., & Armstrong, J. S. (1994). Replications and extensions in marketing: Rarely published but quite contrary. *International Journal of Research in Advertising, 11*, 233–248.

Kerr, G., Schultz, D. E., & Lings, I. (2016). "Someone Should Do Something": Replication and an agenda for collective action. *Journal of Advertising, 45(1)*, 4–12.

Koinig, I., Diehl, S., & Mueller, B. (2018b). "For Risks and Side Effects, Ask Your Doctor or Pharmacist." Cross-cultural consumer responses to pharmaceutical advertising regulation–evidence from Brazil, Germany and the US. In V. Cauberghe, L. Hudders, & M. Eisend (Eds.), *Advances in advertising research IX. Power to consumers* (pp. 243–256). Wiesbaden: Springer.

Koinig, I., Diehl, S., & Mueller, B. (2017). Health communication and integrated corporate social responsibility. In S. Diehl, M. Karmasin, B. Mueller, R. Terlutter, & F. Weder (Eds.), *Handbook of integrated CSR communication* (pp. 471–494). Berlin: Springer.

Koinig, I., Diehl, S., & Mueller, B. (2017). The effects of different Ad appeals in non-prescription drug advertising. A cross-cultural investigation. In M. Eisend, A. Stathopoulou, & G. Christodoulides (Eds.), *Advances in advertising research bridging the gap between advertising academia and practice* (Vol. VII, pp. 265–280). Springer: Wiesbaden.

Koinig, I., Diehl, S., & Mueller, B. (2017). Are pharmaceutical ads affording consumers a greater say in their health care? The evaluation and self-empowerment effects of different ad appeals in Brazil. *International Journal of Advertising, 36(6)*, 945–974. https://doi.org/10.1080/02650487.2017.1367353.

Koinig, I. (2016). *Pharmaceutical advertising as a source of consumer self-empowerment. Evidence from four countries.* Wiesbaden: Springer.

Koinig, I., Diehl, S., & Mueller, B. (2018). Exploring antecedents of attitudes and skepticism towards pharmaceutical advertising and inter-attitudinal and inter-skepticism consistency on three levels: An international study. *International Journal of Advertising, 37(5)*, 718–748. https://doi.org/10.1080/02650487.2018.1498653.

Koinig, I., Diehl, S., & Mueller, B. (2017). Responses to CSR appeals in non-prescription drug Ads: Evidence from Brazil and the United States. In L. M. Gomez, L. Vargas-Preciado, & D. Crowthe (Eds.), *Corporate social responsibility and corporate governance* (pp. 133–155). Bingley: Emerald Publishing Ltd.

Lee, H., Kim, S. Y., & Kang, H.-Y. (2019). Public preferences for corporate social responsibility activities in the pharmaceutical industry: Empirical evidence from Korea. *PLoS ONE, 14*(8), e0221321.

MarketLine. (2016). *Global OTC pharmaceuticals*. Datamonitor Group.

McPeak, C., & Guo, Y. (2014). How the "Go Green" trend influences the automotive industry financial performance. *Journal of Sustainability and Green Business* 2. Available from: https://www.aabri.com/manuscripts/141953.pdf. Accessed: 24. Jul. 2016.

Mohr, L. A., Webb, D. J., & Harris, K. E. (2001). Do consumers expect companies to be socially responsible? The impact of corporate social responsibility of buying behavior. *Journal of Consumer Affairs, 35*(1), 45–72.

Mueller, B. (2011). *Dynamics of international advertising: Theoretical and practical perspectives* (2nd ed.). New York: Peter Lang.

Nielsen. (2012). The global, socially conscious consumer. Available from: https://www.nielsen.com/content/dam/corporate/us/en/reports-downloads/2012-Reports/Nielsen-Global-Social-Responsibility-Report-March-2012.pdf. Accessed: 1. Dec. 2016.

Nielsen. (2014a). Doing well by doing good. Available from: https://www.nielsen.com/content/dam/nielsenglobal/apac/docs/reports/2014/Nielsen-Global-Corporate-Social-Responsibility-Report-June-2014.pdf. Accessed: 1. Dec. 2016.

Nielsen. (2014b). Global consumers are willing to put their money where their heart is when it comes to goods and services from companies committed to social responsibility. Available from: https://www.nielsen.com/us/en/press-room/2014/global-consumers-are-willing-to-put-their-money-where-their-heart-is.html. Accessed: 21. Jul. 2017.

Nielsen. (2015). The sustainability imperative: New insights on consumer expectations. Available from: https://www.nielsen.com/content/dam/corporate/us/en/reports-downloads/2015-reports/global-sustainability-report-oct-2015.pdf. Accessed: 01. Jun. 2017.

Nielsen. (2018). Millennials on millennials U.S. shopping insights in a new era. Available from: https://www.nielsen.com/us/en/insights/reports/2018/millennials-on-millennials-us-shopping-insights-in-a-new-era.html. Accessed: 20. Mar. 2019.

Nosek, B. A., Spies, J. R., & Motyl, M. (2012). Scientific utopia: II. Restructuring incentives and practices to promote truth over publishability. *Perspectives on Psychological Science, 7*, 615–631.

Nussbaum, A. K. (2009). Ethical corporate social responsibility (CSR) and the pharmaceutical industry: A happy couple? *Journal of Medical Marketing, 9*(1), 67–76.

Roblek, V., & Bertoncelj, A. (2014). Impact of corporate social responsibility on OTC medicines consumers. *The Amfiteatru Economic, 35*(16), 12–25.

Royne, M. B. (2018). Why we need more replication studies to keep empirical knowledge in check. *Journal of Advertising Research, 58*(1), 3–8.

Salton, R., & Jones, S. (2015). The corporate social responsibility of global pharmaceutical firms. *British Journal of Healthcare Management, 21*(1), 21–25.

Silverman, E. (2016). The public's view of pharma just keeps getting worse. Available from https://www.statnews.com/pharmalot/2016/08/30/gallup-poll-drug-firms-negative/. Accessed: 21. Jan. 2020.

Sroka, W., & Szanto, R. (2018). Corporate social responsibility and business ethics in controversial sectors: Analysis of research results. *Journal of Entrepreneurship, Management and Innovation, 14*(3), 116–126.

Statista. (2019b). OTC Pharma: Deutschland. Retrieved from https://de.statista.com/outlook/18000000/137/otc-pharma/deutschland. Accessed: 08. Mar. 2019.

Statista. (2019b). OTC Pharma: Österreich. Retrieved from https://de.statista.com/outlook/18000000/128/otc-pharma/oesterreich. Accessed: 08. Mar. 2019.

Statista. (2019b). OTC Pharma: Weltweit. Retrieved from https://de.statista.com/outlook/18000000/100/otc-pharma/weltweit. Accessed: 08. Mar. 2019.

Sternthal, B., Tybout, A. M., & Calder, B. J. (1987). Confirmatory versus comparative approaches to judging theory tests. *Journal of Consumer Research, 14*(June), 114–125.

Wang, X. Q., & Xu, P. (2011). The empirical study on CSR for pharmaceutical firms based on stakeholder theory. *Studies on Industrial Economics, 7,* 97–98.

World Business Council for Sustainable Development. (2000). Corporate social responsibility: Making good business sense. *World Business Council for Sustainable Development.* ISBN 2-94-024007-8.

Yang, M., Bento, P., & Akbar, A. (2019). Does CSR influence firm performance indicators? Evidence from Chinese pharmaceutical enterprises. *Sustainability, 11*(20), 5656. https://doi.org/10.3390/su11205656.

Yoon, Y., Zeynep, G. C., & Schwarz, N. (2006). The effect of corporate social responsibility (CSR) activities on companies with bad reputations. *Journal of Consumer Psychology, 16*(4), 377–390.

Empowering Claims in CSR Tweets: The Moderating Role of Emotion, Fit and Credibility

Paula Fernández, Patrick Hartmann, Vanessa Apaolaza, and Clare D'Souza

1 Introduction

Achieving awareness of a company's corporate social responsibility (CSR) activities is a necessary requisite for CSR's potentially positive effect on customer behavior. CSR awareness is particularly relevant since consumers and other stakeholders have generally little knowledge of most company's CSR involvement (Du et al. 2010). Companies are therefore relying increasingly on social media communication channels to propagate their CSR initiatives. Among different social media applications, Facebook and Twitter are currently the most popular outlets for CSR messages. Using the default tools of these social media applications, companies can directly communicate messages to their followers in these channels without any further media placement and investment. There has been a stream of research on CSR, social media communication and, less abundant, on CSR communication. However, with few exceptions (Fieseler and Fleck 2013; Hartmann et al. 2018; Okazaki and Menendez 2017; Okazaki et al. 2019) there is still a

P. Fernández (✉) · P. Hartmann · V. Apaolaza
University of the Basque Country UPV/EHU, Leioa, Spain
E-Mail: pfernandez023@ikasle.ehu.eus

P. Hartmann
E-Mail: patrick.hartmann@ehu.eus

V. Apaolaza
E-Mail: vanessa.apaolaza@ehu.eus

C. D'Souza
La Trobe University, Bundoora, Australia
E-Mail: cdsouza@latrobe.edu.au

significant lack of research on the specific characteristics and implications of the communication of CSR initiatives on social media. More insight into the factors determining CSR message effectiveness on social media is needed to provide companies with the means to conduct more effective CSR campaigns online.

Our study addresses this gap in the literature by showing how the use of empowering appeals can enhance the attitudinal effects of CSR social media posts. Prior research has shown that psychological empowerment is likely to play a significant role in the effectiveness of both communication in social media and communication of CSR contents (Fieseler and Fleck 2013). In addition to the main effect of empowerment, we also provide a process explanation for this effect by showing thate the feedback of the audience in terms of the number and valence of replies mediates the effect of empowerment on the attitude towards the CSR tweet. Furthermore, we look into how different moderators can affect the strength of the empowerment effect. Drawing on the marketing communications and CSR literature we study whether and how the existence of emotional appeals in the CSR post, the fit of the CSR initiative with company activities and the credibility of the company affect the proposed positive influence of empowerment. To test the hypothesized effects, the study analyses the contents of 840 CSR tweets of five Fortune 500 companies as well as the indicators of their social media performance such as the number of likes and retweets and the feedback of other social media users.

2 Theoretical Framework

2.1 Effects of Empowering Claims in CSR Tweets

Consumer empowerment (Wathieu et al. 2002) has become a significant variable in marketing research. Psychological consumer empowerment refers to the motivational process derived from consumers' subjective experience of influence (Davies and Elliot 2006; Eylon 1998), based on the feeling that they have control of their choices and the power to act on their decisions (Wathieu et al. 2002). Empowered feeling persons believe that they have a greater understanding and control over their environment, including its socio-political dimension. As a consequence, they are more likely to actually intent to exert influence over their environment (Zimmerman and Warschausky 1998). From a communications perspective, consumer's feelings of empowerment can be triggered or reinforced by appropriate communicational claims, for instance through specific information increasing awareness and knowledge of particular issues and situations (Wright et al. 2006).

Psychological empowerment as the feeling that one "can make a difference" is a significant motivational antecedent of prosocial and proenvironmental behavior (Geller 1995). For instance, Hartmann, Apaolaza, and D'Souza (2018) showed that psychological empowerment motivates climate protection and that personal norms have a stronger influence on proenvironmental behavior for consumers experiencing high psychological empowerment than for disempowered feeling consumers. On the other hand, consumer empowerment plays a significant role in social media communication, because consumers can actively participate in the communication process.

Since CSR communication in social media combines both communication related to prosocial behavior and communication in social media, psychological consumer empowerment is likely to play a significant role in the motivational processes triggered by CSR posts. Consumers' feelings of empowerment should, therefore, have a significant influence on the effectiveness of CSR social media communication (Fieseler and Fleck 2013). Hence, appropriate communicational claims that enhance consumer's feeling of empowerment will result in more favorable attitudinal and behavioral responses towards the CSR post:

H1: Empowering appeals in CSR tweets lead to a more positive attitude toward the tweet.

The particular characteristics of social media channels such as twitter imply that users are encouraged to give their feedback to the messages of other social media peers in terms of comments added to the tweet. Most of these comments are generally either positive or negative. The comments, in turn, will affect the attitudinal responses of users that receive the tweet with the previous comments incorporated. We therefore propose that the attitude formation process as a response to a tweet can be explained by the exposure to the audience's feedback to that tweet. We expect the empowering claims in a CSR tweet to lead to a more positive response of other twitter users in terms of the number of positive replies to the tweet, which in turn will lead to a more positive attitude towards the tweet. The effect of a CSR tweet will, therefore, depend significantly on the responses to that tweet by the social media community:

H2: The effect of empowering appeals in CSR tweets on attitude toward the tweet is mediated by the audience's feedback to that tweet.

2.2 Moderating Influences on the CSR Empowerment-Attitude Relationship

2.2.1 Emotional Advertising Appeals

A stream of advertising research has shown the positive effects of emotional advertising claims. Based on a 'transfer of affect' (Aaker and Stayman 1992) and classical conditioning processes (Allen and Madden 1985; Janiszewski and Warlop 1993; Kim, Allen, and Kardes 1996; Kim, Lim, and Bhargava 1998) positive affective communications can enhance attitude towards the advertisement and the advertised brand (Burke and Edell 1989). While research on the emotional effects of social media CSR communication is still scarce, Hartmann et al. (2018) showed that emotional claims in CSR tweets evoking positive affect can increase favorable responses toward the tweet such as positive replies and selecting the tweet as like. It seems therefore likely that additionally including positive emotional claims into the CSR post will strengthen the attitudinal effects of the empowering CSR message. Consequently, we expect a moderating influence of positive emotional appeals on the effect of empowering CSR claims on the attitude towards the CSR tweet.

2.2.2 CSR-Company Fit

The attitudinal effects of empowering CSR claims may also be contingent on the fit, that is, the perceived congruence, between the CSR initiative and the company's activities and brands. Prior research has shown that CSR-company fit plays a significant role in CSR communication effectiveness (Becker Olson et al. 2006; Nan and Heo 2007). The literature has identified different dimensions of CSR-company fit (Menon and Kahn 2003) such as the fit of the CSR initiative with the company's products (for instance, Nestlé participating in nutritional education programs), with the company's clients (McDonald's initiative to lodge the families of children that are hospitalized away from home) or with the existing corporate image (Body Shop sponsoring environmental protection). When a company's CSR activities do not fit in any of these dimensions, consumers may find the CSR involvement artificial and attribute ulterior motives, rather than an authentic concern for the social issue. Engaging in and communicating non-fitting CSR initiatives can have a negative effect on the company's image and stakeholder perceptions. Becker-Olsen et al. (2006) found low-fitting CSR communications to negatively affect consumer beliefs, attitudes, and intentions. The adverse reactions to a lack of CSR-company fit have been attributed to the recipients' increased cognitive elaboration (Du et al. 2010). Such a negative cognitive response will likely also interfere and hinder any possible effects of empowering CSR messages. We therefore expect the CSR empowerment-attitude link to be moderated by CSR-company fit. For non-fitting CSR tweets the positive influence of empowering appeals is likely to be less pronounced, since lack of fit may stimulate cognitive elaboration and consequently critical thoughts.

2.2.3 CSR Source Credibility and Reliability

Source credibility and reliability are considered important requirements for CSR message acceptance and communication effectiveness (Jahdi and Acikdilli 2009). CSR credibility refers to corporate credibility specifically with regard to CSR issues. For companies that have registered major social or environmental scandals, CSR credibility is usually low. Low CSR credibility has been shown to hurt corporate equity, lead to reject CSR claims, decrease resistance to negative information about the company, stimulate unfavorable word of mouth, and affect purchasing behavior (Skarmeas and Leonidou 2013; Bhattacharya and Sen 2004; Du et al. 2010; Yoon et al. 2006). Particularly, the timely concurrence of a plethora of CSR claims and numerous reported incidents of corporate misconduct seems to have contributed to stakeholder skepticism toward corporations (Skarmeas and Leonidou 2013). Consumer responses toward empowering CSR tweets of companies with credibility problems should, therefore, be overall less favorable. Empowering appeals in CSR tweets of such companies are expected to have less positive influences on audience feedback as well as, indirectly, attitude toward the tweet. Figure 1 illustrates the theoretical model.

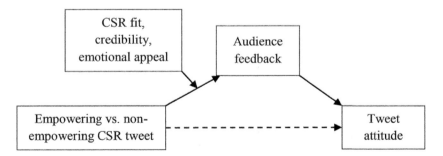

Fig. 1 Theoretical model

H3: The influence of empowering claims in CSR tweets on attitude towards the tweet, mediated by audience feedback, is moderated by a) emotional appeals, b) fit of the CSR tweet and company activities, and c) CSR credibility.

3 Method

3.1 Data Collection

To assess the hypothesized effects with a study of the actual behavior of twitter users, we collected data from a randomized sample of 840 CSR tweets of five Fortune 500 companies. Of the selected tweets all available information was collected and copied into a database. The information collected for each tweet comprised i) the tweet text content itself, ii) all images or video featured in the tweet, iii) links to other tweets or external websites, iv) all replies to the tweet, v) the number of likes and retweets.

3.2 Variables Measurement

To assess the studied variables, the tweet contents were classified and coded. To guide the coders, we developed a coding scheme specifying the characteristics of each coding category. *CSR empowerment* was operationalized as a binary dummy variable. Tweets were classified as empowering $= 1$ versus non-empowering $= 0$ depending on whether the content of the tweet featured any empowering claims in the text message, or in the picture or video included (e.g. "You can contribute to advancing gender equality").

To assess *emotional CSR claims*, tweets were coded as emotional $= 1$ versus non-emotional $= 0$, when the text featured a text message comprising emotional words or the picture showed an emotional stimulus.

CSR-company fit, that is, the congruency between the main activities of the company and the CSR activity featured in the CSR tweet, was assessed as fit $= 1$ in any of the three fit dimensions (product, clients and image) versus non-fit $= 0$ (Nan and Heo 2007).

Since we expected specifically low credibility to negatively moderate the CSR empowerment effect, we assessed the variable *CSR credibility problem* by classifying the tweet as stemming from a company with a credibility problem (a major scandal in the past) $= 1$ vs. no credibility problem $= 0$.

To measure *audience feedback*, for each tweet the replies/comments of other twitter users to that tweet were coded as i) the number of positive replies to the tweet, ii) the number of negative replies, and iii) the number of neutral replies.

To assess the dependent variable *attitude towards the tweet*, based on Kim, Sung, and Kang (2014), we computed the average of the number of likes and retweets of each tweet.

4 Results

Initial correlation analysis confirmed that the empowering claims in CSR tweets (EP) correlated positively with the number of positive replies to that tweet (PO) but not with the number of negative replies (NE), as well as with tweet attitude (AT, Table 1), supporting Hypotheses 1. The number of positive replies also correlated positively with AT.

Furthermore, moderated regression analysis (Table 2) indicated a significant moderation of the effects of empowerment (EP) on positive replies (PO) by emotional appeals, fit between the CSR tweet and company activities, and, negatively,

Table 1 Variable correlations

	EP	PO	NE	NT	AT	EA	CF
Empowering tweet (EP)	1.00						
Positive replies (PO)	0.12^{***}	1.00					
Negative replies (NE)	0.00	0.21^{***}	1.00				
Neutral replies (NT)	0.12^{***}	0.69	0.25^{***}	1.00			
Tweet attitude (AT)	0.08^{*}	0.71^{***}	0.20^{***}	0.50^{***}	1.00		
Emotional appeal (EA)	0.02	0.32^{***}	0.18^{***}	0.26^{***}	0.25^{***}	1.00	
CSR fit (CF)	0.03	0.17^{***}	0.01	0.13^{***}	0.09^{**}	0.06	1.00
CSR credibility problem (CP)	-0.01	-0.08^{**}	0.12^{***}	-0.02	0.01	0.30^{***}	-0.25^{***}

$^{***}p<0.001$, $^{**}p<0.01$, $^{*}p<0.05$

Table 2 Linear regression analysis of interaction effects

Mod	DV	IV	B	SE	t
EA	PO	EP	− 0.09	0.35	− 0.25
		EA	1.72	0.29	6.00***
		EP × EA	3.22	0.59	5.42***
	NE	EP	− 0.06	0.19	− 0.32
		EA	0.71	0.16	4.47***
		EP × EA	0.11	0.33	0.35
	NT	EP	0.02	0.22	0.07
		EA	0.88	0.19	4.76***
		EP × EA	1.77	0.38	4.62***
CF	PO	EP	0.31	0.37	0.85
		CF	0.83	0.30	2.78**
		EP × CF	2.05	0.62	3.31***
	NE	EP	− 0.26	0.20	− 1.35
		CF	− 0.14	0.16	− 0.88
		EP × CF	0.73	0.33	2.22*
	NT	EP	0.03	0.23	0.14
		CF	0.22	0.19	1.16
		EP × CF	1.71	0.39	4.35***
CP	PO	EP	1.77	0.42	4.18***
		CP	− 0.24	0.29	− 0.84
		EP × CP	− 1.41	0.60	− 2.35**
	NE	EP	0.11	0.22	0.52
		CP	0.49	0.15	3.31***
		EP × CP	− 0.24	0.31	− 0.75
	NT	EP	1.15	0.27	4.30***
		CC	0.15	0.18	0.83
		EP × CP	− 1.01	0.38	− 2.66**
	AT	PO	14.50	0.72	20.14***
		NE	1.99	1.04	1.92

(continued)

Table 2 (continued)

Mod	DV	IV	B	SE	t
		NT	0.58	1.15	0.50
		EP	− 1.29	4.61	− 0.28

Note. $^{***}p<0.001$, $^{**}p<0.01$, $^{*}p<0.05$; DV: dependent variable, IV: independent variable, EP: empowering tweet, PO: positive replies, NE: negative replies, NT: neutral replies, AT: tweet attitude, EA: emotional appeal, CF: CSR fit, CP: CSR credibility problem

by the existence of a CSR credibility problem, providing initial and partial support for H3a–c.

To address the moderation of the indirect effect of CSR empowerment on attitude towards the tweet through audience feedback, we conducted bootstrapping moderated mediation analysis by bias-corrected bootstrap confidence intervals with 10,000 bootstrap samples (Hayes 2013). The analysis confirmed a significant index of moderated mediation (95% confidence intervals; Table 3) for the effect of empowering CSR claims (EP) on tweet attitude (AT), mediated by the number of positive replies (PO) and moderated by emotional appeals (EA), CSR fit (CF) and, negatively, by CSR credibility problems (CP), thus supporting the indirect attitudinal effect of empowerment via positive replies (H2), and the moderation of this effect by emotional appeals (H3a), CSR fit (H3b) and CSR credibility (H3c).

The conditional indirect effect of empowering CSR claims on tweet attitude mediated by the number of positive replies (PO) was significant for tweets featuring emotional appeals (EA) ($b_{indirect} = 45.35$, SE $= 18.41$, 95% CI [18.46, 96.12]) but not for tweets lacking such appeals ($b_{indirect} = -1.26$, SE $= 1.12$, 95% CI [−3.96, 0.55]), for tweets with high CSR fit ($b_{indirect} = 34.22$, SE $= 17.21$, 95% CI [10.45, 82.90]) but not for low-fitting CSR tweets ($b_{indirect} = 4.53$, SE $= 4.48$, 95% CI [−2.29, 16.44]), and for tweets lacking credibility problems ($b_{indirect} = 25.63$, SE $= 12.70$, 95% CI [7.96, 62.78]) but not for tweets from companies having such problems ($b_{indirect} = 5.22$, SE $= 5.53$, 95% CI [−3.09, 20.01]). Conditional indirect effects via either negative or neutral replies were non-significant at any value of the three moderators.

Table 3 Moderated mediation analysis of indirect effects of empowering tweets on attitude toward the tweet, moderated by emotional appeals, CSR fit and CSR credibility problems

Index of moderated mediation						
Mod		Med	Mod. med. index	Boot SE	Boot LLCI	Boot ULCI
EA		PO	46.61	18.64	19.10	98.06
		NE	0.23	0.99	− 0.95	3.89
		NT	1.02	8.21	− 16.81	16.23
CF		PO	29.70	18.26	4.99	81.53
		NE	1.45	1.18	− 0.23	4.82
		NT	0.98	7.81	− 18.34	13.95
CP		PO	− 20.41	14.45	− 60.83	− 0.73
		NE	− 0.47	0.73	− 2.48	0.54
		NT	− 0.58	4.77	− 9.06	10.79
Conditional indirect effect at values of the moderator						
Mod	Values Mod	Med	Cond. ind. effect	Boot SE	Boot LLCI	Boot ULCI
EA	0	PO	− 1.26	1.12	− 3.96	0.55
	1	PO	45.35	18.41	18.46	96.12
	0	NE	− 0.12	0.20	− 0.83	0.09
	1	NE	0.11	0.96	− 1.18	3.31
	0	NT	0.01	0.46	− 0.85	1.17
	1	NT	1.03	8.27	− 17.19	16.22
CF	0	PO	4.53	4.48	− 2.29	16.44
	1	PO	34.22	17.21	10.45	82.90
	0	NE	− 0.53	0.41	− 1.55	0.12
	1	NE	0.93	0.97	− 0.13	4.41
	0	NT	0.02	0.86	− 1.37	1.74
	1	NT	1.00	7.95	− 17.76	14.82
CP	0	PO	25.63	12.70	7.96	62.78
	1	PO	5.22	5.53	− 3.09	20.01
	0	NE	0.23	0.33	− 0.10	1.61
	1	NE	− 0.24	0.64	− 1.76	0.78

(continued)

Table 3 (continued)

	0	NT	0.66	5.29	− 12.04	10.08
	1	NT	0.08	1.34	− 1.65	3.38

Notes: 10,000 bootstrap samples for bias-corrected 95% bootstrap confidence intervals, Boot SE = Bootstrap standard error, Boot LLCI = Bootstrap lower limit confidence interval, Boot ULCI = Bootstrap upper limit confidence interval, Med.: mediator, Mod.: moderator, EP: empowering tweet, PO: positive replies, NE: negative replies, NT: neutral replies, AT: tweet attitude, EA: emotional appeal, CF: CSR fit, CP: CSR credibility problem.

5 Discussion

5.1 Theoretical Contribution

With a quantitative content analysis of 840 tweets featuring CSR messages of five Fortune 500 companies, this study shows that empowering CSR tweets lead to more favorable attitudinal responses towards the tweet. In addition, this research provides a process explanation of this effect by showing that the CSR empowerment effect is mediated by the audience's feedback, that is, by the responses of the twitter user community. More empowering CSR posts lead to more positive responses of other twitter users, which in turn results in a more positive attitude towards the tweet. A further finding of this study is to show that this process is contingent on several moderators. The positive influence of CSR empowerment is stronger when the tweet features additionally emotional claims and when the fit of the CSR initiative in any of the three fit dimensions (product, clients and image) is high rather than low. In contrast, the CSR empowerment effect is hindered by a salient credibility problem such as caused by the company registering a major scandal featured in the media.

This research contributes to the further development of CSR and social media communication theory in several ways. Findings confirm the significant behavioral effects of psychological consumer empowerment (Wathieu et al. 2002; Wright et al. 2006; Zimmerman and Warschausky 1998) in the specific context of CSR and social media communication. Whereas prior research has shown motivating influences of empowerment on prosocial and proenvironmental behavior (Geller 1995), such as, in particular, climate protection (Hartmann, Apaolaza, and D'Souza 2018), this study extends the scope of empowerment effects to the attitudinal responses toward CSR posts in social media. Results support Fieseler and Fleck's (2013) proposition that consumers feeling of empowerment will enhance the effectiveness of CSR social media communication.

The process explanation of the empowerment effect based on the mediating effect of audience responses further ads to the existing theory of empowerment effects in communication. By confirming this mediation effect, our study shows that the responses of the recipients to the empowering communication claim are not immediate, but that they rather react to the positive feedback of their twitter peers to the empowering CSR post. Findings, therefore, highlight the significant role of the responses of the social media community in the attitude formation towards CSR tweets.

The findings with regards to the contingency factors of the CSR empowerment effect contribute to several fields of theory development. The positive effect of emotional claims on the empowerment-attitude process is in line with the literature on the favorable attitude effects of emotional communication appeals (e.g., Aaker and Stayman 1992; Allen and Madden 1985; Burke and Edell 1989) and, in particular, with the emerging literature on emotional effects of social media CSR communication (Hartmann et al. 2018). Furthermore, the moderating influence of CSR-company fit extends the scope of prior research showing a positive influence of the fit of the CSR initiative and the company on the effectiveness of CSR communication (Becker Olson et al. 2006; Menon and Kahn 2003; Nan and Heo 2007). The effect found in this study is consistent with Du et al. (2010), who argue that a low CSR-company fit will stimulate adverse cognitive elaboration of the CSR message and consequently lead to an increase in the recipient's critical thought with respect to the company's CSR communications.

Finally, the finding that the empowering appeals in CSR tweets of companies with credibility problems have a weaker positive influence on audience feedback and, in turn, attitude toward the tweet, adds to the stream of literature on source credibility and, specifically, CSR credibility. Our study shows that a low CSR credibility cannot only, as suggested in the extant literature, lead to rejecting CSR claims, decrease resistance to negative information about the company, stimulate unfavorable word of mouth, and negatively affect purchasing behavior (Skarmeas and Leonidou 2013; Bhattacharya and Sen 2004; Du et al. 2010; Yoon et al. 2006), but can specifically moderate the influences of other variables, such as, in the present study, the attitudinal effects of CSR empowerment.

5.2 Practical Implications

The findings of this study provide significant insight for communication managers employing social media such as twitter to disseminate CSR communications. To increase positive attitude toward a CSR post—which may also constitute a significant antecedent and indicator of the attitude toward the company—, communication managers should employ appeals that strengthen the feeling of their target group's psychological empowerment with respect to the CSR initiative featured in the post.

The communicational effect of empowering CSR posts can be further strengthened by including emotional appeals into the design of the twitter message, either as text or emotional pictures, and by selecting CSR activities that fit with the company's products, clients and/or image. Communication managers should also be aware of the detrimental effect of a lack of CSR credibility of their company. The positive effect of an empowering CSR message will be significantly lower or may even backfire as a negative effect for companies with significant credibility problems such as a salient scandal that has been featured in the media.

5.3 Limitations and Future Research

The extended sample of authentic CSR tweets of a selection of Fortune 500 companies contributes to the external validity and statistical power of findings. However, since the data are cross-sectional and based on observational content analysis, our conclusions are limited to correlational inferences and do not allow for a conclusive confirmation of causal effects and their directionality. Because of the level of aggregation of the data, our findings describe the overall behavior of the twitter user community, but do not predict the behavioral responses of individuals. To further confirm the hypothesized causal relationships, the proposed model needs to be addressed with an experimental method where the level of CSR empowerment, emotional appeals, CSR-company fit and CSR credibility are manipulated, and where the behavioral responses of individual twitter users are assessed. In addition, future research should experimentally test different types of empowering verbal and visual communication appeals to determine which type of claims and stimuli are more effective in enhancing the recipients' psychological empowerment.

Acknowledgements This research was supported by the Spanish Government and European Regional Development Fund [grant numbers ECO2016-76348-R, AEI/FEDER, UE], the Basque Government [grant numbers GIC 15/128; IT-952-16] and FESIDE Foundation.

References

Aaker, D. A., & Stayman, D. M. (1992). Implementing the concept of transformational advertising. *Psychology and Marketing, 9*(3), 237–253.

Allen, C. T., & Madden, T. J. (1985). A closer look at classical conditioning. *Journal of Consumer Research, 12*(3), 301–315.

Becker-Olsen, K. L., Cudmore, B. A., & Hill, R. P. (2006). The impact of perceived corporate social responsibility on consumer behavior. *Journal of Business Research, 59*(1), 46–53.

Bhattacharya, C. B., & Sen, S. (2004). Doing better at doing good: When, why, and how consumers respond to corporate social initiatives. *California Management Review, 47*(1), 9–24.

Burke, M. C., & Edell, J. A. (1989). The impact of feelings on ad-based affect and cognition. *Journal of Marketing Research, 53*, 69–83.

Davies, A., & Elliott, R. (2006). The evolution of the empowered consumer. *European Journal of Marketing, 40*(9/10), 1106–1121.

Du, S., Bhattacharya, C. B., & Sen, S. (2010). Maximizing business returns to corporate social responsibility (CSR): The role of CSR communication. *International Journal of Management Review, 12*(1), 8–19.

Eylon, D. (1998). Understanding empowerment and resolving its paradox. *Journal of Management History, 4*(1), 16–28.

Fieseler, C., & Fleck, M. (2013). The pursuit of empowerment through social media: Structural social capital dynamics in CSR-blogging. *Journal of Business Ethics, 118*(4), 759–775.

Geller, E. S. (1995). Integrating behaviorism and humanism for environmental protection. *Journal of Social Issues, 51*(4), 179–195.

Hartmann, P., Apaolaza, V., & D'Souza, C. (2018). The role of psychological empowerment in climate-protective consumer behavior: An extension of the value-belief-norm framework. *European Journal of Marketing, 52*(1/2), 392–417.

Hartmann, P., Fernández, P., Apaolaza, V., & D'Souza, C. (2018): Emotional claims in CSR tweets: The moderating role of CSR message fit. *Advances in Advertising Research, IX*, 231–242.

Hayes, A. F. (2013). *Introduction to mediation, moderation, and conditional process analysis: A regression-based approach.* New York: Guilford Press.

Jahdi, K. S., & Acikdilli, G. (2009). Marketing communications and corporate social responsibility (CSR): Marriage of convenience or shotgun wedding? *Journal of Business Ethics, 88*(1), 103–113.

Janiszewski, C., & Warlop, L. (1993). The influence of classical conditioning procedures on subsequent attention to the conditioned brand. *Journal of Consumer Research, 20*(2), 171–189.

Kim, E., Sung, Y., & Kang, H. (2014). Brand followers' retweeting behavior on Twitter: How brand relationships influence brand electronic word-of-mouth. *Computers in Human Behavior, 37*, 18–25.

Kim, J., Allen, C. T., & Kardes, F. R. (1996). An investigation of the mediational mechanisms underlying attitudinal conditioning. *Journal of Marketing Research, 33*, 318–328.

Kim, J., Lim, J. S., & Bhargava, M. (1998). The role of affect in attitude formation: A classical conditioning approach. *Journal of the Academy of Marketing Science, 26*(2), 143–152.

Menon, S., & Kahn, B. E. (2003). Corporate sponsorships of philanthropic activities: When do they impact perception of sponsor brand? *Journal of Consumer Psychology, 13*(3), 316–327.

Nan, X., & Heo, K. (2007). Consumer responses to corporate social responsibility (CSR) initiatives: Examining the role of brand-cause fit in cause-related marketing. *Journal of Advertising, 36*(2), 63–74.

Okazaki, S., & Menendez, H. D. (2017). Virtual corporate social responsibility dialog: Seeking a gap between proposed concepts and actual practices. In S. Diehl, M. Karmasin, B. Mueller, R. Terlutter, & F. Weder (Eds.), *Handbook of integrated CSR communication* (pp. 225–234). Cham: Springer.

Okazaki, S., Plangger, K., West, D., & Menéndez, H. D. (2019). Exploring digital corporate social responsibility communications on Twitter. *Journal of Business Research, 117,* 675–682.

Skarmeas, D., & Leonidou, C. N. (2013). When consumers doubt, watch out! The role of CSR scepticism. *Journal of Business Research, 66*(10), 1831–1838.

Wathieu, L., Brenner, L., Carmon, Z., Chattopadhyay, A., Wertenbroch, K., Drolet, A., et al. (2002). Consumer control and empowerment: A primer. *Marketing Letters, 13*(3), 297–305.

Wright, L. T., Newman, A., & Dennis, C. (2006). Enhancing consumer empowerment. *European Journal of Marketing, 40*(9/10), 925–935.

Yoon, Y., Gurhan-Canli, Z., & Schwarz, N. (2006). The effect of corporate social responsibility (CSR) activities on companies with bad reputations. *Journal of Consumer Psychology, 16,* 377–390.

Zimmerman, M., & Warschausky, S. (1998). Empowerment theory for rehabilitation research: Conceptual and methodological issues. *Rehabilitation Psychology, 43*(1), 3–16.

A Cognitive Approach to the Argument Strength × Message Involvement Paradigm in Green Advertising Persuasion

Jason Yu

1 Introduction

Today's consumers care about environmental sustainability more than ever. Recent surveys show that a whopping 81% of global consumers across gender and generations feel strongly that companies should help improve the environment (Nielsen 2018), and 73% would change their consumption habits for the environment (Nielsen 2019). In response to this trend, companies' engagement in green activities has been growing rapidly. According to the Governance and Accountability (G and A) Institute's report, 85% of S&P 500 companies published sustainability reports in 2017, drastically increased from only 20% in 2011 (MarketWatch 2018). Accordingly, marketers across the spectrum have widely adopted green advertising as an important marketing communication practice, emphasizing environmental clams in their advertising campaigns to gain consumer brand preference (Yu 2018).

Considerable research has endorsed the attitude-related effectiveness of green ad messages in terms of generating positive attitudes to ads, lifting message and brand credibility (Phau and Ong 2007), forming positive brand attitude (Hartmann et al. 2005; Matthes et al. 2014), boosting the environmental dimensions of brand image, and enhancing brand equity (Benoit-Moreau and Parguel 2011). Various factors have been studied to explain green advertising effects. Along with the research on the properties of the audience including consumer characteristics such as gender, advertising skepticism, green skepticism and environmental concern (for

J. Yu (✉)
Department of Mass Communications, Southern Illinois University Edwardsville, Edwardsville, IL, USA
E-Mail: jyu@siue.edu

a review, see Yu 2018), the properties of the stimulus have been gaining scholarly attention, including the quantity (C. C. Chang 2011; Olsen et al. 2014) and the valence of green claims (H. Chang et al. 2015; Olsen et al. 2014), emotional vs. functional (Hartmann et al. 2005; Matthes et al. 2014), vague vs. false (Schmuck et al. 2018), and verbal vs. visual claims (Schmuck et al. 2018).

However, to date, the role of message strength (or argument strength/quality), a key stimulus property, and message involvement, a key audience property, have not been examined in green advertising research. These two constructs and their interaction have been widely used to predict persuasion in dual-process models including Elaboration Likelihood Model (ELM) (Petty and Cacioppo 1986) and the Heuristic-Systematic Model (Chaiken et al. 1989). More specifically, argument strength has been found to impact consumer attitude toward the ad (A_{ad}), attitude toward the brand (A_b) and consumer purchase intention (PI) in advertising research (e.g., Bee and Dalakas 2015; Drossos et al. 2013; Petty et al. 1983). This study investigated the argument strength × message involvement persuasion in the green advertising scenario. Would strong environmental claims in a green ad excerpt more powerful persuasive impact than weak green arguments? Furthermore, do strong green arguments work more powerfully on the consumers who are highly involved in the ad message when being exposed to the green ad than those who are lowly involved in the ad?

Testing the interaction of argument strength and message involvement is especially meaningful for studying green advertising effectiveness, theoretically and practically. On one hand, some previous studies found that environmental claims in green ads had no impact on consumer responses (e.g., Borin et al. 2011) and could even backfire and cause greenwashing effects (Nyilasy et al. 2014; Schmuck et al. 2018). On the other hand, consumer attitude toward the ad (A_{ad}) has been found to have two distinctive dimensions including utilitarianism and hedonism (R. Batra and Ahtola 1991; Olney et al. 1991; Voss et al. 2003; Yu 2018). This two-dimensional attitudinal construct provides a new arena to examine the interaction as the possible difference of the interaction effect on these two distinctive attitudinal dimensions has not been studied in the past. The purpose of this study was to examine the effects of green argument strength (GAS) and ad message involvement (AMI) and the GAS × AMI interaction on the two-dimensional attitude toward the green ad (A_{ad}), attitude toward the brand (A_b), and purchase intention (PI).

2 Theoretical Development: The GAS × AMI Interaction

The strength of message arguments plays a critical role in persuasive communication. Argument strength refers to the audience's perception that the arguments in a persuasive message are strong and cogent as opposed to weak and specious (Petty and Cacioppo 1981a). A great deal of persuasion research has consistently supported the notion that strengthening arguments in a message leads to greater persuasive impact of that message in general, regardless of the level of elaboration or involvement (e.g., Park et al. 2007; Petty and Cacioppo 1984).

The effect of argument strength has been examined in a number of studies in advertising research. In their experimental study of the interaction of product involvement and ad message quality, Petty and Cacioppo (1981b) found that strong arguments produced more favorable A_b than did the weak ones. A later study found a similar pattern that argument strength in the ad message had an impact on product attitude in both high and low product involvement conditions (Petty et al. 1983). More recent research has further provided evidence showing better A_b and higher PI resulted from the argument strength manipulation, regardless of other factors such as endorser expertise and ad viewing time (Pornpitakpan 2004). A study of consumer responses to mobile phone advertising found that text message ads containing strong arguments led to more positive A_{ad} than did weak-argument ads (Drossos et al. 2013). Another study of the relationship of sports fanship and consumer responses to ads sponsoring teams also indicates a conditioned effect of argument strength on A_{ad}. Bee and Dalakas (2015) found that for low team-identified fans, A_{ad} was significantly more positive with the ad containing a strong argument than A_{ad} with the weak-argument ad.

In green advertising, environmental claims in ads typically contain persuasive arguments promoting the brand's pro-environmental position (Davis 1994). Aligning with the literature, we proposed the following hypothesis:

H1: In general, GAS has a positive effect on (a) A_{ad}, (b) A_b, and (c) PI.

There is considerable agreement that high involvement messages have greater personal relevance and consequences or elicit more personal connections than low involvement messages (Petty et al. 1983). The ELM contends that the audience is more motivated to devote cognitive effort required to evaluate the arguments contained in the message when message involvement is high rather than low. Thus, strong arguments could exert more persuasive power when the perceiver's message involvement is high rather than low. Such an interaction of argument strength and message involvement has been examined and supported in many studies. A meta-analyses of 134 published empirical studies in this subject matter across three disciplines, 93 in social psychology, 31 in marketing and advertising, and 10 in communication, concluded that the findings from these studies are consistent with the ELM's prediction of the argument strength × message involvement interaction (Carpenter 2015).

Particularly in advertising, ad message involvement (AMI) was conceptualized as "a motivational construct embodying the amount of cognitive effort directed by the consumer at processing the contents of an advertising message" (Baker and Lutz 1987, p. 75). MacKenzie et al. (1986) found that AMI affects the structural relationships among ad/brand cognition, A_{ad}, and A_b. Since then, accumulated empirical evidence has shown that AMI has substantial positive impacts on brand-related belief certainty and A_{ad} (Laczniak and Muehling 1993), brand attitude accessibility (Kokkinaki and Lunt 1999), and product evaluation (Polyorat et al. 2007), and purchase intention (Muehling et al. 1991). Hence, we hypothesized that:

H2: In general, AMI has a positive effect on (a) A_{ad}, (b) A_b, and (c) PI.

According to the ELM, particularly in green advertising, under conditions of high involvement, central route to persuasion occurs where stronger arguments in a green ad are more persuasive as the individual carefully scrutinizes the message's arguments or environmental claims, and then favorable thoughts will be elicited that will lead to attitude change in the direction of the advertiser's advocacy. In fact, the persuasive impact of advertising messages has been found to be moderated by the audience's AMI (Andrews and Shimp 1990; Eisend 2013; Kavadas et al. 2007; Y. H. Lee 2000; Muehling et al. 1991; Petty et al. 1983). To examine the argument strength × message involvement interaction in green advertising effectiveness research, a hypothesis was put forward as follows:

H3: AMI moderates the effects of GAS on (a) A_{ad}, (b) A_b, and (c) PI.

Advertising research supports a positive relationship between A_{ad} and A_b. Brown and Stayman's (1992) meta-analysis of the empirical studies of A_{ad} in the past few decades found a rich body of evidence that A_{ad} has a substantial and significant relationship with brand-related cognitions, A_b, and PI. Later studies continued to provide evidence supporting such theoretical relationships (e.g., Y.-J. Lee et al. 2013; Yoo and MacInnis 2005; Zhang and Zinkhan 2006). Research has also shown that A_b is a function of brand beliefs and A_{ad} (Zhang and Zinkhan 2006). Thus, A_{ad} can play an even bigger role in determining A_b when there is a lack of preexisting knowledge of the brand or when the brand beliefs are very limited such as new brands. In fact, substantial evidence has been provided that endorses the mediating role of A_{ad} intervening between ad content and A_b (e.g., Rajeev Batra and Ray 1986; Gardner 1985; Shimp 1981; Zhang and Zinkhan 2006). The following research hypotheses reflect the mediation model:

H4: (a) The GAS effect and (b) the AMI effect on A_b are mediated by A_{ad}.

H5: A_b mediates the effect of A_{ad} on PI.

3 Method

3.1 Design, Subjects, and Procedure

256 students enrolled in a university in China participated in the experiment and were given an environment-friendly facial soap as a gift for participation. They were randomly assigned to the four experimental groups of a 2 (GAS: strong vs. weak) × 2 (AMI: high vs. low) factorial design. Two print ads for ECO, a fictional brand of recycled bathroom tissue, were used in the experiment. All subjects have no experiences either with the brand or with the product category. Subjects' exposure to the ad was immediately followed by a set of questions regarding their attitudes toward the ad and the brand as well as their purchase intention, which were followed by another set of questions about their memories of the arguments in the ad message.

3.2 AMI and GAS Manipulation

The two independent variables, AMI and GAS, were manipulated in the experiment. The AMI manipulation was implemented through randomly assigning subjects to one of the two different instructions for reading the coming ad stimulus. In the high AMI condition, subjects were asked to carefully read all the information carried by the print ad and they were instructed that they needed to answer some specific questions about the ad and the product after the ad exposure. In the low AMI condition, subjects were told to treat the ad just like any ad they happen to encounter in their daily life.

The GAS variable was manipulated by varying the number and content of the arguments in the body copies of the two experimental ad stimuli, with everything else being the same including the logo, headline, slogan, visual elements, and layout. The arguments in both ads are positive and relevant to the product. The body copy of the strong-argument ad contains more arguments in number, and the arguments are more specific and evidence based. The weak-argument ad contains fewer arguments in number, and the arguments are more general and lack supporting evidence.

3.3 Dependent Measures

Three popular dependent variables used in advertising effectiveness research were included in this study, A_{ad}, A_b, and PI. When measuring A_{ad}, we followed the multidimensionality concept that Aad is composed of two dimensions, the hedonic dimension that measures the experiential affect and resembles the entertaining or pleasurable dimension, and the utilitarian dimension that measures the usefulness and relevance perceived by the audience (R. Batra and Ahtola 1991; Olney et al. 1991; Voss et al. 2003; Yu 2018). A 4-item 7-point semantic differential scale were used to measure the utilitarian dimension of A_{ad} (UA_{ad}), informative, useful, important, and helpful, $\alpha = 0.82$. The 4 items used to measure hedonic A_{ad} (HA_{ad}) include entertaining, enjoyable, fun to read, and pleasant, $\alpha = 0.88$. A 3-item 7-point scale was used to assess A_b, on bad/good, unfavorable/favorable, and dislike/like, $\alpha = 0.90$. PI was measured on a 3-item 7-point scale anchored by unlikely/likely, impossible/possible, and improbable/probable $\alpha = 0.94$.

4 Results

4.1 Manipulation Checks

A memorization test consisting of ten questions the ad message was used to check AMI manipulation. The number of correct answers of high AMI subjects ($M = 5.50$, $SD = 2.20$) is significantly greater than that of low AMI subjects ($M = 4.40$, $SD = 2.10$), $t(254) = -4.10$, $p < 0.001$. A separate sample of 198 undergraduates, 121 females (61.1%) and 77 males (38.9%), judged the messages in the two ads, on a 2-item 9-point scale, weak reasons/strong reasons and unpersuasive/persuasive (Lien and Chen 2013; Petty et al. 1983). On the first measuring item, subjects exposed to the strong arguments rated the reasons of the arguments ($M = 6.57$, $SD = 1.81$) as significantly stronger than did subjects exposed to the weak arguments ($M = 5.30$, $SD = 2.03$), $t(1, 196) = -4.61$, $p < 0.001$. On the second manipulation check measure, subjects exposed to the strong arguments rated them as significantly more persuasive ($M = 6.30$, $SD = 1.84$) than did subjects exposed to the weak arguments ($M = 4.96$, $SD = 1.92$), $t(1, 196) = -5.04$, $p < 0.001$. No significant difference either between women's rating of reasons ($M = 6.02$, $SD = 2.00$) and men's rating of reasons ($M = 5.81$, $SD = 2.07$), Welch's $F(1, 157.51) = 0.51$, $p = 0.48$, or between women's rating of persuasiveness ($M = 5.75$, $SD = 1.90$) and men's rating of persuasiveness ($M = 5.44$, $SD = 2.12$), Welch's $F(1, 149.19) = 1.15$, $p = 0.29$.

4.2 A_{ad} Dimensionality

The eight A_{ad} measurement items were factor analyzed using principal component analysis with Varimax rotation to determine A_{ad} dimensionality. An examination of the Kaiser-Meyer Olkin measure of sampling adequacy suggested that the sample was factorable (KMO = 0.87), and Bartlett's test of sphericity was significant, $\chi^2 (153) = 1103.33$, $p < 0.001$). The analysis yielded two factors, which were consistent with the initial assumption of the utilitarian and hedonic dimensions of A_{ad}, explaining 71.47% of the variance for the entire set of items. UA_{ad} accounted for 16.59% of the variance with factor loadings from 0.63 to 0.83 while HA_{ad} explained 54.88% of the variance with factor loadings from 0.80 to 0.87. Two items with the lowest variances were dropped off the measure including "informing" and "fun to read" as a follow-up confirmatory factor analysis showed poor model fit. The modified model fitted the data well, SRMR = 0.03; GFI = 0.98; AGFI = 0.96; NFI = 0.98; CFI = 0.99; RMSEA = 0.05. The AVEs for utilitarian A_{ad} and hedonic A_{ad} were 0.67 and 0.86, and both the composite reliability values were approximately 0.86.

4.3 Hypothesis Testing

Two types of analyses were conducted to test the hypotheses, initial ANOVAs using SPSS followed by structural equation analyses using AMOS. In the ANOVA testing models, the main effects of GAS and AMI and their interaction on the four dependent variables including UA_{ad}, HA_{ad}, A_b, and PI were examined in a parallel manner. The relationships among the dependent variables were not included in the models. Table 1 shows the means and standard deviations. The structural equation analyses consisted of four testing models. Model I and II examined HA_{ad}, A_b and PI while Model III and IV included UA_{ad}, A_b, and PI. Model I and III excluded

Table 1 Means and (standard deviations) of UA_{ad}, HA_{ad}, A_b, and PI

pPI	UA_{ad}			HA_{ad}			A_b			PI		
	Weak GAS	Strong GAS	Total	Weak GAS	Strong GAS	Total	Weak GAS	Strong GAS	Total	Weak GAS	Strong GAS	Total
Low AMI	20.13 (3.95)	20.42 (4.50)	20.27 (4.22)	17.59 (4.72)	18.41 (5.09)	18.00 (4.91)	15.06 (2.59)	14.95 (3.16)	15.01 (2.88)	15.70 (4.60)	15.86 (3.90)	15.78 (4.25)
High AMI	20.75 (4.07)	23.00 (3.04)	21.88 (3.75)	18.39 (4.12)	19.30 (4.66)	18.84 (4.40)	15.05 (3.00)	16.66 (2.74)	15.85 (2.98)	15.92 (4.21)	17.11 (3.67)	16.52 (3.98)
Total	20.44 (4.01)	21.71 (4.04)	21.07 (4.06)	17.99 (4.43)	18.85 (4.88)	18.42 (4.67)	15.05 (2.79)	15.80 (3.07)	15.43 (2.95)	15.81 (4.39)	16.48 (3.83)	16.15 (4.13)

Notes: GAS = Green argument strength; AMI = Ad message involvement; UA_{ad} = the utilitarian dimension of attitude toward the ad; HA_{ad} = the hedonic dimension of attitude toward the ad; A_b = Brand attitude; and PI = Purchase intention.

the interaction GAS × AMI for testing the main effects of GAS and AMI while Model II and IV particularly tested the interaction effects. These two waves of structural equation analyses were performed in tandem. Figure 2 shows the results from testing Model III without GAS × AMI, and (then) Model IV, which added the interaction to Model III.

The initial ANOVA tests showed significant main effects of GAS on UA_{ad}, $F(1, 252) = 4.33$, $p < 0.05$, partial $\eta^2 = 0.02$, and on A_b, $F(1, 252) = 4.33$, $p < 0.05$, partial $\eta^2 = 0.02$, but neither on.

HA_{ad}, $F(1, 252) = 1.84$, $p = 0.18$, nor on PI, $F(1, 252) = 1.71$, $p = 0.19$. As shown in Fig. 1, the tests also found significant GAS × AMI effects on UA_{ad}, $F(1, 252) = 4.85$, $p < 0.05$, partial $\eta^2 = 0.02$, and A_b, $F(1, 252) = 4.33$, $p < 0.05$, partial $\eta^2 = 0.02$, whereas no significant interaction effects were found on HA_{ad} and PI. These findings provided preliminary observations of the relationships among

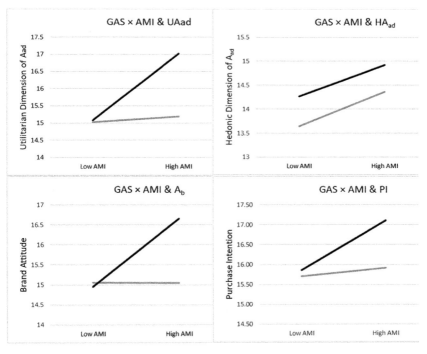

Fig. 1 The GAS × AMI effect on UA_{ad}*, HA_{ad}, A_b*, and PI (*$p < 0.05$)

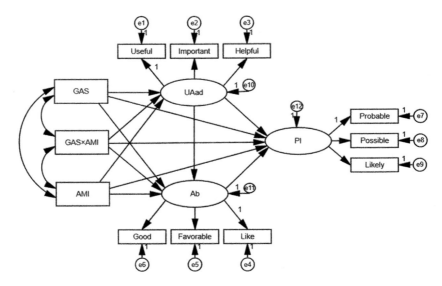

Fig. 2 Model III excluding GAS × AMI followed by Model IV including GAS × AMI (UA_{ad} is replaced with HA_{ad} in Model I and Model II)

GAS, AMI, A_{ad}, A_b, and PI, which were further examined in a series of structural equation analyses.

The results from the structural equation analyses were presented in Table 2. All the four testing models well fitted the data as the table shows. Model I and Model III analyses found that the GAS effect was significant on UA_{ad}, $\beta = 0.14$, $p < 0.05$ marginally significant on A_b, $\beta = 0.13$, $p < 0.10$, but insignificant on HA_{ad}, $\beta = 0.09$, $p = 0.21$ and on PI, $\beta = 0.09$, $p = 0.16$. AMI was found to have a significant effect on UA_{ad}, $\beta = 0.18$, $p < 0.05$, and on A_b, $\beta = 0.15$, $p < 0.05$, but insignificant either on HA_{ad}, $\beta = 0.11$, $p = 0.10$, or on PI, $\beta = 0.09$, $p = 0.17$. Echoing the preliminary findings from the ANOVAs, these structural equation modeling findings partially supported H_{1a} and H_{2a} (i.e. supported UA_{ad} but not HA_{ad}), marginally supported H_{1b} while supported H_{2b}, but did not support either H1cH1c or H2c.

H_{4a} was supported as Model III analysis found a significant indirect effect of GAS on A_b, $\beta = 0.10$, $p < 0.05$, and on PI, $\beta = 0.06$, $p < 0.05$, through UA_{ad} as the mediator. H_{4b} was also supported as the indirect effect of AMI was found significant on A_b, $\beta = 0.12$, $p < 0.01$, and on PI, $\beta = 0.08$, $p < 0.01$. Furthermore,

Table 2 Structural equation analyses: regression coefficients (standardized, unstandardized), p, squared multiple correlations (SMC), model fit

Variable	Model I and Model II			Model III and Model IV		
	HA_{ad}	A_b	PI	UA_{ad}	A_b	PI
Total Effect						
GAS	(0.21; 0.09)ns	(0.24; 0.12)†	(0.23; 0.09)ns	(0.30; 0.14)*	(0.24; 0.13)†	(0.23; 0.09)ns
AMI	(0.25; 0.11)ns	(0.27; 0.15)*	(0.23; 0.09)ns	(0.37; 0.18)*	(0.28; 0.15)*	(0.23; 0.09)ns
GAS × AMI	(−0.02; −0.01)ns	(0.53; 0.24)*	(0.37; 0.13)ns	(0.65; 0.27)*	(0.55; 0.25)*	(0.37; 0.13)ns
HA_{ad}		(0.60; 0.72)***	(0.38; 0.34)**			
UA_{ad}					(0.60; 0.66)***	(0.51; 0.42)***
A_b			(0.56; 0.42)**			(0.41; 0.31)**
Direct Effect						
GAS	(0.21; 0.09)ns	(0.11; 0.06)ns	(0.09; 0.03)ns	(0.30; 0.14)*	(0.06; 0.03)ns	(0.05; 0.02)ns
AMI	(0.25; 0.11)ns	(0.13; 0.07)ns	(0.06; 0.03)ns	(0.37; 0.18)*	(0.05; 0.03)ns	(0.01; 0.01)ns
GAS × AMI	(−0.02; −0.01)ns	(0.55; 0.25)*	(0.07; 0.02)ns	(0.61; 0.25)*	(0.55; 0.25)*	(−0.03; −0.01)ns
HA_{ad}		(0.60; 0.72)***	(0.04; 0.04)ns			
UA_{ad}					(0.59; 0.66)***	(0.27; 0.22)*
A_b			(0.56; 0.42)**			(0.41; 0.31)**
Indirect Effects						
GAS → HA_{ad}		(0.14; 0.07)ns	(0.09; 0.03)ns			
GAS → HA_{ad} → A_b			(0.09; 0.03)ns			

(continued)

Table 2 (continued)

Variable	Model I and Model II			Model III and Model IV		
	HA_{ad}	A_b	PI	UA_{ad}	A_b	PI
GAS → HA_{ad} and A_b			(0.15; 0.06)†			
AMI → HA_{ad}		(0.17; 0.09)†	(0.10; 0.04)†			
AMI → HA_{ad} → A_b			(0.10; 0.04)†			
AMI → HA_{ad} and A_b			(0.17; 0.07)*			
AMI → A_b			(0.17; 0.07)*			
HA_{ad} → A_b			(0.33; 0.30)*			
GAS → UA_{ad}				(0.19; 0.10)*		(0.16; 0.06)*
GAS → UA_{ad} → A_b						(0.12; 0.05)*
GAS → UA_{ad} and A_b						(0.19; 0.08)*
AMI → UA_{ad}				(0.23; 0.12)**		(0.19; 0.08)**
AMI → UA_{ad} → A_b						(0.15; 0.06)**
AMI → UA_{ad} and A_b						(0.22; 0.08)**
AMI → A_b						(0.17; 0.07)*
UA_{ad} → A_b						(0.24; 0.20)***
SMC	0.02 and 0.02	0.55 and 0.57	0.21 and 0.21	0.05 and 0.08	0.46 and 0.46	0.24 and 0.24
Model fit						

A_b was found to mediate both the effect of UA_{ad} on PI, $\beta = 0.20$, $p < 0.01$, and the effect of HA_{ad} on PI, $\beta = 0.30$, $p < 0.01$. Thus, H5 was supported. Beyond testing the hypotheses, it was found that there was a significant indirect effect on PI through both utilitarian A_{ad} and A_b as two mediators in tandem for both GAS, $\beta = 0.05$, $p < 0.05$, and AMI, $\beta = 0.06$, $p < 0.01$.

Adding the GAS × AMI interaction to Model I and III, Model II and IV analyses further partially supported H_{3a} (i.e. the finding supported the interaction effect on UA_{ad} but not on HA_{ad}) and fully supported H_{3b} while the finding did not support H3c. In the analysis of Model IV, the GAS × AMI interaction was found to have a significant effect on UA_{ad}, $\beta = 0.27$, $p < 0.05$, on A_b, $\beta = 0.25$, $p < 0.05$, but not on PI, $\beta = 0.13$, $p = 0.30$. In Model II analysis, the interaction effect was found significant only on A_b, $\beta = 0.24$, $p < 0.05$, but neither on HA_{ad}, $\beta = -0.01$, $p = 0.97$, nor on PI, $\beta = 0.13$, $p = 0.30$.

5 Discussion

One of the key predictions of the ELM (Petty and Cacioppo 1986) is that central route to persuasion occurs when message involvement is high so that strong arguments generate a more positive attitude than weak arguments. This study tested this prediction particularly in green advertising persuasion through examining the effects of GAS, AMI, and GAS × AMI on UA_{ad} and HA_{ad} in parallel, as well as the subsequent effects on A_b and PI. The findings endorsed the important roles of GAS and AMI in green advertising persuasion. Both the main and interaction effects of these two predictors were found significant on the utilitarian dimension of A_{ad} and A_b, while neither main effects nor interaction was found significant on hedonic A_{ad} and PI.

5.1 Theoretical Implications

The current research sheds some light on how green advertising persuasion works in the cognitive sphere by adding a theoretical layer to the ELM's argument strength × message involvement hypothesis. The persuasiveness of strong green arguments in ads was found to depend on the extent to which the ad recipient's ad message involvement when processing the information. This finding supported the interaction hypothesis, i.e. when exposed to a green ad, high involvement individuals are motivated to diligently examine the environmental claims and closely scrutinize the arguments, and therefore form better A_{ad}, A_b, and PI if the arguments are strong enough to generate favorable thoughts about the brand's green position.

However, GAS, AMI and the interaction seem to restrict their persuasiveness to the cognitive processing route only and exert very limited impact on the affective area of attitude formation. Indeed, the effects of GAS, AMI and the interaction were significant on the UA_{ad} but not significant on HA_{ad}. The AMI's indirect effects on A_b and PI through HA_{ad} were also only marginal. With the empirical evidence provided by the present study, the cognitive vs affective theorizing of the argument strength × message involvement hypothesis is compatible with the theory of affective/cognitive matching effects. The theory contends that, in general, cognitive attitudes are more susceptible to persuasion by cognitive messages while affective attitudes are more susceptible to persuasion by affective messages (Petty et al. 2003) and the matching effects have been empirically supported by previous studies (e.g., Drolet and Aaker 2002; Edwards 1990; Edwards and von Hippel 1995; Haddock et al. 2008). Green arguments in ads and ad message involvement are cognitive in nature, and therefore would work more powerfully on cognition-based attitudes such as the utilitarian dimension of A_{ad} than on affect-based attitudes such as the hedonic dimension of A_{ad}.

The principal component analysis and confirmatory factor analysis diagnosed A_{ad} as a multi-dimensional construct. Indeed, advertisements typically carry complex messages that combine arguments, contextual cues, emotional appeals, design and executional elements (R. Batra and Ray 1985) and these different ad components can elicit different audience responses, cognitively and/or affectively, and in turn, generate different brand attitudes and purchase intention. Thus, another theoretical implication of this study is that UA_{ad} and HA_{ad} are independent, though correlated, and both exert persuasive impacts on the audience independently but in differently ways. In the green argument strength × ad message involvement green advertising context, UA_{ad} seems to be more powerful in predicting persuasion as it had a significant direct effect on both A_b and PI whereas no significant direct effect on PI for HA_{ad}. In addition, in this study, UA_{ad} significantly mediated the effects of GAS and AMI on Ab and PI, while HA_{ad} did not mediate GAS' effect and only marginally mediated AMI's effect on A_b and PI. The effect of HA_{ad} on A_b and PI could be explained by the affect transfer hypothesis developed by MacKenzie et al. (1986), which refers to A_{ad} directly influencing brand attitude without going through brand cognition. Exposure to the ad elicits positive affect that will be transferred to the brand through processes of evaluative conditioning, and as a result, the liking for the ad will rub off on the brand and leads to more favorable A_b, which in turn will increase PI.

5.2 Practical Implications

This study offers some managerial implications for green ad design and execution. Strong, cogent, and compelling green claims would exert stronger persuasion than weak claims in general. However, strengthening green claims might be not enough to lead to persuasion as suggested by the effects of GAS × AMI. Advertising practitioners may have to consider the target audience's situational ad message involvement. Evidence from research suggests that AMI could be manipulated by the message developer. For example, AMI can be increased by making the message more personally relevant to the audience (Petty et al. 1983), using fear appeals (Fernando et al. 2016), and designing an unexpected message (Y. H. Lee 2000). However, even carefully considering the GAS × AMI interaction when designing a green ad message may still not be enough as a key variable A_{ad} was found to have two distinct dimensions, UA_{ad} and HA_{ad}, and both impact A_b, which in turn would predict PI. GAS and AMI affect UA_{ad} but remain irrelevant or marginal to HA_{ad}. Other communication techniques such as humor might be used to make ad more enjoyable and the positive feelings may be transferred from the ad to the brand.

5.3 Limitations and Future Research

The main limitation comes from the research model itself. This study focuses on the persuasive roles that GAS and AMI play in green advertising effectiveness. Although the significant interaction of these two factors was found, contextual cues, as suggested by the ELM, were not manipulated so how utilitarian A_{ad} was formed was not clear, while the two A_{ad} dimensions are among the key dependent variables. On the other hand, it was found that the cognition-based GAS had no impact on hedonic A_{ad}, regardless of the AMI condition. This finding indicated that, in addition to cognitive processing that was examined in the study, it might be necessary to include affective processing into research as hedonic A_{ad} was found to significantly affect A_b and purchase intention. However, without including the antecedents of hedonic A_{ad} in the study as independent variables, there is a lack of evidence for this theoretical indication. Investigating the process of affect transfer, along with cognitive processing on either central or peripheral route, was suggested for future research on green advertising persuasion.

References

Andrews, J. C., & Shimp, T. A. (1990). Effects of involvement, argument strength, and source characteristics on central and peripheral processing of advertising. *Psychology & Marketing, 7*(3), 195–214.

Baker, W. E., & Lutz, R. J. (1987). The relevance-accessibility model of advertising effectiveness. In S. Hecker & D. W. Stewart (Eds.), *Nonverbal communication in advertising* (pp. 59–84). Lexington: Lexington Books.

Batra, R., & Ahtola, O. T. (1991). Measuring the hedonic utilitarian sources of consumer attitudes. *Marketing Letters, 2*(2), 159–170.

Batra, R., & Ray, M. L. (1985). How advertising works at contact. In L. F. Alwitt & A. A. Mitchell (Eds.), *Psychological processes and advertising effects: Theory, research and application* (pp. 13–43). Hillsdale: Erlbaum.

Batra, R., & Ray, M. L. (1986). Affective responses mediating acceptance of advertising. *Journal of Consumer Research, 13*(2), 234–249.

Bee, C., & Dalakas, V. (2015). Rivalries and sponsor affiliation: Examining the effects of social identity and argument strength on responses to sponsorship-related advertising messages. *Journal of Marketing Communications, 21*(6), 408–424.

Benoit-Moreau, F., & Parguel, B. (2011). Building brand equity with environmental communication: An empirical investigation in France. *EuroMed Journal of Business, 6*(1), 100–116. https://doi.org/10.1108/14502191111130334.

Borin, N., Cerf, D. C., & Krishnan, R. (2011). Consumer effects of environmental impact in product labeling. *Journal of Consumer Marketing, 28*(1), 76–86. https://doi.org/10.1108/07363761111101976.

Brown, S. P., & Stayman, D. M. (1992). Antecedents and consequences of attitude toward the ad: A meta-analysis. *Journal of Consumer Research, 19*(1), 34–51.

Carpenter, C. J. (2015). A meta-analysis of the ELM's argument quality × processing type predictions. *Human Communication Research, 41*(4), 501–534. https://doi.org/10.1111/hcre.12054.

Chaiken, S., Liberman, A., & Eagly, A. H. (1989). Heuristic and systematic information processing within and beyond the persuasion context. In J. S. Uleman & J. A. Bargh (Eds.), *Unintended thought* (pp. 212–252). New York: Guilford Press.

Chang, C. C. (2011). Feeling ambivalent about going green. *Journal of Advertising, 40*(4), 19–31.

Chang, H., Zhang, L., & Xie, G. (2015). Message framing in green advertising: The effect of construal level and consumer environmental concern. *International Journal of Advertising, 34*(1), 158–176. https://doi.org/10.1080/02650487.2014.994731.

Davis, J. J. (1994). Consumer response to corporate environmental advertising. *Journal of Consumer Marketing, 11*(2), 25–37.

Drolet, A., & Aaker, J. (2002). Off-target? Changing cognitive-based attitudes. *Journal of Consumer Psychology, 12*(1), 59–68.

Drossos, D. A., Giaglis, G. M., Vlachos, P. A., Zamani, E. D., & Lekakos, G. (2013). Consumer responses to SMS advertising: Antecedents and Consequences. *International Journal of Electronic Commerce, 18*(1), 105–136. https://doi.org/10.2753/JEC1086-4415180104.

Edwards, K. (1990). The interplay of affect and cognition in attitude formation and change. *Journal of Personality and Social Psychology, 59*(2), 202–216.

Edwards, K., & von Hippel, W. (1995). Hearts and minds: The priority of affective versus cognitive factors in person perception. *Personality and Social Psychology Bulletin, 21*(10), 996–1011.

Eisend, M. (2013). The moderating influence of involvement on two-sided advertising effects. *Psychology & Marketing, 30*(7), 566–575. https://doi.org/10.1002/mar.20628.

Fernando, A. G., Sivakumaran, B., & Suganthi, L. (2016). Message involvement and attitude towards green advertisements. *Marketing Intelligence & Planning, 34*(6), 863–882. https://doi.org/10.1108/MIP-11-2015-0216.

Gardner, M. P. (1985). Does attitude toward the ad affect brand attitude under a brand evaluation set? *Journal of Marketing Research, 22*(2), 281–300.

Haddock, G., Maio, G. R., Arnold, K., & Huskinson, T. (2008). Should persuasion be affective or cognitive? The moderating effects of need for affect and need for cognition. *Personality and Social Psychology Bulletin, 34*(6), 769–778. https://doi.org/10.1177/0146167208314871.

Hartmann, P., Apaolaza-Ibáñez, V., & Forcada-Sainz, J. (2005). Green branding effects on attitude: Functional versus emotional positioning strategies. *Marketing Intelligence & Planning, 23*(1), 9–29. https://doi.org/10.1108/02634500510577447.

Kavadas, C., Katsanis, L. P., & LeBel, J. (2007). The effects of risk disclosure and ad involvement on consumers in DTC advertising. *Journal of Consumer Marketing, 24*(3), 171–179. https://doi.org/10.1108/07363760710746175.

Kokkinaki, F., & Lunt, P. (1999). The effect of advertising message involvement on brand attitude accessibility. *Journal of Economic Psychology, 20*(1), 41–51.

Laczniak, R. N., & Muehling, D. D. (1993). Toward a better understanding of the role of advertising message involvement in ad processing. *Psychology & Marketing, 10*(4), 301–319.

Lee, Y.-J., Haley, E., & Yang, K. (2013). The mediating role of attitude towards values advocacy ads in evaluating issue support behavior and purchase intention. *International Journal of Advertising, 32*(2), 233–253. https://doi.org/10.2501/IJA-32-2-233-253.

Lee, Y. H. (2000). Manipulating ad message involvement through information expectancy: Effects on attitude evaluation and confidence. *Journal of Advertising, 29*(2), 29–43.

Lien, N.-H., & Chen, Y.-L. (2013). Narrative ads: The effect of argument strength and story format. *Journal of Business Research, 66*(4), 516–522. https://doi.org/10.1016/j.jbusres.2011.12.016.

MacKenzie, S. B., Lutz, R. J., & Belch, G. E. (1986). The role of attitude toward the ad as a mediator of advertising effectiveness: A test of competing explanations. *Journal of Marketing Research, 23*(2), 130–143.

MarketWatch. (2018). Flash report: 85% of S&P 500 index (R) companies publish sustainability reports in 2017. Retrieved from https://www.marketwatch.com/press-release/flash-report-85-of-sp-500-indexr-companies-publish-sustainability-reports-in-2017-2018-03-20-1015745

Matthes, J., Wonneberger, A., & Schmuck, D. (2014). Consumers' green involvement and the persuasive effects of emotional versus functional ads. *Journal of Business Research, 67*(9), 1885–1893. https://doi.org/10.1016/j.jbusres.2013.11.054.

Muehling, D. D., Laczniak, R. N., & Stoltman, J. J. (1991). The moderating effects of ad message involvement: A reassessment. *Journal of Advertising, 20*(2), 29–38.

Nielsen. (2018). *Global consumers seek companies that care about environmental issues.* Retrieved from https://www.nielsen.com/us/en/insights/news/2018/global-consumers-seek-companies-that-care-about-environmental-issues.html

Nielsen. (2019). *A 'natural' rise in sustainability around the world.* Retrieved from https://www.nielsen.com/us/en/insights/news/2019/a-natural-rise-in-sustainability-around-the-world.html

Nyilasy, G., Gangadharbatla, H., & Paladino, A. (2014). Perceived greenwashing: The interactive effects of green advertising and corporate environmental performance on consumer reactions. *Journal of Business Ethics, 125*(4), 693–707. https://doi.org/10.1007/s10551-013-1944-3.

Olney, T. J., Holbrook, M. B., & Batra, R. (1991). Consumer responses to advertising: The effects of ad content, emotions, and attitude toward the ad on viewing time. *Journal of Consumer Research, 17*(4), 440–453.

Olsen, M. C., Slotegraaf, R. J., & Chandukala, S. R. (2014). Green claims and message frames: How green new products change brand attitude. *Journal of Marketing, 78*(5), 119–137. https://doi.org/10.1509/jm.13.0387.

Park, H. S., Levine, T. R., Westerman, C. Y. K., Orfgen, T., & Foregger, S. (2007). The effects of argument quality and involvement type on attitude formation and attitude change: A test of dual-process and social judgment predictions. *Human Communication Research, 33*(1), 81–102.

Petty, R. E., & Cacioppo, J. T. (1981a). *Attitudes and persuasion: Classic and contemporary approaches.* Dubuque: William C. Brown Company.

Petty, R. E., & Cacioppo, J. T. (1981). Issue involvement as a moderator of the effects on attitude of advertising content and context. *Advances in Consumer Research, 8*(1), 20–24.

Petty, R. E., & Cacioppo, J. T. (1984). The effects of involvement on responses to argument quantity and quality: Central and peripheral routes to persuasion. *Journal of Personality and Social Psychology, 46*(1), 69–81.

Petty, R. E., & Cacioppo, J. T. (1986). The elaboration likelihood model of persuasion. In L. Berkowitz (Ed.), *Advances in experimental social psychology* (Vol. 19, pp. 123–205). San Diego: Academic Press.

Petty, R. E., Cacioppo, J. T., & Schumann, D. (1983). Central and peripheral routes to advertising effectiveness: The moderating role of involvement. *Journal of Consumer Research, 10*(2), 135–146.

Petty, R. E., Fabrigar, L. R., & Wegener, D. T. (2003). Emotional factors in attitudes and persuasion. In R. J. Davidson, K. R. Scherer, & H. H. Goldsmith (Eds.), *Handbook of affective sciences* (1st ed., pp. 752–772). New York: Oxford University Press.

Phau, I., & Ong, D. (2007). An investigation of the effects of environmental claims in promotional messages for clothing brands. *Marketing Intelligence & Planning, 25*(7), 772–788.

Polyorat, K., Alden, D. L., & Kim, E. S. (2007). Impact of narrative versus factual print ad copy on product evaluation: The mediating role of ad message involvement. *Psychology and Marketing, 24*(6), 539–554. https://doi.org/10.1002/mar.20172.

Pornpitakpan, C. (2004). The persuasive effect of circadian aroudal, endorse expertise, and argument strength in advertising. *Journal of Global Marketing, 17*(2–3), 141–172.

Schmuck, D., Matthes, J., & Naderer, B. (2018). Misleading consumers with green advertising? An affect-reason-involvement account of greenwashing effects in environmental advertising. *Journal of Advertising, 47*(2), 127–145. https://doi.org/10.1080/00913367.2018.1452652.

Shimp, T. A. (1981). Attitude toward the ad as a mediator of consumer brand choice. *Journal of Advertising, 10*(2), 9–15.

Voss, K. E., Spangenberg, E. R., & Grohmann, B. (2003). Measuring the hedonic and utilitarian dimensions of consumer attitude. *Journal of Marketing Research, 40*(3), 310–320.

Yoo, C., & MacInnis, D. (2005). The brand attitude formation process of emotional and informational ads. *Journal of Business Research, 58,* 1397–1406. https://doi.org/10.1016/j.jbusres.2005.03.011.

Yu, J. (2018). Consumer responses toward green advertising: The effects of gender, advertising skepticism, and green motive attribution. *Journal of Marketing Communications.* https://doi.org/10.1080/13527266.2018.1514317.

Zhang, Y., & Zinkhan, G. M. (2006). Responses to humorous ads: Does audience involvement matter? *Journal of Advertising, 35*(4), 113–127. https://doi.org/10.2753/JOA0091-3367350408.

Printed by Printforce, the Netherlands